Praise for *The Assassination of Fred Hampton*

"This book of the assassination of a sleeping Fred Hampton by Chicago police working for a mad state's attorney is more important NOW than it was THEN. It is a revelation of how the powerful of our city use power—to keep truth distant. The hard truth is that this is a remarkable work."

> —Studs Terkel

"A chilling account . . . essential reading. . . . This book should be read, talked about, and broadcast far and wide, not only to help grasp the government sanctioned tactics of forty years ago, but for its ongoing relevance to seeing what ways ideology has corrupted American political institutions—and what we can do about it."

> —Kathleen Cleaver, Emory University School of Law, former
> communications secretary of the Black Panther Party
> Chicago, former SDS leader, and author

"Required political reading, especially for conservatives who are genuinely concerned about the damage secret government can do."

> —*Chicago Daily Observer*

"Part history, part courtroom drama, part literary memoir, [*The Assassination of Fred Hampton*] evokes with chilling precision a bloody and desperate repressive state apparatus locked in conflict with its greatest fear, a charismatic young black man with revolution on his mind."

> —William Ayers, professor of education, University of
> Illinois at Chicago

"A must-read."

> —Len Weinglass, lawyer and civil rights activist

The Assassination of
Fred Hampton

**How the FBI and the Chicago Police
Murdered a Black Panther**

Jeffrey Haas

Lawrence Hill Books

The Library of Congress has cataloged the hardcover edition as follows:

Haas, Jeffrey.

The assassination of Fred Hampton : how the FBI and the Chicago police murdered a Black Panther / Jeffrey Haas.

   p. cm.

Includes bibliographical references and index.

ISBN 978-1-55652-765-4 (hardcover)

1. Hampton, Fred, 1948-1969. 2. Assassination—Illininois—Chicago. 3. Black Panther Party. I. Title.

HV6289.C4H33 2009

322.4'2092—dc22

                                                                        2009025604

Cover and interior design: Jonathan Hahn

Cover photos: (top) © Bettman/CORBIS; (bottom) courtesy of Chicago Mobile Crime Lab

Photo gallery credits: pages 1–2 courtesy of the Hampton family; pages 4–7, 8 (bottom), 9 (top), 10, 12, 13 (bottom), and 14 © Paul Sequiera; page 11 (top) courtesy Joe Moreno, *Chicago Daily News*, with permission by the Sun-Times News Group; page 16 (top) © Kathy Richland; page 16 (bottom) © Delores Smith

© 2010 by Jeffrey Haas

All rights reserved

First hardcover edition published 2010

First paperback edition published 2011

Published by Lawrence Hill Books

An imprint of Chicago Review Press, Incorporated

814 North Franklin Street

Chicago, Illinois 60610

ISBN 978-1-56976-709-2

Printed in the United States of America

5 4 3

This book is dedicated to the life and memory of Fred Hampton (1948–1969). He refused to compromise in the struggle for justice, equality, and freedom, and he paid the ultimate price. And to those who have been inspired by him to pursue these goals.

In memory of my father, Joseph Haas, and my friend Juancho Donahue, and for my mother, Betty Haas.

To my loving wife, Mariel, and my children, Roger, Andrew, Justin, and Rosa.

To my other family, the People's Law Office, as they continue the legacy of Fred Hampton.

To Iberia and Francis Hampton and Fannie Clark, who endured the loss of a son but persevered to keep the memory alive.

To all those who have died, lost loved ones, or been imprisoned pursuing justice and freedom.

Contents

Introduction

1969: The Year of No Return

While **1969 was pivotal for** me, it was fatal for Fred Hampton. His life moved so much more quickly than mine and burned so much more brightly, only to be extinguished at age twenty-one by two police bullets to the head at four-thirty in the morning on December 4. Yet the story of his life has never been told, and the story of his death, once partially illuminated, has mostly been forgotten. These stories exist in the memories of those who knew Fred, who heard him speak, who respond with excitement and recognition when I ask about him, as though I'm speaking about yesterday or last week rather than forty years ago. The memory of Fred is there in the continuing sadness in Fred's mother Iberia's eyes as she approaches her late eighties.

Maybe we all have points at which our consciousness changes and we cannot return to our former path. For many political activists, that dividing line occurred in the late 1960s. We were fed up with a system that thrived on war, racism, and patriarchy. We were young people who at first hadn't understood why the United States was waging war in Vietnam but who by 1969 believed that it was endemic to an unjust system we felt compelled to stop or overthrow.

Many of the same evils are still with us, as was glaringly apparent in recent years under Bush Jr.: a war of conquest and occupation abroad and ever-growing government eavesdropping and intimidation at home. There is currently a movement to make public U.S. involvement in torture and hold those who authorized it accountable. The Bush-Cheney-Rumsfeld team, with their legal apologists John Ashcroft and Alberto Gonzales, implemented secret domestic and foreign policies in total violation of the constitution and international law and still seek to justify those abuses. Many of the same perpetrators and apologists for Watergate, COINTELPRO, and the Iran-Contra scandal returned to implement even more Draconian measures. If this wrong-

doing is not exposed and those who perpetuated it are not held criminally liable, then it is bound to repeat itself in clandestine programs
like COINTELPRO. The need to protest, expose, and hold accountable
those in power who violate our laws and personal liberties continues
and remains a fundamental struggle of our society and any society.

After the publication of the hardcover edition of this book in 2010, I
learned that in 1995 the FBI declassified memos, which were placed in
the Lyndon Baines Johnson Library and Museum in Austin, Texas. A
researcher discovered the files and sent them to me. J. Edgar Hoover
authored the memos, which he sent to the White House, the Department
of Defense, the Department of State, the Army, and the CIA. They
showed the FBI had informants reporting on Fred Hampton as early as
1967, which was before he was a Black Panther. The memos misrepresented Hampton's words and actions, attributing incendiary speeches
to him that witnesses have told me were never given.

Part I

Rendezvous with Death

Meeting a Revolutionary

The first time I heard Fred Hampton speak was in August 1969. He was the chairman of the Illinois Black Panther Party, and I was at the "People's Church" on Ashland Avenue in the heart of Chicago's black West Side. I was two years out of law school, and it was two days after my law partners had obtained Fred's release from Menard Prison. The sanctuary of the church was filled to capacity with rows of wooden pews going back into dimly lit corners, and it was warm inside.

My colleague Flint Taylor and I found an opening in a row about half-way back. After a few minutes, things quieted down. There was a hush. A moment later Fred emerged from the side and strode to the pulpit. Everyone stood up and clapped. The walls shook with the thunder of three hundred voices chanting "Free Fred Hampton." Unlike at other Panther events, Fred was not surrounded by Panthers in leather jackets and black berets. He stood alone, dressed in a button-down shirt with a pullover sweater. He was twenty years old, with smooth, youthful skin and a boyish smile. He had grown a little goatee in prison and wore a medium-length Afro.

Fred Hampton held the microphone in his right hand and looked out at the crowd.

"I'm free," he began in a loud voice. Then repeated it.

People shouted their approval.

His voice got softer. "I went down to the prison in Menard, thinking we were the vanguard, but down there I got down on my knees and listened and learned from the people. I went down to the valley and picked up the beat of the people." A drumbeat started, and everyone clapped to the rhythm. Fred chanted, a cross between a Baptist preacher and Sly and the Family Stone. "I'm high." Making each *high* into a two-syllable word, he sang, "I'm high—ee, I'm high—ee off the people," and then chanted the words again. It was impossible for me not to join in, and soon I clapped and stomped with everyone else.

When the refrain was over, Fred repeated the most common Panther slogan, "Power to the people," but added his own variation: "White Power to white people, Brown Power to brown people, Yellow Power to yellow people, Black Power to black people, X power to those we left out, and Panther Power to the Vanguard Party." After a volley of "right ons," Fred said:

> If you ever think about me and you ain't gonna do no revolutionary act, forget about me. I don't want myself on your mind if you're not going to work for the people. If you're asked to make a commitment at the age of twenty, and you say I don't want to make a commitment at the age of twenty, only because of the reason that I'm too young to die, I want to live a little longer, then you're dead already. You have to understand that people have to pay a price for peace. If you dare to struggle, you dare to win. If you dare not struggle then damn it, you don't deserve to win. Let me say peace to you if you're willing to fight for it.

Later, Fred asked the audience to stand up. We did. He then told everyone to raise his or her right hand and repeat "I am," and we responded, "I am." He then said "a revolutionary" and some in the audience repeated "a revolutionary." I considered myself a lawyer *for* the movement but not necessarily *of* the movement. The word *revolutionary* stuck in my throat. Again Fred repeated "I am," and the audience responded in kind. This time when he said "a revolutionary," the response was louder. By the third or fourth time, I hesitantly joined in, and by the seventh or eighth time I was shouting as loudly and enthusiastically as everyone else, "I am . . . a revolutionary!" It was a threshold to which Fred took me and countless others. I felt my level of commitment palpably rising.

Fred was speaking in a quieter voice:

> I believe I was born not to die in a car wreck or slipping on a piece of ice, or of a bad heart, but I'm going to be able to die doing the things I was born for. I believe I'm going to die high off the people. I believe that I'm going to be able to die as a revolutionary in the international proletarian

struggle. And I hope that each of you will be able to die in the international revolutionary proletarian struggle or you'll be able to live in it. And I think that struggle's going to come. Why don't you live for the people? Why don't you struggle for the people? Why don't you die for the people?

Fred finished. Everyone stood and applauded again, unaware of the truth of his prophecy. We chanted "Free Fred Hampton," and the church reverberated with the clapping and stamping of feet.

It was cold in the tiny, windowless interview room at the Wood Street police station. I looked across the wooden table at the large-boned woman with a short Afro who was shaking and sobbing. Deborah Johnson's patterned nightgown outlined her protruding belly, revealing her pregnancy.

"Fred never really woke up," she said. "He was lying there when they pulled me out of the bedroom." She paused.

"And then?" I asked.

"Two pigs went back into the bedroom. One of them said, 'He's barely alive, he'll barely make it.' I heard two shots. Then I heard, 'He's good and dead now!'"

Fred's fiancée looked at me with sad, swollen eyes. "What can *you* do?"

I couldn't think of any reply. I couldn't bring Fred back to life.

2

Born and Bred in Atlanta

A **group of young lawyers** opened the People's Law Office (PLO) the same week Fred spoke at the People's Church. We wanted to become lawyers for the movement. Who were we and how did we get there? I begin with me, not because I was the most important; I wasn't. But it's my story. I knew Fred Hampton only briefly, but as with so many others who knew him, he changed my life.

It's difficult to separate the parts of my life that led me to become a Panther lawyer. Who knows for certain how or why we become who we are? I don't. But there were people and events that influenced the course I took.

I was born in Crawford Long Hospital on September 18, 1942. My sister Sue, four years older, and I are from a German Jewish family that settled in Atlanta in the 1850s. My grandfather, Herbert Haas, was one of the lawyers who defended Leo Frank, the Jewish manager of the Atlanta Pencil Factory. In 1913, Frank was falsely accused of murdering a thirteen-year-old, white, Protestant girl named Mary Phagan, whose body was found at the factory on a Saturday morning.

Defending him was so unpopular my grandfather hired a detective to protect his family. The anti-Semitic Hearst newspapers and local press portrayed the murder as a Jewish ritual killing, and with southern resentment against northern carpetbaggers fanned by populist Tom Watson, Frank was convicted and sentenced to death. Governor Frank Slaton, convinced of Frank's innocence, commuted his sentence to life, further angering the riled-up public, and a fellow inmate stabbed Frank in the neck. While he was recuperating, a lynch mob, organized by some of the most prominent families in Atlanta, kidnapped him from the infirmary at nearby Milledgeville, and hanged him outside Atlanta.

My grandfather had been the first person Frank called when he was arrested, and they wrote to each other frequently. The last letter from Frank arrived the day before the lynching. My grandfather refused to discuss the case for the rest of his life, and my father said the Jewish community was traumatized for a generation. Yet as far as I know, and despite the fact that the Anti-Defamation League was born out of this case, the Jewish community failed or refused to make the connection between Frank's death and the lynching of fourteen black people in Georgia alone that year without any trials at all.

My father, Joseph Haas, while primarily a business lawyer, was also the attorney for the Southern Regional Council, a civic organization concerned with racial inequalities in the South. He worked with civil rights organizers including the Student Nonviolent Coordinating Committee's chairman John Lewis to implement the 1965 Voting Rights Act. My dad came up with the name the Voter Education Project to make the group eligible for grants from charitable foundations. The IRS would not have allowed them to fund a voter registration drive. When Dad died in 2000, John Lewis, today a U.S. congressman, wrote the eulogy that I proudly read at the memorial service.

> His work made a major and lasting contribution to the civil rights movement and to liberating white and black Southerners. The Voter Education Project registered more than four million new voters; black voters in the eleven Southern states where it operated. We relied on his legal advice and counsel and "can do" spirit. Without him, those of us on the Freedom Rides and elsewhere on the so-called front lines could not have done what we did.

My mother, Betty Geismer, grew up in middle-class, integrated Shaker Heights, a suburb of Cleveland, where she was a classmate of the track star Jesse Owens. When Mom attended Wellesley College in the early 1930s, the school was swarming with would-be Bolsheviks, socialists, and New Dealers. She fit right in, and became an ardent admirer of Eleanor Roosevelt. She had a shock when she married my father in 1936 and moved to Atlanta, a city still in the long-entrenched throes of segregation. The racial attitudes of most white Atlantans at the time she moved to the South were reflected in the big social event the next year: the grand opening of the movie *Gone with the Wind*, a story of nostalgic longing for a romanticized antebellum South that, of course, included slavery.

In the late 1950s my mother organized the Atlanta Committee for International Visitors (ACIV). Its function was to host persons brought to the United States by the State Department and other governmental agencies. Atlanta was becoming the government's showcase for Southern cities because it had not fought integration with the violence of Birmingham, Alabama, or Little Rock, Arkansas. Rather, a majority of Atlanta's white business leaders united with leaders of the black community to implement slow but peaceful integration. A notable exception was segregationist Lester Maddox. At his Pickrick Cafeteria he sold ax handles to use against blacks who might try to integrate segregated facilities, including his own. This stance got him elected governor of Georgia.

My mother's work for ACIV included hosting African delegations, which put her in touch with Coretta Scott King, Dr. Martin Luther King Jr., and the deans of the Atlanta University colleges. One problem the newly formed ACIV faced was that most Atlanta hotels were still segregated. A few, including the Biltmore, were willing to house all-black delegations from other countries, but they would not allow mixed delegations to stay at their hotels or eat in their restaurants. One day I heard my mother on the phone. "That is unacceptable and simply won't work," she said. "If you want our business you have to accommodate integrated delegations and that includes their black and white hosts." The Biltmore acceded, and soon other hotels became integrated as well.

Like many Southern white kids from upper-middle-class families, I was raised in part by blacks. When I was five, we moved to a farm just north of Atlanta. By the time I was eight, my parents hired Walter McCurry to work the farm. Walter was six feet tall, barrel chested, and muscular, with light brown skin, a small mustache, a round face, and a shaved head. A World War II navy veteran, he returned to Georgia after the war to take up farming, which his family had done for generations. Walter wore overalls and drank sweetened iced tea out of mason jars. He was forty years old when he started working for us.

Our farm consisted of twenty-six hilly acres containing a small lake, a two-acre vegetable and berry garden, several hay fields, a barn with a pasture behind it, and thirty-three pecan trees. With Walter's help we raised chickens, turkeys, and pigs, and kept a horse and a mule.

Walter taught me how to plow behind our mule, Boley—not only how to handle the reins but how to address her with the commands "gee" and "haw" to get her to turn right or left. He chuckled when the plow got stuck or I would get off course.

"Boy, I hope you learn how to plow while we still got some rows left," he would say, adding with a smile, "I spec you ain't done too much damage."

My favorite activity was when Walter put a bridle on Boley and brought her around to the haystack where my two friends and I could get on. Off we'd ride into the woods, where we built forts and kept our stash of sardines and saltines.

I emulated Walter, and he took great pride in showing me what he knew. He was my Jim, and I was his Huck. But unlike our predecessors, the traveling Walter and I did together was to baseball games. My friend Henry lived near Ponce de Leon Ballpark, where the Atlanta Crackers, our local all-white minor league team, played. Only forty years later did I learn that the Black Crackers shared the same ballpark.

The first time Walter took us to a game we were ten. It was a warm, humid evening, and Henry and I went to buy tickets. I looked around and saw Walter was walking off toward the hill in right field, where the black spectators were sitting. I wanted to call out to him, *Come back and sit with us.* But I said nothing.

"Why should he have to sit out there?" I asked Henry.

"Yeah," he replied. "There're plenty of seats here."

There was silence as we each waited for the next thing to be said, but neither of us would take the next step of inviting Walter back to sit with us.

"I hope Country Brown is in the lineup tonight," I finally chipped in. "You got money for lemonade?"

After the game we met Walter outside. We all knew it was wrong and mean that he and other black people were banished to the worst seats. But I never talked about it with him. Nor did he mention it to me. I'm not sure why. I think Walter didn't want to embarrass me.

As for why I didn't say anything, it was probably my fear and timidity, issues that I would confront years later. I was ashamed of the status quo but not willing to take it on. As Alan Paton wrote in *Cry, the Beloved Country* about white South Africans' fear of challenging apartheid, "It was not a thing lightly done."

Lily May Glenn also played a large role in raising me. She worked for us as a maid five and a half days per week, from the time I was six or seven until after I went away to college. Lily had her own small bedroom and bathroom in our house. She was tall and statuesque, with high cheekbones, suggesting some Cherokee roots. She was one of twelve children whose family had been sharecroppers on the remains of a cotton plantation in Georgia.

I loved to hear Lily's stories about growing up in the country, in particular her animated accounts of the horrors of picking cotton. "It was hot and sweaty with long days, dirty work, and boring to beat," she said. "Seemed like the sun would never go down. I'd be sick or hide, anything. If I was forced to pick, I'd put rocks and green cotton boles in my sack to make it weigh more so I could make my quota earlier."

Nearly three decades later, in 1975, one of the main presenters at a radical women's gathering made the mistake of speaking nostalgically about being raised by her parents' black employees. *Servants* was the postslavery word. Her listeners took her presentation to imply that she believed her upbringing was acceptable because it was such a fertile source of memories and support. My friends who attended were appalled at her seeming acceptance of the exploitation of the black people who worked for her family. She was tarred and feathered politically.

As I write about my memories of Walter and Lily, I realize the contrast between the benefits that flowed to me and my family from these relationships and the extreme cost to Walter and Lily. Both worked long hours for low wages with no social security, health, or retirement benefits. They were not equals in our house. They never ate dinner with us, and they addressed my parents as "Mr. Haas" and "Mrs. Haas," while we addressed them by their first names.

I was the first Jew to attend Liberty Gwinn, the county elementary school near our house. My classmates were country white kids, and before they knew I was Jewish, they told me, "Jews have horns."

One day I decided to be bold. "I'm Jewish," I told a group of classmates after school. They looked for my horns and found none. That was the end of the anti-Semitic comments. I liked the kids, they liked me, and I achieved the highest honor, being voted captain of Safety Patrol.

While my classmates withheld name-calling of Jews, they showed no similar restraint with respect to blacks. Like all the other schools in Fulton County, students at Liberty Gwinn went downtown to hear the Atlanta Symphony at least one time each year. Atlanta was totally segregated in the early 1950s. Black kids not only went to different schools but were assigned different times to go to the symphony.

One morning, as my mother was driving my classmates and me back from the concert, we saw three black kids walking on the sidewalks toward the auditorium.

"Niggers, go home," one of my classmates yelled through an open window.

"Y'all niggers don't deserve to go to our auditorium," another yelled.

I was embarrassed. The black kids stopped, hurt and anger on their faces. One of them reached down as if to pick up a rock. Their teacher, who had been walking behind them, intervened and stopped him.

"Roll up the windows," my mother said. "We're getting too much cold air in the car."

And that was that. The racial slurs stopped, but she said nothing more. I too remained silent.

One day in the late 1950s, some teenage friends and I drove to Lake Spivey, a privately owned lake near Atlanta, to enjoy a swim and some relief from the Georgia sun. As we were walking down the beach, a beefy white man in a uniform yelled "Get out of there" to a young black kid knee-deep in the water.

"Why?" the boy asked simply.

"Cause we don't allow no Negras here."

"But this is a public place, ain't it?" the boy replied. Public pools in Atlanta had been ordered integrated and had either integrated or closed down.

"No, this is private, for whites only, can't you see the sign? I don't know how you got in here at all."

We looked past the uniformed man to see a sign on the beach that read **NO COLOREDS ALLOWED**. The boy continued to protest and was dragged from the water crying. His mother came over to comfort him and take him away from the security guard.

As he and his mother started toward the exit, I watched. The security guard weighed more than two hundred pounds to my scrawny one hundred forty. I said something under my breath, low enough not to be heard. When the boy and the guard were gone, I walked to the lake and waded in. I was still outraged and also felt humiliated, having done nothing to stop or even confront the guard. I couldn't enjoy the swim. Our failures to stand up against segregation made cowards of us all.

In 1958 our temple (called the Temple) was bombed because our rabbi, Jacob Rothschild, supported Dr. King's push for integration. Unlike the *Frank* case, where the Jewish community withdrew for a generation, our congregation rallied behind our rabbi and became more committed to civil rights for blacks. Jews in Atlanta were more secure, and many were inspired by the struggle of black people to end segregation.

When I was a high school senior in 1960, one of the few hip things I did was frequenting the Royal Peacock Social Club on Auburn Avenue, where you could drink if you were under twenty-one. It was on the second floor, a couple of blocks from the Ebenezer Baptist Church headed by Martin Luther King Sr. and his son. Lily May had told me about the Peacock and usually knew who was playing there.

The Peacock had the best music in town and was the city's only integrated nightclub. Part of the "chitlin circuit," its patrons were 90 percent black. The white 10 percent was mostly Jewish. Whites were usually seated together, but the warm feelings in that room were unique for me at that time. I think the black people knew we came there to appreciate their music and their scene.

Otis Redding, Sam Cooke, Aretha Franklin, B. B. King, and Marvin Gaye made regular appearances at the Peacock. We brought our own half-pint bottles of bourbon or Seagram's Seven inside our coat pockets and poured generous amounts into the paper cups of Coke we bought for mixers. Packed in there together, at the table or on the dance floor, even I lost my inhibitions, overcoming my self-consciousness enough to do a little making out.

The band I remember best was Hank Ballard and the Midnighters. Hank wrote the original music and lyrics to "The Twist." Unfortunately for him, he let Chubby Checker record it, and Hank never quite made it past being a regional hero. Hank and the Midnighters put on quite a show. Somewhere toward the conclusion of their act, the room darkened. The music started quietly and slowly, and then gradually picked up its tempo. Suddenly a spotlight appeared directly on Hank. He had a pair of women's panties draped over his head. He slowly removed them using his tongue as the music got louder and the beat got stronger. The audience, black and white, clapped to the beat as the panties slowly descended. When they were gone, the audience erupted. It was crude, and I loved it.

At one or two in the morning, climbing down the stairs from the syrupy warmth of the Peacock onto Auburn Avenue, I felt like I was putting on my white skin again and separating into the two familiar worlds of black and white.

After high school I attended the University of Michigan, from 1960 to 1963, where I remained mostly oblivious to political events, disinterested in the formation of Students for a Democratic Society (SDS) on the campus. After I graduated, I sat in my parents' living room, drinking beer and listening to Tchaikovsky and Brahms, conjuring up lofty ideas inspired by my readings of Camus and Sartre, Nietzsche and Kierkegaard. What to be or not to be?

Not quite ready to answer that question, I realized I had lived a privileged life. I needed an equalizer. What better leveler than army basic training at Fort Jackson, South Carolina? There I would be an enlisted man, going through the same physical training as other lowly privates. I wanted to prove to myself that I could survive in a setting without relying on my privilege or my family's money. I had no awareness of the U.S. troop presence building in Vietnam when I enlisted in the Army Reserve in 1963.

I reported to Fort Jackson, near Columbia, South Carolina, on November 19. Three days later President Kennedy was assassinated. Rumors spread on the base that the Russians or Cubans had killed him.

"You men better shape up fast," our drill sergeant, a Cuban exile, yelled on our first day on the tarp. "We're sending you straight off to Cuba as soon as you learn to fire that rifle." He told us with certainty that Castro killed Kennedy and we would soon be invading the Caribbean island. This was not what I had had in mind. All of a sudden I felt like I was in a straitjacket headed for war. This was not the nonthreatening, life warm-up experience I had signed up for.

Young Fred Hampton,
an Early Activist

Fred Hampton, the third child of Francis and Iberia, was born August 30, 1948, in Argo, a suburb on the southwestern side of Chicago. His parents grew up outside the small town of Haynesville in northern Louisiana. Their families farmed the land their great-grandparents had worked as slaves. Fred's father, like many blacks from the rural South, moved to Chicago in the 1930s seeking employment. He found work at the Corn Products Company in Argo.

Among the Hamptons' neighbors in Argo were Mamie Till and her son, Emmett. Mamie Till had come to Chicago from Mississippi a few years earlier. Emmett's father also had found a job at Corn Products. One of Iberia's first Chicago acquaintances was Fannie Wesley, Emmett Till's regular babysitter. Because Iberia stayed home with her three kids until Fred, the youngest, was eight, she helped Fannie by sometimes watching Emmett, whom everyone called Bobo. Iberia told me young Emmett was "curious and quite rambunctious, a handful."

It was difficult for a black family with three kids to find housing in the Chicago area. Black neighborhoods were crowded and expensive. In 1951 the Hamptons moved from Argo to a small house near a lake in Blue Island, a suburb of Chicago.

"I liked the place because it was more like where I grew up," Iberia said. "But there were some rednecks there who gave our kids a tough time."

Dee Dee, Fred's sister, said she and Fred were frequently called into the principal's office for fighting with the white kids after school. "Fred and me never started nuthin'," she said, "but we didn't let them call us names either. We got in a lot of trouble trying to set them straight after school. Together we did all right, but seems like we were always having to explain what happened on the playground to the principal."

Iberia also got a job with Corn Products in 1956, doing quality control on the bottles and caps as they came down the assembly line. "They made me the union steward," she told me. "I loved it. Once we cooked meals at the Union Hall for over seven hundred people, every day during a two-month strike." Talking to Iberia, I got a glimpse of the source of Fred's strength.

In 1958, when Fred was ten, his family moved to Maywood, a working-class suburb, at that time about one-quarter black, west of Chicago. Fred attended Irving Elementary School, across the street from their house. "All the kids loved Fred," Iberia said, smiling. "And the teachers, too. Seems like he was never alone."

Fred, like his mother, had a large head, although I could see from photos that by his teens he had also developed a solid, powerful body. But when Fred was younger, kids teased him, Iberia said. "They called him peanut head and watermelon head. He was upset for a while, but he learned to defend himself with words. He earned the reputation of 'king of signifying.'"

I knew what she meant: called the nines in Chicago or the dozens in New York, signifying meant talking bad to people in an insulting but joking way, like "Your mama . . ." Fred's friends from Louisiana told me, "Nobody wanted to take on his mouth," but they also said a big grin usually followed his put-downs. He'd step back and apologize if he feared he had gone too far.

"When he was very young he fell and landed on his face," Francis told me. This loosened some of his front teeth, and he developed a temporary lisp or whistle sound when he spoke. Francis said he overcame this problem by practicing speaking as clearly as possible. "Even in elementary school everyone recognized he was a sharp talker. He always had a mouth on him. Later he was a genius about speaking."

"On Saturday mornings Fred would round up the neighborhood kids," Iberia said in describing her son. "They would buy food and come back to the house, where they would cook breakfast together for themselves and all of us." Fred knew some of the children didn't get much to eat at home. "Francis and I didn't have to do anything on Saturday mornings but eat," Iberia said pointing to the same table in the dining room where Fred had laid out the food for the kids.

"Fred liked school, especially the social part of it. He was a good, but not great, student," Iberia went on. "But he loved to read, especially history."

One of Fred's friends told me, "He was smart as the dickens, but his grades didn't reflect his smartness."

During the summers, Fred, his older brother, Bill, and Dee Dee visited Iberia's parents at their farm outside Haynesville, Louisiana.

"Yeah, I was a little nervous letting them go back south," Iberia said. "Particularly because Fred had such a big mouth."

She remembered how Bobo Till was killed during a visit to the South. In 1955, when Fred was six, fourteen-year-old Emmett Till left Chicago to visit his mother's family in Mississippi. He was kidnapped from his uncle's home, brutally beaten, and shot because he had supposedly whistled at a white woman outside a local store in the town of Money. His body was found floating in the Tallahatchie River several days after his abduction. His face was so badly beaten he was recognizable only to his mother.

"I couldn't stand going to his funeral and seeing him like that," Iberia said. "I wanted to remember him as the active and saucy kid I babysat for."

When she learned of Emmett's murder, Mamie Till demanded that her son's body be returned to Chicago. She defied the explicit orders of the Mississippi authorities, who had sealed his casket, and ordered that it be opened. Her son's mutilated face displayed to the entire world what Southern racism had done. Thousands of Chicagoans walked by the open casket in 1955 at the Rayner Funeral Home, aghast at what they saw. Years later, Rosa Parks told Mamie Till that the photograph of Emmett's disfigured face in the casket was set in her mind when she refused to give up her seat on the Montgomery bus.

Fourteen years after Emmett's murder, thousands of Chicagoans would walk through the same Rayner Funeral Home to see Fred's body displayed. Many thousands more would take the tour through the bullet-riddled apartment where Fred and Mark Clark were slain by the Chicago police. One of the neighborhood residents described the police raid as "nuthin but a northern lynching."

"Fred, Dee Dee, and I used to talk about Emmett, particularly when we went south," Fred's brother Bill told me. "My mother had told us Emmett had a funny lisp like Fred had when he was younger. We heard that it was his lisp, which sometimes came out like a whistle, that had cost Emmett his life.

"We pretty much stayed out of trouble down South," Bill said. "We couldn't help but notice the **FOR COLOREDS** signs in town over the nastiest drinking fountains and bathroom doors. But generally we kept away from public places."

Fred attended Proviso East High School in Maywood, a huge urban facility with twenty-four hundred students, about one fourth of whom were black. He loved sports and played on the football, basketball, and wrestling teams. On the basketball court Fred was known for being aggressive, and in pick-up games for his "mouth," his trash talking.

In his sophomore and junior years, Fred was reading black political authors, including Marcus Garvey, Malcolm X, and W. E. B. DuBois. Doris Strieter, a Maywood Village Board member, who was taking a course in African American history, asked Fred for advice for a bibliography for her term paper. "In spite of Fred's hectic schedule and his constant harassment by the police, he took the time to come over to our house with a huge stack of books and materials," she said. "Fred was an immensely well-read young man who rose early and read at least two hours before he faced the day."

Fred tape-recorded and memorized the speeches of both Dr. King and Malcolm X. He visited Reverend Clay Evans's church on Drexel Avenue, where Jesse Jackson and Operation Breadbasket and later Operation PUSH were headquartered, and practiced these preachers' techniques.

Iberia and Francis had been churchgoing Baptists in Louisiana, and they joined the Mount Calvary Baptist Church in Morgan Park shortly after they arrived in Chicago. They also attended Reverend McNelty's Second Baptist Church in Melrose Park. Fred liked going to both churches but particularly admired Reverend McNelty's appeals to his congregation to fight racial injustice and inequality. As Fred became more politically active, Reverend McNelty was "right there with him," according to Francis. He frequently asked Fred to address his congregation about issues in the black community.

"Fred was not bashful and did not back down from anything," Francis continued. "He could not tolerate injustice to anyone. Reverend McNelty admired my son."

At Proviso East, Fred encountered inequalities that infuriated him. He recognized that the mostly white faculty and entirely white administration did not adequately prepare the black students for the technological world around them. Black students doing poorly were either counseled out of school or flunked out. They had no remedial programs. He felt that many of the white teachers were tired of teaching and had stopped caring. Some used racial slurs when talking about black students. Fred spoke out, demanding more black teachers and black administrators at the school.

Charles Anderson, a former Proviso East dean, credited Fred's campaign to bring in more black teachers and administrators with his getting a job. "Fred was the reason I was hired at Proviso East High School as dean in charge of attendance," he said. "Until that time, I had been applying for six years and never had been given an interview."

Fred also believed it was unfair that only white girls were nominated for homecoming queen. He organized a student walkout and led a boycott to protest this policy. This resulted in Proviso East students electing their first black homecoming queen. "Some people in Maywood said a black homecoming queen was not worth missing school for," Francis told me. "For Fred it was simply a matter of fairness."

The black and white students at Proviso East seldom mixed socially outside of classes. Because of his popularity and stature with both, Fred was selected to be head of the Inter-racial Council, which met whenever there was racial friction. "Fred's powerful and resonating voice called for calm and discussion," Anderson told me.

The year after Hampton graduated, the principal called Fred back to ease growing racial tensions. White, black, and Latino students participated in a three-day workshop, along with school officials and community members. Fred listened to all the grievances and put together a joint plan to empower each of the student groups and give them a voice in how the school was run.

While in high school, Fred also worked regularly. During the school year, he was a stock boy at the Jewel grocery store in Maywood. When he was older but still in high school, he washed dishes at Dino's restaurant in Elmhurst. In the summers he found factory jobs at the American Can Company and twice at Corn Products. He saved and eventually used his earnings to pay his college tuition.

Fred found jobs for some of the many unemployed black teenagers in his neighborhood as well and successfully pushed the Village of Maywood to fund a summer job program. Of specific concern to Fred was the absence of a municipal swimming pool. Too far from Lake Michigan for trips to the beach, Maywood had no amenities to provide blacks with relief from Chicago's very hot and sticky summers. The white kids went to the pool at the private Veteran Industrial Park in neighboring Bellwood, but black kids weren't allowed. Though Fred couldn't swim, he and his friends carpooled black kids from Maywood to a Chicago Park District pool in the suburb of Lyons, several miles away. He began to talk to the kids and their parents about organizing for a public pool in Maywood.

Fred's outspokenness earned the attention of Don Williams, the head of the West Suburban NAACP chapter. Williams was doing a study of civil rights grievances and identified the same issues Fred had: youth education, recreation, and jobs. There was no active unit of the youth branch of the NAACP in the western suburbs, so Williams asked Fred if he would organize one. He told Fred he could invite his friends to join the NAACP as well. Fred accepted. In 1965 he started the West Suburban Youth Chapter of the NAACP, which drew up a list of grievances. Williams presented the grievances to the NAACP Board, which vowed to support the youth chapter. With Fred as the chair, it grew to more than two hundred members in less than a year.

Under Fred's leadership, young black people in Maywood accelerated the campaign for a public pool and ultimately a recreational center. They were met with a mixed reaction by the Village Board. Some members didn't want an integrated facility, which they feared would result in racial strife. Others didn't want to spend the money. But two members, Reverend Tom and Doris Strieter, were extremely impressed with Fred's presentations and joined him in advocating for the pool. Reverend Strieter had Fred speak at the religious college where he taught; he later wrote, "Fred was a master orator. His rhetoric was stunning as he confronted his white audience with a picture of America's unjust society that most had never imagined before."

4

Chicago, Becoming a Lawyer

In 1964, as sixteen-year-old Fred was speaking out in Maywood, I began at the University of Chicago Law School. On the South Side of Chicago I was surrounded by a poor black community, one being partially displaced by the university I was attending. With black militancy permeating the political atmosphere, amplified by the recent murder of Malcolm X, I could not ignore the blatant inequality between their lives and mine.

At law school I met my classmate Bernardine Dohrn. Intense and persuasive and very attractive, she would become the leader of the Weathermen faction of Students for a Democratic Society. She wore short skirts and high boots and looked you in the eye. Bernardine was passionate and adept at expressing her left politics. She also had a lively sense of humor and an endearing laugh that drew you in and made you laugh, too.

Bernardine chaired the Law Students Civil Rights Research Council (LSCRRC), which provided funds for law students to take summer jobs with civil rights lawyers in the South. In 1965 she matched me with the black law firm of Hollowell and Moore in Atlanta. I had to go to Chicago to take my first steps to confront segregation where I grew up.

My parents knew both Donald Hollowell, a respected older lawyer in Atlanta, and Howard Moore, his younger, more fiery partner. Moore had defended many sit-in protesters and had represented civil rights leader Reverend C. B. King and his followers in Albany, Georgia, when they were beaten for marching and organizing sit-ins to integrate Albany's restaurants and stores. Most of the work I did was on Howard's paying civil cases to free him up so he could do his civil rights work.

But one day Howard Moore called me into his office. "Jeff, I want you to bust Bonners Supper Club," he said. "It's a small restaurant in

Crawfordsville that claims to be a private club. Why don't you take a friend and see if they'll wait on you?"

If we could establish that Bonners served white nonmembers like us, we could prove that their "private club" designation was merely a charade and a way to avoid serving blacks.

I asked my friend Henry Bauer—who had gone to the Atlanta Cracker ballgames with Walter and me—to come along. The restaurant was in a white frame building a block from the central square. Below the words on the painted sign, BONNERS SUPPER CLUB, etched on a separate board, were the words PRIVATE CLUB, MEMBERS ONLY.

We entered the small, plain restaurant, little more than a diner. Its ten round wooden tables were half occupied, as were the bar stools along the side bar.

"Howdy, come on in," the manager said and led us to a table. "How're y'all tonight?" We sat down, ordered chicken something, and waited nervously for the food to arrive.

An eternity seemed to pass. We felt everyone was staring at us. Meanwhile, the town's uniformed sheriff, a middle-aged, husky man with a tin star on his tan shirt and a holstered gun on his hip, entered. He pulled up a chair at the table next to us and began shelling peas with a couple patrons already sitting there. Henry and I were silent after he sat down.

"How y'all boys doin'?" he leaned over and asked us.

I responded in my best and deepest Southern accent. "We're faan."

"Where y'all coming from?" he inquired.

"Atlanta."

I was waiting for the next question, *Why'd you come all the way out here to eat?* It wasn't long coming.

"We got some friends we're going to see in Savannah," I said. That was about as far as I had worked our excuse for being there. Fortunately, I never had to explain why we weren't on the most direct route to Savannah. The sheriff went back to shelling peas.

Finally our food arrived. I pushed it around the plate, eating enough to be polite, and asked the waitress for the check. "Can I have a receipt also?" She looked puzzled.

"Won't that do?" she said pointing at the torn slip from one of those anonymous green pads.

"It will if you sign your name, the name of the restaurant, and the date," I responded.

Again, she gave me a questioning look. After an awkward pause she wrote down the information and gave the receipt back to me. We were out of there before another pea could be shelled.

The next morning I reported what happened to Howard Moore and gave him the receipt. He had me fill out an affidavit about getting served at the restaurant. Three months later, Howard wrote me that Bonners Supper Club "was no longer segregated."

At the University of Chicago, even in our nonradical law school, Vietnam was on everyone's mind. Through 1966 and 1967, the United States steadily increased its troop level and expanded the war. As casualties rose on both sides, students at campuses across the country increased the militancy of their protests. A few University of Chicago students were arrested for seeking to enter the back porch of provost Edward Levi's home. A right-wing law professor threw his radio and struck an antiwar protester at another demonstration. Although I was sympathetic to the protesters' objectives, I wasn't ready to join in and accept the consequence—likely expulsion from school.

At the law school, you were either against the war or you kept quiet. I don't recall any student, not even my classmate John Ashcroft, who would become President George W. Bush's attorney general, vocally supporting the war. Like many of his reactionary brethren, he laid low in the 1960s. His time had not yet come.

I was horrified and found no justification for the napalm and phosphorous bombs being dropped, or for the U.S. presence in Vietnam at all. I read about Ho Chi Minh and the decades of Vietnamese resistance to colonialism—against the French, then the Japanese, the French again, and finally the United States. As I followed the war more closely, I went from ignorance to skepticism to strong opposition. I eventually supported the National Liberation Front, the Vietcong. The Vietnamese wanted not just peace, but liberation.

Our opposition to the war appeared to have little effect on Lyndon Johnson. By 1967 he had a half million American troops in Vietnam and was seeking more. He promised to call up reserve units, and I feared mine would be included. I had joined a military intelligence unit in

Chicago in 1966 because unassigned reservists were the first to be called to active duty. I could not see myself fighting, killing, or being killed in Vietnam.

In March 1967, Dr. King came to Chicago. Together with Dr. Benjamin Spock, he led a five-thousand-person march through downtown to the Coliseum. Bernardine had urged me to come along on King's integration marches the year before, but I wasn't willing to be pelted by rocks in the white ethnic neighborhoods where the marches went. This time I *was* in the Coliseum, when Dr. King spoke about Vietnam:

> Poverty, urban problems and social progress are generally ignored when the guns of war become a national obsession. . . . America is a great nation, but honesty impels me to admit that our power has often made us arrogant. We feel that our money can do anything. We arrogantly feel that we have some divine, messianic mission to police the whole world. . . . We arm Negro soldiers to kill on foreign battlefields, but offer little protection for their relatives from beatings and killings in our own South. I am disappointed with our failure to deal positively and forthrightly with the triple evils of racism, extreme materialism and militarism.

Dr. King went on:

> Those of us who love peace must organize as effectively as the war hawks. As they spread the propaganda of war, we must spread the propaganda of peace. We must combine the fervor of the civil rights movement with the equal fervor of the peace movement. We must demonstrate, teach, and preach, until the very foundations of our nation are shaken.

His speech brought together the black struggles for equality and liberation and the antiwar movement. Both demanded action. Two years later, when I heard Fred Hampton speak with equal fervor, I wondered if he had been in that vast hall of the Coliseum, taking notes.

The press, as well as the leadership of the NAACP and other civil rights organizations, condemned Dr. King for expressing his opposition to the Vietnam War. They thought it would jeopardize his civil rights agenda. A month after his address in Chicago, Dr. King responded to these criticisms at the Riverside Church in New York in his most famous antiwar speech.

> I do feel that the Negro people, because of their peculiar experiences with oppression through the use of physical violence, have a particular responsibility to not participate in inflicting oppressive violence on another people. This is not a privilege but an exceptional moral responsibility. . . . There comes a time when one must have a stand that is neither safe, nor popular, but he must take it because it is right. This is where I find myself today.

Dr. King accepted the responsibility of the formerly oppressed not to be oppressors.

That spring shortly after I heard Dr. King denounce the war, I met Mary Frank. She was twenty-three, a year younger than me, and lived in a studio apartment overlooking the botanical gardens and the grounds of the Lincoln Park Zoo. Mary had recently divorced a brilliant, alcoholic English professor at Northwestern University.

Mary was short, vibrant, and attractive, with an infectious smile, long dark hair, and big brown eyes. She was enthusiastic and warm, given to hyperbole, and had a great sense of humor. We "meshed." Mary's family, like mine, was upper-middle-class Jewish, although she possessed Hungarian passion in contrast to the German reserve I'd inherited from my mother.

Mary had been more precocious and aware than I was in my college years. She had attended Reed College and then Berkeley and participated in the free speech movement. When we met in 1967, she was working for the Film Group, a small progressive filmmaking company. The next year they began making a documentary film about a young charismatic Black Panther leader: Fred Hampton.

When I graduated from law school, I moved into Mary's studio apartment, where we slept in a single bed for almost a year. I decided to stay in Chicago after I graduated law school and took a job with the Legal Assistance Foundation, representing indigent people in noncriminal cases.

In the summer of 1967, I worked half time and studied for the bar exam. When I passed, I took the train to the State Capitol in Springfield for the swearing-in ceremony. We were welcomed by one of the older members of the Illinois Supreme Court. I sat in the large crowd, with my lefty friends from law school and Legal Aid. I expected a bland speech. Instead, we were harangued by a Supreme Court justice, whose welcoming address was a warning:

> As young men and women about to be admitted to the bar, I feel compelled to warn you about the greatest danger to civil liberties and to our peace loving society; that which threatens the very core of our nation, that which can only lead to the destruction of harmony and to the promulgation of violence. I am talking about Black Power.

I sat forward, irritated. Given the escalating war in Vietnam, and the degrading conditions in which urban blacks lived, Black Power hardly seemed the threat we should be worrying about. The justice continued to expound on the duty each of us young lawyers had to condemn Black Power in whatever form it took. His reactionary rhetoric made Black Power more attractive to me. Still, I had no hint that my next ten years would be spent representing some of its strongest advocates.

5

Fred and the Rise of the Panthers

When Fred Hampton turned eighteen in 1966, he refused to register for the draft. The year before, the United States had started bombing North Vietnam. The Student Nonviolent Coordinating Committee (SNCC) led the campaign to register Southern blacks to vote and set up Freedom Schools in Mississippi. They opposed fighting and dying for democracy in Vietnam when registering to vote in Mississippi could be a capital offense for blacks. In 1966, Muhammad Ali refused to register for the draft, declaring, "Why should they ask me to put on a uniform and go ten thousand miles from home and drop bombs and bullets on brown people in Vietnam while so-called Negro people in Louisville are treated like dogs and denied simple human rights?" He also was well known for the more succinct version: "I ain't got no quarrel with the Vietcong. No Vietcong ever called me Nigger."

Fred decided with many others, "Hell, no, we won't go." He was reading Mao Tse-Tung, Che Guevara, and Ho Chi Minh and identified with the socialist struggles of the Third World. Soon he declared he was not just for "peace in Vietnam," but "victory in Vietnam" for the Vietnamese. In 1966, Fred's opposition to the U.S. war effort was contrary to the views expressed by Dr. King's Southern Christian Leadership Conference and the NAACP, the two civil rights organizations with whom he was working.

Fred's evolution cannot be separated from the political events and movements around him. In 1964 riots broke out in Harlem. The following year a riot erupted in the Watts neighborhood in South Central Los Angeles in response to an incident of police harassment. In the five days of looting and setting fires that followed, thirty-six black people were killed, one thousand were injured, and four thousand were arrested. The Public Accommodations Act of 1964 and the Voting Rights Act of 1965 did nothing to change the conditions of blacks in ghettos outside the South. There was a consensus among civil rights groups: they had to confront the poverty and discrimination facing urban blacks—problems caused more by institutional practices and economic inequality than Jim Crow laws.

In 1966, James Meredith, the first black to integrate the University of Mississippi, organized a march from Memphis to Jackson, Mississippi. SNCC organizer Cleveland Sellers described what happened:

> Meredith is shot walking down the highway in Mississippi. Meredith was marching against fear in Mississippi. No better place for us to then . . . introduce Black Power. We had talked about "Freedom Now"; we had talked about anti-Vietnam; we had different issues along the way. So when we talked about Black Power it was in a political context of building political institutions and social institutions in the black community, where we worked. I had no idea, and I'm being honest, that Black Power was going to take off the way it did. The only other incident that I can think of that took off like Black Power was the emergence of Malcolm X.

The response of the media and most whites to the term Black Power was swift, negative, and hysterical. Many saw Black Power as an attack on all white people. Blacks saw it differently. SNCC organizer Courtland Cox explained: "It delivered a positive message to them (the black community). It said 'You are beautiful, you must be strong, you have a proud history, and there's strength in unity.'" The message of Black Power resonated with Fred Hampton. He saw Black Power not as a tool to attack whites but as a concept to bring blacks together and build their confidence. Fred said that "blackness was what was in your heart, not the color of your skin." But any symbol of black unity, including the modest Afro that Fred wore, threatened many whites.

In 1966 high school senior Fred Hampton was working on his own version of black empowerment. He set up a black cultural center in Maywood with a black history section and continued his campaign to hire more black teachers and administrators at Proviso East. During this period two young Californians were similarly engaged. They demanded more black administrators and black history courses at Merritt College in Oakland, California. One was twenty-four-year-old Huey Newton; the other, thirty-year-old Bobby Seale.

Newton and Seale worked at the North Oakland Poverty Center. They went door to door asking residents what they needed and wanted. The information gleaned became the basis of the Ten Point Program when they formed the Black Panther Party for Self-Defense later that year. The program called for 1) freedom to determine the destiny of the black community, 2) full employment for blacks, 3) an end to capitalist exploitation of the black community, 4) decent housing, 5) informed education, 6) exemption for black men from military service, 7) an end to police brutality and murder, 8) freedom for black prisoners, 9) black juries for black criminal defendants, and 10) "Land, Bread, Housing, Education, Clothing, Justice and Peace."

The Black Panthers derived their name from the Lowndes County Freedom Organization, organized by SNCC in Alabama, which formed the Black Panther Party as an alternative to the all-white Democratic Party. The Black Panthers in Oakland adopted Malcolm X's later position that while black culture and black history were beautiful and significant, not all whites were bad, and that whites could be allies as long as blacks controlled the main policies and the agenda for action.

One of the first actions of the newly formed Black Panther Party in Oakland was for members to arm themselves, which was legal in California as long as the weapons were not concealed. They followed Oakland police cars around the ghetto to monitor their treatment of black citizens. This outraged the Oakland Police Department and gave the Panthers immediate visibility. Incidents of police brutality decreased substantially during their patrols, increasing acceptance of the Panthers by the black community.

In Chicago Fred Hampton also spoke out against police brutality. As the leader of the NAACP Youth Chapter, he originally marched for raises of police salaries to get more professional police in Maywood. Later he pushed for changes to make the police more accountable and to give Maywood citizens the power to fire brutal cops.

Dr. King and his organization, the Southern Christian Leadership Conference, accepted the need to confront the issues facing urban blacks. Like other civil rights leaders, Dr. King attempted to address the poverty and discrimination highlighted by the urban riots that by 1966 had spread to Detroit, Michigan; Newark, New Jersey; and many other cities. That year he moved to Chicago to mount a campaign against racial discrimination in jobs, housing, and schools.

Dr. King rented an apartment on the West Side and led marches protesting the exclusion of blacks from many white neighborhoods of the city and its southwestern suburbs. Marchers were met by rock-throwing mobs with people dressed as Nazis. Dr. King was struck by a rock thrown in Marquette Park and later commented, "Swastikas blossomed in Chicago's parks like misbegotten weeds." As Bill Hampton saw it, "In the South the motto is 'you can live near me but don't get too big.' In the North it is 'you can get big but don't live near me'."

In 1966, the summer Dr. King was marching and living in Chicago, Fred graduated high school and worked at Corn Products in a job program designed for high school seniors and college students, earning money to go to college the next year. At seventeen he was supporting himself. One of the people Fred impressed most was Bill Taylor, the president of the Oil, Chemical, and Atomic Workers Union at the Corn Products plant. He describes Fred as "very dynamic, quick witted, and much less focused on himself than on the world around him. He was always trying to bring black people together." He remembers Fred saying, "If you walk through life and don't help anybody, you haven't had much of a life."

Bill Taylor walked with Fred in several of Dr. King's marches. "Fred was enthusiastic for awhile," Taylor said, "but in Jefferson Park, a heckler spit in the face of a woman with us. After that Fred told Reverend King he couldn't keep marching for nonviolence in the face of the violent mobs around them." Fred was not alone. At one rally young blacks booed Dr. King for his nonviolent response to the rock-throwing whites. When Dr. King threatened to march through Cicero, then considered the most racist neighborhood in Chicago, Mayor Richard J. Daley intervened. Dr. King called off the march in exchange for an agreement by the mayor and the Chicago Association of Realtors to promote fair housing practices. Some people in SNCC, the Congress of Racial Equality (CORE), and local organizations saw the agreement as a sellout. They continued with the march.

Dr. King did not achieve the success in Chicago that he had in Alabama. His nonviolent tactics and religious outlook did not attract young blacks in urban areas. Meanwhile, his marches stirred up the whites. I watched on TV as news cameras showed the angry faces and Nazi signs of the white mobs who came out to jeer and attack Dr. King's marchers. Mayor Daley and the Democratic Party were beholden to those Irish, Italian, and Eastern European whites to maintain control of city hall.

After Dr. King failed to make major changes in Chicago, Fred tended more toward Malcolm X's message of self-defense. Still Fred continued to speak highly of Dr. King: "Every time I speak in church, I always try to say something, you know, about Martin Luther King. I have a lot of respect for Martin Luther King. I think he was one of the greatest orators that the country ever produced."

Fred's attention, like many other young blacks, was drawn to an event on the West Coast. In May 1967, thirty Oakland Panthers, twenty-four men and six women, went to the California legislature in Sacramento carrying rifles to dramatize their right of self-defense, as well as to protest pending legislation that would overturn the law allowing them to legally carry unconcealed weapons.

Even though Bobby Seale and many of the other Panthers ended up with six-month sentences for "conspiracy to disturb the peace," and the legislation passed, the photos and TV images of the armed Panthers in leather jackets and black berets at the capitol steps was a shot heard 'round the world. The media responded with horror at blacks with guns invading the legislature. Most whites felt threatened by the images they saw. Many young blacks had a different response and supported the action. Panther chapters started up in Los Angeles, Atlanta, New York, and Detroit.

Black militancy was on the rise in Chicago as well. In the fall of 1967, Fred and Jim Ivory, a respected dentist and NAACP member, addressed a Maywood rally of over a hundred young people. Fred urged his listeners to come to the Maywood Village Board meeting the next night to press their demands for a public swimming pool and recreational center.

The following evening a large crowd, mostly young blacks, went to the Maywood Village Board meeting. Not all were allowed inside. Fred urged the board to find a larger space or let those outside come in, even if they had to stand. The Maywood police panicked, tear-gassing the people who had not been let in. Angered by the police reaction, the young people left the village hall, and ran down Fifth Avenue, Maywood's main street. They broke store windows and threatened residents, including Methodist minister Ron Graham and his wife. A guest at their home was punched by one of the teenagers running from the police.

Seeking a scapegoat, the Maywood police arrested and charged Fred and Jim Ivory with "mob action" because of their speeches the night before, even though they were inside the village hall when the violence took place. Fred stayed in jail for three days before he could post the five hundred dollar bail.

There was disagreement over the tactics of the marches and rallies led by Fred Hampton and the NAACP Youth Chapter. Some NAACP members thought they were too confrontational. The police felt particularly threatened by the sight of large numbers of black youth coming to the village board meetings making demands. While the adult NAACP chapter did not withdraw its support for the youth chapter's activities, neither did it publicly endorse their tactics. As Fred's friend and fellow activist Marvin Carter put it, "They were sort of behind us but not exactly with us."

Following the village board meeting, Fred was targeted by the Maywood police and arrested on several occasions for technical traffic violations. The harassment became so great that Fred stopped driving. The local police were not the only law enforcement agency watching Fred Hampton. After his arrest for mob action, he was put on the FBI's Key Agitator Index, a list of activists that FBI director J. Edgar Hoover ordered FBI agents to monitor closely.

6

Convergence

In the fall of 1967, Army Reserve units like mine were being activated everyday. If I refused to go, it would be desertion, not merely draft dodging. But fighting for the United States in Vietnam went against everything I had come to believe. When I realized this, the decision became easy. I woke up one morning and said to Mary, "I'm not gonna go, no matter what. I won't kill and I won't be killed in Vietnam and I'll take the consequences." The decision behind me, I felt at ease. I never had to decide whether to leave the country or assume a public stance and have a political trial. My unit was never called to active duty.

That winter Mary's mother suggested, since we were already living together, we should get married. Her sister had just died in a scuba diving accident and her family needed something to give them joy. Marriage seemed a rather natural next step, not one I pondered over. Our families loved it, particularly my dad, who shared with Mary's father a great sense of humor and both men enjoyed telling jokes. We had a small wedding at her house and resumed life together in a Lincoln Park apartment, with some new furniture, dishes, and a queen-size bed. Neither of us dwelt much on ceremony in 1968.

A month later, on April 4, I sat behind a desk on the second floor of the Robert Taylor Homes project on the South Side of Chicago. Constructed in the 1950s, Robert Taylor Homes housed over forty thousand African Americans in rows of twenty-five-story, concrete and cinder block buildings extending ten blocks north to south on the east side of the Dan Ryan Expressway.

There were no parks or even trees where we worked, only boarded-up businesses and cement playgrounds strewn with shattered glass and broken equipment. The U.S. Census Bureau had identified the Robert Taylor Homes area as both being the most densely populated and having the lowest per capita income of any community in the country.

I handled landlord/tenant, consumer fraud, and welfare cases, and became particularly skillful at preventing or delaying evictions. I could guarantee my clients several months of extensions before being thrown out on the streets, but I had no way to address the underlying problem of too little money to pay rent and other necessities. In spite of the poverty, many families managed to decorate their homes as refuges of sanity and order in the midst of the gangs, graffiti, violence, and squalor all around them. Inside, many apartments were furnished with comfortable, sometimes even plush, furniture. Pictures of nature, religious shrines, and graduation photos adorned every available wall and countertop, symbols of love and hope amidst despair. Photographs of President Kennedy and Dr. King adorned many mantels.

That morning, Ruth, our paralegal, rushed into my office crying. "I just heard on the radio that Martin Luther King was shot dead in Memphis," she said.

My stomach sank. I flashed on Dr. King speaking at the Coliseum a year earlier.

"What happened?"

Ruth's voice quivered between sobs. She had been a community organizer in Chicago for years and marched with Dr. King two years earlier. "He was shot on a motel balcony. The radio said it was a sniper."

I followed her into her office to hear more on the radio. The announcer reported that Dr. King was standing with SCLC friends when he was shot. He was already dead when he arrived at the hospital.

When I returned to my office, I was shaken, disoriented. *Who really killed him? Was it the government?* I thought of all those apartments with his picture over the mantel, many of them next to President Kennedy. *Now they both had been assassinated, and Malcolm too. Who's left for black people to believe in?* The eviction notices and installment sales contracts on my desk became a blur. I looked out the window at the vast expanse of project buildings with their concrete balconies bordered by chain-link fences and wondered what the reaction would be. I didn't have to wait long. We soon heard reports that African Americans were rebelling on the West Side. They were in the streets, breaking windows, looting, and setting fires. Early in the afternoon, Ruth walked in and told Layton Olson, the other attorney in the office, and me rather firmly, "I think you should leave Robert Taylor Homes. You all might not be safe here, you know what I mean?" We were the only whites in the projects.

"Yeah, you're right," I said. Although I didn't think our office had made enemies, I knew that we were unknown to 99 percent of the people in the area. We heeded Ruth's advice and walked briskly to the parking lot, leaving my files open on my desk and expecting to come back the next morning. Although the South Side remained calm, that office never reopened!

The rebellion on the West Side continued through the night. Mayor Daley issued orders to the police to "shoot to kill rioters, shoot to maim looters." Like the rest of the white people in Chicago, I was hunkered down at home watching the TV coverage of looting and fires and hundreds of spectators. African American teenagers were being arrested and beaten en masse. The broadcasts were frequently interrupted with warnings that it was not safe to go near the rioting—for most white people that meant all black neighborhoods. With news accounts of mounting arrests and high bails, I couldn't stop pacing.

"It looks like they're rounding up every black person on the West Side," I said to Mary, after an eyewitness camera showed the police arresting a group of young African Americans standing a block away from a burning store.

"Yeah, King is dead, and the police are going crazy," Mary said angrily.

"I can't just sit here!" I answered. "I'm going to court. Fuck it. Somebody has to represent those kids."

Her anger turned to apprehension.

"Don't worry, they're not gonna shoot me," I said, fingering the lapel of the suit I had never taken off.

It was after nine o'clock when I drove downtown and parked near police headquarters, a thirteen-story concrete edifice that was also used as the pretrial detention center and bond court. I had to flash my lawyer card to get on the elevator to bond court on the eighth floor. The court was in recess when I arrived. I showed my ID to the bailiff to be admitted to the bullpen area behind the courtroom.

The metallic smell of nervous sweat smacked me in the face. The barred section consisted of a bare room, with cracked linoleum and no chairs and a partially hidden toilet. Wrappers from bologna sandwiches littered the area and I yelled above the din of the prisoners' voices, "I'm a lawyer here to try to get your bond reduced. Come over here if you want help." After a pause, a line formed on the other side of the bars. I began to interview the young men, resting my legal pad on my knee as I took down their personal information.

The men were in their late teens to midtwenties; some attended school and some worked. Most lived with their families and few had criminal records. From the charges against them, mob action and disorderly conduct, I determined almost all were arrested for being in the streets rather than any specific unlawful act. My legal pad was almost full when I saw another lawyer come into the bullpen, a tall, spectacled, thirtyish Ichabod Crane, his thin hair going in all directions. "I'm Dennis Cunningham," he said, shaking my hand. Because of his disheveled appearance, including a well-worn tweed sport coat with reinforced elbows, I assumed he was a hustler lawyer, someone who hung out in the criminal courts to drum up business.

"Judge Bailey has been told to keep these guys locked up until the riots subside," he explained. "We'll be lucky to get a few out. Those with no backgrounds who can show they have a job or school to go to tomorrow are our best shot." We worked for many hours until well after midnight interviewing the arrestees and presenting what facts we could.

"C'mon, Judge," Dennis would urge in his informal style. "It's clear the police don't have anything on this defendant except he was black and in the streets." In a few cases the judge allowed a reasonable bond (one hundred dollars cash) or recognizance bond (no money required). But Dennis was right. In the majority of cases, Judge Bailey, whom I came to know and dislike as an extremely prosecution-oriented judge, set bonds requiring more than the defendant's family could make. These defendants would remain in custody.

As for my initial assessment of Dennis, I was dead wrong. Dennis had grown up in Winnetka, an affluent suburb of Chicago. He attended New Trier Township High School and went to the University of Chicago as an undergraduate in their program for prodigies. He then enrolled at Loyola Law School with the purpose of representing the civil rights movement. After he graduated, four years earlier than me, Dennis began representing movement protesters. He met his wife Mona Mellis at Chicago's Second City, where she was part of the improvisational cast and he was a bartender and part-time actor. That April night I began a friendship and political relationship with Dennis that continues to this day. It led to my joining the People's Law Office.

Six months after our night at bond court, Howard Alk, the film editor at The Film Group where Mary worked, introduced Dennis Cunningham to Fred Hampton. "This is the guy we are making the documentary about," Alk said. "And Fred, this is an attorney who wants to be a people's lawyer."

"That's what I have always wanted to be," said Fred. After a brief conversation, Fred asked Dennis, "What's your phone number? I may need you."

Over two months later, in February 1969, Dennis got a call from a judge in Maywood. "Where are you, Attorney Cunningham? Your client is here. We're ready to start his trial."

Dennis didn't know he had any clients in Maywood. "Can I speak to him, Judge?" Dennis stalled.

"No," the judge said. "But since it's late already, I'll give you until tomorrow morning to be ready to start Fred Hampton's trial."

Dennis hesitated, but he did not disclose his surprise. "I'll be there."

I don't know many lawyers who would have accepted the challenge of going to trial the next day, never having interviewed his client. Dennis didn't want to give up the opportunity to represent the young leader. When Dennis showed up the next morning, he was more than a little nervous—for good reason. He'd never tried a criminal jury case. He had to look at the file to learn the charge was mob action and that it was about some street violence in Maywood. Outside the courtroom in the hallway, Fred told Dennis, "I want the jury to know exactly why we marched to the village board. I wasn't there when the skirmishes happened, but I know the violence was provoked by the police using tear gas."

"I hear you," Dennis said, "and so will the jury."

Despite his inexperience, Dennis's political approach and folksy style were well suited to the task. The attorney representing Jim Ivory, Fred's codefendant, was a smart and savvy African American lawyer named Jim Montgomery. After serving as an assistant U.S. attorney, Jim was rapidly becoming one of the top criminal lawyers in Chicago.

Dennis and Montgomery had to settle for a white jury because prosecutors at that time were allowed to use their peremptory challenges to strike black people without any justification. After the police testified about the violence, Dennis called Fred Hampton to the witness stand. Montgomery later wrote: "When Fred Hampton took the stand and with total frank, honest, confrontational rhetoric denied any criminal activity and conceded what he was doing, you could see the faces of the jurors change."

In his closing argument Dennis echoed Fred's testimony that he was targeted for organizing a march and not for any criminal conduct.

"Not guilty," was the jury's verdict. Afterward, Fred took Dennis aside and gave him the ultimate compliment: "That's the way I would have done it." Fred was still saying he wanted to be "a lawyer for the people," but he had become the leader of the Chicago Panthers and prefaced his stated aspiration with "if I had time."

By 1969 it seemed like none of us had time. We were heading for the rapids, not knowing what was ahead. In March 1968, Stokely Carmichael and H. Rap Brown came to Chicago and shortly thereafter opened a SNCC office on the South Side on Forty-Third Street. Fred went to the office and invited Stokely to speak in Maywood. A few weeks later Fred introduced him at a large Maywood rally. Fred's introduction was so impressive that Bobby Rush and Bob Brown, the two leaders of Chicago's SNCC Chapter, came up to Fred afterward and introduced themselves.

"I was immediately impressed with Fred's ability to speak powerfully and engage and energize the young audience," U.S. congressman Bobby Rush told me over breakfast, thirty-five years later. "He was physically imposing with a powerful personality and deep guttural laugh. I made up my mind I wanted to work with Fred. He was such a magnetic young man." Rush still spoke Fred's name with reverence. "After the rally, I introduced myself to Fred and asked him if he was part of any organization. He said he was the head of the youth chapter of the NAACP."

Later that year Bobby Rush went to Oakland, where he met with the Panther Central Committee. Stokely and Rap Brown had temporarily joined the Panthers, so there was no conflict between the Panthers and SNCC. Rush returned with a mandate to form a Panther chapter in Chicago. The first person he recruited was Fred Hampton, and they opened the Panther office in November 1968. In four years Fred had evolved from organizing for black homecoming queens to becoming chairman of the Illinois chapter of the Black Panthers. By 1968 he was advocating revolution.

Six months later, the Chicago chapter temporarily stopped taking new members so they could integrate all those who had joined. The Breakfast for Children Program, providing free hot breakfasts for kids before school, had expanded beyond its first site, the Better Boys Foundation, to several other locations. Securing the food from merchants, getting it prepared and delivered to the kitchens, supervising the kids eating before school, and cleaning up afterward was major work for many of the Panther cadre. The rest of the day was often spent selling Panther newspapers, interviewing people and filling out questionnaires on their needs and priorities, getting petitions for community control of police signed, attending political education classes, and maintaining the office.

Early on, women in the party, including Joan McCarty, Ann Campbell, Barbara Sankey, Joan Gray, Stephanie Fisher, Beverlina Powell, and Leta Harrison, took the lead and did the majority of preparation for the breakfast program. Panther member Bradley Greene said the women were the hardest and most effective workers in all the Panther programs.

One Panther woman described being in the Panther office when the phone rang. The person who answered it walked over to Fred and said, "The brothers are here from the West Coast and they are staying at a hotel downtown. They want you to send some Panther sisters down there."

Fred responded quickly and curtly, "You can tell them Panther women in Chicago are working on Panther programs, not as whores for Panther leaders."

"Fred was twenty years old," the Panther sister insisted. "It took a lot of courage for him to stand up to the West Coast guys."

A lot has been written about sexism and the role women held in 1960s and 1970s activist groups. Stokely Carmichael's alleged statement, "The only position for women in SNCC is prone" has been widely quoted. It no doubt expressed some men's sentiments. But women I have interviewed from the Chicago Panther chapter said this was not the prevailing attitude in Chicago, nor was it Fred Hampton's.

"There were some guys always trying to come on to women, but they didn't do this when Fred was around," one former woman Panther told me. Another said, "It wasn't perfect, and we could have done more to elevate women, but feminism was just coming to the fore. We weren't immune from the sexism in the culture." Yvonne King said that Fred helped her and other women practice their elocution skills so they could speak publicly for the Party. Women were given leadership positions on both the Chicago and Illinois Central Committees.

Fred went from site to site working at the breakfast programs and talking to the kids and their parents about what the Black Panther Party was trying to do for the community. Kids were taught revolutionary songs. Parents were asked to participate in the programs, although it was not a requirement for their kids to get fed. In one of his later speeches, Fred said:

> The pigs say, "Well the Breakfast for Children Program is a socialistic program, it's a communistic program." And the women say, "I don't know if I like communism. I don't know if I like socialism. But I know that the Breakfast for Children Program feeds my kids." A lot of people think the Breakfast for Children Program is charity. But what does it do? It takes the people from a stage to another stage. Any program that's revolutionary is an advancing program. Revolution is change. Honey, if you just keep on changing, before you know it—in fact, you don't have to know what it is— they're endorsing it, they're participating in it, and supporting socialism."

Doc Satchel, who started the Panther Health Clinic in Chicago, put it another way:

> The Panthers were an armed propaganda unit that raised the contradictions, set the example and provided the vehicle that the people could ride to revolution. We do not say the Black Panther Party will be overthrowing the government; we heighten the contradictions so the people can decide if they want to change the government.

Fred urged Panther members to sell increasing numbers of the Black Panther newspaper throughout Chicago. The paper was printed weekly on the West Coast and delivered to most major cities, where Panther members and supporters sold it on street corners. Party members were given a sales quota. The paper contained articles about Panther activities throughout the country, with a heavy emphasis on the Oakland Chapter, as well as explanations of the Ten Point Program, articles on national liberation struggles, and some straight-up ideological presentations and cartoons satirizing government figures with police sporting pig snouts.

By and large the Panthers advanced a class analysis, with their party representing the vanguard of the proletariat. In one speech that summer, Fred responded to the criticism of the nationalists who had refused to participate with the Panthers, accusing them of being "engrossed with oppressor country radicals, or white people, or honkies." Fred called these critics "dashiki nationalists."

> We got a lot of answers for those people. First of all, we say primarily that the priority of this struggle is class. That Marx and Lenin and Che Guevara and Mao Tse-Tung, and anybody else who ever said or knew or practiced anything about revolution, always said that a revolution is a class struggle. It was one class—the oppressed—versus those other classes—the oppressor. And it's got to be a universal fact. Those who don't admit to that are those who don't want to get involved in a revolution, because they know as long as they're dealing with a race thing, they'll never be involved in a revolution.

Fred frequently spoke about how nationalism could not replace education: "You can't build a revolution with no education. Jomo Kenyatta did this in Africa and because the people were not educated he became as much an oppressor as the people he overthrew. Look at Papa Doc Duvalier in Haiti. He got everyone to hate whites and he turned into the dictator himself. How will people end up without education?"

As for working with whites, Huey Newton relied on white San Francisco attorney Charles Garry when he was charged with killing a police officer because, as he pointed out, Garry was successful in the white judicial system and had never lost a capital case. In Chicago, Fred and the Panthers sought out the services of white progressive lawyers. Four of us responded by creating an independent law collective that could represent them.

Bradley Greene said the Panthers wanted a twenty-four-hour-a-day commitment. "It was hard for people like me to hold a regular job. Many of the new Panther recruits were college and high school students. They often ended up in Panther cribs where the party paid the rent." Bradley went on, "When couples formed in these apartments, they frequently moved out and got jobs. They could no longer do as much work for the Panthers and it led to some of them leaving the party."

While the Panthers' vision of how the revolutionary struggle would actually come about was not always clearly articulated or understood, at least by me, the work of the programs and organizing was always present. They provided a reality check and a complement to the revolutionary rhetoric.

7

Struggle in the Streets— PLO Begins

Panther members in Chicago went door-to-door in many black communities to find out what peoples' complaints and priorities were and to get signatures on petitions for community control of the police. These neighborhood activities sometimes put them in conflict with Chicago street gangs, who considered many areas their exclusive territories. The gangs had become home for many ghetto youth. They were armed and organized. Sometimes they exercised their power to benefit the community. The Black P. Stone Nation, successor to the Blackstone Rangers, carried out a "no-vote" campaign on the South Side to take votes away from the Democratic machine in favor of more progressive and community-oriented candidates. In 1969 members of the Black Disciples, Chicago's second-largest street gang, made up the majority of demonstrators who picketed and actually halted Chicago construction projects in the Loop, Chicago's business center, until they won positions for African Americans in the building trades unions, which had been a bastion of discrimination.

Unfortunately, gang leaders were often focused on controlling the proceeds from the most thriving business in the ghetto, the drug trade. Gang members were encouraged and sometimes required by their leaders to sell drugs and keep rivals groups out of their territory. Everyone assumed the Chicago police were getting their cut.

In 1969, Fred met and worked out a treaty with David Barksdale, the leader of the Black Disciples. The agreement allowed the Panthers to organize and recruit in areas controlled by the Disciples. Fred had been less successful when he met with the leadership of the Blackstone Rangers. One face-to-face meeting took place at the Rangers headquarters in Chicago's Woodlawn neighborhood. Fred and several other armed Panthers went to the meeting but were quickly surrounded by many better-armed Rangers including Jeff Fort, their leader, and other representatives of the Main 21, the Rangers' governing body.

Fred started rapping, making it clear that the Panthers were not trying to control turf. He wanted the Rangers to join in Panther efforts to stop police brutality, as well as join the Party if they desired. At least he wanted an agreement that Panthers could sell their paper without harassment.

Fort told Fred he could be rich if he and the Panthers joined the Rangers' drug operation. Fred refused. Fred did not use drugs and he and Panther policy did not allow Panther members to use them. Drugs and alcohol were prohibited in the Panther office. The meeting ended with Fort acknowledging that the Panthers were not a rival gang but still refusing to permit them to operate in Ranger territory. The meeting lessened tensions only slightly.

Nevertheless, Fred's efforts to work with and organize gang members caused fear throughout the police and FBI. After the meeting at Ranger headquarters, Chicago police, following an FBI tip, arrested a carload of armed Panthers driving away. This resulted in criminal charges against the Panthers and set off speculation that the Rangers had snitched on them. Years later we would learn that an FBI informant in the Panthers had tipped off his FBI control, who then notified the police.

On January 24, 1969, the Chicago police arrested Fred following an FBI tip that he was appearing on a local TV station. In front of the live cameras he was led away on an old traffic warrant. Later, Fred told people that when he got to the police car, he noticed he hadn't been cuffed. When placed in the back seat he saw there was a gun resting there. "I spotted a set-up," he said. "I put my wrists outside the car and started screaming, 'There's a gun in the car that somebody left.'" His quick thinking worked. That day he avoided police bullets.

Fred and the Panthers sought alliances with other groups in Chicago. One of them was the Young Lords Organization (YLO), which had started as a Puerto Rican street gang. In the late 1960s, under the leadership of Cha-Cha Jimenez, they focused on stopping Chicago's Department of Urban Renewal and other city agencies from forcing poor and working-class people, many of whom were Puerto Rican, out of the Lincoln Park neighborhood.

In 1969 the YLO took over Reverend Bruce Johnson's church on Armitage Avenue, and renamed it the People's Church. With Reverend Johnson's support, the church became the headquarters for the Lincoln Park Poor People's Coalition, which included black, white, and Mexican groups who were fighting to keep Lincoln Park from being gentrified. Following the Panther example, the YLO started a Breakfast for Children Program as well as a health clinic in the church. The police were constantly harassing and arresting Cha-Cha for organizing the Puerto Rican community against the city's gentrification plan. For a period in 1969, Dennis went to court regularly to get him released on bond. The Panthers, Young Lords, and Young Patriots, an organization of white Southern youth from Uptown, formed their own Rainbow Coalition, a precursor to Jesse Jackson's, to protest police brutality and abuse in Chicago and support the Panther demand for community control of police.

On April 4, 1969, Manuel Ramos, a Puerto Rican teenager and the minister of defense of the YLO, was shot and killed by an off-duty Chicago police officer at a Young Lords party. Another Young Lord was shot and critically wounded. The police officer's version, that Ramos had attacked him, did not fit with other witness accounts or with the location and direction of the bullets fired into Ramos's body.

The Rainbow Coalition organized a march on May 3 to protest Ramos's killing and demand a new and independent investigation. The police had declared Ramos's death "justifiable homicide," the standard ruling in police shooting cases. In the thirty-five years I practiced civil rights law in Chicago, I don't recall the police ever finding any on-duty police killing anything but "justifiable."

I was growing weary of working at the Legal Assistance Foundation and was drawn more and more to helping organizations such as the Young Lords and the Panthers. And so I was present on that bright and windy spring day in 1969 at People's Park, marching with the Manuel Ramos family. We intended to present a letter to the police demanding a thorough investigation of Ramos' death. In addition to the coalition, the marchers included SDS members and other white leftists. Our march was scheduled to go from Lincoln Park south to the Eighteenth District Police Station on Chicago Avenue.

Dennis and I were among the nearly one thousand protesters who assembled around noon at the plot of vacant land at Halsted and Armitage that the Young Lords had named People's Park. The plot was across the street from where we would open our law collective four months later. We left the park with the Young Lords, in their brown berets with red stars on the front, leading the procession. The march took us through the all-black Cabrini-Green housing project, controlled by the Cobra Stones, part of the Black P. Stone Nation.

As we left the projects heading south, our procession picked up a tail: about one hundred Cobra Stones with red caps turned sideways. Some were holding car radio antennas as weapons and taunting us from behind. When we turned left on Chicago Avenue and arrived at the Eighteenth District Police Station, a hundred cops in formation and full riot gear started marching toward us from the other side. They wore helmets with plastic face guards and carried batons. The Cobra Stones were still approaching us from behind, the gap closing quickly. We were trapped.

I was standing near the Ramos family when I heard, "Join arms together! Protect our march!" I felt paralyzed. My legal training had not taught me how to handle this situation. I considered fleeing but there were no safe havens for legal observers that day. As I deliberated, I saw my friend Ted Stein, another lawyer, unhesitatingly join arms with those on both sides of him. I got a sense of what solidarity means. *Well, Jeff,* I thought, *this is it. There ain't no ducking today. There's only one honorable thing to do.* I locked arms with the people on my right and left, ready to face whatever came. As we stood our ground waiting for the confrontation, Hilda Ignatin, a community organizer working with the Young Lords, left our line and approached the Cobra Stones. They stopped within a few feet of us.

"We're marching to protest a police killing," she said. "Why don't you join us?" They looked surprised and hesitated. Their leaders conferred.

"The police told us the Young Lords were helping the Panthers take over our Projects," one of them said.

"That's not true," Hilda replied. "Our issue is a police killing right here in the Eighteenth District. The same police who brutalize you." The Cobra Stones conferred again. I watched intently. It looked like they were arguing. Then one of them stepped out front. "OK, we'll join you," he said. I relaxed a bit. They stood with us, even joined our chants for justice for the Ramos family. Their presence temporarily stopped the cops coming from the east. Dennis and the Ramos family presented their letter demanding a new investigation to the district commander, who came out to take it, then quickly vanished inside. It was a rare moment when the left and black street gangs connected.

All of us left together. We started walking, but when we turned north on LaSalle Street, it became a trot, and then a run. The crowd smashed store windows with rocks and bottles. I had never been in a group that was breaking windows. My level of alarm rose with each burst of shattering glass. It was electric. I didn't break any windows, but I didn't run away.

The year 1969 was the era of "Street Fightin' Man." The Rolling Stones song was often played as a warm-up for militant demonstrations. Excesses became the norm, whether it was the pulse, passion, and drugs of Janis Joplin and Jimi Hendrix or the increased bombing in southeast Asia. Nikki Giovanni wrote a poem in which she asked, "Nigger can you kill?" Many saw it as a legitimate call to arms for black rage. I too became drawn to the exhilaration of street confrontations and was convinced of their political effectiveness. These were what the press reported and what made headlines. Orderly protests were mostly ignored. However, as a lawyer, the activity was a lot safer for me than the people I supported. I was seldom in the streets, only in court with the unlucky arrestees.

In May 1969, shortly after the Ramos march, Fred had another trial. The summer before, an ice cream vendor in Maywood had been pushed down inside his truck and seventy-one bars of ice cream were handed out to Maywood kids. The police later arrested Fred Hampton after they claimed the victim identified Fred's picture, which they had shown him. Fred always denied he did the robbery. Recently while visiting the Hampton household, I met Thomas Blair, a neighbor of theirs in Maywood since the 1960s. Blair told me he took and passed out the ice cream. His knowledge of the details, as well as his physique, which was similar to Fred's, convinced me he told the truth.

Jean Williams, a female attorney Fred had met on King's marches, represented him. The prosecution brought the ice cream vendor back from Vietnam to testify, an unusual expense and effort in a case with no injuries and so little loss, but Cook County state's attorney Edward Hanrahan wanted Fred in jail. Hanrahan had a broad face and a determined look. He came from Daley's Bridgeport neighborhood and combined Irish appeal with a Harvard Law School education. Ambitious and serious, with a short temper and little sense of humor, he was widely regarded as heir apparent to Mayor Richard J. Daley. In his public speeches after he was elected Cook County state's attorney in 1968, Hanrahan referred to the Panthers as a "gang." This would serve his purpose well when later that year he and Mayor Daley declared a "war on gangs." Hanrahan presented himself as the guardian of law and order, defending society against black chaos and violence.

After he took office in January 1969, Hanrahan created a nine-man Special Prosecutions Unit (SPU) to deal with gangs, even though a similar Gang Intelligence Unit (GIU) already existed in the police department. Hanrahan's SPU was given primarily police functions. Hanrahan had served as the U.S. attorney for Chicago and its suburbs, and he appointed his former assistant, Richard Jalovec, to be in charge of the SPU. In June an additional team of police officers, led by Sergeant Daniel Groth, was added. It included Officer James "Gloves" Davis, a black cop notorious for brutally beating black youth after he put on black leather gloves.

Mayor Daley made the police chief, superintendent of schools, fire commissioner, and head of human resources a top-level committee to direct the city's actions against gangs. Hanrahan, the spokesman for the campaign, promised to increase prosecution of gang members. At one point, speaking to a group of African American mothers, he referred to gang members as "animals unfit for society." He was booed. After that his antigang campaign lost favor among blacks.

Even though Hanrahan vilified Fred and the Panthers publicly, particularly their antipolice rhetoric, many Maywood board members and community activists, black and white, attended Fred's ice cream trial to support him. Some testified as character witnesses. The village board agreed to let Fred do a mock trial using their assembly room as the courtroom. In the mock trial Fred represented himself before a people's tribunal consisting of prominent Maywood citizens and some board members. Exercising the lawyer skills he was never able to utilize in a real courtroom, Fred obtained a "not guilty" from the citizen's jury.

Many of those who acted as jurors and spectators later told me how impressed they had been with the sharpness of his cross-examination and the power of his argument.

At the time of Fred's real trial, I worked with Skip Andrew and Donald Stang, two young lawyers just out of law school in the main Legal Assistance office in downtown Chicago. Skip had spent two years in the Peace Corps in the Dominican Republic. There he witnessed the democratic election of the leftist Juan Bosch, who was quickly overthrown by a U.S.-supported coup. Some of the people Skip worked with were killed in the U.S. invasion. He and other Peace Corps volunteers were so outraged that only a special emissary from the White House talked them out of holding a press conference denouncing the United States.

Skip, the son of a Protestant minister in Iowa, was intense and meticulous, bordering on the compulsive, and took practicing law very seriously. He usually wore a suit and tie, sported a trimmed mustache and goatee, and looked older and more conservative than the rest of us, which added to his credibility in court. Skip and his wife Nancy lived on Burling Street, a few doors from Mary and me in Lincoln Park.

Donald Stang was a Harvard Law School graduate and came from a liberal, Jewish, upper-middle-class family in New York. He was intellectual, cautious, and quiet. He picked his words carefully. Don also had a wry sense of humor and a baby face. His hair was shorter than mine, but we both sported the shorter version of the Afro, a "Jew-fro."

Skip and Don attended Fred's ice cream truck robbery trial. In the small courtroom, they made eye contact with Fred, who later approached them in the hall. Fred pointed a finger at Skip's suit and tie and asked who he was.

"I'm a lawyer at Legal Assistance . . . and so is he," Skip replied, pointing to Don.

"Which side are you on?" Fred asked.

"Yours," Skip responded, assuming Fred was asking whether he was for the prosecution or the defense.

"No, I mean what are *you* two doing for the revolution? Are you for us or against us?"

More than a bit taken aback, Skip and Don sputtered, "For you."

"Then come to the Panther office at nine tonight and knock on the steel door."

No one but Fred could pull off his "in your face" directness without incurring resentment. That evening Skip and Don went to Panther headquarters and knocked. A voice came over a speaker, "Who's there?" They gave their names and were buzzed into a dark vestibule. A speaker from the top of the stairs above them bellowed, "By whose authority are you here?"

"Chairman Fred sent for us" Skip replied.

"Come up one step at a time," the faceless speaker responded. Skip made out a shotgun pointed at them. As they approached the upper part of the stairs, the door at the top opened, and a bright light shined in their eyes. They walked in and Fred greeted them with a grin and a big hug.

That night Fred recruited Skip and Don to be Panther lawyers. Fred's magnetism was irresistible. He laid out the Panther program, told Skip and Don that "the police are trying to destroy the Panthers any way they can. We need your help."

When Don explained that Legal Assistance lawyers couldn't take criminal cases, it didn't satisfy Fred—or Don. After talking with each other, Skip and Don met with Dennis the next week to discuss the formation of an independent law office, one that would be free to represent not only the Panthers but the movement as a whole.

Two days after Fred confronted Skip and Don, he was convicted. Sidney Jones, a black trial judge who was well connected to the Democratic machine, indicated he intended to grant Fred probation, the expected sentence for an offense where no weapon was used, no one was injured, and the defendant had no criminal record. But during the three weeks between the conviction and the sentencing hearing, State's Attorney Hanrahan held a press conference. He blasted the Panthers and Fred Hampton and criticized the trial judge for considering probation. Hanrahan carried a lot of clout in the Democratic Party, and any sitting judge wanted his endorsement for reelection.

On May 27, Fred was sentenced. The prosecutor questioned Fred. His lawyer, Jean Williams, let him answer. "Are your principles consistent and compatible with those of Mao Tse-Tung of Red China?" the prosecutor asked.

"We take things from Mao Tse-Tung and Martin Luther King or anybody else applicable to what we are after," Fred said.

"Do you feel that a legitimate means of obtaining what you are after is armed violence or armed revolution?"

"I believe if we tried anything else we would end up like Dr. Martin Luther King."

Judge Jones had taken his cue from Hanrahan and sentenced Fred to two to five years in the state penitentiary. Fred's bond was revoked and he was taken into custody. He was soon transferred to Menard Prison in southern Illinois, 350 miles from Chicago, to begin his sentence.

On June 4, 1969, a week after Fred went to prison, FBI agents, led by Chicago's Special Agent in Charge (SAC), Marlin Johnson, raided Panther headquarters. They had obtained a search warrant by swearing before a judge that George Sams, a fugitive, was present in the office. Sams had been there but left forty-eight hours earlier. Looking for George Sams was the official reason for FBI raids on Panther offices in at least two other cities. In each instance, Sams left shortly before the raid. It was later revealed that Sams was an FBI informant. He went to these offices to provide the FBI the pretext for a raid.

FBI agents called and told the Chicago Panthers that the office was surrounded, that they had a search warrant, and that no one would be hurt if the Panthers did not resist. Agents then came to the entrance, broke down the front door, and went upstairs, where they pointed their guns at the eight people inside. No one resisted. The FBI seized three thousand dollars in cash and took property and records, including lists of contributors. Food for the breakfast program was dumped on the floor, and legally purchased weapons were confiscated. Nothing was ever returned.

The eight Panthers on the premises were arrested and charged with harboring a fugitive. Skip and Don defended them and procured their release on bond. There were banner headlines that proclaimed the Panthers' arrests for "Multiple Weapons" and "Harboring a Fugitive." These were much more prominently displayed than the back-page news stories several weeks later noting all charges were dropped.

Some Panther members became frightened and left after Fred's incarceration and the FBI raid. Bradley Greene had come to the office to join the Panthers in early May and was told that because there were so many new Panther members, he could only become a "friend of the

Panthers" until the section chiefs had integrated the new members. When he returned in June, he was immediately accepted and soon made a section chief himself.

Skip and Dennis started working on Fred's appeal. They recruited Flint Taylor and Seva Dubuar, two law students, to go to Maywood to get affidavits from community leaders to be used in support of releasing Fred on an appeal bond. Before a trial there is the presumption of innocence and a right to bail except where the defendant is likely to flee or presents a danger to the community. After a conviction, the granting of bail is discretionary. Support and endorsements by community leaders are crucial. Interviewing people in Maywood about Fred was Flint's first experience working closely with black people.

Flint came from an old Boston family that came over on the Mayflower. He attended Brown University and was finishing his first year at Northwestern Law School. His hippy exterior, including long, reddish-blond hair, disguised a tireless work ethic. He was competitive in sports and didn't like to lose at anything. Flint is a person you want on your side whether it's in a lawsuit or a basketball game. His thoroughness and tenacity have made him an indefatigable advocate for civil rights for over forty years and earned him the reputation of being one of the most dogged and successful civil rights litigators in the country. He dates his commitment to civil rights to learning about Fred from his family and friends in Maywood.

In July, Dennis and ACLU attorney Kermit Coleman appeared before chief justice Walter V. Schaefer of the Illinois Supreme Court with the affidavits Flint and Seva had obtained supporting Hampton's release. State's Attorney Hanrahan's representative spoke out vigorously against granting bond, arguing that they "could not keep track of Fred if he was released and he was a risk of flight."

"Are you telling me you don't know where Fred Hampton is every minute of the day?" the chief justice responded incredulously. The state's attorney had no response.

On July 31, while Justice Schaefer was considering granting bail, the Chicago police and the Panthers exchanged gunfire at the Panther headquarters. The police said the incident started with sniper fire, but several witnesses said the police opened fire on the Panther office without provocation. Five police officers were wounded and three Panthers—

Larry White, Dwight Corbett, and Alfred Jeffries—were arrested. Again the office was ransacked and Panther property was seized and never returned. The police formed a gauntlet at the bottom of the stairs. They beat and kicked the three as they walked outside.

Skip showed up in court to represent the Panthers at their preliminary hearing. His cross-examination of the police witnesses exposed so many contradictions in their testimony that charges against all the defendants were dropped.

A few days later Justice Schaefer granted Fred Hampton's petition for an appeal bond, allowing him to be released from Menard Prison. He also set an expedited appeal schedule. On August 13, Fred returned to Chicago, and the next day the Panthers had him speak at the Church of the Epiphany, known as the People's Church, located at Ashland and Adams. It was still warm outside when Flint and I entered to hear Fred. The large stone edifice was in the heart of Chicago's black West Side community, less than a mile from the Panther office. The vestibule was full when we entered. Mike Gray and Howard Alk had set up their filming equipment at the front of the center aisle. Major parts of his speech that evening have been preserved in the Film Group's *The Murder of Fred Hampton*, released in 1971. I have repeated some of them in the opening scenes of this book. Near the end Fred told us we should all say "I am a revolutionary" before we went to sleep in case there was a "revolutionary happy hunting ground" and we might not wake up. Some truth hidden in a joke.

After Fred finished and the church shook with its final reverberation of "Power to the people" and we had all declared "I am a revolutionary," we stood up to leave. Mike Gray turned off his camera. Fred's prophetic words that night, "I'm not gonna die slipping on ice . . . I'm gonna die in the proletarian revolution," became the ending to his film. On the twentieth anniversary of Fred's murder, Mike wrote:

A few months after he died, I began to understand exactly what it was about him that separated him from the rest of us. Watching that footage hour after hour in the editing room with Howard Alk, I finally saw that Fred Hampton was fearless. Literally, without fear. And as we listened to the speeches again and again, it became apparent he had accommodated death. He knew he was going to die. It was OK And so he had set aside the ultimate fear, the one that stopped all of us in our tracks, no matter how courageous, the net fear upon which we base all our other fears, the one that keeps us all in line. Hampton had simply set that fear to rest. He was free. Thus he was able to speak clean simple truths that hit you like a thunderbolt.

If I had not been a lawyer that night I might have gone into the streets or underground. Fred's fearlessness challenged my own fears. Instead, I joined the People's Law Office (PLO). I had been part of the discussions with Dennis, Skip, and Don and was intrigued by the new venture but fearful and hesitant as well. Even with its limitations, Legal Assistance had stability and a paycheck. Income from the new office would be uncertain at best. But the hardest thing was casting my lot outside the mainstream; becoming a lawyer for the movement that challenged the very institutions that most lawyers used their skill to support. Law collectives had formed in New York and L.A., but the concept was still new and no one had enough experience to know how they would fare.

I had to see and hear Fred to overcome my reluctance and my own fear. It's not an exaggeration to say that a part of Fred's legacy is the People's Law Office, which formed a few months after Skip and Don encountered Fred and his "up against the wall" recruitment tactics and when Flint and I heard him speak.

I went home from Fred's speech, grabbed a cold beer, and told Mary we needed to talk. "I want to be part of the new office to represent Fred and the Panthers," I said, as we sat on our living room couch, across from the handmade bookshelves filling up with political literature.

To my surprise, she replied, "Go for it. I can support us for a while on my salary from the Film Group."

"What about film school?" I asked.

"It can wait; I like what I'm doing now." She smiled.

When we opened our new office in the summer of 1969, our clients included the Panthers, the Young Lords, antiwar protesters, and SDS. Chicago's political and social movements were a microcosm of those throughout the United States, if not the entire world. I once was told every generation has its chance to make a revolution. The last had been in the 1930s. This was ours. If we doubted our success, we saw the people in Vietnam, Cuba, and China winning liberation struggles led by revolutionary forces. Many other countries of Africa and South America were also engaged in anticolonial struggles, seeking radical change and separation from the United States. Here we were in the "belly of the beast," where it was most vulnerable.

From today's perspective, what I felt had to be done in 1969 may seem shortsighted and impulsive. This is partly true. I certainly did not appreciate the strength, staying power, and violence the U.S. government would use to suppress our movement. It didn't turn out to be a "paper tiger," as Mao had predicted.

But we did not accept the bourgeois society, imperialism, and patriarchy we encountered. We held the government responsible for the Vietnam War, for buttressing reactionary governments throughout the world, including the apartheid regime in South Africa, and for the continuous oppression and exploitation of blacks, Latinos, and Native Americans as well as women. Like much of the rest of the world, we had come to believe radical, indeed revolutionary change, was necessary.

We divided the world much as Eldridge Cleaver did: "You are either part of the solution or part of the problem." The solution seemed to be revolution "by any means necessary." We felt empowered; we could make history. Only a lack of will or courage could stop us.

As for the personal implications of being a "revolutionary," I, like other "mother country radicals," as we whites called ourselves, had to figure it out. Tennis? OK, but who had time? Tasty food? A hard one to give up and maybe OK if not overindulged, not too expensive, and everyone got to share—potlucks preferable. Maintaining relationships with your parents? The radical movement line was maybe, but my gut said try. My parents were more accepting of me than I was of them. There was a distance, but I didn't burn my bridges. The Weathermen, who had taken over SDS and with whom we had the closest personal relationships, pushed the line. "Smash monogamy!" they cried, arguing it was the source of patriarchy and women's oppression. Yet the alternatives of many partners or serial monogamy had their own problems. I can't say how much we were guided by our theory and how much by our hormones. Sex? No limit. It was free, but of course there could be an emotional toll. Type? Heterosexual not preferred, but allowed, and most of us indulged heartily. Living in nuclear families? The line said no— kids and parents benefit from a communal setting. I had no kids. For a while we helped with Dennis's kids, and I did eventually live in a collective. I had many good and a few bad experiences living in a group scene but found it difficult to maintain over a long period. Mind-expanding drugs like LSD? No prohibition if used to gain better understanding and awareness. Taken infrequently, which I did, they helped me see things I had never seen before and some of these things contained truths even after the trip was over. Like seeing Dennis and his wife Mona as the gurus, those with special insights, at PLO. Money? The line was give it to the movement; share it. I did give up most of mine but held out a little, hedging my bet. Dealing with personal issues? The line said, "the personal is political," which has some truth, but the line didn't take into account the heart, and often neither did I. I left my feelings out of the equation of what should be done.

My cubicle at the newly opened People's Law Office was in the middle of the five other hexagons that made up the interior offices. It was difficult to find enough straight wall to align a desk. A local architect had designed the space to "make us different and to save money," although I never figured out how it did the latter. He also glued egg cartons to the ceiling as noise baffles because the hexagonal walls of each office didn't reach the ceiling. The soundproofing didn't work, but it was a conversation starter with clients.

My first week at the office, we erected a four-foot-high, hollow wooden barricade in front of the glass windows that looked out on busy Halsted Street in Lincoln Park. We filled it with concrete for protection against anyone shooting in from the street. We considered the local police, or their friends, the most likely candidates.

"I wonder how many law offices in Chicago do this," I said to Flint.

We also installed a three-foot-high steel gate between the inner office and entrance door. The gate could only be opened by the buzzer on the receptionist's desk. We took the possibility of a police attack on our office seriously. We had a built-in gun cabinet stocked with a legally purchased and registered shotgun and a nine-millimeter handgun. Some of my partners had taken target practice a few times before I joined PLO, and I went to a private pistol range with the nine millimeter. Firing the gun itself wasn't nearly as uncomfortable as being on the range with a lot of off-duty cops. As it turned out we never had occasion to use or even pull out our weapons. When we moved downtown six years and a political era later, I was surprised to find them still there in the cabinet in the wall. They had become period pieces.

We didn't need a lot of money to live on and the structure of sharing fees, with Dennis getting a little more because he had a family, suited us. We began operating on the Marxist principle "From each according to his ability and to each according to his need," but the complexities of defining *need* quickly caught up with us.

Should we take into account money from a working spouse or parents in determining what each lawyer needed or received? Karl Marx said yes, but we found this impractical and difficult to calculate. Why should a spouse take on onerous work to get more money, if it only resulted in her partner's salary being decreased? I still had some money from my family. Should I work for free until it was gone? These issues became so complicated that after a year we opted for a standard salary, with an increase if you had children. At first legal workers and secretaries earned the same money as the lawyers, but this too changed over time. They continued to earn salaries and the lawyers divided up what was left. In the early years the nonlawyers did better.

Getting paid depended on whether money was coming in. When we started in 1969, we hoped to make two hundred dollars per month each. For me, that was enough for basic living expenses. With money from my family, Mary and I bought a house in Lincoln Park, discounted because it backed on the El, or elevated train. We lived collectively with other PLOers including Flint, Susan Waysdorf and Courtney Esposito, legal workers who did everything from answering phones to investigation, and, later, attorneys Michael Deutsch and Susan Jordan, when they joined the office.

PLO's decision making was democratic. Everyone who worked at PLO had an equal vote at office meetings—even Jim Sorflaten, who swept the office once a week. However, Jim had not been selected because of his activism, and the issues we voted on both confused and bored him. We soon decided that only full-time PLOers got to vote.

Dennis proposed the name People's Law Office because it fit with the times and our mission. Later we realized we had the same initials as the Palestine Liberation Organization. This never proved much of a handicap with our clients, who generally opposed Israel's expansion and sympathized with the other PLO. In Chicago the two organizations were never confused with each other.

Our office was bustling from day one. Defending the Panthers, the Young Lords, and two white groups, Rising Up Angry and the Young Patriots, was a lot of work for four lawyers requiring frequent court appearances. I was quickly drawn into the criminal cases, which sustained the office financially. I became the rainmaker in the office, although for my first twenty years, I would call it a drizzle. We had no shortage of criminal cases, most of which were referred by the Panthers and Young Lords. It was not unusual to have five cases a morning in different courtrooms spread throughout Cook County. Every criminal courtroom was crowded. The only way to cover all your cases, which most often involved continuances, was to get in and out quickly. This required handing the clerk a five-dollar bill under your appearance form to get your case called rapidly.

Another strategy we learned for misdemeanor cases with hostile trial judges was to demand a jury trial. This resulted in the case being sent to Branch 46, a courtroom in the traffic court building. The cops frequently did not follow the cases to the new court and, if they did, often gave up after a few continuances.

I recall the regular Branch 46 judge chiding Dennis as his client's case was dismissed, "Well, Mr. Cunningham, you've outlasted another one."

"Twenty-sixth Street" (2600 South California) was where the majority of the city's felony criminal cases were sent. Cases were often decided at preliminary hearings or at short bench trials. In both situations the judges were in a hurry. If you didn't speak up loudly and quickly, you were overlooked. The hearings and trials frequently turned into shouting matches between the prosecutors and defense counsel, with each using every objection as an opportunity to argue their entire case.

My first political case was defending the twelve SDS Weathermen arrested on September 24, 1969, for demonstrating outside the Conspiracy Eight trial. The Weathermen, who took their name from Bob Dylan's lyrics "You don't need to be a weatherman to know which way the wind blows," were advocating confrontations with the police.

The Conspiracy Eight defendants included Panther chairman Bobby Seale, whose case would be severed on November 5, to be tried later. Those left on trial would become the Conspiracy Seven: Youth International Party leaders Abbie Hoffman and Jerry Rubin; SDS founder Tom Hayden; longtime antiwar organizer David Dellinger; and Rennie Davis, John Froines, and Lee Weiner of the Mobilization to End the War in Vietnam. These seven were among the leaders who organized the thousands of antiwar protesters who came to Chicago and were attacked while protesting outside the 1968 Democratic Convention. Bobby Seale had done nothing but attend the convention and talk with some of the others.

Although the Walker Report, the Illinois governor's investigation of the events outside the convention, concluded it was a "police riot," eight defendants were charged with conspiring to cross state lines with the intent of inciting violence. This was a violation of the new Rap Brown Act, which was passed earlier in 1968 to prosecute protesters for activity otherwise protected by the First Amendment. It forbade crossing state lines with the intent to cause a riot and was an attempt to deter people from or punish them for making radical speeches. The Act was eventually ruled unconstitutional.

On the day the Conspiracy Eight trial started, many protesters, including a small group of the Weathermen, gathered outside the federal courthouse to protest the government's prosecution of the eight for exercising their right to free speech and assembly. When the police pushed the demonstrators up on the sidewalks, some pushed back. One protester was taken into custody and later escaped from the paddy wagon. Twelve other SDS Weathermen were arrested. Video footage showed only minor shoulder shoving between the protesters and the police. Although no one was injured on either side, the arrestees were all charged with at least two felony counts of aggravated battery, a felony count of mob action, and several misdemeanors. One eighty-five-pound demonstrator was charged with offenses carrying up to thirty years for what the videotape disclosed was a light touching of a police officer's shoulder in response to him pushing her. State's Attorney Hanrahan wanted to demonstrate he was tough on demonstrators as well as street gangs.

A few days after the twelve SDS Weathermen were released on bail, we stood in front of Chief Judge Power for the arraignment. The charges against the defendants were read out loud. Judge Power, a small man with a complex to match his name, asked, "How do you plead?"

I gave the standard reply. "The defendants plead not guilty and waive formal reading of the indictment."

Power's next question caught me by surprise. "Who is the leader of this SDS group?"

Before I could respond, Howie Machtinger, one of my clients, replied "Ho Chi Minh." The defendants broke out in laughter.

Judge Power was not amused. "Since you think this is so funny, I find you in contempt. You can spend the day locked up. Sheriff, put them up in the bullpen." The defendants were herded into the lock-up behind the courtroom while I argued on their behalf.

"Your Honor, this was a harmless attempt at humor. There was no disrespect intended," I argued, trying to put the best face on the situation while trying not to laugh myself.

"You can join your friends in the lock-up if you continue arguing, Mr. Haas," was the judge's response.

8

Panthers Versus Police

A **particularly brutal incident occurred on** October 4, 1969. Someone fired at the Panther office, and the Panthers fired back. The Chicago police were called. They broke down the front door, charged inside, and pushed everyone down the front steps. Che (Billy Brooks) was the first to emerge at the bottom, where Officer Richard Curly hit him in the temple with the butt of his shotgun. Panther member Bradley Greene was also struck and beaten outside the front door. The police said they had seen someone on the roof with a shotgun who looked like, but in fact wasn't, Terry Watson, a Panther inside the office. When they arrested Watson, they beat and kicked him more than anyone else.

The police made no efforts to hide what they were doing on busy Madison Street outside the Panther office. When a spectator outside the Panther office objected to the police beatings, he was grabbed and struck as well. In all, six Panthers and the bystander were arrested and taken to the Wood Street station.

In the station parking lot, the arrestees were removed from the police wagon and beaten again. One of the cops, who weighed over two hundred pounds, sat on Watson's back as Watson lay on the ground, and slammed his head into the pavement. Bradley Greene thought they were going to kill him. As Terry lay moaning and crying, one of the other Panthers said he shouldn't be making sounds like that because "He's a Panther." Bradley disagreed and yelled for the cops to stop.

Afterward, the Panthers were picked up and made to run a gauntlet fending off punches and clubbing by the two shifts of officers, one leaving and one coming on duty. The next morning, they were charged with attempted murder of the cops who came to the Panther office. Skip and Don represented them in court. Skip pointed to the defendants' bruised and swollen faces and told the bond judge, "Look at this, this is what the police did to them after the raid." The injuries obviously needed medical attention. The judge reduced their bonds, ordered medical treatment for those who could not make bail, and set a preliminary hearing for November 10. On that date Skip cross-examined the arresting officers so skillfully that the contradictions between their testimonies and their arrest reports, as well as between each other, became so obvious that all charges except those against Terry Watson were dropped.

During the October 4 raid, the police had again ransacked the Panther office, and important files containing lists of members and contributors were confiscated or destroyed. William O'Neal, who joined the Panthers shortly after they opened their office in November 1968, voluntarily took charge of repairing the damage. He was one of the few Panthers with mechanical and carpentry skills and he was able to repair even the walls damaged by the police.

Flint and Seva, PLO's law students, brought Fred Hampton to speak at Northwestern Law School later in the fall. Flint drove out to the suburbs to pick up Fred and during the ride, Flint said, "Fred was speed-rapping about the cops, describing them as out to get him."

Flint had expected a few students to show up for the talk. When they walked into Northwestern's Robert McCormick Hall, it was packed with over three hundred people. Flint had never spoken before a large audience. He stumbled through his introduction of Fred. Humiliated, he turned the podium and microphone over to Fred, who received a standing ovation. Fred chided Flint about his awkwardness, but he added that Flint was part of the reason he was out on bail. Fred said that Flint, and the rest of the lawyers who wanted to help the Panthers, had better get their act together because "what the Panthers are doing is serious, and the police are serious about trying to stop us."

Fred described the police raid on the Panther office a few days earlier. He told how Panther members had been taken outside and beaten and how the police had gone out of their way to dump out the kids' food in the Panther office. Fred talked with particular satisfaction about seeing the children eating and Panther members serving them. He explained this was how people could understand socialism, "through participation and serving the people."

Fred ended by telling the law students and lawyers that they had a role to play in helping make revolutionary change and that he particularly respected lawyers who had gone South to represent civil rights activists.

Fred adapted his talk to law students without diluting the militancy and energy I had witnessed at the People's Church in August. When Fred ended with "Power to the people," the normally staid law school audience responded in kind, loudly, mesmerized. After the speech Flint and Seva proudly introduced Fred to the dean and faculty. Fred was at home in any conversation. But during the ride back with Flint, Fred switched into his earlier mode, talking continuously about how the police were targeting him and the Panthers.

In October, Fred was still spending some nights at his parents' home in Maywood and some in other Panther apartments. Deborah Johnson was seven months pregnant with Fred's baby; she and Fred wanted to live together. When he had gone to prison in May, Fred had asked his friends, including Che, to look out for her. Later Che warned Fred against getting his own place in the city, urging Fred to get an apartment in the suburbs, further from the Chicago police.

Despite the warnings, Fred and Deborah rented a small five-room apartment on the first floor of a two story flat at 2337 West Monroe, one street over from the Panther office. It quickly became a Panther hangout where Che, Doc, and others often stayed with them. Sometimes, Deborah and Fred moved to other Panther cribs as a cautionary measure.

The FBI and local police immediately took note of Fred's new address. In retrospect, it's a little hard to understand why Fred, who was so conscious of being a target of the Chicago police, did not see the danger of living so close to the Panther office. They were in the heart of a community that was in a virtual state of war with the police. Guns, usually registered, were often kept at the apartment. While they may have given an illusion of security, there seems to have been little control over who brought what weapons into the apartment and how they were accounted for and maintained.

The Panthers, including Fred, used rhetoric that increased hostility with law enforcement. Expressions such as "You kill one pig, you get some satisfaction, you kill all the pigs, you get complete satisfaction," were taken literally by some police. The Panthers also didn't heed their own words for the truth they contained. Fred and the Panthers knew that J. Edgar Hoover and the FBI as well as the local police were out to get them. Fred understood he was a marked man, but the security at the new Panther crib was irregular and haphazard.

A few blocks away from Hampton's new apartment, residents of Henry Horner Homes, an all-black housing project, were having their own confrontations with the police. For over a year teenagers from the projects had been petitioning for the installation of a traffic light at a corner where people crossed to get to local schools and the neighborhood health clinic. In September, one month before Fred moved into his new apartment, two young kids had been killed on separate days crossing the intersection. The city still refused to install the light.

Seventeen-year-old John Soto became the leader of the campaign to get a traffic light put in and organized protests in the neighborhood. His brother, Michael Soto, a twenty-year-old decorated Army sergeant, came home on leave from Vietnam to visit his family and participated in the protest led by his brother in September.

On October 5, the police killed John Soto. The police version was that John Soto had been stopped by the police and when he fought with them, an officer's weapon went off "accidentally" firing a shot into the back of Soto's head. Several witnesses denied that John had fought with the police and said he had been shot without provocation.

Community anger grew and Michael extended his leave to attend his brother's funeral. On October 10, Michael Soto was also shot and killed by the Chicago police, who claimed they shot him after he pulled a gun. Again, the police version contradicted that of civilian witnesses, who said the incident started when a police squad car blocked the path of Michael Soto and two friends. When the youths separated, the police chased Michael to the second floor of the projects, where they shot him. People on the second floor said Michael had been unarmed.

Immediately the community became more outraged and rioting escalated into gunfire. In the exchanges of gunfire ten police officers and a twelve-year-old were reported wounded. According to the NAACP's Commission of Inquiry set up later, "The Commission discovered that a substantial segment of the community believed that, contrary to all police reports, John and Michael Soto had been murdered by the police because of their participation in the traffic light protests."

The coroner's inquests were delayed; meanwhile the internal police investigation found John's death to be "accidental homicide," and Michael's "justifiable homicide." The Soto killings were well publicized locally. They took place in the same neighborhood as the Panther office and confirmed for many people the Panthers' view that the police were licensed thugs, who served as an occupying army in their community. There was no effective means of redress for the victims of police abuse. The prosecutor and the internal police investigative agency invariably closed ranks to support the cops. It is hard to overestimate the effect the Soto brothers' deaths had on both the community and the Panthers. In speeches, Fred spoke about the incidents repeatedly. They became exhibit number one in the Panthers' demand for community control of police and added credibility to their call for armed self-defense.

Ten years later, our office could well have been the one called to represent the family of John and Michael Soto. By then we had learned how to prosecute a civil rights case. High profile cases against the police became our specialty. The transparently implausible police explanations of the Soto killings matched the patterns we would come to recognize later. But in 1969 we had neither the experience nor the reputation as civil rights lawyers to attract these cases, and few Chicago lawyers wanted to sue the police without an airtight case. We felt as helpless as everyone else when we read that no action, either disciplinary or criminal, was being taken against the cops responsible for the Soto brothers' deaths. A few weeks after Michael Soto was killed, Fred spoke at Northern Illinois University in DeKalb, about eighty miles from Chicago, and devoted a substantial part of his speech to police abuse and killings:

> You've got Bobby Seale being chained and gagged at the federal building. You've got John and Michael Soto, who were murdered in two days. We need some guns, we need some guns, and we need some force. Now they brutalize without even arresting them. They shoot somebody with no intention of arresting them.

After specifically attacking Mayor Daley and "Hammerhead" Hanrahan, Fred continued with the words that were often quoted after his death. Words that inspired his audiences and that we very much wanted to be true:

> Don't worry about the Black Panther Party. As long as you keep the beat, we'll keep on going. If you think that we can be wiped out because they

murdered Bobby Hutton and Bunchy Carter and John Huggins, you're wrong. If you think because Huey was jailed the party's gonna stop, you see you're wrong. If you think because Chairman Bobby was jailed, the Party's gonna stop, you see you're wrong. If you think because they can jail me you thought the Party was gonna stop, you thought wrong. You can jail a revolutionary but you can't jail revolution. You can lock up a freedom fighter, like Huey Newton, but you can't lock up freedom fighting.

Looking back on history, it's not so clear that you can't kill a revolution or a movement if you assassinate its leaders. It's unlikely the Chinese Revolution would have succeeded with Mao dead, or that the Vietnamese would have obtained their independence without Ho Chi Minh. The latter continued successfully after Ho died, but only after he had put in forty-six years of organizing and fighting. The Cubans would not have driven Fulgencio Batista out and gotten rid of his oppressive government without Fidel Castro and Che Guevara. The Colonists may not have been successful in establishing a democracy without George Washington's determination and leadership, particularly when he stopped his rebellious unpaid soldiers from their attempt to impose military rule after defeating the British. The murder of Patrice Lumumba in the Congo in 1961 and Salvador Allende in Chile in 1973 are examples of freedom struggles that were defeated because the CIA determined to kill their leaders.

In another part of Fred's November speech, he said:

And when pigs move on our cribs, we have to protect our cribs with gun force. Pigs don't move on Panther cribs, they make sure the Panther's out of town. . . . Because they know when they comin' to a Panther crib that we might talk a lot of rhetoric, but we deal with the same basic jargon that the people in Babylon dealt with. It takes two to tango, motherfucker. As soon as you kick that door down, I have to kick it back on you. We don't lock our doors. We just get us some good guns and leave them motherfuckers open.

It's hard to imagine Fred believed the police were afraid to raid an apartment with the Panthers present. So what was he saying? Knowing the police were listening, was he warning them the Panthers were armed? Was he telling Panthers they should have guns in their homes to protect themselves or was he signifying big time with the police? The rhetoric that energized the Panthers was often the same rhetoric that the police used to justify attacks on them.

From the time Fred and Deborah moved in, there were guns kept at 2337 West Monroe. While the outer doors were locked, the tiny locks at the front and rear were not reinforced. As for security, people with guns were normally assigned to stay awake by the front door when Fred slept there. But even later, after I interviewed the Panther survivors, I never heard of any drills or preparation for an actual raid, or any specific instructions of what the Panthers were supposed to do if the police came.

Fred ended his speech to the students at Northern Illinois with the Panther refrain, "Time is short, let's seize the time."

It's often difficult to separate Fred's rhetoric from what he believed. I have wondered if *he* was always able to make this distinction.

9

Last Glimpse

In late November we got word from the appellate court that Fred's ice cream robbery conviction had been upheld. He had to serve the rest of his two-to-five-year sentence. His appeal bond would be revoked within ten days. Rumors spread that Fred might go underground, or leave the country. Some believed that he would return to the penitentiary, where he had organized several prisoners.

At our December 1 PLO meeting, Dennis announced Fred had the six thousand dollars needed to buy the Panther headquarters building. The Chicago police had consistently put pressure on the Panthers' landlord to evict the Panthers. Owning their own building made sense. Because I had done some housing work, I volunteered to go and help complete the purchase. I relished the idea of working with Fred, though I was a bit intimidated by the reverential respect people had for him. I called the Panther office and set up a meeting with Fred for the next day.

I went there the following afternoon and stood on the street outside the steel door. Bullet holes from the previous police attacks marred the building's facade. Two faded posters with the Panther emblem hung on each side of the door. I pushed the buzzer and cleared my throat.

"This is Jeff from the People's Law Office and I have a meeting with Chairman Fred at four o'clock," I said.

After a pause the door was buzzed open. At the top of the steep staircase another door opened and I was led into the large, open space that made up the main office. It hummed with noise and activity. Around me people were criticizing each other about a snafu that morning getting the food delivered on time to one of the breakfast program locations. There were stacks of Panther newspapers on the floor in the corner and on some of the desks I saw piles of signed papers titled "Petition for Community Control of Police."

Boxes of cereal and pancake mix, donations to the breakfast program, were piled in another corner. Familiar posters of Ho Chi Minh, and the

Vietnamese woman carrying a rifle with a baby slung from her shoulder decorated the walls. The famous poster of Huey Newton and Bobby Seale with leather jackets, black berets, and rifles, one standing, one sitting on a fanned-back wicker chair, hung on the back wall. A Panther I didn't recognize told me Fred was talking to people in the back and would be out soon. Someone stood next to a chalkboard containing a listing of the breakfast sites and was filling in names for tomorrow's assignments.

A few minutes later Fred emerged. Before I could introduce myself— I wasn't sure if he knew who I was—he smiled. "Hello, Jeff, come on in." I followed him to the office in the back where he sat down behind a wooden desk. It was hot in the office and Fred wore a T-shirt. I took off my suit jacket and faced him.

"I got the person who's giving us the money ready to go. Can we close tomorrow?" he asked, clearly in a hurry to complete the purchase.

"I have to draw up a deed and get the owner to meet us and sign it," I explained. "I've got court in the morning and the coalition's housing proposal to finish after that. How about—"

"How's that housing plan coming?" Fred interrupted, referring to the proposal for low- and moderate-income housing sponsored by the coalition of the Panthers, Young Lords, and Young Patriots.

"I have to file our proposal with the Department of Urban Renewal on Thursday morning. It really looks good. If the City follows its guidelines, we should get the money to build, but that's a big 'if,' given who we are. How 'bout if I meet you and the owner here Thursday afternoon?" I asked.

Fred agreed. Buying the Panther building was not the kind of real estate deal where an inspection was required. The Panthers knew every crack in the plaster and bullet hole in the ceiling, because they had repaired the office after each of the three police raids.

"How's the boiler, have you checked that out?" I asked.

"You can see, we get plenty of heat, except when the police bullets give us too much ventilation," he replied, a slow smile spreading across his face.

"We put some cement in our walls when we opened the People's Law Office last August. Maybe you should try that," I said, only half joking.

"It's the windows they shoot at, not the walls," Fred said, "but I'll check it out."

I showed Fred the completed real estate papers. "Here's where you sign. I've listed you as the chairman of the Panthers, to make it legal."

"That's accurate," he smiled again. "Let's get this done quick." He signed and I gathered up the papers and slipped them into my briefcase. As we were walking up to the front, Fred paused in our conversation to talk to some Panthers who had entered the office. This handsome, powerfully built man of twenty-one, six years my junior, was giving instructions. "Show up on time for the breakfast program; sell your quota of Panther papers; be at political education class on Monday and Wednesday nights." Fred was talking continuously, asking questions and answering them. His voice had the staccato tempo and energy of a rapper. There were few pauses and a lot of rhythm. He seemed to be driven by some inner force that created a continuous flow of orders and encouragement. Even though he appeared relaxed and jovial, there was a sense of urgency to his directions. The Panthers appeared to run on Fred's energy.

He stopped for a moment to thank me. "I'll see you Thursday. Power to the people."

I answered, "Power to the people." Opening the door and leaving, I hoped I was playing a small role in helping the Panthers gain self-determination—at least over their own building.

It was late in the afternoon when I left, so I went home instead of returning to work. "Fred is amazing," I told Mary as soon as I walked in. "He's in perpetual motion. I wish I had half his energy. I feel like I have to run in place to keep up with him."

"I know what you mean," she replied. "Some of the footage we've shot of Fred makes him look like he's on speed; but it's a natural high."

"You should see the way he gets people around him motivated," I said. "I don't know what they'll do when he goes back to finish his prison term."

We went out to eat that night, as neither of us had time to shop. Over flautas and beer we talked more about Fred. "You know he's only twenty-one. At his age I was nowhere," I said, still impressed over my recent encounter with him. "If he can avoid the police and prison, he's going to be a great leader."

"We're trying to figure out how to end our documentary," Mary said. "We want to complete the film so more people in the country see him in action. We've got some wonderful footage of Fred speaking outside the Conspiracy trial about freeing Bobby Seale, and also of his August speech at the People's Church. We also took a lot of him serving breakfast to the kids. We need an ending."

"I'm sure it will come to you. If you capture half his dynamism, you'll have a great film."

The next morning I went to court and then to the office to make the final corrections in the coalition housing proposal. The deadline for filing was the next day, Thursday, December 4, at 9:00 A.M. I worked all afternoon handwriting my corrections on the typed draft. In this precomputer era everything was done on typewriters with corrections painted on carbon copies with White-Out. If a document had to be flawless, like a court paper or housing proposal, corrections meant retyping the entire document. We kept the typist-secretary–legal workers at our office busy. We were fortunate to have a steady flow of movement people, mostly women, type for us; some even volunteered to work evenings. One thing the computer age corrected was our sexist division of labor. We all learned to type and correct our own court submissions. I learned later that while I was working on the paperwork for the housing proposal, Fred, with William O'Neal by his side, was meeting with Conspiracy Seven lawyer Lenny Weinglass on the South Side, inquiring about getting an extension on his appeal bond from the Illinois Supreme Court, which would allow Fred time to decide if he wanted to flee the country to avoid going back to prison.

By six o'clock Wednesday evening I was still laboring over the housing document. Liz Stern, the wife of a friend, had offered to help type the final draft at her home. I went over to Liz's apartment about eight o'clock that night to give her handwritten edits and corrections. We worked through the night keeping awake on coffee, cookies, and cigarettes. In that partially unenlightened era, I was still smoking, which today seems as much an anachronism as White-Out. At five o'clock in the morning the final draft was done. I was exhausted. It was still dark when I got home. I climbed the outside stairs, walked into our second-floor apartment, threw off my clothes, and collapsed on the couch.

10

A Knock at the Door

I'd just fallen asleep when I heard a loud knock at the front door. Dazed, I got up and opened it. My partner Skip Andrew was standing there dressed in suit and tie.

"Chairman Fred is dead. I just got a call from Rush. The pigs vamped on the chairman's crib this morning."

I remained stuck on the words "Chairman Fred is dead."

"Someone else was killed and a lot of people were shot. Deborah Johnson and some others are at the Wood Street police station; the people wounded are at Cook County Hospital."

"What should *I* do?" I asked.

"I'm meeting Rush at the morgue and then we are going to the chairman's crib. Why don't you go to Wood Street and try to talk to some of the survivors?"

"Sure," I stammered. He turned abruptly and was gone down the steps.

Fred Hampton dead? I had just seen him at the Panther office, looking bigger than life. I couldn't imagine him motionless. I went to the bedroom and shook Mary.

"Fred Hampton's been killed."

Mary stirred, coming out of sleep. "Huh, what?"

I repeated the news. She bolted upright. "Noooo!" she cried, shaking her head back and forth.

"I don't want to believe it either, but I think it's true. I'm going to interview some of the survivors at the lock-up."

"How can I help? What can I do?" Mary pleaded.

"I have to go," I urged. "I'll call you later if you can help."

I went back to the living room and put on the same suit I had just thrown off. I grabbed my briefcase, the housing proposal inside, and walked out the door before seven o'clock.

I replayed Skip's words in my mind. "The chairman is dead." It was Fred who made us believe we were strong and unstoppable. Now he was dead.

It was well below freezing and the snow was piled up on the edges of the streets. Francis and Iberia Hampton approached the entrance gate to the Corn Products plant in their 1966 green Ford. They'd been expecting Fred to come home when they went to bed the previous evening, but Fred's bed was still made and the chitterlings they'd left on the stove for him were untouched when they got up in the morning of December 4. Francis dropped Iberia off at the front gate and parked. Iberia's shift started at seven o'clock, a half-hour before his.

Francis worked as a painter, glazier, and repairman in the maintenance section. After dropping Iberia off at the entrance gate, he usually parked the car and went to the paint shop where he made coffee for everyone and put the place in order before his shift started. As Francis walked toward the entrance gate, the gate did not open as it usually did. Tilman Malrey, the middle-aged security guard whom Francis had known for years, came out of his booth and walked up to him.

"I think you and your wife need to go home. We heard on the radio there was a police raid and I think your son was shot."

Francis looked at Malrey. "What happened to him?"

"I think you need to go home," Malrey repeated. "Maybe you can find out more on the radio." Although Francis sensed Malrey was trying to help him, he also thought Malrey was withholding information. Francis knew his son had become the target of police raids. He had told Fred when he joined the Panthers that he did not want him to be violent. Fred responded, "I will defend myself if I have to."

He remembered his son's speech at Reverend McNelty's Baptist Church four weeks earlier. Fred had told the large and enthusiastic crowd, "The next time you see me I may be in a collar and tie." Fred seldom wore a dress shirt or tie, and Francis assumed his son was talking about being dressed for burial. Indeed, since Fred's release from prison in August, and even more recently he had said things that made Francis believe he knew he might not live much longer.

Francis asked Malrey if he would put in a call to Iberia's workstation and tell her that she should come outside to meet him. As he waited in the car, he heard on the radio that his son was dead. The reporter from WBBM "All News Radio" said that Black Panther leader Fred Hampton and another unknown Panther were killed at four thirty that morning in a shootout at 2337 West Monroe. Francis recognized the address. The radio announcer went on to say that the police entered the Panther apartment with a search warrant looking for guns, that the Panthers had opened fire on the police after the officers announced their presence, and the police had responded with gunfire of their own. Two police officers were injured, along with four Black Panthers who were taken to Cook County Hospital.

The report continued, indicating that the raiding police officers were assigned to State's Attorney Hanrahan's office. Francis knew Hanrahan was the prosecutor who had campaigned on the platform "war on gangs." He also knew Fred had repeatedly criticized Hanrahan in his speeches for using antigang rhetoric to carry out what Fred called "a war on black youth."

Before Iberia could punch the clock on the way to her assembly line post, she saw a slip of paper with a message for her to call her daughter Dee Dee at home and the other message from Malrey. She called her daughter. "The police killed Fred. You gotta come home," Dee Dee told her.

Francis saw Iberia walk slowly past the entrance gate looking down at the ground. He knew from her slow pace that she had heard about their son. They didn't have to say anything. Francis opened the car door for her and they drove home in silence. She had wanted Fred to come home to Maywood the night before. Although he was spending the night with his parents less and less, Iberia still considered him to be living at home and kept his bedroom intact. Even when he had introduced Deborah to her a month earlier and said "This is my baby" pointing to Deborah's pregnant belly, Iberia did not envision Fred moving out completely.

Iberia was upset when Fred became a Black Panther. She felt uncomfortable with their talk about guns. She was afraid he would become a police target. Why was he was always the one to be out front, the spokesperson? But she also was proud of Fred. He was doing what he believed in, standing up for black people. Iberia herself was a seasoned union steward. She had cooked for seventeen hundred striking workers at the union hall during a five-month strike several years before. She knew where Fred got his courage and determination, and she had shown her support by cooking for the Panthers' Breakfast for Children Program.

By the time Francis and Iberia arrived home, the radio had identified the other Panther killed in the raid as eighteen-year-old Mark Clark from Peoria, Illinois. A spokesperson from Hanrahan's office was on TV saying the police had been fired at from the back bedroom where Fred was found dead.

When a close friend of the Hamptons came over to their home, she saw Iberia sweeping the floor looking stone-faced. She hardly spoke. Francis was trying hard to hold back tears. Later on, Iberia would tell the friend that Francis wasn't tough enough to handle their son's murder. His face would get sad and tear up when Fred's death was brought up.

On my way to the police station, I heard the news flash: "Fred Hampton and another Panther member were killed this morning in a predawn raid by police officers assigned to state's attorney Edward Hanrahan. Hanrahan's office indicated the officers were serving a search warrant for weapons when they were fired upon by the occupants and returned the fire." *Why was Hanrahan the prosecutor in charge of a police raid?*

I arrived at the Wood Street police station at 7:30 A.M. I parked on the street and walked a block to the dilapidated building. I entered through the glass door on the side and approached the counter that separated me from several uniformed officers. It looked like business as usual, with the cops behind the counter filling out forms and talking on desk phones. A middle-aged sergeant approached and asked what I wanted.

I showed him my attorney identification card. "I want to see Deborah Johnson, and anyone else arrested after the police raid on Monroe Street." The sergeant looked as though he was expecting me. "State's Attorney Hanrahan has given orders that the prisoners arrested after the raid are not to be seen by anyone, including attorneys."

I wasn't surprised that Hanrahan would give such an order, but it was illegal. "Hanrahan's order violates an Illinois criminal statute specifically forbidding anyone to interfere with the right of a person in custody to see their attorney," I said as authoritatively as possible. As a practicing criminal law attorney, I carried a paperback copy of the Illinois Criminal Code in my briefcase. I pulled it out and read the sergeant the statute

Hanrahan *and he* were violating. He wouldn't budge, and he wouldn't call Hanrahan. Frustrated and outraged, but with a 9:00 A.M. deadline for filing the housing proposal, I left and drove downtown to the City Urban Renewal Office. This project, which had been many months in the making and had successfully brought together black, Latino, and white community groups, suddenly seemed distant and insignificant.

After filing the housing proposal, I was driving back to the police station when I heard two police officers interviewed over the car radio. They claimed they had been on the raid but hadn't known it was a Panther apartment. Suddenly shots were fired at them from the rear bedroom where they said they later found Fred's body. They made it sound as if they barely escaped alive.

Back at the counter inside Wood Street, I heard the same response from a different sergeant. He was shorter and stockier than the first one but had the same look of satisfaction when he turned down my request to see the people arrested. I went over to the pay phone next to the lock-up and called Hanrahan's office. Sheldon Sorosky answered. I knew him as a "special state's attorney" assigned to prosecute political cases. That fall I had argued against him in bond court and at preliminary hearings defending the Weathermen. He was a slim, Jewish guy who liked to schmooze. He had been defensive about the tough positions his boss Hanrahan had required him to take and let me know by inference that what went on in court was just a job and less important than maintaining our Jewish professional acquaintance in the hallway outside.

"Shelly," I said, "What the fuck's going on? The police here won't let me see the Panthers in the lock-up based on orders from your boss. You know you can't do this."

"Hold on," he said. I could hear Sorosky conferring with someone I was certain was Hanrahan. When the muddled voices ceased, Shelly got back on the line.

"It's all right." Apparently Hanrahan had given in. "You can visit them."

"How 'bout telling the cops here that. They think they're under orders from your boss not to let me in."

"Will do, Jeff," he confirmed. Then added, "You owe me one."

A few minutes later, a patrolman came out from behind the counter and led me to the back of the station. He unlocked the door to a tiny, windowless interview room, with a small wooden table and two wooden chairs on either side.

There was a knock at the door. The patrolman unlocked it and Deborah Johnson was brought into the cramped room. This was our first meeting. She leaned over, crying and shaking, supporting herself with one hand on the table. Slowly she sat down. She looked at me guardedly, not quite fathoming who I was or why I was there.

"I'm Jeff Haas with the People's Law Office." The mention of my PLO connection and my Afro appeared to relax her a little.

"How are you and your baby?" I asked.

There was a pause as if she didn't hear me, then she responded, "I wasn't shot like a lot of the others. The pigs pushed me around, but I think my baby is OK." She paused again. "Fred never really woke up. We were sleeping. I woke up hearing shots from the front and back. I shook Fred but he didn't open his eyes." Deborah demonstrated how she had pushed against Fred several times trying to wake him. "At one point he sort of raised up and then lay back down again." She repeated that he never opened his eyes. "I got on top of him to try to protect him from the gunshots. The bed was shaking from the bullets." She said the shooting stopped only after someone in the bedroom with her yelled, "We got a pregnant sister in here." She told me two "pigs" came into the bedroom. One of them pulled up her nightgown and called out, "Look, we got a broad here." Then they pulled her out into the kitchen.

Deborah stopped talking as she wiped her eyes on the sleeve of her nightgown. I was nodding my head trying to be supportive, "Fred never really woke up," she repeated. "He was lying there when they pulled me out of the bedroom." She paused.

Then she described two police officers going into their bedroom, hearing one of them fire two shots, followed by, "He's good and dead now." Deborah put her head down. A moment later she raised it suddenly and looked at me. "What can you *do*?" she asked.

Indeed, what could I do about the horrible murder she had just described?

Not knowing what to say, I wrestled with the idea of putting my arm around her but instead asked her, "Did it look like Fred had been shot already when you were pulled out of the bedroom?"

"He didn't have any blood on him that I could see," she replied. "I crawled on top of him during the shooting to try to protect him." She showed me her patterned blue and white nightgown. There was no blood. Deborah's description of Fred rising up but not opening his eyes, then lying back down, seemed strange. I couldn't understand why he appeared dazed and semiconscious when he had not been shot.

"Were the men who raided the apartment in uniform?"

"No, but they were definitely the pigs." She described how, after she was taken out of the back bedroom, she and other Panthers were pushed into the kitchen, handcuffed, and made to stand facing the back door. They were ordered not to turn around. She knew they had killed Fred because the police were bragging to each other, "Fred Hampton, the Panther chairman, is dead." They told the occupants to keep their heads down as they took them outside and put them in police cars.

"Are you injured?" I asked.

"I guess I'm OK, but my baby could come any time."

Even though by her account she was innocent of any criminal acts, I knew the police would try to justify what they did by accusing the victims of being the aggressors, initiating the gunfire.

"I'll do everything to get you out as soon as possible and try to make sure you and the baby get medical care until you're released. Some of the doctors who work at the jail hospital work at the Panthers clinic. I'll ask them to look in on you."

I wrote down Deborah's mother's name and phone number. "I'll call and tell her you weren't wounded and seem to be OK. She should start raising money for bail." We shared a brief hug. She had never stopped crying.

I tapped the door to indicate that the consultation was over. In the next thirty-five years, I interviewed more than a hundred people in police lock-ups. None imprinted on my memory as strongly as Deborah Johnson, pregnant, in her nightgown, sobbing, and telling me that the police had just murdered her boyfriend in their bed.

After Deborah was led out, I sat down and tried to picture what she had described. It was difficult to imagine the scene. I had never been to the apartment and I was determined to get a sketch of the layout.

A few minutes later there was another knock. This time the lock-up keeper brought in a tall, square-shouldered man with short hair, about my age and another man, short and in his late forties with graying hair. Their handcuffs were removed and the keeper brought another chair to the table.

The tall, younger man introduced himself. "I'm Harold Bell from Rockford." He said he was a Vietnam veteran and a college student. The other man was Louis Truelock. He told me Fred recruited him when they were in prison together at Menard and he had joined the party after his release, a couple of months after Fred's. Both Bell and Truelock were trembling and looked in shock. Truelock was particularly anxious to tell what happened. He described how he had been asleep in the living room at the front of the apartment when he heard footsteps in the entranceway and a knock on the front door. Truelock said he asked who it was and he heard somebody say "Tommy," followed by gunfire from outside. Harold said he heard "two thuds in the entrance hallway and then two shots." I was writing furiously on my legal pad trying to keep their accounts straight.

Truelock and Bell said they immediately left the living room and ran to the back bedroom to wake up Fred. Bell saw "men with guns coming in the back through the kitchen door," as he reached the entrance to Fred's bedroom. He got on the bed with Fred and Deborah and shook Fred, yelling, "Chairman, the pigs are vamping!" But Fred would not wake up. "He only raised his head and slowly put it back down." Bell saw pistols and shotguns being fired into the rear bedroom; he could also hear firing from the front of the apartment. He spoke in a formal, stiff way that partially covered his fear.

Bell told me that as he huddled on the bed with Fred and Deborah, "A hand reached in the room and pulled me out. I was pushed onto the floor in the dining room where I was told to lie spread-eagled. Then someone kicked me really hard in the groin. The police shooting in the apartment was like a firefight. They moved to strategic positions. It seemed to last forever. The police definitely knew what they were doing."

Bell said after he, Truelock, and Deborah were in the kitchen, two police officers returned to the bedroom. "I heard more shots from the back bedroom. I could tell those were shots from a handgun." Then he heard the police yelling, "That's Fred Hampton, that's Fred Hampton."

Truelock said he also went to the bed where Fred and Deborah had been sleeping. After a brief pause in the shooting, he yelled, "We have a pregnant sister in here!" The police entered the back bedroom, pulled Deborah and him out, and pushed them toward the kitchen. Truelock heard more gunshots from inside the rear bedroom. When the gunfire finally stopped, Bell, Deborah and he were being held in the kitchen. "We were handcuffed and told to look at the floor."

Truelock continued: "A policeman dragged Fred's body out of the back bedroom and onto a door lying on the floor of the dining room. He wasn't moving."

As they were being led out of the apartment, Bell saw Fred lying in his underwear with a pool of blood around his head. "I saw where he had been shot in the head. I was told to keep moving, look straight ahead," while the police were taunting, "Chairman Fred Hampton is dead." I was trying to write down everything, but I finally stopped. I asked Bell to draw a sketch of the apartment from front to rear, from the north entrance and vestibule on Monroe Street to the kitchen door at the rear. His diagram depicted an entrance door off the vestibule into the living room and a hallway to the right of the front door, heading south toward the back of the apartment. The hallway lead past a small bedroom on the left, and then past another one, also on the left, where Deborah and Fred had been sleeping. Toward the rear of the apartment the hallway opened on the right into a dining room, followed by the kitchen. The kitchen was at the rear of the apartment with the kitchen door opening onto a landing and then the back stairs.

"Mark Clark . . . was lying on the floor in the living room after the raid," Truelock added, pointing inside the living room square on Bell's sketch, next to the front door. "He wasn't moving." Truelock said the police kept firing even after they had been brought out of the back bedroom.

Then Truelock pointed to the front bedroom on the diagram. "The people in there, Doc, Verlina Brewer and Blair Anderson, were all shot, and so was China Doll in the living room. Doc looked really bad. He was bent over holding his stomach. We were all told to shut up, look at the floor and not talk to each other."

Bell asked me if I knew what happened to the people who were wounded. I told him they were at Cook County Hospital, but no one had been in to see them yet. Both Bell and Truelock were particularly concerned about Doc.

"His shirt was covered in blood. He could hardly stand up, but the pigs kept shouting at him not to lean over and stand up straight. He was trying, but he kept falling down," Truelock said.

"What about Deborah? How's she doing?" Bell asked.

I told him Deborah was still crying when I saw her a few minutes ago, but I thought she and her baby were OK.

Bell and Truelock explained that things happened so fast, they never even picked up or fired a gun. Instead, they were trying to wake up Fred to figure out what to do. Someone must have been assigned security, with so many Panthers sleeping in one place. Because of their location in the living room by the front door, it was likely Bell or Truelock or both. I didn't ask them specifically whether they had been assigned security. They were miserable enough. They kept repeating how quickly the gunfire had followed the knock, and that they ran to the back to wake up and warn Fred. I thought they were embarrassed that they had done nothing to defend the apartment, but they didn't try to make themselves look better.

Suddenly, as though he had just remembered something, Truelock leaned over and whispered, "Look out for Rush."

"What do you mean?" I whispered back.

"One of the police officers here was bragging 'Rush is next,' and they said something about another raid."

"Can you identify the cop who said this?" I asked instinctively. He said that although he could hear the police voices from his cell, he couldn't see who was talking.

"I'll warn him," I said.

At the time of my interview, Bell and Truelock had been in custody four hours. They told me the police officers at Wood Street were laughing and gloating about Fred's death. I told both of them that I didn't yet know what charges would be placed against them but that our office would try to get them bail. I wrote down the necessary information to fill out petitions to reduce bond and collected the names of their people to contact about bail money and to inform them of their court date when it was announced.

I rapped on the door to signal the guard to let us out. "Try to get permission to call me at PLO later on in the afternoon," I advised, as the door was being opened. "We will know more about your charges and the conditions of the people at Cook County Hospital."

On my way out I checked at the front desk to find out if specific charges had been filed (they had not), and drove back to PLO.

I'm a slow emotional processor, gleaning the facts and ruminating over them before responding with my feelings. Not a bad trait for a lawyer, but not so helpful as a human being or spouse. It took awhile for me to comprehend the full impact of what the survivors had told me. What they described was nothing short of deliberate murder, certainly by the two officers who had gone into the bedroom and executed Fred. The raid looked like an assassination, something I had connected with the deaths of Malcolm X, Dr. King, and the Kennedys. Now I was staring at one up close.

Part of me wanted to gather evidence to help the survivors win their criminal trials and, if possible, prove through the courts that Fred was intentionally killed. The other side of me believed Fred's murder proved the legal system didn't work. What good did it do to have lawyers and courts and a constitution and legal precedent if the police under the direct control of the prosecutor could murder you in your bed? I wasn't sure whether I wanted to be a lawyer fighting for justice inside an unjust system or on the outside exposing the legal system as a fraud, taking direct action against Fred's killers. In the 1960s we used to repeat Lenny Bruce's words, "In the halls of Justice, the only Justice is in the halls." As lawyers for activists, it took us awhile to discover that in most cases, we could both participate in the legal system and expose its inequities.

When I left, I called Bobby Rush, the Panther defense minister, at the Panther office. I told him what Truelock had said about the police coming to his apartment next.

There was a pause. "Those motherfuckers will do anything. Don't worry. I won't go home." Then, his voice crackling with emotion, he added, "Jeff, when I was at the apartment with Skip this morning, I saw the bloody mattress. Did they really shoot Fred in his bed?"

"That's what Deborah said, and Bell and Truelock too. They said the police came in shooting. They went into Fred's room and executed him right there on his bed. Deborah said he never really woke up."

There was another long pause. "That fits," Rush finally said. "The bullet holes at the apartment show they were shooting towards Fred."

"They urged me to get the word out about what happened," I added.

"I'll do that," Rush promised.

11

Hanrahan Versus Panthers

When I got back to the office there was a message from Skip that said he was still at Fred's apartment and was working with Mike Gray, who was filming the scene and recording Skip's gathering of bullets and shell casings. Apparently the police had not sealed off Fred's apartment—a striking departure from police rules. The police had a duty to protect a crime scene where people were shot and killed. I wondered if they'd abandoned the premises because, having accomplished their dirty work, they did not want to face the community's response. I was amazed that Skip had the presence of mind, after hearing that Fred had been killed, to call Mike Gray and bring him to the apartment to film evidence collection.

"Hanrahan's about to hold a press conference!" someone yelled from the next cubicle. Everyone ran next door to Glascott's Groggery and I asked the bartender to turn the TV on.

Edward Hanrahan was sitting in the library of the State's Attorney's Office behind a dark mahogany table covered with rifles, shotguns, handguns, and many hundreds of rounds of ammunition, all arranged in neat rows. He began reading from a sheet of paper in an authoritarian, indignant voice.

As soon as Sergeant Daniel Groth and Officer James Davis, who were leading our men, announced they were policemen, occupants of the first-floor apartment attacked them with shotgun fire. The officers took cover, and the occupants continued firing at our policemen from several rooms in the apartment. Three times after that Sergeant Groth ordered all his men to cease firing and told the occupants to come out with their hands up. Each time one of the occupants replied, "Shoot it out," and the police officers continued firing at the occupants. The immediate, violent criminal reaction of the occupants in shooting at announced police officers emphasizes the extreme viciousness of the Black Panther Party. So does their refusal to cease firing at the police officers when urged to do so several times. We wholeheartedly commend the police officers for their bravery, their remarkable restraint, and their discipline in the face of the Black Panther attack, as should every decent citizen in our community.

While speaking, Hanrahan frequently pointed to the weapons in front of him, indicating the police had seized them from the Panther apartment. Police procedures required that contraband confiscated be inventoried and taken directly to the crime lab. This was the only way to maintain the chain of custody as well as to preserve the condition of any evidence that had to be tested. Hanrahan bypassed that procedure so he could display the weapons to the press. He appeared confident that if he could show weapons seized from Panthers and remind the public of the Panthers' "extreme viciousness," then "every decent citizen" would support the police actions without challenge.

Hanrahan was not only taking responsibility for the raid but also praising the raiders for their courage. Hanrahan's statement that each time after the police officers called for a cease-fire the occupants answered with shouts of "shoot it out," sounded more like the lingo in a TV Western than what a Panther, or anyone, would yell in the middle of a gun battle.

In answers to reporters' questions, Hanrahan said Fred Hampton was found dead in a back bedroom near a .45-caliber handgun. He indicated a similar handgun had been seen firing from that room at the police in the rear. He stopped and pointed to a .45-caliber pistol on the table, indicating this was Hampton's weapon.

Sergeant Daniel Groth, the apparent leader of the raid, also spoke: "There must have been six or seven of them firing. The firing must have gone on ten or twelve minutes. If two hundred shots were exchanged, that was nothing." The tall deep-voiced sergeant acted as though he had miraculously escaped an ambush.

When I went back to my office, I called the news desk at the *Chicago Daily News*, the more widely circulated and liberal of Chicago's afternoon papers. I told the person who answered they should send a reporter to Hampton's apartment and that Bobby Rush, the Panther defense minister was holding a press conference there shortly. I also told them

Hanrahan had originally denied me access to talk to the Panther survivors, because he did not want his version to be challenged.

Of course I didn't know for sure exactly what did happen during the raid, only what the Panthers had told me. But there was a spontaneity and consistency to what they said. I thought they would have been proud to defend Fred's apartment and told me if they had. Their admissions of being caught unprepared, even frightened, and putting up no resistance had the ring of truth.

Later that afternoon I bought the *Chicago Daily News*, which carried two very different versions of the raid. Under the front-page banner headlines, "Panther Chief, Aide Killed in Gun Battle with Police," there were two subheads. One was titled "Six Injured in Shootout." The other was "Police 'Murdered' Hampton—Panther, We Can Prove It."

The first one repeated much of Hanrahan's press statement and added that he was going to charge all the surviving occupants with attempted murder of the police. An additional statement from Sergeant Groth was included: "As we entered, a girl who was lying on a bed in the living room fired a blast from a shotgun at us," and "a .45-caliber pistol was found in Hampton's hand, when officers entered a rear bedroom and found him lying in a pool of blood on a bed. A shotgun was found next to the bed." Two other raiders, Detectives Carmody and Ciszewski had synchronized their stories with Groth. They told the *Daily News* reporters that "a man later identified as Hampton had fired at them with a shotgun and a pistol from the rear bedroom." Deputy Police Superintendent Nygren supported Groth's account: "Miss Harris touched off the gun battle by firing at the police with a shotgun."

The other version in the *Daily News* was based on information I had provided Rush from my interviews with the survivors:

Bobby Rush, deputy minister of defense for the Black Panther Party said Thursday that Panther chairman Fred Hampton was "murdered while he slept in bed." "We can prove that," Rush said at a press conference on the steps outside the blood-spattered first floor apartment at 2337 W. Monroe, the scene of Thursday's Panther police shootout. "This vicious murder of Chairman Fred and Mark Clark, our defense minister from Peoria, was implemented by that dog Nixon and Hanrahan and all the rest of the pigs. Hampton never fired back when the pigs came into his back room and shot Fred in the head. He couldn't have fired because he was asleep."

The *Daily News* article stated that Rush took reporters on a tour of the apartment and "showed them bullet holes that he said indicated that policemen had fired into rooms, but no shots had been fired out."

A growing chorus in the black community rejected the raiders' accounts. It was clear to anyone viewing the ravaged apartment that Fred was shot to death on his bed. By late Thursday the Panthers were leading tours for the press, neighborhood residents, and interested civic leaders, pointing out the locations of the bullet holes as well as the bloody mattress. Observers demanded an independent investigation. One organization that immediately challenged Hanrahan was the Afro-American Patrolmen's League, the black police union that regularly spoke out against police brutality. Their leader, Renault Robinson, went to 2337 West Monroe, and held a press conference the night of the raid. He declared unequivocally that Fred had been "murdered."

 Part II

Exposing the Murder

"A Northern Lynching"

Skip pushed open the door to the living room and Mike Gray turned on his camera as they entered the ransacked apartment. Skip and Rush cleared a pathway through the debris toward the rear. When they came to the back bedroom, they stopped. Skip leaned down and peeled a blood-soaked poster from a door lying unhinged on the floor. He looked at the coagulated pool of blood below him and pointed. "This is where the chairman must have died."

Mike Gray's camera captured the condition of each room and the bullet-pocked walls as well as the overturned dressers and clothes strewn throughout, exactly as the police had left them, just four hours earlier. Then, Skip went to work. Forensics had been his favorite course at Northwestern Law School and he had learned the art of evidence gathering and preservation from Fred Inbau, the legendary expert on police techniques. Mike Gray filmed each shell casing or bullet fragment as it was picked up. Skip described the object, the location where he found the object, and then placed it in an envelope that he marked "2337 apt, exhibit number 1, 2, 3, etc." Jim Reed, a minister who also had come to the apartment at Skip's urging, signed the outside of the envelope as a witness. Soon Flint, Seva, and Ray McClain, another law student from PLO joined Skip, and in the following days my wife, Mary, and Skip's wife, Nancy Dempsey, helped pick up and mark bullet fragments and shell casings.

Viewing Mike Gray's film later, as I have many times, I continue to be astounded at how Skip had the presence of mind and the self-control to react so calmly and methodically to Fred's death. He appears so technical and matter-of-fact, standing there inserting each metal fragment into an evidence folder. He reacted professionally and clinically while the rest of us were trying to decide what we should do. Years later I asked Skip what he felt when he saw Fred's body at the morgue that morning and how, an hour later, inside the apartment he was able to respond so methodically.

"My lawyer training came out," he said. "Something from law school kicked in and I just automatically applied what I had learned about gathering evidence and the chain of custody." He agreed that my characterization of him as "cold, calculating, and efficient" was probably accurate. He said he hadn't thought about his feelings.

Skip and Rush were not sure when or if the police would come back to seal the apartment, so Skip worked pretty much around the clock for two days, gathering, identifying, and filming the physical evidence. That afternoon Rush directed Panthers to lead guided tours for the neighborhood residents gathered outside. The apartment was freezing cold even with the space heater in the living room on. It was also quite dark, until Mary and Nancy, Skip's wife, brought in more lamps.

When I went to 2337 a couple of days after the raid, it was still freezing and the new lamps only partially illuminated the rooms. I knew there had been nine Panthers in the apartment at the time of the raid, and I was struck by how small the five rooms were, and the thinness of the walls, which looked as if they were made of cardboard. The run that Truelock and Harold Bell made from the living room to Fred's bed was no more than ten feet. I walked to the back. The blood-soaked mattress took up most of the bedroom. The wall to my left, which separated the two bedrooms, was riddled with bullets holes coming from the living room.

The bloody door on which Fred's body was dragged was lying in the doorway, plainly visible throughout the apartment. It indicated his executioners wanted to show off their "kill" to the other raiders as one might show off the carcass of a slain deer. A police photo showed Fred's body on the door in polka dot underwear and a T-shirt, with blood pouring from his head wounds. Another photo showed the uniformed police officers carrying Fred's body down the front steps on a stretcher. They smiled for the police photographer. Their grins reminded me of the spectators' smiles in the lynching photos from the South, including the people photographed standing around the just-lynched body of Leo Frank.

The Panthers started leading tours through the apartment even before the physical evidence had been analyzed. These tours were compelling because there were almost one hundred bullet holes in the east walls of the apartment where the police had fired at the Panthers, and none on the west walls where shots would have impacted had the Panthers fired at the police. "People looked different after they walked through the apartment," one of the Panthers who led the tours said. "They were angry."

The Philadelphia chapter of the Panthers sent two members to Chicago to assess what happened. One of them, Mumia Abu-Jamal, described what he saw: "People were lined up in the bitter Chicago cold in a way that made the apartment building resemble a movie theater." After the visit he wrote, "We had seen with our own eyes the walls cut through with cop machine gun fire. We had seen the mattress where Fred and his woman had lain, blood caked like tomato soup deep into the material." He described the effect it had on Rosemary, the other person who came with him. "When Rosemary came out, something in her had changed. When she entered the apartment, she was a supporter of the BPP. When she left the building she was a Panther."

An elderly woman touring the apartment shook her head and commented, "This was nuthin but a Northern lynching."

Fred's body was sent to the Rayner Funeral Home on Friday, December 5, after a very hurried autopsy by Dr. Constantinou, a Greek-born physician with a temporary Illinois medical license. His protocol showed he found two bullet wounds in Fred's head. He did no analysis on the contents of Fred's stomach or his blood. He determined that Mark Clark was struck and killed by a single bullet through the heart.

Not satisfied, Skip asked the Hamptons for permission to have an independent autopsy done at the Rayner Funeral Home. The Hamptons gave their consent.

On Saturday morning a second autopsy was done by Dr. Victor Levine, a former Cook County coroner, with two physicians and Skip present. Dr. Levine found that both head wounds came from bullets fired from the top right side of the head in a downward direction. One shot entered directly in front of the right ear and exited from the left side of the throat, and the other entered the right forehead and was probed to a point behind the left eye. They were consistent with two shots to the head at point blank range from the doorway to the south bedroom. The downward angles of the bullets were inconsistent with the horizontal shots that came through the wall from the front.

Dr. Eleanor Berman, the Cook County chemist retained by Dr. Levine, tested Fred's blood. In two separate tests she found a high dosage of the barbiturate Seconal, enough to make him unconscious or very drowsy. The barbiturates explained why Fred never woke up. Fred did not use drugs, so the question was, *how did the barbiturate get there?*

On Saturday, December 6, Skip and Dennis asked Herbert MacDonnell, a prominent firearms expert in Corning, New York, to come to Chicago. Two days later MacDonnell examined, measured, and photographed the locations, directions, and diameters of the bullet holes throughout the apartment and gathered what remained of bullet fragments and shell casings.

MacDonnell determined that the upper panel of the living room door contained two bullet holes, not one, as the police found. The smaller hole on top indicated a shot fired in, and the larger one several inches below was made from a shot exiting. The smaller bullet hole was chest high and it lined up with a bullet found in the rear living room wall that matched Sergeant Groth's handgun. The larger hole was made by a shotgun slug and matched up with a shotgun wad found high up in the ceiling of the anteroom. This type of ammunition matched that found in the shotgun attributed to Mark Clark.

MacDonnell measured the upward trajectory of the deer slug as seventeen degrees and determined it was fired from a place near the floor in such a manner as to strike the door at waist level and then impact high on the ceiling outside. The strange upward angle would be consistent with a shot being fired by Mark Clark as he was falling to the ground.

MacDonnell also measured the angles of both shots through the front door and concluded that the door was more open for Mark Clark's shot than it was for Sergeant Groth's. Thus, if the door was opening when the shots were fired, Groth's shot came first.

Skip removed this panel to preserve what he recognized as a critical piece of evidence, one that might reveal who fired the first shot at the front. He stored the front door panel, together with the bloodstained mattress, at the home of Reverend Reed.

MacDonnell noted another entrance hole in the vestibule. A wad found inside the hole matched up with the ammunition in the shotgun carried by Officer Jones, who had entered the front. One of these three shots was the first one fired. Which came first cannot be conclusively proven from the physical evidence alone. We later concluded that the most likely scenario was that Jones's shot, fired in the crowded entrance foyer either as a signal to the police at the rear or by accident, set off the other two.

MacDonnell showed Skip that a bullet makes a larger hole as it exits a wall than when it enters and the wood is splayed outward at the exit hole. Thus, we could look at the bullet holes in the apartment and determine the direction from which they had been fired. MacDonnell confirmed that except for one of the two bullet holes in the front door, all the eighty or more shots poured in from the direction of the police entering the apartment.

13

The Battle for Hearts and Minds

On December 4, while Hanrahan was giving his press conference, members of his office were drawing up felony charges of attempted murder, aggravated battery, and unlawful use of weapons against each of the survivors. The raiding officers prepared sworn complaints that each of the occupants had fired at them. Bonds were set at one hundred thousand dollars each.

Following his interview with the *Daily News*, Bobby Rush was interviewed on camera. He declared that Fred had been "murdered in his bed" and called the raid an "assassination" ordered by J. Edgar Hoover. Although the press quoted Rush, much of the public dismissed Rush's charges as Panther rhetoric.

Donald Stang went to Cook County Hospital later on December 4 to check on the four wounded survivors. When he returned to PLO, he reported Doc Satchel—nicknamed for his role in organizing the Panther health clinic—had the most serious injuries. He had four bullets in him, including two in his abdomen. He was just coming out of surgery.

"He'll probably survive, but it's not clear in what condition," Don said.

Doc was no more than five feet six inches tall and weighed maybe one hundred and forty pounds. It was hard to imagine him being hearty enough to survive two bullets in his abdomen.

Verlina Brewer, a student from Ann Arbor, Michigan, was shot in her left buttock and left knee. Don said she was doing OK, but the knee wound could give her some trouble. Blair Anderson, a young guy who was a former Blackstone Ranger whom they call BJ, was hit in both thighs and his penis. Don said the other person was a student from Champaign, Illinois, Brenda Harris, whom he described as a tiny woman with a big Afro known as China Doll. She was shot two times in the thigh and in her hand.

Doc was the only one I knew. He was always so positive and enthusiastic.

"They're all handcuffed to their hospital beds, and I don't think they're going to bring them to court until they've improved," Don added.

Later that day someone talked to Fannie Clark, the mother of Mark. She told us Mark had been one of many black children mistreated in the Peoria schools. He had started a Panther chapter and breakfast program in Peoria the previous summer and came up to Chicago at Fred's urging to find out how the Panthers there ran their chapter and program. Mark had been traveling around the state attempting to organize more Panther chapters. He was one of eighteen children. Now his mother was contacting the coroner to take his body back to Peoria for burial.

On the afternoon of December 4, Brian Boyer, a young reporter for the *Chicago Sun-Times* reported to work at about four o'clock. Boyer asked for permission to visit the apartment. His editors said it was too dangerous for a white reporter to go there and that no black reporters were available. Boyer went anyway.

"I guess my first reaction was to check the walls again to see if they'd plastered anything over," he said. "Then I called in and said they weren't going to believe it, but it looked like murder to me. I asked for editors and other reporters to come down and go through the apartment, but they weren't interested." Boyer returned to the paper and reported what he had seen.

One of his editors responded, "If we run that story and the West Side burns down, we'll be responsible." Jim Hoge, the *Sun-Times* chief editor ordered the story to run, but in the next day's edition it was buried on page thirty-two.

Brian Boyer responded, "I quit."

On December 5, Deborah Johnson, Harold Bell, and Louis Truelock were brought to preliminary hearing court on Twenty-Sixth Street. The press sat in the front row, and Panthers and their supporters filled the rest of the wooden spectator benches. Skip, Don, and I stood up as the defendants were led out from the holding cell into the courtroom. Shouts of "Power to the people" came from the rear, and Harold Bell raised his fist in the defiant Black Power gesture.

Skip, Don, and I handed up written appearance forms, and when our clients names were called we answered, "Ready for trial." We had chosen this strategy because we wanted to show the world and the press that our clients were eager and prepared to confront the state's so-called evidence. By answering "ready," we also began the 120-day term for the prosecutor to bring our clients to trial.

"The State is not ready and is seeking a continuance," Nick Motherway, one of Hanrahan's subordinates, replied. In a political case like this, the prosecutor generally does not want his witnesses, the police officers, subjected to cross-examination at a preliminary hearing. By continuing the case he'd be given time to get a direct indictment from the grand jury. In that circumstance he would be allowed to present testimony of the police officers with no cross-examination. The indictment would then supersede the need for a preliminary hearing.

"Continuance granted for two weeks until December 19," the judge responded.

"Then we move that our clients bonds be lowered," Skip said. "Deborah Johnson is eight months pregnant, Your Honor."

"Denied," Judge Epton answered again. "Bond will remain at one hundred thousand dollars." There was hissing from the back. "I will order that Deborah be seen by a doctor at Cermak Hospital. Next case."

Skip was interviewed in front of the TV cameras just outside the courtroom. I was a couple feet away as he stood in front of the cameras and declared, "Hanrahan is guilty of murder." A day of looking at the blood and bullet holes in the apartment had shocked and outraged Skip. "Let's tell it like it is," he said afterward. I congratulated him.

Our office took responsibility for defending the survivors. As we heard their accounts and saw the apartment, we knew the truth had to be told. We lost our innocence on December 4.

When I lived in Chicago, in the middle of the cold, gray winters people would ask me why I stayed. Over time I had an answer: "I was bitten by Chicago and in particular the murder of Fred Hampton. I have been trying to bite back ever since."

Bobby Rush was not home early in the morning on December 5 when the police raided his apartment in the projects at 2040 South State. The police claimed they found marijuana and put out an arrest warrant for Rush. It's doubtful that was true, both because Rush didn't use marijuana and because I had warned him the police were coming.

We wanted to devise a way for Rush to surrender himself safely and publicly so that the police would not use his arrest as an opportunity to harm him. One of the Panthers suggested we ask Jesse Jackson to accompany Rush when he turned himself in. We reasoned that if Rush turned himself in with a public figure and in front of the media that Jackson would attract, the police could not say he resisted.

I didn't understand why PLO was selected to make the liaison with Jesse Jackson, but I made the contact more than willingly. I wanted to meet this great orator. I phoned Jackson, told him Flint and I were Panther attorneys and needed to meet with him. He invited us to come to his Hyde Park apartment early the next day.

Jackson's apartment was on the second floor of a three-story Victorian building. A very large and muscular black man, whom we took to be a bodyguard, opened the door and let us in. The apartment was modest in size but well furnished. We sat down on the couch in the small living room and waited. Jackson came out in silk pajamas, a bathrobe, and slippers. Flint and I introduced ourselves and stood to greet him. He asked why we had come.

"We represent the Panthers and the reason we're here is that Bobby Rush has an arrest warrant for marijuana. He's hiding out, and we're afraid if the police find him they might kill him. We would like you to be with him when he turns himself in," I said.

"So now the Panthers are coming to me," Jackson said. "When Fred was alive, the Panthers spent a lot of time attacking me; some of them even called me a sissy. Are they going to keep that up?"

I knew Fred had accused Jackson and Operation Breadbasket of developing programs focused primarily on helping black businessmen rather than poor and working-class people, but I was surprised by Jackson's response. Fred criticized many black organizations, although the criticisms I heard had been on political, not personal, grounds.

"I'm sure the Panthers would be very grateful if you helped to protect Rush, and I certainly doubt if any personal attacks would continue," I answered.

Jackson walked back and forth in the small open space in the living room, pondering our proposal. Then he stopped.

"You know what? Rush should come to Breadbasket and turn himself in when the Saturday morning service at the Drexel [Avenue] church is televised at eleven o'clock." He looked pleased with his suggestion and continued, "I'll make an introduction and then welcome Rush as he comes onstage."

"Sounds like a good scenario to me," Flint said.

"Thank you, and I'm sure the Panthers will appreciate your gesture. We'll make sure he's there tomorrow morning," I added.

Renault Robinson, president of the Afro-American Patrolmen's League, was more than willing to assist us. He agreed to accompany Rush to the Operation Breadbasket meeting. The black police commander from the district nearest the Drexel Church also assured us he would accept Rush into his custody and vouch for Rush's personal safety. He acceded to our plan, no questions asked.

On Saturday morning Kermit Coleman, the ACLU lawyer who had worked with us on Fred's appeal, picked up Rush in his red two-seater sports car. They then picked up Renault Robinson, who carried Rush on his lap as they headed for Operation Breadbasket.

There were more than five hundred people in the Drexel Church when Flint and I arrived at ten o'clock. We were among the few whites, and we sat in the third or fourth row, with a good view of the stage. We waited, listening to the glorious sound of the choir singing hymns from the balcony in the rear of the church.

At 10:30 A.M. Reverend Jackson came out to the pulpit area as the singing ended. The program was being broadcast live on WVON radio, and the next hour segment would be televised. Jesse spoke with his usual dramatic flair, giving an earlier version of his "I am somebody" speech, and the audience responded enthusiastically. At 11:00 A.M. a group of police officers from the Afro-American Patrolmen's League, all in uniform, came up on the dais with Renault Robinson. Shortly afterward Rush came from the side, accompanied by Kermit Coleman.

Jesse put his arms around Rush. "You belong to the community," he said, and he warned the police not to harm him. The audience stood and applauded. Jesse preached that the attack on the Panthers was an attack on all blacks, and he expressed the sentiment I had heard from many black people: "If it happened to Fred, it could happen to us." Most whites didn't see it that way.

Jackson praised Fred as a courageous and inspiring young leader who had been taken away from the people he served by Hanrahan's murderous raid. Again, the audience clapped as Jackson and Rush stood together. The police commander, who had joined them, repeated his vow to protect his new prisoner. Rush surrendered himself, his fist in a Black Power salute. "Power to the people," he shouted as he was led away.

Jackson's public pronouncements condemning the raid were echoed by virtually all civil rights organizations in Chicago. Hanrahan had counted on the black community denouncing the Panthers after the raid. Instead, like the people in this enormous church, they condemned Hanrahan and the raiders. For many, Hampton was seen as yet another young black leader who, like Malcolm X and Dr. King, had fought against injustice and was assassinated because of what he stood for. Only this time, the government's connection to the murder was more apparent. The fatal bullets had come from the police under the command of the local white prosecutor. The fact that Fred was killed in his bed at four o'clock in the morning continued to horrify the majority of black people in Chicago. To them it was a political assassination.

One of the strongest reactions to Fred and Mark's deaths came from Maywood mayor Cabala and the Maywood Village trustees. They visited the site of the raid and called for Illinois attorney general Scott to seek indictments against the officers for "a blatant act of legitimized murder." The national NAACP called for an inquiry, which led to a large-scale investigation cochaired by former attorney general Ramsey Clark and Roy Wilkins, the head of the NAACP. Former Supreme Court justice Arthur Goldberg joined several black congressman, aldermen, and state senators calling for an independent inquiry. Many community leaders came to Chicago on December 20 to participate in a public forum. They heard testimony from elected officials, civil rights leaders, businesspeople, and Panthers who reiterated their demand for an independent investigation. The steady pressure from civil rights groups kept the question of how Fred died in the public eye in Chicago.

The police never explained why they departed from police procedure and vacated the apartment rather than sealing it, at least until the evidence was gathered. The raiders claimed Richard Jalovec, Hanrahan's assistant, ordered them to leave, although he does not recall this. Later Jalovec said the police feared retaliation. Like the thousands of people who walked past Emmett Till's casket at the Rayner Funeral Home in 1955 and remember his swollen, beaten face as a stark symbol of white Southern violence, the people who filed through 2337 fourteen years later saw the large number of bullet holes and the bloodstained mattress as symbols of Chicago police violence.

Chicago political analyst and campaign strategist Don Rose was interviewed twenty years later in the Medill School of Journalism's student paper, the *Monitor*. In the article (part of a Fred Hampton commemoration issue), entitled "After Raid, Blacks Leave Democrats' Machine," he described the political fallout after December 4:

> The raid and the cover-up were probably pivotal in galvanizing the black community. They had not, for years and years, had an issue this offensive stir this many people. A fury built up as events unfolded. The unveiling of the assassination and the cover-up turned the black community around. There was a lot of anger against the machine and against Daley in particular.

Mayor Daley supported the police after the raid, as he did in all their confrontations with civilians, and condemned the Panthers, but he didn't go out of his way to publicly stand up for Hanrahan. Chicago's black aldermen, state representatives, and congressman Ralph Metcalfe—all loyal to and dependent upon the Democratic machine in the past—bolted, openly condemning Hanrahan. This was the same machine that in November 1968, a year earlier, had made electing Hanrahan state's attorney a higher priority than getting Democrat Hubert Humphrey elected president. Hanrahan won, and Nixon carried Illinois and the election.

West Side alderman Danny Davis described, in the above-mentioned *Monitor* article, how the raid impacted the black community: "[The raid] instilled a sense of militancy and resistance, that certain things would not be tolerated. It sparked a determination that had not existed before." The only black person in Chicago with an official position who publicly supported the police action was United States district judge William Parsons, who was contacted by the FBI to be its mouthpiece.

In law we have a term, *res ipsa loquitur*, "things speak for themselves." This was true of 2337. TV and newspaper reporters viewed the premises and came away disbelieving Hanrahan's claims that there had been an extended shootout. Black reporter Lu Palmer of the *Chicago Daily News*, one of the few black writers with his own column, visited the scene on the day of the raid. His job was to comment on the news from a black perspective, and he had written several columns before December that were sympathetic to the Panthers. Fred warmly called him "the Panther with the pen." In his column the day following the raid—entitled "Is There a Drive to Get Panthers?"—Palmer answered his question with an emphatic *yes*. He wrote that when he visited the apartment, "it was immediately clear that this was murder."

John Kifner, the Chicago correspondent for the *New York Times*, also described going to the apartment:

> The crowds were a cross section of the black community: workmen in paint-stained clothes, angry young men and women, elderly people, middle-aged women in flowered hats, people in coats and ties and others in Army jackets, a smattering of whites. In the late afternoon there would be lines of small children in their bright school clothes. "Right here is where the first brother Mark Clark was murdered," a young man in the Panthers black leather jacket would say just inside the front door, gesturing with a thin pointer. "The pigs say that a girl fired a shotgun at them and they started shooting. Now you can see, ain't no bullet holes around the door." He would go on, "no shooting coming out; all the shooting coming in." The reaction was particularly strong when people gathered around the bloodstained mattress in the back bedroom where Hampton died. "They killed him when he was asleep, he never had a chance," was the response of a middle-aged woman.

On December 8, Hanrahan held another press conference to counter the snowballing criticism. He again portrayed the Panthers as the aggressors, responding to the officers' calls for cease-fires with continuous firing. He said a "more detailed statement would be improper in view of the criminal charges pending against the survivors." He added, "We were then and are still convinced that our officers used good judgment, considerable restraint, and professional discipline."

Shortly thereafter, reputed *Daily News* columnist Mike Royko, an iconoclastic reporter but no friend of the Panthers, went to the premises and responded to Hanrahan's claims:

State's Attorney Edward Hanrahan says it was only through the "grace of God" that his men escaped with scratches in their predawn raid on a Black Panther flat. Indeed, it does appear that miracles occurred. The Panthers' bullets must have dissolved in the air before they hit anybody or anything. Either that or the Panthers were shooting in the wrong direction—*namely, at themselves.*

Years later I learned that the Panthers had considered retaliation against the police, but they decided against it when they saw so much of the public and media condemning the raid.

After the private autopsy on Saturday, December 6, Fred's body was laid out for public viewing for two days at Rayner Funeral Home. Thousands of people walked past. He was dressed in a dark suit with a pale blue turtleneck shirt, not the way he would have dressed a week earlier. His wounds had been hidden by the mortician's impressive skills. Unlike Mamie Till, Iberia and Francis Hampton did not tell Sammy Rayner to show the wounds. Panthers in leather jackets stood at each end of the coffin, and there were bouquets of flowers, some dyed black. A ribbon on one said YOU CAN KILL A FREEDOM FIGHTER, BUT YOU CAN'T KILL THE FIGHT. On Fred's chest were political buttons, rosary beads, even class rings people had dropped into the coffin.

Many of Chicago's top criminal defense lawyers volunteered to represent the survivors. James Montgomery, who defended Fred's codefendant in the Maywood Mob Action case, agreed to represent Deborah; and Eugene Pincham, probably Chicago's most prominent criminal defense lawyer, became counsel for Verlina Brewer. Warren and Jo-Anne Wolfson filed appearances for Brenda Harris and Blair Anderson. Warren wore a crew cut, was very calm, and was known for his precise, stilettolike cross-examination, while his red-haired, flamboyant wife Jo-Anne added fire to the defense. Kermit Coleman from the ACLU's prison project became Doc's attorney, and we continued as counsel for Truelock and Harold Bell.

Standard defense strategy was to wait for trial to present your defense. "We don't tell them a damn thing until they finish putting on their evidence," one of the lawyers said at a hastily called meeting with the Panthers to discuss strategy.

"You haven't seen the horror on the faces of people coming through the apartment," one of the Panthers responded.

We were faced with the seeming contradiction between the need to tell the public what happened, and thus provide support for the growing tide of opposition to Hanrahan or, alternatively, to provide what some considered the best legal defense for the survivors. Our group decision was to take the offensive, to tell the press what happened as recounted by the survivors and as demonstrated by the physical evidence. This public approach became critical in determining how PLO would represent the movement and victims of police and official misconduct in the future. We presented the case in a political, not a criminal, framework. "Putting the state on trial" is the way we came to characterize this strategy. We learned it was the best strategy to expose government wrongdoing and educate the public. It was also the best strategy to win.

Following the meeting Dennis talked to *Chicago Daily News* reporter Hank Di Sutter and told him the survivors' version of the raid. Di Sutter reiterated the Panther accounts in detail in the *Daily News* the next day, on December 10, under the headline "Panther Story of Killings."

Hanrahan went into a rage, a state even his friends say was common. He called the *Daily News* story "an obvious effort by the counsel of the Black Panthers to try their case in the press. It is outrageous." Hanrahan felt he had the exclusive right to present his case publicly, but we were in a duel with Hanrahan to win public support.

That afternoon, responding to what he termed "an orgy of sensationalism in the press and on TV that has severely damaged law enforcement and the administration of justice," Hanrahan and his top assistants Jalovec and Boyle called the *Chicago Tribune* editors. They offered to make the police raiders available for exclusive interviews with their reporters. They also provided photos that they said "conclusively proved the Panthers opened the gun battle by firing a shotgun blast through the front door." The *Tribune* accepted.

The next morning, December 11, the *Tribune*'s front page contained headlines, one and one half inches high, labeled EXCLUSIVE. In the police version printed in the *Tribune* exclusive, Sergeant Daniel Groth and many of the officers gave their detailed stories of what transpired at 2337. The article went for several pages.

Sergeant Groth said that he picked the early morning hour for the raid to catch the occupants by surprise, after an informant told him there was a cache of weapons in the apartment. He knocked on the door and announced they were police and said they had a search warrant. He heard movement inside and called out, "Police! Open up!" After a person responded, "Just a minute," Groth ordered Davis to kick the door open. Groth claimed that as they entered the anteroom he heard a shotgun blast that was fired through the closed living room door, just missing Officer Davis and himself. After Davis crashed through the living room door ahead of him, Sergeant Groth saw a woman on the couch fire a second shotgun blast at him as he was standing in the doorway, just missing him. "The flash of her weapon illuminated her face," he said. Groth fired two shots at the woman.

Gloves Davis told the *Tribune* reporters the light from Sergeant Groth's shot allowed him to see both the woman on the couch, whom he shot with his .30 carbine, and a man in a chair with a shotgun in his hands ready to fire. "I don't know for sure if he ever got a shot in at me or not. I fired twice and hit him. He stood up and I jumped up too, struggling with him until he fell. Then I fell across his body." The person on the ground was Mark Clark.

Sergeant Groth said the first time he called for a cease-fire, "the words were barely out of my mouth before there was the whomp of a shotgun blast from the front bedroom that slammed into the bathroom door almost directly across the hall." Hanrahan gave the *Tribune* reporters photos of the bathroom door to show where the shotgun pellets struck the wood.

In his account, Officer Carmody said Panther fire was directed at him from the rear bedroom as he entered the back of the apartment. He returned the fire with his .38-caliber snub-nosed pistol. During one of the cease-fires, Carmody heard someone in the back bedroom yell, "We're coming out, don't shoot. We've got an injured man back here." Carmody said Truelock and Bell came out of the back bedroom. He then said he ran into the back bedroom and found a man later identified as Hampton lying face down on the bed with his head facing the bedroom door.

He was lying with his arms hanging over the foot of the bed. On the floor at his right hand was a .45-caliber automatic and at his left a shotgun. I could see he's been hit but I didn't know if he was alive or dead. All I know was that room was full of shotguns and rifles and ammo. So I grabbed him by a wrist and dragged him into the dining room away from all those guns.

Officer Joe Gorman's account in the exclusive followed Groth's. He described shooting each of the three people in the front bedroom just as they were rising to shoot him. To back up the raiders' accounts, Hanrahan and Jalovec gave the *Tribune* three police photos. One depicted the living room door with one rather large hole circled on it. The photo was offered to prove the Panthers fired the first shot. The second photo, mentioned earlier, was represented as being the bathroom door. It had numerous bullet holes in it and in the exclusive was captioned "Hail of lead tore thru bathroom door in fire from opposite bedroom, according to police." The third photo was the inside of the kitchen door. Carefully circled on the photo were two black dots to highlight that they were bullet holes from shots Fred had supposedly fired.

The same night as the *Tribune* exclusive ran, Hanrahan offered each of the major TV stations the unprecedented opportunity to come to his office in the Daley Center and film the officers staging a reenactment of the raid. Hanrahan's office had hired carpenters who used two-by-fours to construct a mock up of the apartment. Hanrahan required the TV stations that participated to air the entire police version without interruption. Only WBBM, the local CBS affiliate, accepted Hanrahan's conditions.

Despite a careful rehearsal, the raiders had to do several takes to get the version they wanted. Fortunately for us the outtakes were kept and became valuable sources for cross-examination of the raiders. The final twenty-eight-minute version, gleaned from more than five hours of filming, aired on WBBM-TV the same day the *Tribune* "Exclusive" was published.

The TV reenactment was much like the story theater staged by Paul Sills of the nearby Second City, where each character tells his story as he acts it out. "I took my handgun and knocked loudly against the front door," Groth began, and then struck the wooden mockup with a real automatic. "I took my machine gun and I put it on automatic fire," Gorman later continued, moving the mock machine gun across the pretend living room wall. The officers' descriptions of a plethora of Panther shots were almost amusing. They were lies, and we could prove it by the absence of bullet holes lining up with the supposed shots.

Careful readings of the *Tribune* exclusive and the transcript of the reenactment have Brenda Harris firing two shotgun blasts at the police while sitting on the living room couch; enough shotgun blasts and other fire emanating from inside the front bedroom to break the cease-fire "on three separate occasions"; at least one shot at the police from Panthers running down the hallway; and several shotgun blasts and handgun fire from the rear bedroom and from Hampton himself as the police entered from the kitchen door.

Angered at being scooped by the *Tribune, Chicago Sun-Times* reporters came to the apartment the next morning, December 12, to compare the police photos displayed in the *Tribune* with the actual scene. Skip and the Panther guides demonstrated that the *Tribune* photo of the two black spots on the kitchen door, supposedly proof of Panther firing, were actually the dark heads of nails near the doorknob. There were no bullet holes near the kitchen door where the raiders had entered. Skip also stood in the kitchen and demonstrated to the reporters that Carmody could not have seen Hampton or any Panther firing from the back bedroom because the kitchen wall blocked the entire line of vision between where Carmody had entered and the back bedroom.

At the front of the apartment Skip sat on the couch exactly where the raiders placed Brenda Harris in their staged reenactment. "Come sit here and you can see Brenda could not have fired a shotgun at the officers from here without striking one of them or the walls behind them. Yet look, there are no bullet holes there." Skip pointed to the entrance-way and living room walls around the front door, which had no impact points. "As for the front door, if you look carefully in this photo, you can see there are two bullet holes, one made by Groth's revolver firing into the living room."

One of the Panther guides led the reporters to the door Hanrahan had represented as the bathroom door to prove the Panthers fired out of the front bedroom across the hall into that door. "Hanrahan's photo is not the bathroom door he claimed. It's this door to the north bedroom," the guide showed. "It was flush against the living room wall and those holes line up with the police firing from the living room."

The reporters saw that he was right. "This is the real bathroom door and you can see there isn't a single bullet hole in it," the Panther continued. When Skip told me the *Sun-Times* photographer took a snapshot of the nail heads and the real bathroom door with no impact points, I couldn't wait to see the article.

Sure enough, there was a gleeful tone in the *Sun-Times* headlines that same day: "Bullet Holes Were Nail Heads." The article, complete with photos, showed not only Hanrahan's misrepresentations but that the raiders' stories about the Panthers' firing from the two bedrooms and Brenda's firing from the couch had to be lies. Other newspaper reporters came to see for themselves and echoed the *Sun-Times* accusations that Hanrahan and the raiders were lying. The account of the raid offered by the police officers became the *Tribune*'s most infamous front-page story since their misinformed headlines in November 1948: "Dewey Defeats Truman."

Hanrahan's rapid decline in credibility vindicated our decision three days earlier to force his hand by going on the offensive. The UPI was sending out a "mandatory kill" order on transmission of the photos Hanrahan had provided the *Tribune*. He called another press conference to denounce "trial by the press." We went to Glascott's to watch.

Hanrahan was in the library where he first displayed the Panther weapons. He told the now cynical TV and newspaper reporters, "I have made no evaluations of the pictures other than to say they portrayed the scene accurately. We have made no characterization of the pictures." Hanrahan disclaimed any responsibility for the captions, snapping back at one questioner, "We are not editors."

With the TV camera going, another reporter asked, "Do you intend to resign?"

Hanrahan stopped. He glared at the questioner who dared ask such an impertinent question. Then he calmed himself and looked away with an air of disgust, before refocusing on the reporters in front. "Are there any serious questions?"

"That one sounded pretty serious to me," I said to Flint.

Enraged that he was being challenged, Hanrahan continued indignantly, "I would have thought our office is entitled to expect to be believed by the public. Our officers wouldn't lie about the act. I'm talking about the credibility of our officers here and myself." Then, in the middle of his own press conference, Hanrahan stomped out.

14

Farewell to a Revolutionary

Thousands of people went to see Fred's body lying in the Rayner Funeral Home on the South Side on the weekend after the raid. On the following Monday, five thousand more walked past the open casket at Reverend McNelty's church in Melrose Park. After the procession, the church was filled to capacity for the memorial service. Mike Gray's documentary film about Fred's life had become a film about his murder. He filmed the service and I have watched his documented footage many times.

The pallbearers were Panther men in black leather jackets. William O'Neal had visited the Hamptons the night after the raid and begged them to allow him to serve as a pallbearer. They consented. He joined Rush and four other Panther men around the coffin. Together they wheeled the casket into the sanctuary to begin the service with the church chorus singing "Onward Christian Soldiers." The flower bearers were eight Panther women, who were stalwarts in the party. They sat in the front row in dresses and joined in the singing.

The Honor Guard was composed of Hanrahan's Most Wanted list. It included David Barksdale, the chief of the Black Disciples; Jeff Fort, the leader of the Black P. Stone Nation; Cha-Cha Jimenez, chairman of the Young Lords Organization; Obed Lopez of the Latin American Defense Organization (LADO); and a representative from the Latin Kings. Father Clemens, the popular black priest from a South Side Catholic church, read the obituary prepared by Fred's family.

In 1967, Fred became president of the Maywood NAACP Youth Chapter, leading, without fear for personal safety, protest marches for recreational activities for black youth of Maywood who had none, for open housing and improvement of school relationships at Proviso East High School. In November 1968, Fred became chairman of the Illinois chapter of the Black Panther Party, working with superhuman strength and dedication to better the lot of black people. On Thursday morning, December 4, 1969, his life was ended, but his dedication and passion for freedom lives.

Father Clemens, known for his advocacy for black youth, ended with the refrain familiar to everyone who knew Fred:

You can kill the revolutionary, but you can't kill the revolution. You can jail the liberator, but you can't jail the liberation. You can run the freedom fighter all around the country, but you can't stop freedom fighting. So believed Fred—so said Fred—so say we all.

Father Clemens was followed by eulogies from Reverend Ralph Abernathy, leader of the Southern Christian Leadership Conference, and Russell Meek, a well-known Chicago journalist and media commentator. Skip spoke next. We had just received the informal report of the independent autopsy a few hours before his speech, which confirmed Deborah's account that Fred died of two shots fired into his head when he was in a reclining position. With the self-righteousness and fire inherited from his Calvinist preacher father, Skip declared: "What Hanrahan and Jalovec don't understand, and what those police officers who put those two bullet holes in his head don't understand, and what Nixon and John Mitchell [the attorney general] don't understand, is that you can't kill the chairman, and anyone who tries is an enemy of the people and is a pig. Pigs die, but Chairman Fred lives."

Jesse Jackson gave the main eulogy, proclaiming again that "the police attack on Fred and Mark was an attack on the entire black community." He called for the community to work to get rid of racist politicians like Hanrahan.

Bobby Rush and Reverend McNelty delivered the last remarks and benediction. Rush reiterated Fred's admonition to "Be strong" and to carry on his work. In spite of his entreaties, Rush had noticed a change in the party, which was to increase in the coming weeks and months. He described this to me years later: "Fred's death played a tremendous role in destroying the party. After that night, the party slowly declined and members left one by one."

In the pageantry of Fred's death, this decline was not immediately discernible. We hid the devastating effects by repeating the slogan, "You can kill a revolutionary, but you can't kill the revolution." It's what we wanted to believe, but that didn't make it true.

Fred's casket was taken from the sanctuary by the pallbearers and placed in a hearse, where it was driven to O'Hare airport. It was flown to Haynesville, Louisiana, for a final service before burial at the Bethel Baptist Church cemetery.

Panthers Indicted

All of the other survivors were released on bail by the end of the month. Deborah gave birth to Fred Jr. on December 18. Doc was recovering slowly after much of his colon was removed in surgery. He was left with an eight-inch scar extending from his abdomen to his chest. The wounds of the other survivors had mostly healed, although with her permanently stiff finger, Brenda Harris would never play the violin again.

Following the raid, members of the heavily rigged police Internal Investigations Division (IID) exonerated the raiders after asking them only three questions and furnishing them with the answers. Then there was a coroner's inquest, led by an old Democratic Party loyalist, Martin Gerber. Not surprisingly, it found Fred and Mark's deaths "justifiable homicide." Their decision was based on two police accounts. First, a Chicago crime lab technician swore there was only one hole in the front door after the raid (the one going out), and John Sadunas, another technician, testified that two shotgun shells found by the police were fired from the Panther weapon held by Brenda Harris.

During the inquest a showdown occurred between Gerber and our office. Skip was held in contempt and spent a weekend in jail for refusing to produce the front door panel. He didn't bring it in until the raiders' had testified that no police officer fired through the front door. The panel clearly contained the bullet hole of an incoming shot.

The IID investigation and the coroner's inquest findings convinced almost no one of the raiders' innocence. Rather than easing public pressure, they added to the momentum for an independent investigation. This led the U.S. Justice Department to announce in December that a federal grand jury would convene in Chicago to determine if there was sufficient evidence to indict the police and their supervisors, including Hanrahan, for violating the civil rights of the Panther occupants, both during the raid and with their false accounts afterward. The Grand Jury started hearing testimony in January 1970.

Each of the Panther survivors was indicted by the county grand jury on January 31 on at least one count of attempted murder, one count of armed violence, and numerous other weapons counts. Hanrahan had presented the grand jury with the raiders' stories and Sadunas's report. The defendants were required to appear in court on February 11.

Thousands of people go to trial at the Twenty-Sixth Street building and even more thousands plead guilty to crimes to avoid the harsher penalty meted out if you lose at trial. Twenty-Sixth Street was my main workplace for many years. There was always a funny smell in the seven-story building. People said it was tears. I believed them.

When PLO and the other Panther defense lawyers arrived at Twenty-Sixth Street on February 11, the press was there en masse, with the reporters and sketchers in the courtroom and the TV camera crews on the first floor. Our case was assigned to Judge Epton, a moderate but often self-righteous judge, who sat in one of the spacious courtrooms on the higher floors of Twenty-Sixth Street.

"*People v. Johnson, et al.*," the clerk called as we and the Panther survivors stepped up before Epton. The courtroom was full of Panther supporters and sympathizers and again I heard some of the spectators in the back call out "Power to the people" as we stepped forward. Hanrahan was absent, keeping a lower profile after his press debacle.

Judge Epton handed the lawyer for each defendant a copy of the charges. As was the custom, we waived formal reading of the indictment and entered pleas of not guilty. I was representing Harold Bell. The lawyers had collaborated on a set of pretrial motions. In addition to the standard discovery requests (which asked for the names of all the state's witnesses and any documents the prosecution intended to use), we asked for disclosure of all information about informants, police infiltration, and surveillance relating to the raid. We argued that we could not properly prepare the defense if one of the survivors was collaborating with the police or prosecutors. Judge Epton looked at Bob Beranek, the heavyset prosecutor, and ordered the prosecution to disclose if any of the defendants or witnesses were informants.

Judge Epton continued the case until May to give both sides time to comply with the other's discovery requests. We had asked the state to tell us if any of the defendants were in fact informants. There was widespread suspicion inside the party that one of the people in the apartment during the raid was an informant. This suspicion was fed by the reports of Seconal in Fred's blood as well as the fact that the people on security in the front room had failed to protect the chairman.

O'Neal directed the distrust toward Truelock. Not only had Truelock been stationed near the front door on security, but he was an ex-con who met Fred in prison and was released shortly after Fred and then joined the party. We were familiar with jailhouse snitches who fabricated testimony about their cellmates in exchange for early release. Truelock, at least superficially, fit the profile.

But our investigation demonstrated Truelock had completed his original sentence. It was he who'd told me he'd overheard the police saying Rush's apartment would be next, which allowed me to warn him. Truelock's tip may have saved Rush's life, and seemed inconsistent with being a police informant. Also, Truelock appeared so upset and forthcoming when I interviewed him originally, that I never believed he was working for the police. We never uncovered any evidence that he was.

Fred's murder had pushed the Weathermen further toward furtive political activity. The United States was set to invade Cambodia and expand the war. Nonviolent opposition seemed to have had no effect in stopping the escalation. Mary and I had opposite reactions to the swell of political events. I was getting drawn in more just as she began pulling back from what she saw as a one-dimensional and increasingly threatening and maybe dangerous political life.

Two police cars were firebombed at the Nineteenth District Police Station on December 6, two days after the Panther raid. The Weathermen later claimed credit, stating it was a response to Fred's murder. In a statement issued clandestinely in early 1970, the group called itself the Weather Underground Organization (WUO) for the first time and issued a "Declaration of a State of War" against the U.S. government. Its members were adopting fake identities and pursuing covert activities.

Skip had a different reaction to the police raid than did the rest of us at PLO. His response was to become the best prepared—indeed, the consummate—criminal defense lawyer, which he believed was necessary to defeat Hanrahan and the police in court. Don, Dennis, and I had less and less confidence in the legal system. For the time being, my increasing disillusion with the political system and the courts was consistent with representing the sectors of the movement seeking the most radical change. Similarly, while the Weathermen sought to win converts to their politics and actions, they also wanted lawyers to represent them and were content that we remained in our roles.

The issue of "armed struggle" was of primary importance to a large number, if not the majority of movement people in 1970. Most of us supported the Vietnamese, the African National Congress in South Africa, and the other liberation movements who, in President Kennedy's words, had found no nonviolent means of struggle open to them. But support for armed struggle in the United States, as well as the wisdom of carrying it out, was widely debated and we liked to say that it was the "cutting edge" issue of the time.

I supported the need, necessity, and rightness of armed struggle because I saw it winning and freeing people around the world. I felt the frustration of seeing all the nonviolent antiwar work we had done appear to have little effect on Nixon and Kissinger's pursuit of the war. The "Vietnamization" of the war, where Vietnamese bodies would be substituted for Americans, and the Phoenix Program of targeted assassinations were not progress. As a movement attorney, I had the luxury of supporting armed struggle by defending its adherents, without the personal risks inherent in carrying it out. I was not underground and did not even have to sacrifice a generally comfortable lifestyle for my political beliefs.

Many of the Weather people who went underground came from middle- and upper-middle-class backgrounds similar to my own. The challenge to give up what was a privileged life was part of the motivation and allure of both the Weather people and myself toward armed struggle. They did it, at least for a while, and I didn't. I still believe in the rightness of armed struggle in certain circumstances. I don't think the leaders of the slave rebellions, John Brown, Nat Turner, or Crazy Horse were wrong. Nor were Patrick Henry and George Washington, who were hardly nonviolent. And I respect the partisans who resisted the Nazis with guns.

The Weathermen and Panthers both wanted revolution. Both believed, with substantial historical and contemporary proof, that it would not come about nonviolently. Not in the violent United States. Today I realize our revolutionary vision did not take into full account the strength of the forces against us. No strategy would have succeeded. Our position inside the United States made it easier to expose and sometimes block U.S. military actions abroad, but it did not mean we could successfully use the tactics of those we supported to fundamentally change this country. In different ways the Panthers and the Weather people risked their safety and their lives to bring about the change we all believed was necessary. I want to understand both their mistakes and their contributions. I have learned it's far easier to review history than to make it. I'm not sure what I would have done had I not had a law license and been using it to defend those who espoused revolutionary change. Would I have had the courage to take up armed struggle even if I had been willing to risk imprisonment? Could I actually commit violent acts that were so antithetical to the liberal, nonviolent, and rational way I was raised? Even if I could screw up my courage, would it have been right?

It was difficult in those days to balance political effectiveness and personal challenges. Indeed, have we not all imagined ourselves behind the telescopic sight of a rifle aimed at Hitler's head as he rose to power in the 1930s and wondered if we could pull the trigger? I think there were mistakes made when peoples' desires to challenge their own limitations overshadowed the political correctness or viability of what they were attempting. I can understand this. It does not condemn all violent acts or actors, but it's something to watch out for as you head for the point of no return.

The People's Law Office survived and grew because we did not require uniformity on political issues. It was a delicate balance at PLO to stay politically involved, aware, and participating, without requiring support of the same movement factions.

On March 6, 1970, three Weathermen were killed in an explosion inside a townhouse in Greenwich Village in New York City, when a bomb they were making accidentally detonated. Ted Gold, who was killed, and Cathy Wilkerson who was reported fleeing, had stayed with Mary and me a week before when they came to Chicago for their court dates. The war had come home.

16

The Survivors Go Public

As we sat on the modern couches facing each other at the Wolfson's townhouse in fashionable Sandburg Village, Jo-Anne wore an Afro wig and twirled the chamber of an empty revolver. Although a very serious and skillful defense lawyer, she was also caught up in "Panther chic." We were at a meeting of the Panther defendants and their lawyers to decide if Panther survivors should tell their stories publicly.

The indictment of the survivors had created more resentment in the black community. Hanrahan was trying to bolster the credibility of the prosecution with public statements that "the only people with actual knowledge of the raid, who had talked publicly, were the police officers." The survivors had only spoken through their lawyers. The Panthers proposed a people's inquest at Malcolm X College, with Chancellor Charles Hurst presiding. The tribunal would take place in a large auditorium open to the public, and the testimony would be transcribed.

Some of the defense lawyers objected to our clients testifying publicly. "My client won't testify unless and until I tell him too, and that decision will be made after the state rests its case," one of the lawyers said. There was a murmur of agreement. This was the conventional wisdom. "We've been able to build a consensus in the black community and large segments of the public that the raid was not a shootout but a shoot-in," Dennis answered. "We did this by speaking out. We can't pull back now."

We at PLO, and the Panthers, wanted more than a "not guilty" in criminal court. We wanted to continue the public condemnation of Hanrahan and the raiders enough to get *them* indicted on criminal charges. "The people's inquest will keep up the pressure to bring criminal charges against Hanrahan," I said. The Panthers argued it would also demonstrate how an alternative institution could work. In spite of the reluctance expressed by many of the other defense lawyers, PLO and the Panthers prevailed. The survivors would testify publicly.

To build support for the people's inquest, the Panthers issued a "Statement to the Black Community" that read: "Daley and Hanrahan, following the orders of Nixon and Agnew, sent their pigs to murder Chairman Fred. They broke into his home, murdered him in bed while he slept. But that was not enough; they decided to try to kill everyone there." The Panther communiqué continued, "We demand the decentralization of the police so that the people can control the pigs in their neighborhood and no pigs would get the opportunity to murder our people and kill our youth."

Referring to the police as "pigs" was also a Panther trademark. While this terminology obviously led to some loose rhetoric—as in the chant "oink, oink, bang, bang, dead pig"—the term was generic for police who preyed on the community, not a personal attack, although I don't think many law enforcement officers made the distinction. Certainly the term *pig* was intended to vilify the police, but the Panthers' main objective was to organize community opposition to police abuse and gain control over what they saw as the "occupation" of their neighborhoods by police, who showed no respect for them.

The Panther bulletin concluded: "The People Must Indict Hanrahan and Impeach Nixon and Agnew." These goals were obviously ambitious, but the authors of the communiqué rightly sensed the raid was more than a local effort.

The Panthers were looking to the black community for some form of justice. On March 8 the people's inquest convened at the First Congregational Church at Washington and Ashland. Six of the seven survivors testified in the converted lecture hall, where a large audience of spectators and some press had assembled.

A tribunal of six community leaders was picked to hear the testimony and determine the guilt of Hanrahan and the raiders. There was substantial interest and curiosity on the part of the public and the press to hear the first-hand accounts of the raid from the Panthers who survived.

Doc's description of waking up in the dark, ducking, and being hit by machine gun fire had moved the spectators and the jury. Deborah spoke of Fred's death publicly for the first time. Her testimony was the most moving. Without using the word, Deborah described what could only be termed an execution. There was silence in the room after she reported hearing the two gunshots from the bedroom followed by the words of Fred's slayer, "He's good and dead now."

The tribunal was also given the pathology report of former Cook County coroner Levine that indicated that the parallel nature of the shots and the closeness of their entry points in Fred's head made it likely that they were fired at close range from the same spot while Fred was not moving. Hanrahan and the police were invited to testify at the people's inquest but refused. Their prior public statements at the reenactment were made available to the inquest jurors. After the testimony ended, the tribunal members recessed to discuss the evidence. When they returned they announced a "peoples' indictment of Hanrahan" and the raiders for murder. The mainstream press reported the verdict dutifully. The tribunal's verdict carried no legal effect and was symbolic, but it was important to the Panthers' goal to educate the community. Just as Fred had done a mock trial following his conviction for the ice cream truck robbery, the people's inquest suggested a system where power was in the hands of the people. Each gave a vision of something that was possible and could work, and each was an example of the Panthers' efforts to involve people in police issues.

On April 30, the month after the people's inquest, Nixon went on TV to report that the United States was expanding the Vietnam War by invading Cambodia. Lon Nol, the puppet the United States had installed to replace a popular government in Cambodia, was so uniformly hated that Pol Pot was able to ride anti-U.S. feeling to seize power and eventually carry out the extermination of over two million Cambodians, a third of the population.

Students across the country reacted to Nixon's announcement with rage and immediate mobilization. I, like many of them, saw it as proof that he and Kissinger were only making a pretense of seeking peace, but were still seeking victory. If victory was not attainable, they would substitute the annihilation of the Vietnamese people and their neighbors. "We're going to bomb them back into the Stone Age," General Curtis Lemay had threatened in 1964, and the B-52 bombing of Hanoi was now happening. Three days after the invasion of Cambodia, there was a call for a national student strike at a mass meeting at Yale University.

Immediately, student protests and strikes spread throughout the country. On some campuses, such as Kent State in Ohio, the National Guard was summoned. But the antiwar and anti-ROTC protests continued.

On May 4, members of the National Guard, without warning, fired sixty-one shots into a demonstration of approximately two hundred Kent State students. Within thirteen seconds four students were dead, and nine wounded. One would remain paralyzed for life. None of us in the antiwar movement could remain still or silent when we heard this. Nixon further fueled our outrage by casting the students as the violent ones when he declared, "When dissent turns to violence, it invites tragedy." The protesters had not turned to violence, the National Guard had. In Chicago I joined demonstrations protesting the Kent State killings, which were part of over 350 protests in the country. More than half of all U.S. colleges and universities were shut down, and more than 60 percent of the students joined in student actions and strikes. Some of the universities remained closed for over a year. Two thousand protesters were arrested.

It was disclosed later from notes and memoirs of cabinet members that Nixon and Kissinger had considered dropping nuclear bombs on Vietnam. Fear of campus rebellion was one of the reasons they decided against it.

A week after the Kent State shootings, a National Guard building was bombed in Washington, D.C. The Weathermen took credit and issued a communiqué stating it was in retaliation for the killing of the four Kent State students. The small amount of physical damage caused by the bomb seemed a justified response to the deliberate shooting and killing of four students, not to mention the daily munitions being dropped on the Vietnamese. I did not question the bombing. In fact, it gave me pleasure to think there was some retaliation for the escalation of the Vietnam War and the killing of the Kent State students. If they could raise the stakes, perhaps so could we.

Ten days after Kent State, two more students were killed when white state police officers opened fire on an unarmed group of black students at Jackson State University in Mississippi. There was much less outcry, but there were demonstrations at many black colleges. I joined a small protest in Chicago. By the end of the month, the National Guard was patrolling over twenty university campuses in sixteen states. The massiveness of the insurrection can hardly be comprehended today. For a moment it appeared campus radicals were a new revolutionary class.

The escalation of the political climate tore at the fabric of my marriage. Mary and I began to realize that we were not going to make it. I was pulled in more, politically, as she retreated. My overall feelings during that period were a mixture of exhilaration and hope, loss and tragedy: a sense of empowerment sometimes shaken but not gone; a pessimism and anger about the United States, and still a hope and belief that our movement would change things.

17

A Puzzling Victory

There was a strange hush in Epton's courtroom on May 8 when the Panther defendants returned. "They've got to produce the names of informants today," Skip said as we entered. He had his yellow pad out with his argument outlined in case the state refused to disclose the informants. Judge Epton was finishing his morning call, and nodded to us that he would call our case shortly. Our clients sat nervously in the front row of the spectator section.

Nick Motherway, one of Hanrahan's top assistants, came out from the rear and stood next to the court stenographer. One of the defense lawyers approached him, but he waved him off. "*People v. Deborah Johnson, et al.,*" the clerk announced. Seven defendants and seven defense lawyers stood up and we walked forward to stand in front of the bench. The clerk called each defendant by name and each answered "here." Motherway addressed the court: "Because our evidence, gathered by our police, may prevent us from meeting standards satisfying judicial standards of proof, we are compelled to dismiss the indictment."

"Motion granted," Epton responded, in a perfunctory tone. Clearly, he had been forewarned.

We looked at each other and at our clients, too stunned to smile. A few seconds later Jim Montgomery broke the silence: "On behalf of my client Deborah Johnson, I hereby answer ready for trial and demand trial." This trial demand would prevent the state's attorney from ever reinstating the case, at least after the 160-day speedy trial period had run. Each of the defense lawyers made a similar trial demand for his or her own client. Epton's clerk then declared, "Court is in recess."

We turned and walked through the court to the hallway, followed by a slew of spectators yelling "Indict Hanrahan." We and our clients huddled in one corner of the tiled vestibule. "After all his huffing and puffing about the Panthers' attacks on the police, Hanrahan has dropped the charges," Skip said triumphantly, a smile emerging.

"Maybe he didn't want to have to expose the informant," Dennis said. "Or maybe the federal grand jury pressured him into dismissing the cases."

"It's not what Motherway said," Warren Wolfson chimed in. "The state frequently gathers evidence improperly. There's something else."

"Don't look a gift horse in the mouth," chimed in Eugene Pincham, the most senior and prominent lawyer among us.

By this time the press was begging us to go downstairs for a comment in front of the TV cameras. We descended to the first floor. The defense lawyers said the charges were dismissed because the Panthers were innocent and the evidence proved it. Skip added, "The same evidence shows Hanrahan and the raiders are the ones who should be indicted for murder."

It was true: the physical evidence showed the survivors' innocence, but it would be another five years before we found why the indictments were dropped so abruptly. The same day our clients charges were dismissed, they were handed subpoenas to appear in front of the federal grand jury the following Tuesday. Failure to appear would be contempt of court and they could be jailed until they complied. But the Panthers were hesitant to give the federal grand jury credibility by testifying before it.

Milton Branch, a black assistant U.S. attorney from Denver, who was on loan to the federal grand jury, urged us to have our clients participate. But we distrusted the federal government. The head of Chicago's FBI field office, Marlin Johnson, had personally led the FBI raid on the Panther office the previous June. He gave the orders as the FBI agents tore up the office. FBI chief J. Edgar Hoover had publicly declared the Panthers to be "the greatest threat to the internal security of the country," and John Mitchell, the attorney general, put the Panthers on his hit list and determined they posed a sufficient enough threat to justify wiretapping them without warrants.

We got together with the survivors to weigh the options. I still had some hope the grand jury might indict Hanrahan and the raiders. I knew if the Panthers refused to testify, the government would blame us for failing to indict Hanrahan. As we reviewed and discussed the history, it seemed that no matter what we did, indictments by this grand jury were unlikely.

At the meeting, Skip repeated what Jay Miller, head of the ACLU in Chicago had told him about Jerris Leonard, the deputy attorney general in charge of the federal grand jury: "Jerris Leonard told me to my face that Bobby Seale was added as a defendant in the Conspiracy case, because 'The Panthers are a bunch of hoodlums,' and 'We've got to get them.' Miller would not have made this up." We told the survivors what we knew about some of the FBI actions against the Panthers, which included its raids on Panther offices across the country.

Dennis brought up the federal grand jury in San Francisco that was investigating the Panthers. It was still sitting. "The black U.S. attorney in San Francisco, Cecil Poole, charged that their objectives were 'to get the Panthers and harassment.'"

We were in a no-win situation. If the survivors testified and no indictments were returned, which was likely, then the grand jury would have appeared to have weighed all the evidence and found no wrongdoing. If they refused to testify, then the grand jury would blame them for their failure to return indictments, even though the survivors' testimony at the people's inquest in March was available to the grand jury.

On Tuesday, May 12, the day the subpoenas were returnable, Rush held a press conference announcing the survivors' decision, with Skip and Doc by his side. He told the press "It has been our experience that grand juries, including the one that indicted the seven survivors and refused to indict the police who took part in the raid, are illegal shams used to excuse illegal actions of the police. We want to testify, but we feel the grand jury is rigged." He also pointed out that there were only two blacks on the twenty-three-member federal grand jury.

Three days later, a TV reporter called Skip at PLO to say the federal grand jury had just issued a 132-page report and no indictments. We huddled around Skip after he yelled the news into our open cubicles. "He wants to know if we have ever heard of a report with no criminal charges," Skip inquired. We shook our heads, disgusted. Skip told the reporter, "No, they're supposed to return indictments or do nothing."

When Skip hung up, Dennis said, "I'd bet the purpose of this report was to justify their failure to indict."

Someone went to the Dirksen Federal Building and returned with four copies of the official-looking, blue, bound report and a copy of the *Sun-Times*. The headlines were "U.S. Jurors Assail Hanrahan's Raiders," with the subheadings: "Rip Panthers, Crime Lab, IID; Only One Shot Fired at Police." Flint, Dennis, Skip, and I each took copies of our report to our cubicles to read before we reconvened in Skip's office.

The report began with an introduction citing the "nearly 100" witnesses called and "over 130 exhibits" examined, whereby its authors claimed a thorough and exhaustive investigation. Robert Zimmers, the FBI's firearms expert, testified that the two shotgun shells, which the Chicago Police Crime Lab had positively identified as coming from Brenda's shotgun, were fired from Officer Ciszewski's shotgun. The Chicago Crime Lab must have fabricated their test results to fit the officers' stories.

Zimmers also concluded from the configurations of the bullet holes, as well as the bullet fragments and shell casings recovered, that there was only one Panther shot fired and it came from the gun held by Mark Clark. The police fired at least ninety times.

A third autopsy, performed by a new pathologist working for the federal grand jury, confirmed that the fatal shots were fired into the top of Fred's head downward from right to left with roughly parallel trajectories. Other than these bullet holes, the only physical marks on Fred were a bullet found imbedded in the exterior of his shoulder and a graze wound in his leg. The exact caliber of the bullets that went through Fred's head could not be determined from the holes but were consistent with the diameters of the .38-caliber bullets fired by Carmody and also with the .30 carbine bullets fired by Gloves Davis. Nevertheless, the federal prosecutors never sought to determine who fired the fatal shots, where they were fired from, or whether they were fired deliberately to murder Fred.

The chemist advising the grand jury disputed our chemist, Dr. Berman's, findings that Fred's blood contained Seconal. He testified that the blood samples he examined showed no traces of Seconal and that the drug would not have dissipated between Berman's testing and his own, done a month later, after Fred's body was exhumed in Louisiana. But he could not offer an explanation why the Seconal showed up both times in her tests.

In spite of the physical evidence, the grand jury report blamed the deaths and injuries on Panther provocations and hostility toward the police, as much as on the actions of the police themselves. A large part of the report was an indictment of the Panthers, portraying them as a violent revolutionary organization that sought confrontation with the police. Ultimately, Jerris Leonard and the other authors of the grand jury report claimed they could not charge Hanrahan and the raiders "without the testimony and cooperation" of the survivors, even though they had access to the transcripts of the survivors' people's inquest testimony. "Given the political nature of the Panthers," the authors said, "the grand jury is forced to conclude that they are more interested in the issue of police persecution, than they are in obtaining justice. It is a sad fact of our society," they continued, "that such groups can transform such issues into donations, sympathy and membership, without ever submitting to impartial fact-finding by anyone. Perhaps the short answer is that revolutionary groups simply do not want the legal system to work."

A footnote at the end of the grand jury report states: "Finally, the grand jury wishes to acknowledge the invaluable investigative contributions of the Federal Bureau of Investigation. Without the cooperation, professionalism and proficiency of this agency, the grand jury could not have completed its assignment." The irony of this statement became much clearer years later.

"Well, the FBI's firearms examination supports our clients' accounts," Skip said, after we came back together.

"If the raiders fired ninety to ninety-nine shots to the Panthers' one, then what happened at 2337 was a massacre, not a shoot-out." Flint added.

"But the grand jury, or I should say the federal prosecutors and FBI case agents directing the grand jury, refused to draw the obvious conclusions from what the physical evidence demonstrated," Dennis responded.

"They never answered or even addressed the most important question of how Fred died. Was he deliberately assassinated?" I joined in.

"The report indicates there was an FBI informant who provided the same info as Groth's informant. It would be good to find out who that is. Maybe there's a connection between the disclosure of that informant and the dismissal of the Panther cases," Flint said.

The worst thing was that the report's heaviest criticisms of Hanrahan and the raiders were for their lack of care in planning the raid and their efforts to prejudice prospective jurors afterward rather than for their killing two people. The grand jury leveled stronger criticism at the Internal Investigations Division than at Hanrahan, calling it "so seriously deficient that it suggests purposeful malfeasance."

"Well at least the grand jury recommended that police functions be done by the police, not the state's attorney," Flint said. "Taking guns away from Hanrahan is positive."

"You know what?" Dennis said. "This report and its conclusions were written before the Panthers refused to testify three days ago. It's too lengthy to have been written after. They had made up their minds not to indict anyone whether the Panthers testified or not, and then blamed it on the Panthers' noncooperation. This is bullshit."

The federal grand jury report satisfied neither side. While the headlines gave us some solace, the report ultimately equated the conduct of the police during the raid with the Panthers' "antipolice" rhetoric. Hanrahan and the raiders had still gotten away with murder. Large segments of the black community reiterated their demands that the raiders be brought to justice. The Afro-American Patrolmen's League continued to push for prosecution; the NAACP was pursuing its own investigation. Black community groups and liberal whites joined in demanding the appointment of an independent prosecutor.

Black politicians loyal to the Democratic Party withdrew their support for Hanrahan and joined the call for justice. Alderman Ralph Metcalfe, previously a staunch supporter of the mayor and the Democratic Party, led the movement of black politicians away from the Daley Machine. That fall Metcalfe's independence got him elected United States congressman.

What could we do next? We were criminal defense lawyers who defended the movement. But now no criminal charges were pending against the Panthers, the raiders faced no charges, and there would be no trial to expose the police as the attackers.

18

Sue the Bastards

"What about a civil rights suit?" Dennis threw out at our next office meeting. The dropping of criminal charges made it possible for our clients to testify without fear of prosecution. Suing the perpetrators of the raid would put us on the offensive, but we lacked the know-how, the resources, and the permission of our clients. These formidable obstacles were exacerbated by the ambivalence of many of us about using the courts at all. Still, as plaintiffs, we would be the moving party; we could make the claims and define the issues. On the other hand, we would have the burden of proof and the responsibility of carrying the case forward.

We had never done a complex civil case, much less a civil rights claim against powerful and well-funded government officials. We were just beginning to learn how to poke enough holes in a prosecutor's case to raise reasonable doubt. We had never written a civil rights complaint. Moreover, civil rights cases were brought in federal court under the federal civil rights laws. To sue there, we'd have to learn an entirely new court system and set of procedures.

The prospects for winning a judgment at the end of years of legal wrangling seemed remote. We needed the unanimous verdict of a jury, and the December 4 raid remained as controversial and divisive as ever. Many, if not most, white people still supported Hanrahan. Jurors for federal trials were picked from the registered voters who lived not only in Chicago and Cook County, but the white suburbs in DuPage and Lake Counties as well as rural areas extending as far north as Wisconsin. We would be lucky to get one black juror. Filing a civil suit could be setting the survivors and the families of Mark and Fred up for another defeat.

Into this chasm between what was needed and what we knew how to do stepped Arthur Kinoy. With short legs and a slightly hunched upper torso, he was an elf of a man of some fifty years. He taught constitutional law at Rutgers Law School and came to Chicago as an emissary from the Center for Constitutional Rights in New York. The National Lawyers Guild spread the word that we were considering filing a civil rights suit.

Arthur had traveled to the South during the late 1950s and the 1960s. He and his cohort Bill Kunstler, had represented Dr. King, Fannie Lou Hamer, and the Mississippi Freedom Democratic Party. They also represented the families of James Chaney, Andrew Goodman, and Michael Schwerner, three civil right workers kidnapped and slain by Klan members after they went to Neshoba County, Mississippi to investigate the burning of a black church that was being used as a freedom school.

"You can do it," Arthur kept repeating. He stood and leaned forward, waving his closed right hand for emphasis. The rest of us were sitting on the window ledges, countertops, and a few chairs at the front of our office. This was the biggest meeting space we had preserved in our converted sausage shop.

Arthur continued: "In the South, the civil rights activists we worked with were constantly being harassed and jailed. Some were beaten and even killed. We had to figure out ways to protect them." He said they had found an old statute that allowed them to remove cases to federal court and get away from the more racist state judges. "We sued local police and officials for denying our clients the right to vote, or march, or even sit at a restaurant. We forced Southern courts to issue orders protecting the civil rights workers." He was cooking—nodding his head and pounding his knee. I felt like I was right there with Arthur in a North Carolina jail, strategizing with the people arrested at a lunch counter, or in Mississippi advising people turned away from voting. He believed using the Constitution to help the movement was what radical lawyers should be doing.

There was no "I can't" with this salesman for "taking 'em to court." His infectious excitement, as much as his arguments, made us believe we could win too. For the moment I put aside my skepticism about using the courts. A few days later we suggested filing a civil rights lawsuit to Iberia and Francis, and they wanted to know more. Dennis, Flint, and I then called Mark's mother—Fannie Clark—Doc Satchel, and the other survivors to a meeting at the Hamptons' home in Maywood. Iberia served lemonade as we sat on upholstered chairs and the living room sofa arranged in a rough circle.

Our clients were skeptical of obtaining any good outcome from the courts. They had seen Hanrahan manipulate the criminal process to indict them, while he and the raiders went uncharged. Dennis attempted to answer their misgivings: "A civil suit will allow *us* to be the prosecutors," he argued. "We go first and put on the evidence. We will be able to define the issues and set the terms for the trial. Also, we get to question each of them in depth under oath about what happened. They've told so many lies there's no way they can look believable."

"Who do we sue?" Verlina asked.

"We want to sue everyone responsible; the planners, the raiders, and those who lied to cover up what occurred. This includes Hanrahan, his assistant Jalovec, and of course the police." I added. "We would also try to include as defendants the people in the Chicago Police Crime Lab and the state's attorneys who did the phony investigation."

Flint, who was still a law student and didn't often speak up, added, "Our legal research shows we can charge them all with conspiracy together in one suit."

The argument that won the day was Fannie Clark's: "We can't just do nothing. Mark and Fred should still be alive. I want to bring their killers to trial." Nobody countered what she said.

"Let's go ahead. We're in," Iberia Hampton said. I saw the determination on her face and knew, despite the difficulties, we had to go after everyone responsible for Fred's murder and the cover-up afterward.

Iberia had another reason for wanting to file a civil suit: "The way he was described in the papers, people didn't really know who my son was." She didn't like the way he was constantly portrayed with his fist in the air and talking about "pigs." She wanted the lawsuit to show her son as the young organizer, the gifted speaker, the would-be lawyer, the young man on whom she and Francis had placed so much hope. Fred was a combination of her own ability to bring people together and Francis's quiet but resolute militancy.

Doc was also anxious to begin a lawsuit. The pain and medical complications from his gunshot wounds were still with him. "Let's go all the way. Whatever it takes," he urged. After only partial recuperation from his injuries, Doc had resumed responsibility for running the Panther medical clinics and was back on a fourteen-hour-a-day work schedule. "I'm going to have these scars and the pain for the rest of my life," he said. "Why shouldn't the people who shot me and their bosses pay?" After he spoke, all the survivors agreed to sign up for the lawsuit.

Deborah had been quiet, but she was moved by the resolution of the others. "I want Little Fred to be proud of his father," she said. "I hope the suit will show how great he was and make the pigs answer for what they did."

As we lawyers overcame our fears, we began to focus on the positive. In civil cases, extensive discovery is allowed. We would get to cross-examine all the defendants under oath at depositions, with court reporters recording what they said. The contradictions between Hanrahan's and the raiders' accounts and the physical evidence made the prospect of confronting the defendants a trial lawyer's dream.

Arthur Kinoy's experience in finding solutions that protected civil rights workers in the South, even in the most racist courts, gave me hope. Wasn't this our job? I would learn that civil cases, where we were on the offensive, actually gave lawyers the best opportunities to expose government wrongdoing. There were also provisions in the Civil Rights Act that required the defendants to pay our attorneys fees if we won. This allowed us to support ourselves without burdening our clients. But then we only got paid if we won.

Having decided to proceed with civil litigation, we needed to write the complaint to combine the claims of the survivors and the deceased into one lawsuit against all the perpetrators. We didn't have the resources or the desire to bring nine separate suits, nor did we want to sue each set of prospective defendants separately. The legal construct we had found was to charge all the actors in a conspiracy to act together. That way we combined Hanrahan, Jalovec, the fourteen raiders, the crime lab people, and those who falsified the investigation into one lawsuit.

Skip, who had carried the burden of the criminal defense and who knew the evidence best, did not assist in the filing of the civil case. As I mentioned earlier, he was moving in the direction of becoming a top criminal defense lawyer—not only one who would win but one who could charge big bucks. Years later he told me with some regret that he had always feared being as poor as his family had been when he grew up, and that money and reputation were important to him. He left PLO because we refused to open a second office on prestigious LaSalle Street.

Flint and Dennis drafted a complaint using our facts and language and Arthur's prior pleadings. Ray McClain, a bright University of Chicago Law School student, assisted them. Finally, the Center for Constitutional Rights sent Bill Bender, an experienced civil rights lawyer, to Chicago regularly to help draft pleadings and oversee the legal work.

After a week of drafting, we all pitched in and reviewed the complaint for its factual accuracy, tweaking it where necessary. Dennis added some purple prose to spice up the allegations. Essentially, we were charging the defendants with conspiring to deprive our clients of their constitutional rights to life, liberty, due process, and equal protection, and the right to be free from illegal searches. In May of 1970 we filed our complaint. We had no idea we were embarking on a thirteen-year battle.

On June 27, 1970, Chief Criminal Court Judge Joseph Power bowed to the pressure from the coalition of forces dissatisfied with the federal grand jury and appointed a special prosecutor. This was only the second time this had ever occurred in Cook County. It is nearly impossible to get the chief judge, selected for that position by the local Democratic Party, to rule that the local prosecutor, elected by the same party, is not fit or has a conflict of interest in a criminal prosecution. Judge Power appointed Barnabas Sears, an elderly, white-haired lawyer with a patrician manner who was well respected by the legal establishment and who had gained fame prosecuting the Summerdale police scandal, to investigate Hanrahan. While not known for representing blacks, Sears was viewed as independent of Daley. Sears hired two assistants—Weyland Cedarquist, an experienced trial lawyer, and Ellis Reid, a young, progressive black lawyer, to help him.

In spite of what I believed were his good intentions, I didn't think Sears had enough energy or trial savvy, not to mention killer instinct, to prevail. He was too much of a gentleman to win against the down-and-dirty tactics he would face. But the Panthers had been among the groups calling for the special prosecutor and wanted us to assist Sears in any way possible.

Mary and I separated in 1970. As I was being pulled more and more into the most radical sectors of the movement, she was looking for other friends and stepping back from what seemed to her like the rapids before the falls. We had started our marriage believing we could live a middle-class life but still support radical groups. Looking back, I think this might have been possible. But in 1970 I didn't want a separation between my personal and political lives. It was hard to tell my dad about the breakup. I knew he really loved Mary and was sad about the breakup, but I think he hid his feelings out of loyalty to me. As for me, I'm ashamed to say I was too caught up in events to feel the pain of separation and the loss of what we had both hoped would be our partnership for life.

When Mary moved out of the Bissell Street house in 1970, other people moved in, and we operated more as a collective. Flint came to live at Bissell Street after his girlfriend, Seva, left the office and Chicago. Liza Lawrence, a close friend of Courtney Esposito's who, like me, sported a large Afro, occupied one of the bedrooms in our house. Susan Waysdorf, another temporary dropout from the University of Chicago, occupied another. All the bedrooms were on the second floor, but movement people coming into town for court dates or just needing a place to crash frequently occupied the couches in the living room or the spare bedroom at the back of the house, four feet from the El tracks.

Courtney Esposito had been part of a Weatherman collective in Chicago, but after the townhouse explosion, she left SDS and started working at PLO in 1970. She and I began a relationship after Mary and I split up. Courtney soon moved into Bissell Street. Olive-skinned with green eyes and light brown hair, she had a tough outwardly manner reinforced by a sarcastic tongue. We shared a bedroom most of the time. I say "most" because we, the men, were constantly being lectured to (justifiably) about our failure to do our share of the housework, particularly the cleaning. The withholding of sex was a frequent punishment.

We had weekly meetings, and chores were parceled out, from shopping and cooking to cleaning. Everybody pitched in for food, and I paid the utilities and mortgage. As a movement person with access to money and in this case the ownership of the house, I felt hypocritical. I got some consolation from a saying attributed to Ho Chi Minh: "You can't control what life you were born into, you can only control what you do with it."

PLO's first woman lawyer, Susan Jordan, came to live in our house shortly after she joined the office. She was my age, in her late twenties, and had just graduated from Northwestern Law School. With a sharp tongue and a very self-assured manner, Susan could more than hold her own with the men. She quickly established herself as a very competent criminal lawyer. There were few women criminal lawyers at that time, and shortly after she joined the office, she teamed with Jo-Anne Wolfson to defend a prisoner at Stateville Correctional Center, in Joliet, Illinois, who was accused of assaulting a guard. It was our introduction to prison work.

Susan also began a relationship with PLO partner Don Stang. Don's wife Laura Whitehorn had left Chicago to join a women's collective in Pittsburgh. Don remained with PLO until 1973. Don and Laura had started with many of the middle-class assumptions that Mary and I had, but their comfortable Hyde Park apartment, filled with the books of their Harvard-Radcliffe educations, was a shell that no longer fit.

Don rented an apartment directly across Bissell Street. We learned later when we got our FBI files that FBI agents occupied an apartment directly above his. They monitored and recorded our comings and goings with great interest and took photos of everyone who visited.

The Hampton civil suit was assigned to Joseph Sam Perry, an old, feisty judge, much like his cohort Julius Hoffman, who had presided over the Conspiracy Seven trial. Perry grew up in Alabama, was diminutive in stature and imperial in style. Both Hoffman and Perry were bad draws for civil rights plaintiffs.

Hanrahan, and indeed all the defendants, moved for more time to obtain lawyers and answer our complaint. Subsequently, they persuaded the county to appoint John Coghlan and the city to appoint Camillo Volini, two private attorneys, to represent them. There was no limit on their expenses or on the hours they could bill. It was a payoff for two Democratic Party loyalists.

John Coghlan was a rough-and-tumble, red-faced Irish lawyer. He wore glasses, and could be tough, dramatic, or sarcastic, as the occasion required. He had been a cop, and was at his best portraying police as the unsung heroes of our society. He would represent Hanrahan, his assistant Jalovec, and the seven raiders who were permanently assigned to the State's Attorney's Office.

Camillo Volini, an overweight Italian lawyer with a round face and flabby jowls, was appointed for the other cops and the crime lab personnel. He was less intense and confrontational than Coghlan, and even had a jocular side. Both Coghlan and Volini were seasoned in the politics of Chicago's white ethnic communities and knew well how to appeal to their fear of blacks. Although Coghlan and Volini were appointed solely so they could receive public monies, they used their titles as "special state's attorney" and "special corporation counsel" to claim governmental status, seek privileges from the court, and intimidate witnesses.

Perry allowed Coghlan and Volini substantial time to respond to our complaint. We were still awaiting their answers that fall.

19

Shootout in Carbondale

On November 12, 1970, Chicago newspaper headlines described an early morning shootout between the Panthers and the local police in Carbondale, Illinois, at a house the Panthers rented. Amazingly, no one was killed, although the confrontation was reported to have lasted several hours. Bullets struck two Panthers and one police officer. Neighbors, awakened by the gunfire, came out and urged the police to stop firing, and a truce was arranged. Four Panthers were arrested inside, and two some distance away. All were charged with multiple counts of attempted murder and were being held on one-hundred-thousand-dollar bond.

Because we had come to be accepted as the "Panther lawyers," Bobby Rush asked PLO to go to Carbondale to represent the men arrested. Their families had contacted Chicago lawyers, and they were asking twenty-five thousand dollars apiece to represent the defendants. They didn't have that kind of money.

"Anyone able to go to Carbondale?" Dennis asked at the impromptu meeting put together at the front of the office after Rush's call.

Susan Jordan said she wanted to go, but she and Jo-Anne Wolfson were preparing their defense for their Stateville prisoner client.

"I'll go," I said.

"Me too," added Flint, who was taking the semester off from law school.

Courtney Esposito said she would go also.

To my surprise and delight, Michael Deutsch said he'd help with the trial. We were hoping he would join PLO, and he had started attending our office meetings. He had been an academic standout at the University of Illinois, as well as at Northwestern Law School, where he was on the law review. When he graduated in 1969, he had taken the prestigious position of clerking for Seventh Circuit Justice Otto Kerner, the former Illinois governor.

Moved by the tumultuous events of 1969 and 1970, Michael became more interested in PLO's work than rising in the professional or academic world. He is one of the most incisive thinkers I've ever known. My dad used to say the most important thing in law is determining what is relevant. Michael does this as quickly as any lawyer I've met. Flint and I immediately accepted Michael's offer to help at trial.

Among the three of us I had the most experience even though I was only three years out of law school and had only one felony trial under my belt. I had no idea what the courtroom atmosphere in southern Illinois would be like.

I asked my partners what we should charge. I was the most hard-nosed about finances. For Dennis, money was an afterthought, if considered at all. We decided we would offer to represent everyone for a total of ten thousand dollars. We had never taken money for defending the survivors of the December 4 raid, but we were often covering five cases a day per lawyer, in different courthouses around Cook County, just to pay the rent and our three-hundred-dollars-per-month salaries.

Two days later, Flint, Courtney, and I drove to Carbondale in southern Illinois. It was closer to Mississippi than Chicago, so I anticipated a very racist environment. In Cairo (pronounced *Kayro*), Illinois, fifty miles south of Carbondale, white supremacists had been driving around the black housing project shooting into it nightly. However, we found Carbondale, home to Southern Illinois University, less like the Old South than we expected. Most of the students were from the Chicago area.

Our first stop was the Panther office located in an unheated storefront at the edge of the small black community. I introduced myself to Jimmy Brewton, an intelligent former student who had started the Carbondale Panther chapter, and Paul Atwood, a white guy in overalls in his early twenties. Paul was missing his right forefinger; I later learned he had cut off his "trigger" finger to avoid being drafted for Vietnam.

They offered to walk with us the three blocks to the Panther house. The neighborhood consisted of two-story wood-frame houses in reasonably good condition. They reminded me of neighborhoods in Atlanta where even the poorest blacks owned their own homes. The

Panther house was also two stories, with windows on all sides of the second floor. I saw bullet holes in the glass panes of some of them. I also saw the outlines of sandbags above the window frames. Paul said they had been put there weeks before the shootout.

"That's where the Panthers were defending themselves," Jimmy said, pointing to the second floor. "And the cops were spread out behind their squad cars and those trees."

A white-haired black man in work clothes came out of his house and asked who we were.

"We're lawyers from Chicago, who may be representing the Panthers," I answered. "Did you see the shootout?"

"Part of it," he replied. "I was sleeping when shots woke me up. I looked out and saw all these cops running around in the dark with guns. I thought they were going to kill us. I didn't know what was going on. I grabbed my shotgun and looked outside from behind my curtain."

"Did you see who started it?" Courtney asked. "Did you hear the police give any orders over bullhorns before the shooting started?"

"No, first thing I remember hearing was shots from around my house and then some shots from this house right here, where those Panther boys stayed."

"Would you be willing to testify at a trial?" Flint asked.

"Sure. I don't want the police coming in here shooting," he said, angrily. "Some kids could end up getting killed." We had found our first witness.

Later that afternoon, Flint, Courtney, and I went to see the men in custody at the Murphysboro jail, fifteen miles from Carbondale. The sheriff let Flint in as a law student, but not Courtney, even though I told them she was our paralegal.

An hour later Flint and I were led to a small dingy room with a card table and a couple of chairs. We sat down. After a few minutes, four men were brought in. We introduced ourselves, shook hands, and stood around the table, a little awkwardly.

The men looked haggard and exhausted after three days in jail. Three of them were SIU students from Chicago. In the newspaper accounts the authorities claimed the shootout had started when the police followed a burglary suspect to the house. The police said when they surrounded the house and ordered the occupants out, the Panthers started firing.

The most vocal of the men in custody was Leonard Thomas, dark skinned and handsome, with a finely featured face and horn-rimmed glasses. Even though his clothes were ruffled, he looked as if he would be more at home in a classroom than firing a rifle.

"It was a real firefight, but they started it," Leonard said. "Bullets were flying everywhere. I don't know why nobody got killed."

"'Cause we were prepared to defend ourselves," Milton Boyd (nick-named Houseman) jumped in. He was tall and slender, with very dark skin and cheeks that pumped in and out when he talked. "We had our place barricaded. We weren't going to be ambushed and killed in our beds like the brothers in Chicago."

"Most of us were asleep when somebody from the front yelled that the police were surrounding the house. We heard shots and we went to our battle stations," Leonard added.

We later learned that Elbert Simon, the black postmaster general of Carbondale, had entered the Panther house and convinced the Panthers to surrender after he received assurances from the police that they would not fire as the Panthers came out.

The men in custody wanted to know more about us. I explained that we represented the Panthers in Chicago, including the Hampton family, and we had been asked by Bobby Rush to help them. They looked skeptical. We were dressed in jeans and looked more like hippies than lawyers, with Flint's ponytail and my Afro. They thanked us for coming down, but I sensed we would have to prove our merits in court.

"How about bail?" Leonard asked. "If you get us out, we can earn money and pay you without burdening our parents."

This was not the type of agreement most criminal lawyers relished. They wanted cash up front. Sometimes we did too, but we weren't going make them sit in jail. Getting your client out on bond is the first, and often most critical, step in a criminal case. With a client out of jail, there's no pressure to go to trial quickly. Generally the defendant benefits from postponing the trial, particularly when there is a lot of publicity around the event that led to the arrest. Clients can assist in finding witnesses, working out the necessary defense, and preparing courtroom testimony. Also, it makes a much better impression on the judge and jury for your client to be free. Not only can he go to and from court without a marshal escorting him, but the jury knows he has been trusted enough to be released and is voluntarily appearing for trial. Unless we got the bond lowered, these defendants would be in custody at the time of trial, several months away. Because they were Panthers, getting the bond reduced would be difficult. This was the test for the defendants of whether we could deliver.

The bond hearing took place in Murphysboro in the regular courtroom in the old courthouse, located in the middle of the town square. Flint and I sat down at the counsel table in the empty, cavernous, wood-paneled courtroom.

Richard Richmond, the prosecutor, arrived shortly thereafter. He was a stocky but handsome man in his late thirties who came from a prominent local family. He walked over, introduced himself, and shook our hands. He was friendlier than I had anticipated. The judge, who arrived shortly thereafter, was less cordial.

The defendants were led into the courtroom shackled hand and foot. I stood up. "Your Honor, it's demeaning for the defendants to be brought into court like this. I move to have the marshals remove their handcuffs and leg chains." The judge looked at Richmond, who said he had no objection. The judge looked annoyed that Richmond had acceded to our request but begrudgingly ordered the sheriff to remove the handcuffs and leg chains.

I stood up and explained that the defendants had no criminal backgrounds, were students who came from working- and middle-class families, and had not sought this confrontation with the police. At worst, some of them had defended themselves when the police attacked. Richmond opposed our motion to reduce bond based on the length of the standoff, the number of shots fired, and the danger to the officers. To my surprise, he didn't focus on the defendants being Black Panthers.

The judge quickly ruled: "Motion to reduce bond is *denied.*"

Back in our tiny visiting room in the jail, our clients were understandably upset. They were facing six months or more in custody before trial.

"We're not giving up," I said. "There was too much pressure on this judge for him to let you guys out."

"We'll appeal his decision," Flint rejoined. "I've already started drafting a petition to the Supreme Court to ask for a bond reduction."

We called some local activists together to set up a defense committee. Somebody had a photograph of the six Panthers chained together in handcuffs and leg restraints after the shootout. The men in the photo looked like slaves being led to a slave ship or an auction block. The photo with the words "Free the Carbondale Six, Stop the Railroad" in bold letters under it became the official poster of the defense committee.

Flint and I spent two days drafting and filing the appeal. Within a couple days, Justice Goldenhersh's clerk called to say the Illinois Supreme Court justice set a hearing at his Mount Vernon office the following Monday. He had a reputation for being open-minded, even liberal.

The next Monday morning Flint and I were called into Justice Goldenhersh's law office along with the prosecutor, Dick Richmond. Flint introduced himself as a third-year law student and obtained permission to participate in the hearing. I repeated my arguments from the earlier bail hearing but emphasized that the defendants were or had been college students with firm family roots in their communities. They were not going to break contact with their families and flee. I argued that Illinois law includes the presumption of innocence before trial, which requires releasing defendants on bail unless the state demonstrates they are a danger of flight or a risk to the community, which these defendants were not. Flint cited cases to support me.

"Do you agree with their premise, Mr. Richmond?" Justice Goldenhersh asked.

Richmond said that he accepted our formulation of the law and he didn't argue against bail very forcefully. Here was a prosecutor unlike those in Cook County's criminal courts: a prosecutor with a conscience.

Shortly after we left the judge, his clerk brought out his order. I glanced at the bottom line: "The Appellants Motion to Reduce Bond is hereby granted. Bond is set at $10,000." Our clients would be released as soon as their families put up 10 percent, or one thousand dollars.

Flint and I were exuberant. "Let's get out of here before he changes his mind," I said.

At the Jackson County Jail we reported the good news. There is nothing more satisfying than seeing the smile when you tell a client in jail he or she is going home.

"You guys really did it," Leonard said.

"You the one," Houseman joined in, giving us a high five.

James Holley, nicknamed Blood, was short and stocky. He had hardly said a word on any of our earlier visits. This time he gave us our biggest compliment: "You guys are our trial team."

20

Vietnam and Protest

Back at **PLO, Flint and** I were greeted with congratulations. We wanted to push the Hampton case, but it seemed stuck in slow motion. The defendants filed motions to dismiss, challenging the sufficiency of our conspiracy allegations and claiming Hanrahan was immune from civil suit because he was the prosecutor. Judge Perry was in no hurry to decide the motions or to allow us to begin deposing the defendants.

By 1971 the Panthers in Chicago and nationally had diminished in size and influence. They weren't recruiting new members and the Chicago chapter never regained the size it was before Fred's murder. No one could replace Fred's charisma, energy, or organizing ability.

The Panthers' primary activities became the selling of the Black Panther paper, the maintenance of the office on Madison Street, and administering a now-diminished breakfast program and health clinic. Many municipalities, including Chicago, began to implement their own free breakfast programs, taking away one of the Panthers' primary sources for community outreach and support. While the Panthers could rightfully claim they had initiated the breakfast programs, they received only the continued harassment from the city officials who had copied them. Years later, with the community pressure gone, the city abandoned the breakfast program.

The split between most of the West Coast Panthers, including Huey Newton and Eldridge Cleaver, who was living in exile in Algeria, took its toll on all the Panther chapters. Many Panthers left because they sympathized with Eldridge, who espoused the need for underground armed units. The Chicago chapter allied itself with the West Coast Panthers, who had given up much of their militancy. With their leadership constantly being arrested and put on trial, the West Coast Panthers devoted most of their energy to freeing them.

Some revelations in 1971 suggested additional reasons for the Panthers' decline. In March antiwar protesters who later identified themselves as the Citizens Committee to Investigate the FBI broke into an FBI office in Media, Pennsylvania, a suburb of Philadelphia. After the break-in, they clandestinely began releasing documents they had seized. These documents exposed the secret FBI Counterintelligence Program (COINTELPRO). One of the documents they released was a memo from FBI director J. Edgar Hoover to all FBI offices, ordering FBI agents in all cities with Panther chapters to develop "hard-hitting programs designed to expose, disrupt, misdirect, discredit, or otherwise neutralize" black nationalist organizations, including SNCC and the Nation of Islam. Another stated objective was to "prevent the rise of a messiah who could unify and electrify the militant black nationalist movement." Stokely Carmichael, Dr. King, and Elijah Muhammad were named as potential "messiahs." Hoover ordered that COINTELPRO's existence be kept secret. Every office was to report directly to him on its efforts to carry out the program's mandates.

"Do you think this COINTELPRO had something to do with the raid?" Dennis asked Flint and me when the documents were first published.

I was wondering the same thing. "We always thought this was Hanrahan's thing," I answered. "But maybe he had help."

In 1971, William O'Neal left the Panthers. He became the lessee and manager of an Arco gas station in Maywood, only a few blocks from the Hampton home. When Dennis and I visited O'Neal, he told us "this gas station supports Panthers involved in underground activities." He said he was sure clandestine work was "what Fred would have wanted" and he was carrying out Fred's intentions. He claimed a vague connection to the politics of armed struggle that Eldridge Cleaver espoused. O'Neal was particularly vehement in denouncing the Chicago Panthers for having no military capability.

Even with his businessman aura, O'Neal tried to impress Dennis and me by bragging about how he could go in and out of the business and criminal worlds. He claimed he and his friends Robert Bruce and Nathaniel Junior, two ex-Panthers, were regularly committing burglaries.

In June of 1971 the *New York Times* and the *Washington Post* printed the Pentagon Papers. These were top-secret documents smuggled out of the Defense Department and copied by Daniel Ellsberg while he was working for the Rand Corporation. The files demonstrated that military advisors in the Johnson administration understood that the war could not be won and that continuing would lead to many times more casualties than the government admitted publicly. Ellsberg faced possible life imprisonment if he released the documents but took the risk because he was convinced the war in Vietnam had become so destructive that militant and courageous resistance was needed.

The Pentagon Papers confirmed everything we in the antiwar movement already believed about the government's willingness to carry out heinous crimes and inflict mayhem in a war it knew it could not win. The publication of these documents greatly increased the antiwar movement's credibility with the media and intelligentsia.

Nixon's paranoia about leaks brought on by Ellsberg's release of the Pentagon Papers led to the creation of the White House–directed "Plumbers unit." These ex-CIA recruits carried out the burglaries at Watergate and at Ellsberg's psychiatrist's office, which led to Nixon's impeachment when he tried to hide his knowledge of the burglaries. The country's repulsion for the government overreaching and the intrusions of the Plumbers and the cover-ups that followed eventually created the atmosphere for uncovering other clandestine government activities, including COINTELPRO.

Years later, Ellsberg said it was the daily, relentless protesters outside the Rand Corporation where he worked that caused him at first to question, then repudiate his role in supporting the war in Vietnam, and ultimately to risk years in prison to help end it.

21

The Carbondale Trial

In the summer of 1971 the Center for Constitutional Rights was help-ing us answer Hanrahan's motions to dismiss. They had generously provided us with assistance from Bill Bender, one of their most skilled lawyers. Hanrahan's lawyers took the position that as a prosecutor, Hanrahan had absolute immunity for any actions he took. We argued that executing a police raid was a police function, not a prosecutorial one, thus Hanrahan was not entitled to complete immunity. The law was on our side, but out of deference to Coghlan and Volini, Judge Perry wasn't.

More briefs and memos were still due on both the immunity and conspiracy issues as Flint, Michael, and I went to trial in August in the Carbondale Panther case. Judge Perry stopped our discovery while the special grand jury considered criminal charges against Hanrahan. There was nothing to do but answer their motions and wait for Perry to rule.

The Carbondale Six became the Carbondale Three after the prosecu-tor decided to indict the Panthers separately. The first trial would be for Leonard Thomas, Milton "Houseman" Boyd, and James "Blood" Holley, all of whom were arrested inside the house after the shootout.

Though we feared the Carbondale Panthers would not get a fair trial in front of the humorless and prosecution-oriented Judge Prosser, we were hopeful about the jury. Michael and Flint had opened a PLO branch in Carbondale that spring, and had become familiar with the jury pools there. A lot of SIU students, faculty, and ex-students were on the registered voting lists in Jackson County, along with a lot of weed-smoking folks who didn't love the police. We wanted a young jury, which in that period meant an iconoclastic jury.

Our understanding of the law was that the prosecutor had to prove that an individual defendant fired at a specific police officer with the intent to kill him in order to prove any of the seven attempted murder charges pending against each defendant. It would be nearly impossible for any of the police officers to identify which individuals had fired at him. If we could pick a jury that would hold the prosecution to its legal burden, we thought we had a good chance of winning.

For jury selection, the spectator section of the courtroom was packed with supporters, mostly current or recent college students or those who had taken a brief respite from the university. The Carbondale Six Defense Committee, which comprised primarily student activists and was formed shortly after the shootout, had done its work. It makes a huge difference for a jury to see there are people in court who care about the defendants on trial. This is particularly true in a political case, where the prosecution invariably tries to show the defendants to be on the fringe.

As the trial began, our clients were dressed in sports clothes, and Michael and I had on court suits. Flint was wearing a tan sport jacket and a red, curly-haired wig to cover his shoulder-length reddish-brown hair. From a certain angle he looked a little clownish. The wig did not quite fit and had an orange tint.

Eleven of the twelve white jurors selected were in their twenties. In 1971, age was a strong indicator of one's sympathy toward change and to political movements in general. We assumed most of the jurors would relate to our youthful and iconoclastic style and exuberance, not to mention our suspicion of the police.

Michael made our opening statement; it was the first time he'd ever spoken to a jury. Nervous at first, he quickly got into the rhythm, presenting the case from the defendants' perspective. They woke up in the early morning hours to flashes and the sounds of gunshots coming from the darkness. Without indicating whom, he acknowledged that some of the people inside had fired back to protect themselves. While an opening statement is not the time for argument, it is a time when defense lawyers talk about reasonable doubt, and Michael told the jury that the state couldn't meet its burden on any of the twenty-one attempted murder counts because they couldn't show who had fired any of the shots or at whom they were fired.

After openings, Richmond called the first of the seven officers. He testified that he and the other officers surrounded the Panther house after chasing a burglary suspect they had seen run inside. It had been early morning and still dark. The police had given warnings over a bullhorn to the occupants to come out. After that, the officer testified, he'd seen and heard shots from the second floor of the house, and returned the fire from behind a tree a hundred feet away.

When I questioned the first police officer, he admitted he could not identify who had fired at him. He also acknowledged he knew the house was where the Panthers lived and the police had contingency plans for a raid. I was trying to establish a motive for the police firing and picked the obvious one—they knew they were Panthers.

Michael and I took turns cross-examining each of the other six police officers. Their testimony was similar to the first, but one of the officers was especially adamant that following a particular flash from the house, he felt the bullets "whizzing past" him as he ducked, and he could tell from which window the shots came. Although the officers got occasional views of the Panther house, they could not identify the persons firing. Still, I feared the jury might sympathize with these young, white, earnest-sounding cops and find our clients guilty, even if the jurors could not identify who fired at which police officers.

On the Saturday after the trial's second week, Flint, Michael, and I drove the fifty miles to Mount Vernon, Illinois. It was a hot, humid afternoon with only a few clouds to protect us from the sun. We stood in an open area next to a freshly dug grave. It was the final resting place of George Jackson, shot and killed two days earlier on August 21, 1971, by guards at San Quentin State Prison. Jackson had served more than ten years of a one-year-to-life sentence for stealing seventy-one dollars from a gas station. He was the Malcolm X of the prison movement. Like Malcolm, he had educated himself in prison and become a compelling writer and spokesperson for black revolt. He had also been a Panther.

Jackson's book, *Soledad Brother*, gives a gripping account of the racism in the criminal justice and prison systems. Like Malcolm's biography, Jackson's contains vivid descriptions of the development of consciousness of a black revolutionary; his life was a symbol of resistance. Jackson's death resulted in work stoppages, memorial services, and teach-ins at prisons throughout the country. The men inside Attica Correctional Facility in New York declared a day of silence during which no one spoke. They also stepped up their demands for humane treatment and set a timetable for the administration to meet with them.

The San Quentin guards who shot Jackson claimed he'd been trying to escape using a pistol that he had concealed in his Afro, supposedly passed to him in the visiting room. Other reports raised the questions of whether he was trying to escape at all and whether the pistol was planted. Jackson had become a particular target of the guards because they suspected that he and two other prisoners, known collectively as the Soledad Brothers, were involved in the killing of a guard in retaliation for another guard's killing of three prisoners at Soledad Prison. George's brother, Jonathan Jackson, had entered the Marin County courthouse a year earlier demanding freedom for the Soledad Brothers. He was shot and killed leaving the courthouse, as were the judge he'd taken hostage and two other prisoners who had been on trial and left the building with Jonathan.

George Jackson's burial took place in a cemetery in an open field, surrounded in the distance by pine trees. From there FBI agents dressed in suits were peering at us through binoculars. George and Jonathan had grown up in Mount Vernon. George's freshly dug grave sat next to Jonathan's, and their headstones were only a couple feet apart. We were sweating in our suits. Of the fifty people there, Flint, Michael, and I were the only whites. Georgia Jackson, a stately woman, asked the three of us as we stood next to her sons' graves who we were.

"We're Chicago lawyers, defending the Panthers on trial from Carbondale," I answered.

She told us that what we were doing was important. "You would have liked my son. He was so strong. He taught himself to be a writer. He could have been greater," she said. "It was such a waste, him spending all those years in prison for nothing. He wasn't the way they portrayed him. He was smart and read a lot. He was a natural leader and could have helped a lot of people. He had courage. There wasn't anything he wouldn't do, if he thought it was right." She reminded me of Iberia talking about Fred.

Georgia Jackson urged the three of us to continue fighting to keep black people, particularly Panthers, out of jail. I went back to the trial feeling blessed and inspired, and even more keyed up to free the Carbondale Three.

In court the following Monday, I called the neighbor we had met on our first day in Carbondale. He had a practical, down-home air about him that made his testimony about waking, hearing gunshots, and reaching for his gun, that much more credible. On cross-examination Richmond asked him if he would have shot if he knew it was the police. "Yeah, if they were firing at me," he replied. We hoped with similar testimony from other neighbors, we would convince the jury that the Panthers' defending themselves was reasonable and justifiable.

In the closing argument I attempted to go into the history of white violence against black groups, including the December 4 raid by the Chicago police. Richmond objected but I kept talking, finishing my sentence. I tried to put the jurors in the shoes of the neighbors, and by implication, the Panthers. "What would you do if you woke up and heard shots, looked outside, and saw people shooting at you?" I asked. The issue of whether the police announced their office and ordered people to surrender was very much in dispute. I reiterated the defense's position that this had never happened. The jury went out to deliberate early in the afternoon.

Four hours later we received a call from Judge Prosser's clerk. The jury had reached their verdict. We hoped the short deliberation could be taken as a sign that we had won without much dissent. On the other hand, it could mean the jury felt the state's case was clear-cut and that the Panthers were guilty.

I called the defense committee and our friends so that they could come to court for the verdict. Opposite us as we sat down was Dick Richmond, looking weary after the three-week ordeal. The jury came out, not smiling exactly, but not looking at the ground as juries with guilty verdicts frequently do. They looked at the defendants.

The foreman of the jury stood up and announced, "We have reached a verdict."

The clerk took the jury form and went to the witness stand to read it. "As to count one, the charge of attempted murder against Leonard Thomas, we the jury find him not guilty." One down and forty-one to go. The clerk continued reading, describing each count. They were each followed by "not guilty."

When the clerk read the last "not guilty" verdict and started to put the paper down, a spontaneous shout went up from the defendants and spectators. The hugging and crying of relief began. I couldn't hold back my own tears of joy. Hugging my clients, realizing we had kept them out of prison and that they were going home was spectacular. Flint took off his wig and threw it in the air.

I went over to thank the jury and learned they not only were on our side but wanted to come to the victory party we had announced for that night. They told us one of the four hours they spent deliberating was trying to decide whether Flint's red curly hair was a wig. They had guessed right.

Later that night we went down to Little Grassy, a lake just outside Carbondale. We shed our clothes and sang and shouted in the warm water well into the night.

The next day we drove back to Chicago. "Panthers Acquitted in Carbondale" was the banner headline, even in the Chicago newspapers.

22

Prosecuting Hanrahan

"**G**rand Jury Indicts Hanrahan" was the headline that greeted us after we returned to Chicago. The indictment charged Hanrahan, his assistant Jalovec, the fourteen raiders, and the police personnel who conducted the investigation with "knowingly and willfully, fraudulently and deceitfully, conspiring, combining, confederating, and agreeing to obstruct justice," to prevent the criminal prosecution of Daniel Groth and the other raiders as well as to obstruct the criminal defense of the survivors. Police Superintendent James Conlisk was named as a coconspirator but not indicted.

Hanrahan and company would have to face criminal charges, but the obstruction of justice charges hardly matched the seriousness of what they had done.

"I don't understand how the grand jury could believe that Fred's death from the two parallel gunshot wounds to his head at close range could be anything but deliberate murder," I said to fellow PLOers congregated at our office the day after our return.

"Who knows?" Dennis responded. "Maybe Hanrahan or the police had a grand juror or two in their pockets from the start."

"Or maybe they recruited some along the way," I answered.

"Well, I think it's amazing Hanrahan was indicted at all," said Susan Jordan.

When I considered the events of the previous year and how long it took to get Hanrahan charged, I realized she was right. The time frame was in stark contrast to the five minutes of a cop's grand jury testimony that had been sufficient for Hanrahan to indict our clients.

In December 1970, Barnabas Sears convened a special grand jury, and the survivors testified for the first time before a government body. Publicly, Sears kept his distance from us at PLO. He didn't want to be tainted by appearing to be too close to our radicalism or a Panther sympathizer. Privately, we worked with Cedarquist and Reid, his assistants. This cooperation included allowing them to review our files on the raid. We didn't give their access a second thought.

In April 1971, when rumors were circulating that the special grand jury was about to return indictments, Hanrahan and the other targets of the grand jury hired attorneys to represent them: Thomas Sullivan, the former U.S. attorney; George Cotsirilos, one of the best and most polished criminal lawyers in Chicago; and John Coghlan, the infighter from Daley's area of Bridgeport who already was representing Hanrahan in our civil suit. Sullivan had distinguished himself as U.S. attorney, and later as an advocate for civil liberties in representing protesters from the 1968 Democratic Convention. His background as well as his cool, precise courtroom style added prestige and skill to Hanrahan's defense.

In May, at Sullivan's urging, Judge Power ordered the grand jury to stop deliberations and hear Hanrahan and the raiders' side of the story. This was unprecedented. Persons being investigated have no right to present any evidence to the grand jury. When Sears criticized Judge Power for this intervention, he was fined for contempt.

In June, despite Power's efforts to prevent it, the grand jury announced they had returned an indictment. Judge Power immediately ordered the indictments sealed and suppressed, another outrageous and unprecedented act. Not only the liberal Chicago Council of Lawyers but also the more staid Chicago Bar Association condemned Judge Power for his interference and urged Hanrahan to step down as state's attorney until the grand jury was completed.

The position of presiding judge of the Cook County Criminal Courts, the largest criminal court system in the United States, was a political appointment directed from the mayor's office and Judge Power knew who provided his gavel. He was a close friend, neighbor, and former law associate of Mayor Daley. Clearly, Daley and the machine did not want Hanrahan charged, and the usual prohibitions against interference with the grand jury did not apply.

At one point, Power even cut off funding to the special prosecutor, and went so far as to appoint Mitchell Ware, head of the Illinois State Police, to investigate Barnabas Sears. Fortunately, Ware never got started. On August 24 the Illinois Supreme Court overruled Power. Their unanimous opinion, written by Justice Schaefer, the same justice who had granted Fred Hampton an appeal bond, concluded that "the interests of justice would best be served by opening the indictment and proceeding pursuant to the law." The opinion further ordered that Mitchell Ware's appointment be revoked.

Unfortunately, the Supreme Court turned down Sears's request to appoint a trial judge from outside Cook County. Judge Power's last ruling before transferring the case was to appoint Judge Philip Romiti, a friend of Mayor Daley and former dean of DePaul Law School, to be the trial judge.

"What's Judge Romiti like?" I asked, continuing the conversation with Dennis and Susan. "I've never had a case before him."

"He's pretty tough on defendants in a regular criminal case," Dennis said. "But here, with Hanrahan on trial, and Romiti's ties to the Democratic Party, I'll bet the defendants are licking their chops. I'm sure they'll take a bench trial."

I didn't feel optimistic, either. "I think Sears is outgunned, particularly if, as you say, the defense lawyers have Romiti in their pocket."

"Thomas Sullivan is as good as they get," Susan pitched in. "He's cool and calculating and Coghlan will be the hatchet man."

"Romiti will be looking for any excuse to acquit Hanrahan," Flint said.

Sears had an uphill fight. To my knowledge, cops had been charged with bribery, drugs, and burglaries but never for incidents where they wounded or killed civilians while on duty. State's attorneys worked with the police in their criminal prosecutions. Hanrahan, like all the Cook County prosecutors before and after him, granted police officers *de facto* immunity from criminal prosecution, no matter what they did on the streets.

23

Revolt at Attica

On **September 9, 1971, as we** contemplated how we could assist the special prosecutor, twelve hundred prisoners seized control of one quarter of New York's Attica Correctional Facility. The prisoners took thirty-nine guards hostage and demanded to meet with Commissioner Russell Oswald and that Warden Mancusi be fired. For over a year the prisoners had put forth a list of demands for humane treatment including decent food and medical care, educational and occupational programs, and an end to overcrowding and guard brutality. George Jackson's death in San Quentin the month before accelerated their demand to meet with the head of the Department of Corrections. Their pleas had been ignored, but with the takeover of the prison, they were finally being heard.

Observers were called in: *New York Times* reporter Tom Wicker, New York assemblyman Arthur Eve, and New York congressman Herman Badillo. Bill Kunstler came to Attica after the prisoners requested he represent them. I watched the confrontation on television, moved by the bravery of the mostly black and Latino prisoners and by the reasonableness of what they sought. I had visited enough Illinois prisons to know that the conditions they protested were endemic to the entire prison system.

Over the next four days, negotiators and observers were televised entering and leaving the prison gates. For a moment it seemed negotiations might succeed, but they then reached an impasse. While the prison administration said it would comply with some of the demands, they were adamant about no amnesty for the rebellious prisoners. The prisoners who led the takeover would be criminally prosecuted.

A deadlock loomed. Tensions grew. The prisoners asked for Governor Nelson Rockefeller to come to Attica and meet with them. He refused. Instead, he ordered hundreds of state police to surround the prison.

On September 12, Bill Kunstler, the chief lawyer at the Conspiracy Seven trial, who had decried Fred's killing as "murder," came out of Attica begging for more time. "I fear the worst," he said. His passionate plea went unanswered.

The next morning a light rain fell at Attica. I watched on TV as hundreds of state police wearing yellow raincoats and armed with rifles entered the front gate. A few minutes later the television crews picked up muffled sounds of gunfire. Cold-blooded murder, I thought. The prisoners have no way to defend themselves.

A couple of hours later the media reported twenty-nine prisoners shot dead and ten hostages killed; scores of other prisoners were wounded. The prison had been retaken, but it took a massacre to do it.

There was an immediate lockdown. No one was allowed in the prison except employees. A spokesperson for Warden Mancusi reported that the dead hostages' throats had been cut and many had been castrated. It sounded terrible, but then I wondered if their reports were true.

That night, as the National Lawyers Guild in New York was calling for lawyers to go to Attica to interview and assist the prisoners, we held a meeting at Dennis's house. I'd come to the meeting prepared to argue that since Attica was near Buffalo, lawyers from New York should be the ones to go. But Dennis, always the visionary, spoke most eloquently.

"Attica was about rebellion, black rebellion," he argued. "Those men were murdered and somebody has to tell their story. We have to go there. We told the Hampton story and we have to go there to be the witnesses to tell this one."

He was right. I was too cautious. It was a time for action.

Perhaps it was as arbitrary as who had the lighter court schedule the next week, but I was selected to drive to Attica and interview the prisoners along with Mzizi Woodson, an outgoing and enthusiastic twenty-one-year-old African American woman working at PLO as a legal worker. She sported a big Afro and a warm smile. As soon as we decided that PLO would send someone to Attica, she volunteered.

"Let me go," she said. "I can leave tomorrow." I knew seeing Mzizi would be a welcome sight for the men inside. They were calling themselves the Attica Brothers.

Mzizi and I left Chicago on September 15, two days after the assault. We drove all night. The next morning we met Dan Pachoda and Eliot

Wilk, National Lawyers Guild lawyers from New York City, at the entrance gate of the huge concrete-walled prison. The administration had just begun to allow lawyers inside the day before. Pachoda and Wilk had the list of those who led the rebellion. These were the prisoners most in danger of reprisals by the guards. We divided up the list so that between us we could see all the leaders in the next two days. I also copied down the names of the prisoners killed, knowing the people we visited would want to know who died.

"We're here to see Frank Smith," I told the guard at the front desk. His name came from the top of our list. Frank had been in charge of security during the takeover. I was afraid they wouldn't let Mzizi enter, but I explained she was a paralegal and she was admitted.

We were led to the interview room, where a glass barrier two feet high ran across the middle of the table, separating visitors from prisoners. We sat down in the hard plastic chairs on our side and waited. I could hear guards' voices echoing from outside, the clang of gates slamming shut. The room was dingy and smelled of sweat.

An hour later the guards brought in a huge bear of a man. He was just over six feet tall with broad shoulders and a huge chest and belly. His neck was thick like the rest of him, his face round, and his head was shaved. He was wearing only boxer shorts and a T-shirt. As soon as the guards unshackled his hands, he stuck one out in our direction around the glass.

"I'm Big Black," he said, in a deep, rumbling voice, looking us directly in the eye. He was indeed big and very dark skinned. There was something disarming in his straightforwardness.

After the guards left, I explained that we came from a movement law office in Chicago at the urging of the National Lawyers Guild to help the Attica Brothers. He looked at both of us: I had an Afro, the Jewish, curly kind. It was a little shorter than Mzizi's.

"Y'all came all the way from Chicago for us? Ain't that something!" He shook his head in disbelief. He looked at Mzizi. "Are you a lawyer, too?"

"No, but I work with them. We're here to help you if we can." Her simple words seemed to relax him.

Big Black began his story. He sat back and gave us some background. Because of his size and the fact that he got along with everyone, including the Black Muslims, he had been chosen as head of security for the yard. He oversaw the protection of the hostages. "The hostages got the same food and water as everybody else, and we didn't let anyone bother them. No one got near them without my permission. We even shared our blankets with them." He said the guards/hostages wanted the administration to work out the demands "as much as we did."

He went on to describe the siege. When the state troopers appeared above them on the walls with rifles, Frank ordered the hostages be taken to different parts of the yard and the catwalk. He told the men leading them to stand close by. "I figured the police wouldn't fire at the brothers, for fear of hitting the guards. The hostages were blindfolded and clearly identified."

"First came the tear gas," he said. "People looked for something to cover their face. When I first heard shots, I thought they were blanks. Then the people around me in the yard started dropping. I realized they were real bullets, and everyone ducked and ran for cover.

"L. D. Barkley [a main inmates spokesperson who'd declared, 'We are men, not beasts, and we will not be driven and beaten as such'] was one of the first persons I saw go down, like he had been targeted.

"When I looked up on the catwalks," he went on, "I saw the hostages lying on the ground next to the men guarding them. Some weren't moving and I saw blood around them."

I asked Frank, "What about the stories that the hostages had been castrated?"

"That's total bullshit and they know it. The hostages were shot down like dogs, like the rest of us. The troopers had all the guns. It was a slaughter and they didn't care who they hit."

As with Hampton, the official version was a cover-up to hide deliberate killing.

"I'm sorry about the underwear," Frank said to Mzizi. "It's the best I could do."

"Where are your clothes?" she asked.

"The guards stripped us naked after the shooting. Then they made us crawl naked in the mud through a gauntlet where they beat us. They've only given us back underwear and T-shirts."

"It's been three days," I said. "You should have some pants and a shirt by now. Maybe I can do something about this."

"Well, you see what clothes I got," he said. "Some men don't even have T-shirts yet." Leaving them in underwear looked like retaliation by the prison administration.

Frank went on to describe how all the prisoners were made to lie on the ground. Some of them had an *X* drawn on their back and were marched off in a different direction. He wanted to know what had happened to them. I said I didn't know but would try to find out when we interviewed more prisoners.

Frank tried to continue. Then his powerful, booming voice stopped. Tears came. Mzizi's and my eyes met, searching for something to say. Frank's tone turned quieter, almost pleading.

"They took me out of the line. They made me lie on a table naked on my back and put a football under my chin. They put their burning cigarettes out on me. Some dropped them from the catwalk above and were laughing. They told me if I moved and the football hit the ground I was dead. I tried not to move. I was sure they were going to kill me. They knew that I was in charge of security and used me as an example to scare everybody else, because nobody else got this treatment."

Frank raised his shirt and showed us the reddish, blistered burn marks on his stomach, shoulders, and arms. There were a lot of them. He lowered his shirt, his eyes full of tears. I reached around the glass and put my hand on his broad shoulder. Mzizi was also crying. She leaned over and hugged the part of his upper body she could reach.

I felt an immediate bond with Big Black. He reminded me of Walter, with his broad shoulders and warm manner. There was an openness in Frank, a willingness to share his life and his feelings. Later on, I realized what it was. Frank trusted me, trusted us.

Before we left, Frank described what it was like in the yard during the four days when the prisoners were in control. "We set up our own government," he said. "We voted on things: what the demands would be, who would negotiate, and how to divide the food and water we got. Everybody was treated equally and the guards got as much as everyone else, including food, water, and blankets. When the troopers pointed their guns and opened fire, the guards were just as scared and were crying like the rest of us."

Our time was up. We had been allowed nearly two hours with Frank, and wanted to see other prisoners. We stepped to the side of the table. I put my arms around Frank and he hugged me back. I'd never done that with a prisoner. He and Mzizi exchanged a longer hug. "We will tell the story of you and the Attica Brothers," she vowed, as he was shackled and led away.

We came out of the prison late in the afternoon, charged up after seeing more prisoners who gave us similar accounts of what happened in the yard. "We've just got to tell what happened," Mzizi said. "What the state troopers did was nothing but a cold-blooded massacre."

"Rockefeller ordered them to do it," I said. "He should be held responsible."

That night Mzizi and I went to a meeting at the home of Herman Schwartz, an ACLU lawyer and professor at the University of Buffalo Law School. All the lawyers who had been inside that day were there, along with Schwartz and some of his law students. He had a reputation as an expert in prisoner rights and ran a clinic at the law school.

For the meeting, he arranged the chairs in his living room in rows facing a large cushioned chair where he would sit. Before the meeting started we proposed putting the chairs in a circle so that we faced each other. We were used to the more equal arrangement from our collective's meetings. One of the law students, Mara Siegel, agreed with us. Professor Schwartz seemed reluctant but agreed and we rearranged the chairs; the meeting began.

Mzizi and I were adamant about going to the press right away. Schwartz wanted to keep a tight rein over what was said and avoid anything too inflammatory, or too political. "Let's be careful about what we say," he said. "So far, everything's been cleared through me." It reminded me of the lawyer meetings after the Panther raid, when some of the lawyers urged too much caution.

We'd learned from the Hampton case that the battle for the public's mind was critical; most people formed their opinions based on the early reports. Rockefeller's office and the prison administration were trying to justify the orders to fire based on the supposed threats to the hostages, but they had discarded the castration and throat-cutting stories after the coroner reported they all died of gunshot wounds. None of the lawyers who had visited the prisoners after the assault had talked to the press about the gauntlet or prisoners being singled out for more beatings with an X placed on their back or even the lack of proper clothes.

At the meeting we obtained a consensus that the prisoners' stories had to be told, and soon. Schwartz agreed to hold a press conference. One of the New York lawyers who'd been inside and heard accounts similar to ours would tell what happened.

After the meeting Mzizi, Mara Siegel, and I went to the local motel/restaurant for a drink.

"So what do you do in Chicago?" Mara asked. She had huge brown eyes, long, straight, dark hair, and a contagious laugh. She spoke with excitement. The more we told her about the history of the People's Law Office, the more interested she became.

I was explaining how it was that we came to Attica, when I noticed five or six guys crowded around the table next to us. They were noisy, a little drunk, and appeared to be celebrating, with their glasses of beer raised high as if in a salute to something. I leaned over to hear what they were saying.

"It was like shooting fish in a barrel," one of them said.

"Yeah, I know I got a few of them," the guy next to him responded. "You should have seen them running, trying to get away." They all laughed.

It took me a moment to realize what they were talking about. These were the state police, now in civilian clothes. Seventy-two hours earlier they'd come into the prison firing their assault rifles. I listened to see if I could pick up any more of the details of what they were saying.

They saw me looking at them and lowered their voices. When I told Mzizi and Mara what I'd heard they didn't believe it. Then they did. Shocked, we paid our check and got out of there. I'm pretty sure I heard Mara say "killers" under her breath as we walked past them to leave. We should have said it out loud.

Mzizi and I spent two more days interviewing the Attica prisoners, returning once to see Big Black who was still in his underwear. It was like visiting an old friend. We communicated greetings to him from other prisoners and told him what we had learned. He asked us when we were coming back and I said somebody from our office would return soon.

"Don't forget me and what we did," he said.

I never have.

I returned from Attica ready to pass on the powerful but tragic stories told to me by the men inside. I spoke at a rally outside of Cook County Jail from the back of a pick-up truck. My message—in reality their message—was a call to prisoners, and indeed to all of us, to stand up and rebel against brutality and inhumane conditions, and to people on the outside to support prisoner demands for humane treatment.

"Who is Attica?" I asked, after recounting the stories of Big Black and the other Attica Brothers.

"Attica is all of us!" The crowd responded enthusiastically (I've never had a more receptive audience). The conditions at Attica were no worse than the conditions in Illinois prisons or the Cook County Jail, and many in the audience had friends or relatives inside.

Everyone at PLO agreed we should continue representing the Attica Brothers. In the short term this meant working to improve the conditions for the men in the prison, which was on lockdown. On the not-too-distant horizon, it meant criminal defense. It was a certainty that the leaders of the rebellion who had survived would face criminal charges including murder. The administration was blaming the *prisoners* for the guards' deaths, rather than the state troopers who shot them.

For the next five years, we and many other Guild attorneys, including Bill Kunstler, who had been an observer during the takeover, worked for the Attica Brothers defense. Liz Fink and Danny Meyers from New York eventually made representation of the Attica Brothers their full-time work along with Dennis and Michael from PLO.

I returned to Attica several times, but eventually my major responsibility shifted to the Hampton case. I was building a private practice in Chicago to support the office financially, and also became more involved in the local issues of urban renewal, police brutality, and prison conditions in Illinois. And, I confess, Michael and Dennis were more willing to travel than I was. They put the fate of the Attica Brothers ahead of everything else.

There was plenty to do in Chicago. In addition to the Hampton and Clark cases and our regular criminal cases, the People's Law Office represented the antiwar movement, Weatherman fugitives, grand jury resisters, Puerto Rican political prisoners, the Young Lords Organization, and prisoners who challenged the poor conditions in Illinois and federal prisons in court. We could not have taken all this on without being a collective, sharing both a common political commitment as well as work and money. I could pull back on representing the Attica Brothers because Michael and Dennis took over. Dennis could stop working on the Hampton case when he moved to Buffalo because Flint and I made it our priority.

24

Two Bad Decisions

By the fall of 1971, our civil suit against Hanrahan was over a year old but still barely moving along. Hanrahan's lawyers, Coghlan and Volini, had now moved to stay discovery until the completion of Hanrahan's criminal case. Judge Perry's resulting order barred us from both written discovery and taking the oral depositions of the defendants. Judge Perry was angered by our straightforward accusations against Hanrahan and the raiders, labeling our claims that they conspired to murder Fred Hampton "outrageous." He seemed more intent on denouncing our allegations of murder than in determining their truthfulness.

When we filed the civil suit, I didn't understand how important the politics and demeanor of a federal judge could be in determining the outcome. Had we known how much of an adversary Perry would become, we may not have continued in federal court at all. The federal suit could have been voluntarily dismissed and filed in state court but without the constitutional claims. In later years we would sometimes take this route when assigned a judge as hostile to civil rights cases as Perry.

Perry focused on the defendants' lengthy motions to dismiss as well as their accompanying briefs. Fortunately, Bill Bender and Jon Hyman, the head of Northwestern's legal clinic in Chicago, helped us research and draft opposing memos and briefs. PLO had limited time and resources to counter the myriad pretrial motions filed by the well-paid defendants' lawyers, all designed to defeat or slow down the litigation. At that time we also had little knowledge of federal civil rights laws. Coghlan and Volini challenged and moved to strike each paragraph of our complaint, even though civil rights pleadings are supposed to be construed broadly, which means you don't have to describe every factual allegation in detail. Judge Perry took all their motions seriously, no matter how baseless.

The defendants' lawyers also pushed the very substantial legal issue that, as the state's attorney, Hanrahan was immune from prosecution and thus could not be sued. The law was clear that prosecutors had total immunity from civil liability for decisions they made prosecuting criminal cases, even including situations in which they intentionally directed their witnesses to commit perjury. Our response was that Hanrahan was acting *not* as a prosecutor but as a law enforcement official supervising the state's attorney's police. It was his function, not his title, that should determine whether he had immunity. There was no clear legal precedent on the issue.

Coghlan and Volini made huge sums of money billing for hundreds, and ultimately thousands, of hours defending Hanrahan and company. Coghlan took perverse pleasure in filling out his time sheets while sitting in court at the counsel table next to Flint and me. If the judge hadn't arrived in the courtroom, Coghlan would whistle as he completed each form. He knew Flint and I were being paid little. He and Volini made in an hour what we earned in a week.

On February 3, 1972, Judge Perry ruled. He dismissed Hanrahan and Jalovec and the other assistant state's attorneys, saying they were entitled to full immunity. "Obviously he cared more about their title than what they did," Flint said to me at PLO.

I was even more cynical: "I think if Hanrahan ordered Groth to kill Fred and gave him the gun, Perry would find him immune."

Perry also dismissed the defendants from the crime lab and Internal Investigations Division and threw out our entire complaint, saying our allegations were scandalous and our language was improper. "What they did was abhorrent, not our naming it," I continued.

"He did say he might allow a new complaint, if we used the proper wording. How do you say *murder* in a nice way?" Flint asked.

"We'll appeal his ass," Dennis said.

I was outraged by the rulings of this capricious, conniving judge. Our only option was to appeal Judge Perry's dismissals to the Seventh Circuit. This would take six to eighteen months. Bill Bender and Tom Geraghty, head of the Northwestern Legal Clinic, agreed to take the major role in writing the appellate brief. Meanwhile, Hanrahan and the other defendants in our civil suit were set for trial on their criminal charges of obstructing justice.

On July 10, 1972, the long-awaited criminal trial of Hanrahan and company for conspiracy to obstruct justice began before Judge Romiti. Hanrahan's lawyers could have delayed the trial past July, but Hanrahan was running for reelection as Cook County state's attorney in November. He wanted to be acquitted before the election. I was still skeptical that Sears and Cedarquist were a match for Hanrahan's lawyers, nevertheless we supported them and continued to allow them access to our Panther raid files. These were being kept in Tom Geraghty's office in the legal clinic at Northwestern Law School, because Geraghty and his students were working on the civil appeal.

On a warm Saturday afternoon, two weeks after Hanrahan's trial started, Flint called me in Wisconsin, where I had gone for the weekend. "Jeff, listen," he said frantically. "Cedarquist found a signed statement from Louis Truelock in our files. Truelock claimed to have fired two shots at the police from a pump rifle as he ran down the hall to wake up Fred. Cedarquist wants permission to copy it. He's threatening to get an order requiring us to produce it. What do we do?"

I vaguely remembered there were survivors' statements taken, but I never saw them or knew their contents and had forgotten they existed until Flint's call. Truelock's statement was totally different from what he'd told me four hours after the raid. If Truelock had fired a rifle anywhere on his path from the living room to the back bedroom, there would have been shell casings, bullet fragments, and resulting bullet holes at the rear of the apartment or in the hallway. None of these were ever found, nor was a pump rifle found.

"Truelock must have lied in the statement because he wanted to take suspicion off himself. Everyone was calling him an informant then," I said to Flint. Regardless of discrediting the accuracy of the statement, I knew its discovery was huge. Cedarquist was acting as the prosecutor, and the criminal rules required it be turned over to Hanrahan.

"We don't want to be the ones hiding evidence," I finally responded. "But I think Skip took the statement and knows more about it. You should call him."

"Will do," he said. Flint hung up.

Skip had been gone from PLO for over a year. He didn't want to be accused of withholding evidence. Without consulting Truelock or the other survivors, he agreed to allow Cedarquist to copy the survivors' statements in our files and turn them over to the defense.

We should have asked Truelock, not Skip. We lost sight of the simple legal principle that the attorney-client privilege belongs to the client, not the lawyer. Even if we had inadvertently disclosed the statement to Cedarquist, it was for Truelock to decide whether the statement should be released beyond that. Instead of upholding our client's privilege and refusing Cedarquist's request, Flint and I hesitated and let Skip decide. It was a big mistake. When Jim Montgomery, who had been representing Deborah Johnson, refused to turn over her statement, Judge Romiti upheld his position.

Hanrahan's lawyers were given Truelock's statement and it was big news. The criminal trial was suspended; suddenly we were the ones who had to answer questions. Skip and Donald Stang, who had witnessed Truelock's statement, and Flint were subpoenaed to a hearing on how, why, and where the statement was taken and whether Truelock had, in fact, said what was contained in it. Skip could only say he presumed Truelock did make the statement because it was written down and signed on every page by Truelock. He couldn't remember Truelock's words and of course he couldn't say whether Truelock was telling the truth. Flint testified that he did not know the contents of the statement, which was true, and that he was as surprised as I was about Truelock's claims. Don Stang refused to testify.

The defense knew that Truelock could explain away the statement's contents as boasting to make himself look less culpable for Fred's death and to take suspicion off himself as a possible informant. So they focused on the "hiding" of the statement by Skip and Sears, rather than relying on its contents, which were in conflict with the physical evidence.

When the trial resumed, Hanrahan's lawyers had everyone's statement except Deborah Johnson's. Sullivan and Coghlan accused Sears of the "deliberate and dishonest cover-up" of the statements, although only Truelock's asserted that its author ever fired.

The overall defense strategy was to downplay evidence of what actually happened. Instead, they contrasted the Panthers, whom they portrayed as dangerous, malevolent black revolutionaries, with their clients, whom they characterized as the zealous, brave, unheralded protectors of our safety. It was a strategy likely to succeed because Sears, their opponent, never challenged and probably believed it.

I was excluded from the trial because, like other PLO lawyers, I was a potential witness. Unfortunately, the accounts we read in the newspapers and from those who attended the trial made it painfully clear that Sears was losing.

Michael Arlen, a well-known essayist and journalist, came to Chicago to observe and record Hanrahan's trial. The next year he published *An American Verdict*, an impressionist view of what he saw in court, a montage set against Chicago's political landscape.

Arlen wrote about how Harahan's attorneys portrayed the two sides: "One [myth] was the racist objectification of the Panthers as threats to everything civil, and the other was the bravery of the police when forced to carry out their ultra-dangerous duties."

In contrast, Arlen wrote: "The prosecutors only had the physical evidence drily presented and no sustaining myth." Sears had the facts but no clear theory of why it happened, and Arlen points out that the white, aged, formal Chief Special Prosecutor Sears was not about to embrace the Panthers.

Every trial lawyer learns that a case is a combination of the evidence and the theory that ties it together. Without a myth or theory, Sears's presentation carried no punch.

During the last week of October 1972, the prosecution rested its case. There would be no time for a defense if the trial were to end before the elections. The defendants filed motions for acquittal, arguing the state had failed to prove them guilty. Judge Romiti scheduled the oral arguments on the motions to begin on October 26.

Arlen gave detailed accounts of the lawyers' closing arguments:

The defense argument begins with Thomas Sullivan, dressed in a serious suit, who . . . proceeds to bring up once more the Panthers' predilection for violence, their antisocial habits, and their dishonesty as indicated by the changed testimony—a revelation, as he now construes it, that had been extracted from an unwilling and probably dishonest prosecution by the aggressive, truth-seeking tactics of the defense.

But it was likely Coghlan who stole the show in that courtroom packed with prosecutors, police, and Democratic Party loyalists. From court transcripts, Coghlan's closing words:

> You know, we all understand—as men and policemen—that it's open season these days on policemen, and they know it from the day they put on the star. . . . There's only one way that I know of for a copper to prove that he's on the square and that is to die. . . .
>
> There's a funny thing about being a policeman. A policeman has the same fears for his life that any of the rest of us have. But he has one more thing that only a policeman understands, and that is: if he goes yellow on his partners, he is through on the job. He never gets another partner. . . . I'll tell you right now we wouldn't be here today if Officer Davis had taken a shotgun deer slug through the belly as he went through that door. . . . When Joe Gorman followed him with his machine gun, he didn't know what he was going to find in there. There was action, there was shooting, there was darkness. But Joe Gorman knows that if he doesn't go through that door, he is through as a policeman. He'll never be able to hold up his head again. And he'd sooner die. If Duke Davis hadn't been bent over with that alley-wise cunning that comes from twenty years on the force, part of him would have been up there on the stairway. He'd have proved then he was an honorable man. In this town, about the only way a copper can prove he's an honorable man is by dying.

A masterful argument from the cop's perspective. Of course it had nothing to do with the facts.

Hanrahan spoke for himself, something not normally allowed a defendant with three attorneys. Hanrahan spoke, not only to the judge but to the electorate:

> We have listened to the philosophy of the Black Panther Party describing the mandate that every member of the organization have a gun, be able to use it, and know how to defend his pad. We listened this morning to Mr. Sullivan recall the testimony of Deborah Johnson when she related the poem by Fred Hampton—that revolting poem—expressing satisfaction from killing a police officer. And when I listened to that evidence, and I think about Duke Davis and these other officers—well, I believe that the

people of Cook County owe a medal to every one of these officers who had the integrity to go into that apartment under fire to seize those weapons, which, if the Black Panther philosophy had been allowed to continue in force, would have undoubtedly been used to kill other people.

In fact this is an outlandish case—and how easy it is to make these false allegations, and how difficult to disprove the falsity—that is so easily leveled at men who have no defense except that they come here to trial, or else die.

Thank God Duke Davis did use his twenty-four years of police know-how to come in low. Thank God Joe Gorman did have the guts to follow him. And thank God for men like Ed Carmody.

Hanrahan went on to equate criticisms of the raiders' actions with a criticism of law enforcement in general, referring to the accusations of misconduct in the press as, "These irresponsible statements that undermined public confidence in law enforcement."

Unrepentant to the end, in fact congratulatory of the raiders' actions, Hanrahan remained indignant that anyone had the temerity to accuse him of wrongdoing.

Arlen writes:

Sears rose to answer. "Your Honor, I suppose the next thing I will hear from the defense is that I have some communion with the Panthers." This communion or connection was the last thing Sears wanted to be tainted with, so he went on to establish his credentials: born and bred in North Dakota. Sears was anxious to show he was from the same white, male, professional, law-abiding world as were the defendants and their lawyers and the Judge.

On the morning of Wednesday, November 1, as Romiti was scheduled to announce his verdict, Donald Stang and I were about to start a murder trial one floor below Romiti's courtroom. I had seen the camera crew poised in the lobby when I arrived. By eleven o'clock, reporters, cops, and state's attorneys were heading for Romiti's courtroom to hear the ruling.

I was still sitting on the wooden bench in the front row waiting for my trial to begin when I heard a commotion in the hallway outside. I walked to the rear of the courtroom, opened one of the large paneled doors, and looked out. The stairways in the middle of the floor were filled with people heading down toward the lobby.

"What happened?" I asked.

"Not guilty! Everybody!" someone descending the stairs yelled. I ducked back into my courtroom. I didn't want to see the smiling faces of Hanrahan, the raiders, or their supporters.

Was this it? I wondered. Three years after the raid, no federal prosecution, not guilty on the state prosecution, and our civil case dismissed. Would Hanrahan ever have to pay?

I walked over and told Don what I just learned.

"They got away with it," he said.

The newspapers later reported that Romiti said he had to vote his conscience and not respond to pressure, comments that must have momentarily given Sears and his team some hope. But Romiti had quickly followed with, "This court can only conclude and does conclude that evidence is not sufficient to establish or prove any conspiracy against any defendant. A judgment of acquittal is entered as to each defendant and each defendant is discharged."

Six days later blacks in Chicago delivered their verdict. They voted for Democrat George McGovern for president, Democrat Daniel Walker for governor, and regular machine candidates for judge and lower county offices. But they didn't vote for Hanrahan: Bernard Carey became the first Republican state's attorney in Cook County in recent history.

Part III

The FBI's Clandestine Operation

The Snitch

On a cold **Saturday morning** in February 1973, I was drinking my coffee while sitting on the bench Dennis had built in the alcove in the kitchen. I picked up the paper. The *Chicago Tribune* headline read, "Informer Aids FBI in Quiz." The article stated that a Chicago police sergeant was a suspect in the kidnapping and murder of two drug dealers on Chicago's South Side. The person named as the witness against the sergeant was William O'Neal.

The article indicated O'Neal had been an FBI informant since 1968. I looked to see if it was the same O'Neal I knew, the former Panther chief of security. A picture on the second page of the article confirmed it. *That motherfucker*, I thought. I pictured O'Neal, smiling, joking, cynical—always seeking the upper hand, constantly claiming he knew how to get over on the man. The article continued. O'Neal and a former Chicago vice detective, Stanley Robinson, had been detained in the kidnapping of several drug dealers, some of whom had been murdered and dumped in the Chicago River. A confidential FBI report quoted in the article said Robinson had executed Jeff Beard while O'Neal "drove the death car and witnessed the murder."

Could the guy I knew with the disarming smile and casual attitude be involved in murder for hire? More important, did he drop the dime on Fred? O'Neal's self-satisfied grin stuck in my mind. His swagger. His flashy clothes and big ride. Did the FBI pay for those? Robinson told the *Tribune* reporter that he had infiltrated O'Neal's criminal enterprise and was about to arrest him when he was apprehended. O'Neal countered that he had infiltrated Robinson's extortion ring, which was involved in shaking down and killing drug dealers. The *Tribune* reporter was uncertain whether Robinson or O'Neal would be charged.

"I got the techniques down," O'Neal used to say, bragging about how he got away with burglaries and stickups. His fascination with criminal activity seemed inconsistent with him being an informant. Then I realized maybe not; it made his cover that much better.

Deborah told me O'Neal had driven her to Fred's apartment the night of the raid, but O'Neal left before they went to sleep. Did he know what was coming? Would the FBI risk disclosing the raid plan to an informant? Would it risk its informant getting shot and possibly turning on it if he was inside and survived? Had he drugged Fred with the barbiturate found in Fred's blood?

O'Neal didn't talk politics. He proposed actions, frequently armed ones. This conflicted with my image of an informant as the silent, observant type, following orders from his control to remain inconspicuous. Looking back, he was clearly a provocateur, but I hadn't realized then that this could be a good cover for an informant.

Like a lover who discovers betrayal, I reconsidered O'Neal's behavior in light of the new disclosure. It fit uncomfortably well. He always had money; he was constantly offering to chauffeur Fred and Rush and later Deborah in his big car; he never attended political education classes and pushed actions over thought and politics; he advocated the most militaristic line; he often carried a gun; he was constantly suggesting other Panthers engage in criminal activities; he was at Fred's apartment the night before the raid when everyone ate dinner. Then he left.

The *Tribune* article reported the FBI had first contacted O'Neal because he had flashed phony FBI identification at a Chicago cop arresting him for driving a stolen car. The Chicago police had turned the matter over to the FBI because impersonating an FBI agent is a federal crime. No one heard anymore about the case. Somebody in the FBI must have recognized his knack for deceit and recruited him.

Dennis was finally getting up. As he came into the kitchen in his bathrobe, I held up the newspaper.

"Check this out," I said. "O'Neal was working for the FBI."

Dennis winced. The news hit him like a slap in the face. He took off his glasses and wiped them with his T-shirt as though he needed a clean lens to comprehend what I had said. Even more than me, Dennis had befriended O'Neal, invited him to his house, hung out with him, and trusted him. Dennis reached for the newspaper and read the article. He didn't say anything for a while, but his brow remained creased. For once he had a puzzled look unlike the usual calm and gleam in his eye that came from having anticipated the situation. This time he clearly had not. He'd been deceived like the rest of us.

After a long pause Dennis said, "I've gotta say he was good at his game. He took me in. There was enough there to be suspicious, but I have to admit I wasn't."

"Me either," I admitted. We all had heard, even repeated, the common refrain that the party was infiltrated, but I was still alarmed to discover it was someone we knew. It made me feel more vulnerable.

I also felt critical of myself, not because I had ever confided anything so damaging to O'Neal but because I had congratulated myself on being able to maintain a friendship with a black person with street savvy.

That day I realized Dennis was not invincible. I had seldom challenged his perceptions or even his prophesies. He had been the first to recognize the need for an independent law office to represent the Panthers, and the first to conceptualize and implement it. He had proposed People's Law Office as the name we carry to this day. Dennis had advocated going on the offense with our evidence and accusations after Fred's death, which had caused Hanrahan to respond and lose his credibility, and Dennis immediately saw the need for our office to get involved in Attica following the assault and killings by the New York State Police. But on this day, I realized that Dennis, like me, was capable of being deceived. I can't attribute all of our being taken in to our pride. O'Neal had fooled the Panthers themselves and was good, very good, at his game.

Later that morning Dennis and I got over venting our anger and frustration at being so effectively hoodwinked and tried to figure out how O'Neal really worked.

"He used his car, his supposed street smarts, and his mechanical skills to get near the leadership," Dennis commented. "None of these required any political understanding."

"And because he was always the first one to build some military device or advocate some military action, people didn't suspect him. We should know better," I said. "And frankly, I thought it was cool to hear this streetwise guy supposedly telling it like it is."

"Do you think he provided the information for the raid?" I continued, thinking out loud.

It had come out at the federal grand jury that Jalovec's tip came from the FBI, but Sergeant Groth swore he had his own source. A valid search warrant had to be based on information that the informant had personally provided the officer who was signing the affidavit. If Groth didn't have an informant, then the warrant would be invalid and the search and raid illegal.

"I think O'Neal told them there were guns in Fred's apartment." Dennis said. "And if he was working for the FBI, I doubt he would be working for Groth as well." If we could prove Groth had no informant, the raid per se would be unconstitutional; that is, without probable cause. We could win the civil case on legal grounds and at least get sanctions against Groth. The jury would only have to decide the amount of damages. However, proving Groth's informant did not exist would be difficult. Thus far neither the federal grand jury nor Judge Perry had demanded Groth name his informant or offer proof that he even existed.

"Kind of interesting, in six months of investigation, that the grand jury overlooked O'Neal," I said, "and never interviewed his FBI control agent."

All of us had been suspicious that the federal grand jury was mostly about blunting public outrage, giving the appearance of a fair investigation without doing anything. I now began to see its function as hiding the FBI role.

"The FBI might be behind this whole thing. It's outrageous, they pretend to be the impartial fact-finders for the raid, and really they're covering their own ass. I think we should take O'Neal's deposition," Dennis said, once again thinking ahead.

"At the moment we don't have a lawsuit in which to depose anyone," I reminded him. "Unless the court of appeals reverses Perry, we may never learn what the FBI did."

When the article exposed O'Neal, documents had already surfaced that demonstrated Hoover and the FBI had targeted the entire black movement, from Dr. King and the Southern Christian Leadership Conference to the Muslims. The FBI had blackmailed Dr. King by threatening to release tapes showing his infidelity if he didn't kill himself. "There is only one thing left for you to do. You know what it is," the cryptic FBI note attached to the tapes read.

Although Hoover consistently sought to defame and discredit Dr. King and other black leaders and organizations, it was the Panthers whom Hoover labeled "the biggest threat to the security of the United

States." We had copies of the FBI memos in which Hoover ordered FBI agents to attack the Panthers with "hard-hitting programs to destroy, disrupt, and neutralize" them. These directives, including using local police to achieve their aims, were contained in the FBI documents released by the antiwar protesters who carried out the burglary of the FBI's office in Media, Pennsylvania. In 1971, when they were first circulated, we didn't know how to connect them to our case. O'Neal might well be the link.

We understood that Fred, with his charismatic appeal, bringing hundreds of young blacks into the movement, was a threat. Why wouldn't Hoover perceive that as well? Of course he did. The question was what did he do to "neutralize" Fred?

By the middle of 1973, the Watergate scandal was exploding, and it became clearer that the break-in was connected directly to the White House. Public interest in uncovering government wrongdoing increased dramatically. Disclosure was at the top of the national agenda as well as our own. We already knew the outlines of the FBI's Counterintelligence Program. We wanted to find out what steps were taken by the local FBI office in Chicago to implement the program, and ultimately to learn if the December 4 raid was a COINTELPRO operation.

Subsequently, we began to receive FBI COINTELPRO documents released by the Senate Select Committee on Intelligence, known as the Church Committee. It was holding open hearings investigating the break-ins at the Democratic headquarters at Watergate and at Daniel Ellsberg's psychiatrist's office. After Ellsberg had released the secret documents nicknamed the Pentagon Papers to the *New York Times* and the *Washington Post*, the White House was so infuriated that not only did they order Ellsberg be prosecuted for espionage, but Nixon's top advisor, H. R. Haldeman, ordered a break-in to Ellsberg's psychiatrist's office to try to find data they could use against him at his criminal trial.

The Church Committee's mandate went beyond investigating Nixon's "Plumbers" and included uncovering all illegal government spying and dirty tricks. They began asking questions and started the subpoena process for obtaining documents on the FBI's formerly secret Counterintelligence Program.

Interest in government malfeasance is cyclical. Gaining the momentum to get to the bottom—or actually the people at the top—of the illegalities depends upon many factors. Watergate was now two years old, but only after the disclosure of the Plumbers breaking into Ellsberg's office did it gain momentum. Years later, in the 1980s, our office exposed that Chicago police commander Jon Burge had tortured black suspects to get confessions from them, but it took over fifteen years before Mayor Richard M. Daley, who at the time was the prosecutor who used the tainted confessions to get convictions, was confronted. In 1973 we were finally getting a real national investigation of COINTELPRO, after many of its victims were dead or in prison and its existence had been public knowledge for two years.

Soon after O'Neal's exposure, Flint pointed out to me that the Church Committee had uncovered that Jerris Leonard—the head of Nixon's Civil Rights Division of the Justice Department and coincidentally the person who led the federal grand jury investigation of the December 4 raid—also headed a secret intelligence unit charged with gathering information on black militants and passing it on to law enforcement. He was supposed to be looking into civil rights violations against the Panthers, yet he had the responsibility to help the FBI and other law enforcement agencies monitor and destroy them. "Talk about the fox watching the chickens," Flint said. "Jerris Leonard had no intention in 1970 of exposing the then secret COINTELPRO, no matter how large a role it had in the raid."

The pieces were beginning to fit. "Now we know why the federal grand jury he led never uncovered O'Neal, and never examined the details of Fred's death to see if it was murder. Probably because they were behind it," I said, getting hotter as I realized they had successfully kept the FBI role in the raid hidden for four years.

"And worst of all, that sanctimonious bastard Leonard blamed the Panthers for both causing the raid and preventing the grand jury from learning the truth. I gotta admit he was clever," Flint responded.

Things changed as the public and media came to understand the danger represented by clandestine government spying and dirty tricks. We benefited from that national momentum. We needed the help. We were working to uncover an outrage even bigger than the Plumbers;

a deliberate political killing, set in motion from FBI headquarters in Washington.

In May, three months after we learned about O'Neal, the NAACP Commission of Inquiry released their book-length report on the December 4 raid. It was aptly titled *Search and Destroy*, the name given to military missions in Vietnam to ferret out and kill Vietcong. The commission was cochaired by former attorney general Ramsey Clark and NAACP chairman Roy Wilkins. Law professor Herb Reid from Howard University wrote the report. The commission examined every bit of physical evidence and scrutinized all the prior testimony as well as the existing expert opinions. Where the facts were in dispute (for example, who fired the first shot, how Fred was killed, and whether or not he was drugged), they not only analyzed the existing expert opinions, but when they felt those were deficient, they retained experts of their own.

The commission ridiculed the federal grand jury report because it had been more critical of the Panthers for their violent rhetoric and for their refusal to trust the federal prosecutors leading the grand jury than it was of the police actions.

The commission understood the police were viewed skeptically in the black community and the issue of police abuse of citizens was much more important to blacks than to whites. They documented the reasons for, rather than criticized, the Panthers' lack of trust of law enforcement. As a result, they gained the cooperation of the Panthers, and the survivors willingly testified before the commission. However, as the NAACP report explained, if federal prosecutors had really been interested in determining if criminal conduct, including murder, took place, they could have relied on the transcripts of the survivors' testimony at the people's inquest.

Search and Destroy noted, "The federal grand jury's *Report* scarcely deals with the precise manner of Hampton's death except to assume that Fred was killed by one of the bullets coming through the wall." To the befuddlement of the NAACP commission, the feds were inexplicably not interested in learning how Fred died or who killed him.

In contrast, *Search and Destroy* began, "Those of us who want to love our country are not anxious to ask whether our police are capable of murder. So we do not ask. We do not dare concede the possibility."

Unlike the federal grand jury, the NAACP report delves directly into how Fred was killed.

Search and Destroy reached four conclusions about the raid. The first one was that the police fired all but one shot. This was largely conceded by the federal grand jury and supported by the findings of Robert Zimmers, the FBI's firearms identification expert.

The second conclusion was that Officer Jones most likely fired the first shot in the hallway next to the front door. This was based on the shotgun impact hole and shotgun wads found outside and to the left of the living room door, which matched Jones's shotgun and was where the raiders forced their way in. The commission concluded that Jones's shot led to a second shot, by Sergeant Groth, through the front door and a third shot from Mark Clark, quite possibly after he had been mortally wounded. This sequence, they found, best fit the angles of Groth's and Clark's shots through the front door, because Groth's shot was fired as the door was opening and Clark's after it was opened further.

The commission's third and most dramatic conclusion was:

> The shots in Hampton's head, their closeness to each other, and their proximity to the shoulder wound indicate they were fired by persons who could see their target. If Hampton could be seen and was then shot it was likely that Johnson and Truelock, if on the same bed, could also be seen and shot. It is therefore probable either that Fred Hampton was shot after the occupants were removed from the room by an officer or officers who could see his prostrate body on the bed, or that Hampton was deliberately selected as the sole target. . . . The death of Fred Hampton appears to the Commission to have been isolated from the killing of Mark Clark and the wounding of Brenda Harris on the one hand, and from the wounding of Ronald Satchel, Verlina Brewer, and Blair Anderson on the other. The Commission has concluded that there is probable cause to believe that Fred Hampton was murdered—that he was shot by an officer or officers who could see his prostrate body lying on the bed.

The fourth finding was, "The Commission has been unable to determine whether Hampton was drugged at the time of his murder, but considers it more probable than not that he was." After an exhaustive analysis of all the pathologists' reports and testimony, the commission found the most reliable report was done by Eleanor Berman, the former Cook County Deputy Coroner retained by PLO. They also acknowledged that discrepancies in the handling of the blood and the first autopsy made it more difficult to reach a definitive conclusion.

Search and Destroy concludes, "Summary execution is not acceptable and summary punishment cannot be condoned."

Finally, they named it. Not murder or assassination (killing for a political purpose) but summary execution, an alternative but accurate description of what happened. "They laid it out," I said to Flint after I finished the report. "It took them more than two years, but they got it."

"I'd like to wave this in Perry's face," Flint answered. "He won't even let us suggest Fred's death was deliberate. I hope the Seventh Circuit reads this before it decides our appeal. Better yet, I'd like to get the report into evidence after they've ordered Perry off our case."

Search and Destroy was widely quoted in the Chicago papers. Its condemnation of Hanrahan and the raid, as well as its finding of summary execution reignited the public's, and in particular the black community's, skepticism about the police version. Roy Wilkins, Ramsey Clark, and Jesse Jackson, as well as some white leaders, called for reopening a federal criminal investigation.

Back in Court

It was August 4, 1973, already a warm morning and the office air conditioner was barely holding its own against the muggy heat. I was in my cubicle when I heard Flint yell from the front of the office, "We won!" I ran out to find him talking on the phone by the front desk. He put the receiver down to his waist. "It's the *Tribune*. The Seventh Circuit just handed down their decision. They reversed Perry. We're back in court."

He picked up the phone. "As soon as we get the opinion, we'll make a comment." By this time a crowd had formed.

"Take that, Judge Perry," I said. "You can't get rid of us that easy."

Forty-five minutes later we assembled again. "Here it is," Flint said, reading from the unanimous opinion. "The state's attorney's alleged participation in the planning and execution of a raid of this character has no greater claim to complete immunity than activities of police officers allegedly acting under his direction."

The Seventh Circuit reinstated our case against all the cover-up people too. They found that as long as we alleged the conspiracy to hide the facts prolonged the prosecution, they are legitimate defendants. The decision gave us new life. We could confront the defendants in depositions and at trial and probe O'Neal about his and the FBI's role. One problem remained. The court refused to get rid of Perry. We would be back before the cantankerous old man with the spotted hands.

"At least they are ordering Perry to let our case go to the jury, not dismiss it," Flint said. "I hope he listens to them, 'cause he sure don't listen to us."

"I hope this ain't a Pyrrhic victory," someone said. "Perry may be down, but he's not out."

We decided to go after O'Neal first. We knew what the raiders were going to say, but we didn't know what his story would be. We needed to learn how deeply the FBI was involved. And so we began the torturous process called discovery to find out the FBI's role in the raid.

Discovery in federal civil cases is different from criminal cases, where neither side has the opportunity to depose the other side's witnesses. In a civil case every witness is deposed (questioned under oath in front of a court reporter), and there are not supposed to be any surprises at trial. At a deposition you are allowed to ask a witness anything that might lead to evidence, even if the answer itself would be irrelevant or inadmissible at trial. Thus, the scope of questioning is quite broad.

The thoroughness allowed in a deposition permits you to explore all the information and opinions the witness has. If it is done carefully and you have anticipated every way the witness might try to hurt you, then you should not be surprised by their answers at trial. You can also avoid asking the questions that lead to answers you don't want the jury to hear. The courts are supposed to assure full disclosure. The premium is on preparation. Before trial both sides are supposed to know all the evidence the other side has.

Our plan was simple. We would subpoena the FBI for all the documents that showed the FBI's involvement in the raid. The first and most obvious connection to the FBI was O'Neal. In October, two months after our case was reinstated, we subpoenaed him to a deposition and subpoenaed the FBI record keeper in Chicago for documents concerning the raid.

The response was a motion to quash the document subpoena. Sheldon Waxman, the U.S. attorney representing the FBI, also resisted complying with our subpoena, claiming O'Neal was no longer in government custody and his identity might be jeopardized if he appeared, even though we had agreed not to ask him his current name and address.

Perry ordered Waxman to produce O'Neal but then reversed himself when Waxman refused to comply. We reissued the subpoena several times, but Perry refused to enforce it, although it was very likely O'Neal had information relevant to the planning and perhaps the execution of the raid. Perry had no real legal basis for denying us access to O'Neal, but protecting the FBI was an instinct that ran deep for Perry. Flint, who prepared the motions to compel after the government refused to produce either documents or O'Neal, would return to the office frustrated and angry but always with the will to continue. A few days after being turned down, a new, sharply worded motion to enforce the subpoenas would appear bearing his signature.

Perry seemed as resolute as Flint, but public pressure was building to interrogate O'Neal. The press was hungry for information on the informant who had sent Stanley Robinson to prison for life and who had infiltrated the Black Panthers. Perry didn't like to buck the press. The NAACP report suggesting Fred was probably drugged added to the public sentiment to uncover O'Neal and the FBI's role in the raid. Locally, Jesse Jackson focused on the FBI and the drugging in demanding another investigation, while Roy Wilkins and Ramsey Clark echoed his demands nationally.

At every court date, we characterized the government's refusal to produce O'Neal as a "cover-up," which it was. The press picked up on our characterization, and newspaper editorials echoed our demand to expose the FBI role.

In January 1974, after six months of wrangling, U.S. Attorney Waxman summoned us to Perry's courtroom for an unscheduled court date. When the case was called, Waxman stepped up to the bench. "We've agreed to produce O'Neal for a deposition," he announced. No reason was given. Perry frowned and shook his head. He'd gone out on a limb to protect the FBI and now it was yielding to public pressure. "The government will inform counsel of the date and location of the deposition shortly," Waxman continued. "We want this information kept under protective order for O'Neal's safety."

"We'll agree," I blurted. I looked over and Waxman gave me a nod. I wasn't completely surprised. Waxman was the garrulous type and had given me the impression he did not like his job, which mostly involved fighting off our requests for evidence connecting the FBI to the raid. Still, the decision to produce O'Neal was probably made at a higher level.

Meanwhile, Waxman claimed the FBI's record keeper could not locate any FBI files about O'Neal or the raid. We wanted to question O'Neal after we had the documents, but we didn't want to miss the opportunity to depose him. We reluctantly agreed to take O'Neal's deposition without the FBI reports. Shortly thereafter we got a call from Waxman directing us to be at the U.S. Attorney's Office at the Federal Building in Detroit on January 12.

We all wanted a piece of O'Neal but we decided that Bill Bender would lead off questioning, and Dennis and I would follow. Flint, just recently admitted to the bar, would help on preparation and slip us questions if we missed something.

"It's going to be strange seeing him now, knowing he was an informant," I said, as we rode the elevator to the U.S. Attorney's Office in Detroit's Federal Building. "We knew him, or thought we knew him, pretty well."

Bender had a full goatee, dressed in suit and tie, and showed the confidence in court of the legal expert he was. Bill was only a little older than me but seemed much more adult and experienced. Bill had briefed and argued many civil rights cases. He was married to Rita Schwerner, widow of slain civil rights worker Michael Schwerner.

"I know you guys feel he chumped you," Bender said. "But he'll be more forthcoming if we're not too hostile."

"We won't attack him, at least not physically," Dennis said. "I just want to see what makes him tick."

"Bill, I don't think I can shake his hand," I said. "Is that all right? Strangely enough I still believe O'Neal admired Fred. He told me in almost every conversation I had with him after Fred's death how much he respected Fred and how the Panthers went downhill after he was killed. I don't think he was just making it up."

"We don't know what he made up," Dennis reminded me. "How 'bout those tears after Fred was killed. O'Neal was inconsolable."

"Maybe we'll see the real O'Neal, today," I said, "if there is one."

We checked in at the U.S. Attorney's Office and were led to a small windowless room, somewhere in the bowels of Detroit's Federal Courthouse. When we entered, O'Neal was sitting at a table with Waxman, Volini, and Joe Witkowski, Coghlan's young associate. A court reporter had set up his stenographic machine at the end.

Dressed in a tweed sport coat and tie, O'Neal turned toward us but did not stand up. His expression was amazingly relaxed. "Hello, Dennis, Jeff, Flint. How are you guys doing?" he asked, as if nothing had changed. To my relief he did not offer his hand.

"Hello, Bill," Dennis nodded his head.

"Long time," I said, as neutral as possible. "This is Bill Bender. He'll begin the questioning.

Bill Bender nodded also but didn't offer his hand. "Let's begin," he said.

O'Neal testified that he joined the Panthers in 1968 at the request of FBI Agent Roy Mitchell. Mitchell paid him one hundred dollars per week at the outset. He became Fred and Rush's bodyguard and ultimately chief of security. His job was "ferreting out" informers and making sure the Panthers had their weapons in working order. "From March 1969 on," he said, "guns weren't too much of an issue because he [Mitchell] knew they had a lot of guns. It wasn't that important unless a trainload of guns or something came in, and that never happened." O'Neal's testimony conflicted sharply with Jalovec and Groth, who claimed it was the sudden appearance of guns at 2337 that led to the raid.

O'Neal testified that Mitchell had been interested in Fred's apartment as soon as Fred moved in and O'Neal told him who lived there. His tone was nonchalant, even when he described being in Fred's apartment the night of the raid. He calmly denied drugging Fred but admitted Fred never took drugs on his own. Finally, Bender asked him how he felt after he learned Fred was killed.

O'Neal shrugged his shoulders and responded coolly: "I knew another agency had made the raid, so I wasn't concerned with it." His answer was a little too glib to believe. O'Neal said he was "surprised" when the raid happened, but when Mitchell assured him he had not passed O'Neal's information on to the police, he was satisfied. O'Neal was no dummy, and I doubted that Mitchell could have so easily convinced him that his information was not used.

O'Neal displayed no sense of guilt or responsibility or even satisfaction. When we asked him what he thought of Fred and the Panthers, he answered, "I respected them, I respected what they were doing. I respected them, period." I had expected O'Neal to denounce Fred at the deposition to justify his informing on him. But his endorsement was worse, more outrageous. I wondered who this moral eunuch was who could betray Fred for money and then praise him.

Without FBI reports documenting his activities as an informant, it was difficult for any of us to challenge O'Neal's general assertions and often vague memory. I left the deposition frustrated. We had not obtained a clear picture of how O'Neal and his informing fit into the raid or COINTELPRO. He did not come across as either the boasting beast or the remorseful penitent. He had successfully walked the line.

After the deposition Flint wrote an article for our local National Lawyers Guild paper irreverently titled "Up Against the Bench," which ended, "There are too many unanswered questions about the government's actions against the Black Panthers, specifically their involvement in the December 4 raid. . . . For in an event such as the murder of Fred Hampton lies the true meaning of Watergate."

27

Floor Plan for Murder

Following O'Neal's deposition, we were even more determined to overcome the FBI's stonewalling of our document requests. Flint put together an amended subpoena *duces tecum* for Mitchell's deposition, which we served on the FBI in March. *Duces tecum* means that, in addition to appearing to answer questions, the person must bring along documents designated in the subpoena. Flint characterized the documents we were seeking broadly as "all FBI documents concerning O'Neal, the Black Panther Party, and the raid." He described the documents and the files in every way imaginable so that the lawyer or FBI agent responding could not credibly avoid locating what we were seeking. Flint attached a twenty-six page legal memo in support of enforcing the subpoena. The law was clearly on our side, even if Judge Perry wasn't.

One might wonder why the FBI didn't just purge its files of all inculpatory material. The FBI filing system made this almost impossible. For example, an FBI memo from headquarters titled "Counterintelligence Program—Black Nationalist Hate Groups" or "COINTELPRO—Black Extremists" would be routed to files in more than forty local FBI offices. Similarly, if an FBI agent in Chicago wrote a document about Fred Hampton, one copy went into the Fred Hampton file, another into the Black Panther file, and yet another into the Racial Matters Squad (RMS) and local COINTELPRO files.

Not only were multiple copies produced and maintained, but also each copy displayed the routing of all the other copies. Purging the Black Panther file in Chicago would only dispose of one copy. The routing on the copy in the Washington, D.C., file would show that a copy should exist in the Chicago Black Panther file unless the file had been purged. Purging all the dispersed files required collusion on a massive scale by many people. The FBI preferred stonewalling to destruction.

After Flint argued the law in court on March 11, Sheldon Waxman responded that the government had found and intended to produce a "truckload" of documents. Maybe the FBI realized that Flint was a bloodhound on the scent of a conspiracy and wouldn't quit until he got what he was after.

On April 9, Flint and I came to court with a shopping cart in place of a truck. "How are we going to have time to read this stuff before Mitchell's dep?" I asked Flint, as we approached the outer doors of the courtroom.

"We'll get some help from people in the office. We can do short abstracts of the important documents." We parked the cart in the corridor and entered the courtroom.

When the case was called, Flint and I went up to the podium before the bench. I saw no truckload. I thought Waxman might have left the documents in his office. Then he approached the bench with a stack of papers about one-half-inch thick.

"What are those?" Flint asked.

"These thirty-four documents are all we have," Waxman said apologetically.

Flint and I looked at each other in disbelief. *This is total bullshit*, I thought. Flint and I were about to explode. Perry recognized our fury. He called his next case.

"Maybe big things come in small packages," I said to Flint.

Still curious about the contents of the new disclosures, Flint and I rolled the empty cart down the hall until we found an open witness room. We sat down at the circular table inside. Flint divided the stack in half, and we began to read through them. The FBI had blacked out such large portions that some contained nothing more than headings such as "Black Panther Party."

One document in the middle of the stack caught my eye: a hand-drawn sketch that looked like Fred Hampton's apartment. At the bottom of the diagram were the hand-printed words "1st floor, 2337 W. Monroe." Every room in Fred's apartment was carefully diagrammed. Even the location of the furniture in each room was noted. The entranceways at the front and back were also marked. Above the square marking the rear bedroom was hand printed, "Room of Hampton and Johnson when they stay here." Inside the bedroom were broken lines in the shape of a rectangle, and inside the lines was the word "bed." It was the exact location where Fred was lying when he was shot and killed.

I handed Flint the sketch.

"This could only have been made to use in the raid," Flint said.

"We got 'em," I said. "The attachment says they furnished the information in this diagram to the state's attorney two weeks before the raid." My jubilation over the discovery overshadowed my outrage at how intricately they had set things up. "They can pretend the FBI didn't initiate the whole thing, but this proves them liars."

Flint agreed. "It's the closest thing we'll get to a smoking gun."

There was no indication on the diagram of who made it or what file it had been pulled from. These would be questions we would put to O'Neal's control, Roy Mitchell, and to O'Neal if we got another crack at deposing him. The information on the floor plan came from "CGT-1," which we had learned meant Confidential Government Informant 1.

"I'm sure O'Neal was CGT-1," Flint said.

Below the floor plan, on the same page, was a map of the neighborhood highlighting the relationship of 2337 West Monroe to the surrounding streets.

"The FBI didn't leave anything to chance. They made sure the raiders could find 2337," I said.

The other document of the thirty-four that had not been totally deleted and that contained real, substantive information was dated November 21, 1969. It was from Special Agent in Charge Marlin Johnson to J. Edgar Hoover. It was partly excised but indicated that CGT-1 had provided information on November 19 that a large number of weapons were being stored at 2337 West Monroe, "a Panther crib, that is available to any BPP member for use such as sleeping and eating." Included among the weapons listed were several rifles, shotguns, and two handguns.

The FBI memorandum continued: "Source stated that all these weapons were allegedly purchased on local Illinois Gun Registration cards." It named the persons "most frequently seen" at the address: Fred Hampton, Billy Brooks, Doc Satchel, and Louis Truelock and Debra Johnson, who is allegedly pregnant by Hampton.

It was clear the FBI was zeroing in on Fred at 2337 two weeks before the raid. O'Neal told us Mitchell wasn't really interested in weapons, but either he was lying or Mitchell used old information about weapons to lure the police into a raid.

The memo concluded, "The Chicago Police Department and AFTD [the Bureau of Alcohol, Tobacco, Firearms and Explosives of the Treasury Department—commonly known as the ATF] has been furnished the contents of information set forth in this LHM [letterhead memorandum] as well as the Illinois State's Attorney's Office."

I flashed on Carmody's press interview a few minutes after the raid, at which he claimed complete surprise that there were Panthers there. "That was bullshit what Carmody said—that they didn't even know it was a Panther crib. They knew they were raiding *Fred Hampton's* apartment and knew exactly where he would be sleeping," I said. I imagined Carmody coming in the rear, knowing Fred's bed was only a few feet away.

"The FBI set Hanrahan up pretty good," Flint answered. "Everything he needed for a raid plus FBI endorsement."

28

On the Trail of COINTELPRO

With the floor plan as our main exhibit, Flint and I set out to prove the raid was a COINTELPRO action planned and initiated by the FBI. If we could prove this, then the illegal goals and methods explicitly endorsed in the program would provide the necessary intent to show FBI participation in an illegal conspiracy. We also needed to get enough information on individual FBI personnel to add them as defendants, as we could not sue the FBI directly.

Our first federal deposition after O'Neal was Roy Mitchell. For two days in May 1975, Bill Bender, Flint, and I questioned Mitchell in downtown Chicago in an office larger than any of our cubicles, loaned to us by the Lawyers' Committee for Civil Rights (LCCR). LCCR also had a copy machine, something PLO couldn't afford, and which we needed to duplicate documents.

Mitchell came into the deposition room with Arnold Kanter, a young, clean-shaven, and overly earnest U.S. attorney who had suddenly replaced Sheldon Waxman. Agent Roy Mitchell looked like a marine recruiter. He was in his late thirties, had a straight jaw, and wore his light brown hair in a crew cut. He sat straight up in his chair during his deposition, as if at attention. He did his best to come off as a "Yes sir, no sir," by-the-books kind of FBI agent. He presented a stark contrast to the freewheeling O'Neal, his informant.

Mitchell never offered information beyond what we asked for, yet he prided himself on his memory, part of his professional competence. So when we pinned him down and asked specific questions, we learned many of the details of his relationship with O'Neal as well as his role in initiating the raid.

Mitchell recruited O'Neal in 1968 while investigating an auto theft. In exchange for his testimony against the other car thieves, charges were dropped, and O'Neal became a paid informant. Several months later, after the relationship had lapsed, O'Neal was arrested for impersonating a federal officer by possessing phony FBI identification. Again Mitchell intervened, and soon thereafter he asked O'Neal to join the Black Panther Party and resume his informant status.

Mitchell claimed he gave no specific instructions to O'Neal as to how to act in the Party. Nevertheless, he admitted he was aware of O'Neal's construction of an electric chair, his advocacy of violent and illegal acts, and his obtaining of weapons for the Panthers. COINTELPRO memos directed agents to use provocateurs to incite Panther members to violence, but Mitchell claimed his work with O'Neal "had nothing to do with COINTELPRO." Judge Perry's refusal to enforce our subpoenas for COINTELPRO documents made it impossible to challenge his assertion.

Nevertheless, Mitchell provided a critical link in our conspiracy when he admitted he shared information with Richard Jalovec, the supervisor of Hanrahan's Special Prosecutions Unit, about the Panthers, including the fact that O'Neal was working for him as an informant. Sharing an informant's identity was not routinely done and was a strong indication of the regular communication between Mitchell and Jalovec as well as between the FBI and Hanrahan's office.

Conspirators seldom admit planning illegal acts together. Usually the most you can do to prove a conspiracy is show regular contacts and a common purpose, then ask the jury to draw the necessary inferences. Mitchell made our case substantially stronger by acknowledging his close ties and regular meetings with Jalovec.

Mitchell also testified that he obtained a floor plan from O'Neal of the Panther office in June 1969, which led to the June 4 raid. At the outset, the FBI called the Panther office and got the Panthers to agree to not resist. After arresting everyone inside, the FBI trashed Panther headquarters and stole their records. Mitchell was in radio contact with Marlin Johnson as the trashing went on.

Mitchell also testified that he regularly kept his superiors, Robert Piper, the head of the Racial Matters Squad, and Marlin Johnson, the Special Agent in Charge (SAC) of the Chicago FBI office, informed about Fred Hampton and the Panthers through conversations and memos.

In early October 1969, Mitchell wrote a memo to SAC Johnson and FBI headquarters that said Hampton and Deborah Johnson had rented the apartment at 2337 West Monroe. In early November, Mitchell learned that Hampton had visited the West Coast, and reported to Piper and Johnson that Fred was about to become part of the national leadership of the Black Panther Party. The more Mitchell implicated Piper and Johnson, the easier it would be to show they were part of the conspiracy.

"Mitchell and his bosses certainly understood that a national role would push Fred's charisma and influence beyond Chicago," I said to Flint at the break.

"And make him the type of leader, or 'black messiah,' Hoover ordered all the FBI offices to target," Flint agreed.

"I believe Mitchell's Chicago and D.C. superiors were following the information he was getting from O'Neal about Fred very closely and were giving Mitchell instructions," Bill Bender added.

Mitchell's supervisors had approved O'Neal receiving three hundred dollars per month, a relatively large payment for informants at that time, as well as additional payments when his information was particularly useful. Every time Bender asked Mitchell about the parallel between his and O'Neal's activities and the mandates of the Counterintelligence Program, Mitchell repeated in robotic fashion, "The raid had nothing to do with COINTELPRO." On the instruction of U.S. Attorney Kanter, he would then refuse to answer any more questions about COINTELPRO.

Our questioning of Mitchell proceeded chronologically up to the middle of November 1969. I jotted down notes, waiting to confront him with the floor plan and trying to anticipate how he would explain its evolution. Up to this point Mitchell had remained unruffled.

As we approached the days leading up to the raid, Mitchell took more time to answer the questions, and he consulted with his attorney, Kanter, more frequently. He testified that on the evening of November 13, 1969, the day Chicago police officers John Gilhooly and Frank Rappaport were slain in a gunfight with ex-Panther Jake Winters, he met with O'Neal at the Golden Torch restaurant in downtown Chicago. That day the newspapers covered the police deaths with banner headlines, and it was the lead story on all the TV network stations. Mitchell had to know that evening when he met with O'Neal that the police and state's attorney would be anxious to respond to the police killings and get revenge.

Mitchell said he brought graphic pictures of the slain officers to the meeting and showed them to O'Neal, who reported that the Panthers were naming the medical clinic after Jake Winters.

O'Neal and Mitchell met six days later, on November 19, again at the Golden Torch restaurant. There, while sitting at a table, they constructed the floor plan. Mitchell claimed he had not asked O'Neal to get the floor plan and "couldn't recall" whether he or O'Neal suggested making one. I sat there staring at Mitchell, knowing that there was no way that such an orderly and detail-conscious person would not remember who suggested the floor plan, or that O'Neal could have proposed it. (O'Neal wasn't going to initiate the raid.)

Mitchell claimed it was the newly acquired information from O'Neal on November 19—that there were weapons at 2337—that caused him to construct the sketch and ultimately to disseminate the "information in the floor plan" to the Cook County State's Attorney's Office. If he had admitted ordering the floor plan six days earlier, before he said he learned about weapons in the apartment, it would have been tantamount to admitting the weapons were merely the pretext for the raid. The extremely detailed nature of the floor plan, however, disproved that it could have been constructed spontaneously from memory by O'Neal. He clearly had been ordered to focus on the layout of the apartment after the deaths of Gilhooly and Rappaport.

Mitchell's opportunistic seizing of the November 13 shootout to initiate a raid plan for the local police employed a tactic very similar to the stated COINTELPRO objective of using local law enforcement to harass and confront the Panthers. I again asked Mitchell about his knowledge of COINTELPRO and its objectives. Following the advice of his lawyer, Mitchell refused to answer, repeating, "COINTELPRO had nothing to do with the raid."

"That was not my question, Mr. Mitchell. What did you know about COINTELPRO?" I still got the same answer, but Mitchell was becoming restless.

"He's a lying sack of shit," I said to Flint in the bathroom at the break, after checking the stalls to make sure no one else was present. "And he tries to come across as the straight guy just doing his job. Maybe that's what's so maddening. He never expresses any emotion, or even suggests the ability to be so manipulative."

"But he doesn't look good," Flint answered. "As Fred said, when you lie, 'you come up with answers that don't answer and with explanations that don't explain.' His denials of COINTELPRO playing a role look flaky."

Mitchell testified that O'Neal told him on November 19 that among the weapons in the apartment was a sawed-off shotgun and a stolen police riot shotgun. He passed this information on to the Gang Intelligence Unit at a face-to-face meeting that very day. He said the GIU then scheduled a raid for November 25.

This contradicted Mitchell's November 21 memorandum, which stated that all these "weapons were allegedly purchased on *legal* [emphasis added] Illinois State Gun Registration Cards issued to female BPP members who have never been arrested."

When I asked Mitchell why he had not included the information about the two illegal weapons in his memo to his superiors, he replied it was an "oversight."

Oversight, my ass, I thought. This guy does not have oversights, certainly not involving such critical information. Here was another moment when Mitchell's meticulous manner and recall of details undermined the credibility of his testimony.

As my probing continued, the slight talkativeness with which Mitchell had described his meetings with O'Neal disappeared. His answers became sharper. He began to shift in his chair.

Mitchell testified that the Gang Intelligence Unit had originally planned a raid based on the information he provided them but had called it off when he advised them the weapons were removed. He then told the State's Attorney's Office the weapons had been returned, but he never told the GIU this.

My hunch then was that the FBI preferred the raid be done by Hanrahan's office; perhaps because the GIU was suspicious they were being set up to do the FBI's dirty work. They may have questioned why Mitchell passed his information to them rather than sending it to the ATF. Perhaps Mitchell picked up on their suspicions and felt Hanrahan's Special Prosecution Unit would be more anxious to do the raid and ask fewer questions. He no doubt realized Hanrahan would like to get credit for a Panther raid.

Mitchell admitted that he placed the *only* copy of the floor plan in the O'Neal confidential informant file, to which only he, Piper, and

Johnson had access. Copies of other documents containing significant information from O'Neal about Fred Hampton were routed at least into the Fred Hampton and the Black Panther files in Chicago. Mitchell couldn't explain why only one copy of this document was made, but he admitted this made it possible to destroy the floor plan without leaving a trace that it ever existed. I believed that Mitchell was scheming from November 13 not only how to provoke a raid but how to hide the FBI's role in initiating it. He might have succeeded, but for Sheldon Waxman.

In an interview years later over lunch, Waxman, now a former U.S. attorney, told me with a very satisfied expression, "They [the FBI Agents who brought Waxman the diagram of 2337] looked at me as if to say, 'you know what to do with this.' But I didn't want to take the weight for them and destroy it. They were pissed when I turned the document over to you guys. After that my days in the U.S. Attorney's Office were numbered."

During the next break I asked Flint what he thought of Mitchell's credibility. It's difficult when you're asking the questions to comprehend the full effect of the answers.

"He looks totally ridiculous telling Hanrahan the weapons were illegal and writing a memo saying they weren't. It also looks like the raid was a COINTELPRO action to me, despite his lame denial," Flint surmised.

After we learned of the FBI floor plan, we wanted to add O'Neal and his FBI controls as defendants so they would go to trial with Hanrahan. Conspirators belong together, particularly in court, and maybe by now Hanrahan was beginning to realize he had been set up. Perhaps he'd join us in pointing a finger at the FBI. We were actually shooting (figuratively of course) for adding Hoover as a defendant, and attorney general John Mitchell, who was overseeing the operation of the government's illegal intelligence operation.

We didn't know how far we could get up the chain of command, but we were aiming high. Our conspiracy, like the one that resulted in the Watergate break-in and the burglary of Ellsberg's psychiatrist's office, started at the top. The cover-up reached to the top as well. The question was whether Perry would allow us the documents to learn what Hoover and the attorney general knew about Fred Hampton and the plan to kill him. Meanwhile, I had to finish Mitchell's deposition.

John Coghlan, Groth's attorney, was shouting something at Mitchell and his lawyer when Flint and I reentered the deposition room. He stopped short when he saw us. Coghlan's face was more flushed than usual, and his jaw was tense. He was not wearing his cocky smile. Camillo Volini, the other lawyer for the cops, was frowning and shuffling his oversized body in his chair.

Earlier, I had hardly noticed Coghlan and Volini. Because Mitchell was not their client, they couldn't direct him to refuse to answer questions. Coghlan was accustomed to running the show and wasn't pleased that Mitchell admitted such a close relationship with Jalovec.

After the break, Mitchell testified that he had talked to Jalovec, Hanrahan's assistant, "five to seven times" between November 26 and December 2. The subject matter of all these conversations was Fred Hampton's daily movements, his apartment, and the fact that weapons were being stored there. Mitchell's communications with Jalovec culminated in a face-to-face meeting on December 2 with both Jalovec and Sergeant Groth at the Cook County State's Attorney's Office.

Coghlan and Volini remained uncharacteristically quiet as I continued questioning Mitchell. Now I understood why they had been so riled up earlier. They knew Mitchell was directly contradicting their clients. Jalovec had never admitted continuous collaboration with Mitchell and had denied any face-to-face meeting with him before December 4. Groth had claimed he'd *never* talked to Mitchell, not even on the phone. Trying to appear unconcerned, Coghlan scratched the inside of his ear with a pencil and looked toward the ceiling. Volini attempted a look of boredom as he rocked back and forth in his chair, but a discernible frown made its way across his face.

Mitchell testified that at their half-hour meeting on December 2 at Hanrahan's office, he again told Jalovec and Groth about the large cache of weapons at 2337. He also told them for the first time that there was a sawed-off shotgun and a stolen police riot shotgun in the apartment. Mitchell specifically informed Groth and Jalovec the apartment would be vacant on Monday, Wednesday, and Friday evenings when Fred led political education classes.

I asked Mitchell if he had shown Jalovec and Groth anything. Volini's chair stopped rocking. Mitchell didn't hesitate. He testified that he brought and showed O'Neal's floor plan to the two men. I went through the details of the plan, asking him if he had specifically mentioned particular items. "I may have pointed out the bed where Hampton would be sleeping," he admitted. The "may have" was the best I was going to get, but it was all I needed to argue that the raiders knew exactly where to go.

Neither Groth nor Jalovec had ever admitted to seeing O'Neal's floor plan, although Mitchell had admitted the floor plan would be "invaluable" for anyone conducting a raid. For five years the FBI and Hanrahan's office had maintained the fiction that it was a call to Groth from his informant that had provided the information for the raid. Groth had testified numerous times that Jalovec's information from the FBI came later, was secondary, did not include a floor plan, and had merely corroborated the data from his own informant. Within fifteen minutes Mitchell had totally contradicted Groth and Jalovec's accounts.

Every lawyer has a way of disguising his chagrin when a witness gives testimony damaging to his case. I look down at my legal pad to avoid eye contact with the jury or the other lawyers and pretend to be writing away. Coghlan had gone to his other ear with his pencil, looking distant and inscrutable. Volini sat there with a blank stare, rocking.

Mitchell seemed to enjoy describing his critical communications with Hanrahan's office, taking credit for what followed, while suggesting Groth's claim of having his own informant was a lie. Mitchell wanted to get credit for his work setting up the raid. He avoided eye contact with Coghlan and Volini during this questioning. I thought we had gotten just about everything we could expect from Mitchell. But there was more.

On the morning of December 4, Johnson and Piper sent Mitchell to Hanrahan's office to "determine additional information about the raid." Mitchell testified that he met with Jalovec and Hanrahan in the library, where the Panther weapons had been put on display. In just a few minutes Hanrahan would hold his first press conference there. It was about 10:30 A.M. and already Jalovec and Hanrahan had put together their story, which they repeated to Mitchell: the Panthers opened fire on the unsuspecting police, they continued firing throughout the ordeal, and Hampton himself had fired at the police from his rear bedroom.

"What else did they tell you at that meeting?" I asked.

Coghlan tried to interrupt, but I instructed Mitchell to answer.

"Jalovec asked me if I minded if it got out that I was the source for the raid."

If he was "the" source, there wasn't any other. Mitchell was not careless with his words. I couldn't avoid turning and winking at Flint. Coghlan and Volini glanced at each other and quickly looked away. Jalovec's acknowledgment that Mitchell's information *alone* had led to the raid indicated that Jalovec and Groth were guilty of perjury. In his affidavit for the search warrant, prepared by Jalovec, Groth swore under oath that he relied on information from his own informant.

The creation of an informant for Groth was necessary because if Groth had told the truth, that his information came from the FBI, no judge could have legally signed the warrant. A search warrant can only be issued on probable cause. This was then interpreted by the Supreme Court to mean that law enforcement officers seeking warrants must swear that they are either an eyewitness to the information they are reporting or they have a reliable informant who saw it and reported it directly to them. If Groth had told the truth and swore he got his information from Jalovec who got it from Mitchell who got it from O'Neal, it would have been triple hearsay. He and Jalovec knew such an affidavit, a truthful one, would have been insufficient to obtain a search warrant.

Jalovec told Mitchell he did not mind if it got out that the FBI was the source of information for the raid. Yet for five years, and through two grand jury investigations and Hanrahan's criminal trial, the FBI never admitted this. In fact, Hanrahan, Jalovec, and Groth had repeatedly denied it under oath.

"Why have you never told anyone that the FBI was the source for the raid?" I continued.

"No one ever asked *me*," Mitchell explained, incredibly.

At the next break Flint and I found an empty room, closed the door, and did high fives. "Mitchell's killing them," Flint congratulated me. "I never dreamed he would contradict Jalovec and Groth so much."

"He wants to show off. He's had to hide his role for so long. He can barely contain himself," I agreed, smiling.

"That's definitely part of it, but I think what he's testifying to must also be laid out in FBI documents. He's chosen to go with what's in the files rather than what Jalovec and Groth want. We've got to get the FBI memos," Flint insisted.

We went back into the deposition room with a bit of a swagger. I couldn't help shooting Coghlan a knowing glance. "Informant, indeed," I whispered. He and Groth were manipulating the claim of informant's privilege not to protect an informant but to protect Groth from perjury.

Coghlan put on his pugnacious grin, which I took to mean, "You may be right, but you'll never prove it."

Mitchell had revealed a lot, but he continued to deny the raid had any connection to COINTELPRO. He also refused to produce the FBI documents showing payments to O'Neal. Instead, he gave us an affidavit showing how much he paid O'Neal. Flint and I suspected the payment documents themselves would be more revealing, perhaps containing an evaluation of O'Neal and summaries of the information he provided. We had to rest on speculation. Perry continued to uphold their objections to payment records, but at some point the dam had to crack open.

In 1974, PLO was in its fifth year. Our clients included the Attica Brothers, Puerto Rican Independentistas, the Hampton plaintiffs, and the antiwar movement. Arthur Kinoy said that movement lawyers had to be twice as good because we started with the judicial system against us. Charles Garry, the Panther lawyer in San Francisco, said he was a better lawyer than Perry Mason because Mason's clients were innocent. Our cases were never easy, whether our clients were innocent or not.

I worked to recruit other lawyers and law students for the movement through the National Lawyers Guild, which experienced a great influx of young, progressive, and sometimes radical lawyers and legal workers in the late 1960s and 1970s. We started the Guild Anti–Police Brutality Project in Chicago in 1972, and Flint and I met Peter Schmiedel there. He joined our office the next year.

Later, we obtained our own Chicago police "red squad" (intelligence division) files, which showed the police had sent an undercover recruit (under the false name Kostro, ironically) into the Anti–Police Brutality Project. We had wondered what happened to "that Castro guy," as he'd introduced himself. The files showed he had taken quite thorough notes and regularly reported on Flint's and my activities there. I've never known whether the police were looking for an inside view of our Hampton strategy or just a clearer profile of us.

By 1974, I had a good bit of court experience, but it was mostly in criminal cases. Flint had less, having passed the bar two years earlier. We were already spending half our time on the Hampton civil case. Dennis and Michael were spending two-thirds of their time in Buffalo working with other lawyers defending the sixty indicted Attica Brothers.

This left Peter Schmiedel and Mara Siegel, who had recently joined the office, as our only other full-time Chicago lawyers. Peter Schmiedel, tall and handsome with premature salt-and-pepper hair, was just getting used to going to court. He had already taken some assignments researching and writing motions on the Hampton case under Flint's tutelage. Mara continued to be the fire-eater she had been when Mzizi and I met her at Attica. Her style was flamboyant, and she was the first person I remember wearing a nose ring. Mara had a robust and sometimes crude sense of humor. She kept us men, whom she frequently referred to as "the boys," on our toes by chiding us on our sexism. Mara liked going to court and was getting more confident and effective by the day. (She removed the nose ring after she passed the bar.) Pat Handlin, more conventional and sober than Mara, came to Chicago after graduating from SIU and became a legal worker in the office. At SIU she had been an antiwar student activist and a strong supporter of the Panther defendants in the Carbondale trial. She later started a prison project supporting women prisoners and jailhouse lawyers at Dwight Correctional Center.

29

Groth's Informant

"Who's gonna try the Hampton case?" Flint asked at the PLO meeting in early August 1974. We were sitting in the small area at the back of the office, baking in the Chicago heat. The air conditioner was broken and the one small, portable fan didn't have a chance.

"I want to be involved, but the Attica cases will keep Michael and me in Buffalo most of the time," Dennis said. I had assumed Dennis would try the Hampton case. Now it was up to Flint and me.

I realized then with both trepidation and excitement that I would be the most experienced PLO lawyer at the trial. I would have to take the lead in court: the backup quarterback who finds himself in the big game. I was not as good at strategizing as Dennis, nor as incisive at articulating the law as Michael. With only one civil rights case behind me, I didn't know the civil rules of discovery very well. I had no experience proving damages and felt awkward and slightly ridiculous asking for money to compensate for someone's life or injuries.

But the challenge was as exciting as it was daunting. Our accusations were more significant than Watergate: the murder of Fred Hampton, a promising young leader, was a greater crime than burglarizing the Democratic headquarters. The orders for both emanated from the same seat of power. It wasn't Nixon aides H. R. Haldeman and John Ehrlichman giving them as in Watergate, instead it was J. Edgar Hoover and Nixon's attorney general, John Mitchell.

I was happy to resolve my criminal cases and focus on Hampton. Uncovering government wrongs was PLO's mission, and our lawsuit fit with the angry mood in the country. The week before our meeting, two thousand of us stood and applauded at the National Lawyers Guild convention in Minneapolis, Minnesota, as we watched Nixon resign.

The Senate Intelligence Committee, led by Democrat Frank Church, was holding public hearings investigating and exposing illegal intelligence operations. Their purview included the FBI's Counterintelligence Program, which Hoover claimed had been disbanded in 1972. Nevertheless, the Senate committee was looking for ways to outlaw similar abuses in the future. The FBI's role in the Hampton assassination, when fully exposed, should be exhibit number one. All we had to do was follow the evidence up the chain of command. Unfortunately, Judge Perry stood in the way.

After it was decided that Flint and I would lead the trial team, Peter Schmiedel and new attorney Holly Hill indicated they wanted to work on the Hampton trial as well. "It's why I joined the office," Holly said, and they both were already well grounded in the facts. The plan was for them to work their way into taking depositions and eventually speaking in court. They would even participate in the trial if we had the resources to support four of us in the courtroom.

I had become the chief rainmaker at PLO. But I was less and less available to do paying criminal cases as the Hampton case moved toward its trial date in January 1976. The income stream to the office became a trickle.

When Holly and Ralph Hurvitz graduated from Northwestern Law School, they turned down the opportunity to make a minimum twenty-five thousand dollars per year, even at a Legal Aid job. They could have earned two or three times that in private practice. Instead, they accepted the one hundred dollars per week that PLO would try to pay them.

Charles Hoffman, nicknamed Chick, joined PLO shortly after Holly and Ralph. Chick grew up in Maywood, where he hung out mostly with black kids. He knew and emulated Fred at Proviso East High School. He joined us as part of Fred's legacy. Chick was particularly adept at research and writing. He also was refreshingly even-keeled in the midst of the tensions our practice engendered.

We used to say that satisfaction from our work was our real compensation. I still feel that way. In the late 1960s and early 1970s we were part of a movement. We had sympathetic ears to listen to our struggles and had the added compensation of feeling we were making a difference.

With Dennis in Buffalo, Flint shared major responsibility for the case with me. If he felt any apprehension, he didn't show it. He was an indefatigable scrapper, a battler. I knew this from playing basketball with him. He was the driving point guard, passing or taking it to the hoop, whatever was necessary to score and to win. He was just as relentless when he was on the trail of documents or tracing the FBI's devious efforts to avoid discovery. He wasn't yet sophisticated or smooth in court, but his persistence and his loyalty made up for it.

I mentioned that Holly and Ralph had joined PLO after graduating from law school. When I first met Holly, with her warm brown eyes, high cheekbones, and mischievous smile, I became infatuated with her, and we started a relationship. A year later she moved into Seminary Street, where she, Michael, Mara Siegel, and I each had our own bedroom. My relationship with Holly was tempestuous from the get-go. I protected myself from the vulnerability of love by deciding Holly wasn't political enough. She protected herself as well. After we broke up I realized my feelings too late. There was tension as we both continued to work together. But despite broken hearts and hurt feelings the show went on, and so did our pursuit of Hampton's killers.

All of PLO remained committed to the Hampton case, even if Flint and I took primary responsibility. When we needed to write motions, others in the office helped with the research and drafting. PLO was far from perfect, but in retrospect I don't think any one or two or three of us could have worked so hard and so long had we not had the collective to support us. It was the retreat where we found camaraderie and sympathy after a tough day in court, the place we came to tell our stories and be tended to, and where we got help with legal strategies. It gave us the strength to endure.

"How come you guys are so down in the mouth?" Mara Siegel would ask, mimicking our "serious selves." "Doing time in the courtroom can't be as bad as time behind bars."

Of course, she was right. We'd lick our figurative wounds and go on.

Flint asked about moving the office downtown for the trial later that fall. It was a burden bringing boxes of files downtown for every court date. At trial we couldn't retreat to our office for lunch breaks, or go there as easily in the evenings after court. Looking around at our hexagonal cubicles with dirty, plasterboard walls that were four feet short of the ceiling and egg cartons above to muffle the sound, I realized we could never do depositions at our current location. Also, the neighborhood had become increasingly gentrified. The struggle to maintain Lincoln

Park as a place affordable to Puerto Ricans and other working-class people had been lost. There was less and less reason to stay.

I liked being able to walk to work in blue jeans and walk home late at night. There would be a different atmosphere in an elevator building in the Loop. Despite my reservations, I could see the move was going to come before the Hampton trial started.

The Hampton team—Flint, Dennis, Holly, Peter, and I—stayed together after the regular office meeting. We decided to work in three major areas to get ready for trial. One was proving what happened during the raid. We could rely on the plaintiffs' accounts, the ballistics evidence, and the testimony of Robert Zimmers from the FBI crime lab as well as the many false stories of the raiders.

I agreed to handle the firearms evidence although technical detail was not my strength. I accepted the assignment with some trepidation. Unlike Skip, the fine points of evidence gathering and testing were not my forte. Not yet anyway.

The second area of work was obtaining the evidence to prove the raid was part of COINTELPRO. Flint had renewed our requests for FBI and COINTELPRO files after Mitchell's deposition. Without stating it, we understood Flint would continue to take the lead in enforcing our document demands and uncovering the COINTELPRO connection to the raid.

And finally there was Groth and his supposed informant. His deposition was scheduled for the next week. John Coghlan, Groth's attorney, had already stalled Groth's deposition for six months. We had gotten a hint of his reason earlier that summer: Coghlan was trying to find a dead Panther who might qualify as Groth's informant if Groth were ever ordered to name someone. A live person would obviously be harder to control and would likely dispute Groth's claim. From his questioning of the survivors at their depositions, we knew Coghlan was considering Clifton Morgan, aka Babatunde Omowale Babatunde, who had died in July 1970 in an explosion near some Illinois Central Railroad tracks. The police, FBI, and coroner had concluded he blew himself up accidentally, carrying or trying to detonate a bomb.

Coghlan asked every plaintiff at his or her deposition if they knew Babatunde and if he had been at 2337 West Monroe the week before the raid. Most of the plaintiffs did not know him and none of them said he was present in early December, when Groth claimed his informant viewed the weapons in the apartment. This didn't deter Coghlan. We later learned he was secretly taping interviews with other witnesses, trying to find someone who would say Babatunde had been in Fred's apartment.

When we finally got the transcripts of these interviews after the trial, they showed Coghlan suggesting, begging, and even threatening witnesses to place Babatunde at 2337 prior to the raid. "I don't recall seeing him there," was the universal response.

Holly agreed to work on the Groth issue and Peter on amending the complaint to add the FBI higher-ups. "Groth is lying about having an informant to protect," Flint said as we ended the meeting. "He's protecting his own ass from perjury."

On August 24, Sergeant Daniel Groth entered the deposition room of the Lawyers' Committee for Civil Rights, with Coghlan at his side. Groth refused to look toward Flint and me, and didn't say hello. Several minutes later his nostrils flared when he finally turned in our direction and shot us a nasty sneer. PLO had been a thorn in his side ever since we exposed his trumped-up version of the raid delivered to the newspapers and TV stations in December 1969. I remembered his televised words: "It was fifteen minutes of hell, and a miracle not one policeman killed, not one policeman shot. It only stopped because their arsenal was not equal to our police arsenal."

Sergeant Groth was tall, with dark hair, a bony, angular face, and a deep voice. He spoke like someone used to giving orders and not being questioned. Groth would have been tough to question on his own, but with Coghlan running interference, it was even harder. Coghlan often interrupted our questions with objections and instructions to Groth not to answer. Sometimes he signaled Groth: "Sergeant Groth has already answered that question and told you . . . " adding what Coghlan wanted Groth's answer to be.

Nevertheless, Groth took responsibility for many of the questionable police actions. He unapologetically stated that he authorized his officers to carry their own personal weapons on the raid. This included shotguns, automatic pistols, and Gloves Davis's .30-caliber rifle. He also approved Officer Gorman being issued a .45-caliber machine gun, although he admitted no one had ever taken a machine gun on a previous raid led by him. Groth said he hadn't run the raid at 8:00 P.M., when his informant had told him the apartment would be vacant, and instead changed the raid time to 4:00 A.M., because he wanted to use "surprise." He chose not to take bullhorns or make a phone call to announce the police presence, although he knew that when the FBI had done this in June it had led to the Panthers not resisting their entry. He also decided against tear gas.

Groth called the raiders together at 4:00 A.M. on December 4. In his early statements, Groth, like the other raiders, pretended it was a routine search and they were totally surprised to find armed Panthers there. That didn't look credible given the arsenal of weapons they took on the raid. Moreover, it conflicted with their defense at their criminal trial, which focused on how dangerous the Panthers were. Groth's current testimony fit our conspiracy claim quite well. He admitted informing the raiders that 2337 West Monroe was the apartment frequently occupied by Fred Hampton, and he told them that there was a large cache of weapons there. Groth testified that he warned the raiders, "Hampton sleeps with a .45 by his bed."

I kicked Flint under the table. Groth had not mentioned this most provocative detail in his previous testimony. Telling the raiders this at the preraid briefing and showing them where Fred slept on the layout was an invitation to murder. Groth also admitted he had referred to a "rough sketch" when describing the layout of Fred's apartment to his officers.

Flint then asked Groth what transpired at the meeting on December 2 when, Mitchell had testified, Mitchell showed Groth and Jalovec the floor plan. "I have no recollection of the meeting," Groth answered. Flint stared at him. Flint kept pressing Groth for what he did recall about his contact with Mitchell. Groth pushed the lie more: "I never met or spoke with Roy Mitchell."

I looked at Flint, rolling my eyes and nodding sarcastically. Coghlan threatened to terminate the deposition, commenting that Flint and I were showing his client disrespect. We didn't respond. Instead, Flint formulated the next and most obvious question: "Where did you get the information for the search warrant?"

Groth hesitated, looked at Coghlan, and then began to testify. It sounded like even the cadences had been rehearsed. Groth said that on the night of December 2 he received a call at home "out of the blue" from an informant who told him there were weapons at 2337—the same information that Mitchell testified he gave Groth and Jalovec at their face-to-face meeting on the same day.

When Flint probed Groth on when his informant saw the weapons in Fred's apartment, Coghlan interjected authoritatively, "I order Sergeant Groth to refuse to answer on the grounds that to do so would endanger the lives of other persons."

"Is your informant alive or dead?" Flint asked Groth, which elicited the same objection from Coghlan.

"Is it the informant or someone else Groth is protecting?" Flint turned and asked Coghlan.

Coghlan [*ignoring Flint*]: "I order Sergeant Groth to refuse to answer."

The only question Groth answered was, "Did you pay him?" He said he didn't pay him. The informant provided Groth with information for "advancement in other areas."

Groth testified that he took notes of his conversation with his informant and made a sketch on a yellow pad from his informant's description of 2337. He used both to brief the other raiders, and he had them with him when he briefed Hanrahan on December 3. He kept his notes and his sketch of the layout of 2337 in a file with information from other informants.

"And where are those notes and sketch today?" Flint asked.

"I destroyed them immediately after the raid," Groth responded.

"And the larger 'informants' file?"

"I destroyed that also."

After Groth's deposition, Flint, Holly, and Peter drafted a motion to compel the court to order Groth to answer questions about his informant. The law was clear; the informant's privilege protected only the safety of the informant, not "other persons."

Four months later we got a hearing. Because of the importance of the motion, Morty Stavis, a seasoned constitutional lawyer and a founder of the Center for Constitutional Rights, came to Chicago to argue for our side.

Flint introduced Morty Stavis to Judge Perry, highlighting some of his many accomplishments, including briefing and arguing several U.S.

Supreme Court cases with important constitutional issues. Judge Perry couldn't have appeared nicer or more open-minded as he welcomed Stavis and said he looked forward to hearing his arguments.

Morty Stavis, approaching sixty, was short and stocky, with curly hair and a well-trimmed goatee. He was wearing a herringbone sport coat and had a relaxed confidence as he approached the lectern to address the judge.

His argument was both impassioned and simple. The informant, if he was alive, had critical information that could decide many of the factual issues in dispute, such as whether Fred was drugged and what the police knew before the raid, and possibly what took place during the raid. The law required a balancing test between the interests of the party seeking the information and the need to protect the informant. In this instance, the very existence of the informant, whether he was reliable, and his value as a witness to the events of December 4 greatly outweighed law enforcement's interest in keeping his identity secret. If the defendants intended to name a dead man, then of course there was no legitimate law enforcement purpose or legal basis to refuse to disclose his identity. If the informant never existed, then the claim of privilege was being put forth in bad faith, and sanctions were appropriate against the defendants and their lawyers.

When he sat down, I thought maybe even Judge Perry had been convinced. Coghlan and Volini responded in their most indignant, pontificating rhetoric. Volini went first: "The county of Cook is a political subdivision of the state of Illinois, as is the city of Chicago, and the privilege was asserted by Sergeant Groth upon direction by me and Mr. Coghlan for the protection of the citizens of the city of Chicago, and it was asserted by the government and has been consistently asserted by these two governmental agencies."

Not to be outdone, Coghlan stood up and stressed that Groth had refused to answer based on Coghlan's instructions as "the state's attorney of Cook County as far as this case is concerned." They puffed themselves up, pretending to speak on behalf of government entities rather than as the court-appointed private lawyers they actually were.

Judge Perry ordered us to return the next day, when he would make his ruling.

"For once I think Perry is taking our arguments seriously," Flint said as we left.

When we returned the next morning, Morty Stavis had flown back to New York. Judge Perry began, "I am concerned with the naming of the informant because of the danger that counsel for the defendants have stated they believe honestly and sincerely would result."

Coghlan: "And danger to the lives of other persons."

Judge Perry: "Oh, yes, the danger to the lives of the informer and maybe other persons."

Perry raised our hopes when he ordered Coghlan to bring Groth to court that afternoon so he could question him about the identity of the informant in chambers. Coghlan and Volini were surprised by the judge's order. They objected, but when Perry appeared determined, Coghlan asked that the interview be conducted without a court reporter. Flint and I immediately objected to this private *ex parte* interview with a party to the lawsuit without a record being made. I didn't trust Perry to accurately report what happened, and we would have no transcript of Groth to impeach him with later. Perry overruled our objections.

After lunch, Coghlan brought his client to court. Groth looked a bit miffed but determined as ever. Flint and I were waiting expectantly, hoping for a breakthrough.

Judge Perry asked Groth to come with him through the rear door toward his chambers. We didn't know what Perry would do.

"If Groth names Babatunde as his informant, they have a problem," Flint said. "They can't prove he was an informant or was even in Fred's apartment in December."

"Do you think Groth will take contempt to cover up his lies?" I responded.

A few minutes later the rear door opened. Groth followed Perry into the courtroom and the judge ordered Groth to take the witness stand. Groth stood by the witness chair without sitting down. He seemed to know the questioning would be brief.

Judge Perry: "Will you refuse to reveal the informant's identity even if ordered to?"

Groth: "I will continue to refuse. (*pause*) I am refusing to answer based on my experience in this case as a police officer."

Judge Perry: "Even though I should commit you to custody, would you still refuse? Is that your position?"

"I would respectfully decline, yes sir." This could be the record a judge made before finding a witness in contempt. I was getting excited.

Judge Perry: "The witness may step down. The plaintiffs motion is denied."

Flint and I both jumped up, fuming. This was a new one. The court was not going to require Groth to answer his question because Groth was willing to take contempt. Based on this logic, why would any witness answer any question he didn't like?

"Sit down," Perry ordered. He threatened us with contempt.

Groth hurried for the exit doors at the rear of the courtroom, shooting Flint and me a sadistic grin as he passed.

Perry scuttled off the bench a moment later.

Outraged by his decision, we filed a mandamus asking the court of appeals to reverse him. We argued that Perry's ruling was so significant to the case, and so far off on the law, it constituted an abuse of discretion. Unfortunately, the higher courts gave trial judges a great deal of leeway on discovery issues.

Judge Perry responded with a vengeance to our accusation that he abused his discretion. "So you guys want to play hardball," he challenged us on the next court date. He rescinded his previous order allowing us to take depositions by tape recorder, which we had sought in order to save court reporter's fees.

The court of appeals turned us down. We went to trial under Perry's order that we could not challenge Groth on the witness stand about the existence or identity of his informant. Orders we were determined to disobey.

Hiding COINTELPRO

The purpose of discovery is to make trial less a game of blind man's bluff and more a fair contest with the basic issues and facts disclosed to the fullest extent possible. —Supreme Court Justice William O. Douglas, 1958

In general, FBI agents do not voluntarily admit wrongdoing. They must be confronted with one or more documents they wrote or approved. We had the memos Agent Mitchell had authored, stating that he told State's Attorney Hanrahan's office about guns at Hampton's apartment, and that he had shown Hanrahan's assistants the floor plan designating the bed where Fred and Deborah slept. Mitchell sent these memos to his supervisor, Robert Piper, and to the head of the Chicago FBI office, Marlin Johnson. Flint and I intended to confront Piper and Johnson with these at their depositions to make them admit their knowledge and approval of Mitchell's actions. That would be the easy part.

We also had COINTELPRO documents with orders from FBI director J. Edgar Hoover to the heads of all FBI field offices, including Marlin Johnson, to come up with "hard hitting programs" to "disrupt, expose, misdirect, discredit, or otherwise neutralize" the Panthers and "prevent the rise of a messiah who could unify and electrify the militant black nationalist movement." We planned to cross-examine Piper and Johnson using these documents, which they had read and initialed, and force them to acknowledge their roles in executing the Counterintelligence Program. This would be harder.

Flint and I deposed Robert Piper in the unadorned but cramped conference room loaned to us by the Lawyers' Committee for Civil Rights. From the windows of the room, you could see the midriff of several Chicago office buildings. We had arrived first and were sitting at the Formica conference table talking to Julian Carter, our court reporter.

He had just set up his stenograph machine when Piper and Assistant U.S. Attorney Arnold Kanter entered. After perfunctory introductions, I asked if they were ready to start. Kanter nodded.

"Would you swear the witness?" I asked the court reporter.

"Do you swear to tell the whole truth, the honest truth, and nothing else but the truth?" Carter asked hurriedly, typing as he spoke.

"I do," affirmed Piper. He was tall and gaunt with an aloof, erudite manner.

I opened with the preliminaries, questioning Piper about his training and background in the FBI. Before answering each question, he lifted his bony nose and looked at me as if I were an irksome child.

"Were you aware that your subordinate, Roy Mitchell, provided Hanrahan's office with a floor plan, in fact this floor plan?" I asked, picking up the diagram of Hampton's apartment. "Let the record indicate I am showing the witness Piper Deposition Exhibit Number 1."

"Yes, I was," he stated. He had initialed Mitchell's memo.

"Did you approve Mitchell meeting with members of the State's Attorney's Office and giving them information about guns in Hampton's apartment?"

Again, he replied, "Yes." He had initialed that memo as well.

"And were you aware they intended to use this information to conduct a raid on Hampton's apartment?"

He hesitated but admitted that the "information would be valuable in conducting a raid."

Piper acknowledged speaking with Mitchell the morning following the raid. He testified that he had "no particular concern" when Mitchell told him about the Panther deaths and injuries. He recalled the Mitchell interview with satisfaction. His coldness was disturbing, even to me, who did not expect a show of compassion from FBI officials.

Piper testified that he was head of the Racial Matters Squad, charged with monitoring the Panthers and other black groups. Thus, he would have been the likely person to supervise the agents and their informants carrying out COINTELPRO. "Were you and Mitchell acting pursuant to the Counterintelligence Program when you provided Hanrahan with the floor plan?"

He sneered. I was about to comment sarcastically that the court reporter couldn't take down his expression, he would have to answer

From left: Fred's brother Bill, Fred, sister Dee Dee circa 1950.

Birthday gathering for Fred's uncle Roosevelt White. Seated at the table are Roosevelt, Fred, and brother Bill; behind Fred is sister Dee Dee, mother Iberia, Francis, and Iberia's brothers, sisters, and spouses.

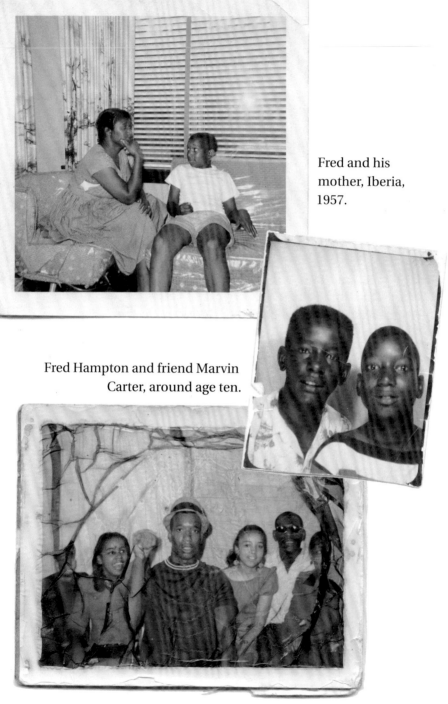

Fred and his
mother, Iberia,
1957.

Fred Hampton and friend Marvin
Carter, around age ten.

Fred Hampton's twenty-first birthday party.

Airtel to SAC, Albany
RE: COUNTERINTELLIGENCE PROGRAM
BLACK NATIONALIST-HATE GROUPS

nationalist activity, and interested in counterintelligence, to coordinate this program. This Agent will be responsible for the periodic progress letters being requested, but each Agent working this type of case should participate in the formulation of counterintelligence operations.

GOALS

For maximum effectiveness of the Counterintelligence Program, and to prevent wasted effort, long-range goals are being set.

1. Prevent the coalition of militant black nationalist groups. In unity there is strength; a truism that is no less valid for all its triteness. An effective coalition of black nationalist groups might be the first step toward a real "Mau Mau" in America, the beginning of a true black revolution.

2. Prevent the rise of a "messiah" who could unify, and electrify, the militant black nationalist movement. Malcolm X might have been such a "messiah;" he is the martyr of the movement today. Martin Luther King, Stokely Carmichael and Elijah Muhammad all aspire to this position. Elijah Muhammad is less of a threat because of his age. King could be a very real contender for this position should he abandon his supposed "obedience" to "white, liberal doctrines" (nonviolence) and embrace black nationalism. Carmichael has the necessary charisma to be a real threat in this way.

3. Prevent violence on the part of black nationalist groups. This is of primary importance, and is, of course, a goal of our investigative activity; it should also be a goal of the Counterintelligence Program. Through counterintelligence it should be possible to pinpoint potential troublemakers and neutralize them before they exercise their potential for violence.

4. Prevent militant black nationalist groups and leaders from gaining respectability, by discrediting them to three separate segments of the community. The goal of discrediting black nationalists must be handled tactically in three ways. You must discredit these groups and individuals to, first, the responsible Negro community. Second, they must be discredited to the white community,

- 3 -

Ralph Abernathy, Fred Hampton, and Jesse Jackson at the Southern Christian Leadership Conference office in 1967.

Hoover's outline of COINTELPRO objectives, including prevention of the "rise of a 'messiah'" in the black nationalist movement.

Fred Hampton, 1969.

Bobby Rush and Fred Hampton,
Chicago, 1969.

Fred Hampton in the Black Panther office, 1969.

Fred Hampton presiding at a Black Panther wedding, Chicago, August 1969.

Black Panther headquarters on Madison Street, 1969.

Black Panthers free breakfast program, Chicago, 1969.

Aftermath of October 1969 police raid on the Black Panthers'
headquarters.

FBI's "anonymous"
letter intended
to ignite violence
against the Black
Panthers within the
black community.

Consequently, Chicago now recommends the following
letter be sent FORT, handwritten, on plain paper:

"Brother Jeff

"I've spent some time with some Panther friends on
the west side lately and I know what's been going on. The
brothers that run the Panthers blame you for blocking their
thing and there's supposed to be a hit out for you. I'm not
a Panther, or a Ranger, just black. From what I see these
Panthers are out for themselves not black people. I think
you ought to know what their up to, I know what I'd do if I
was you. You might hear from me again."

"A black brother you don't know"

The above would be sent to FORT in care of the First
Presbyterian Church, 6401 South Kimbark, the widely publicized
headquarters of the Rangers.

It is believed the above may intensify the degree of
animosity between the two groups and occasion FORT to take
retaliatory action which could disrupt the BPP or lead to
reprisals against its leadership.

Consideration has been given to a similar letter
to the BPP, alleging a Ranger plot against the BPP leadership
however, it is not felt this would be productive, principally
since the BPP at present is not believed as violence-prone as
the Rangers, to whom violent type activity, shooting, and the
like, are second nature. There is also the possibility that
if a future contact between the two were to take place, and it
became apparent that both had received such communications,
then an outside interest would be somewhat obvious.

Chicago will take no action regarding the above,
pending Bureau authorization.

Street door to the Black Panthers' headquarters after the October 1969 police raid

Chicago police removing Fred Hampton's body from his apartment.

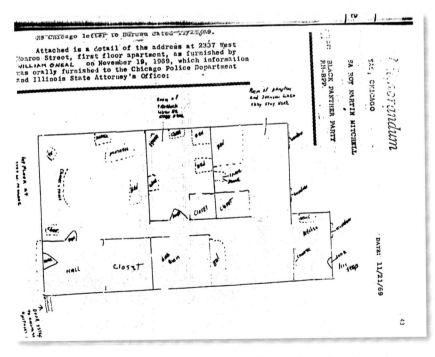

Enhanced FBI floor plan provided to police raiders showing where
Hampton slept.

Fred Hampton's bedroom after his assassination.

Nail heads (circled) claimed by state's attorney to be bullet holes and proof of Panther firing.

Line of people waiting to pay their last respects to Fred Hampton at the Rayner Funeral Home, Chicago, 1969.

Fred Hampton, Rayner Funeral Home, Chicago, 1969.

44

12/11/69

AIRTEL

TO: DIRECTOR, FBI ~~████████~~

FROM: SAC, CHICAGO ~~████████~~

SUBJECT: ~~████████████~~

Re·Bureau airtel 12/8/69 and Chicago letter 11/24/69.

Information set forth in Chicago letter and letterhead
memorandum of 11/21/69, reflects legally purchased firearms
in the possession of the Black Panther Party (BPP) were stored
at 2337 West Monroe Street, Chicago. A detailed inventory of
the weapons and also a detailed floor plan of the apartment
were furnished to local authorities. In addition, the identities
of BPP members utilizing the apartment at the above address
were furnished. This information was not available from any
other source and subsequently proved to be of tremendous value
in that it subsequently saved injury and possible death to
police officers participating in a raid at the address on the
morning of 12/4/69. The raid was based on the information
furnished by informant. During the resistance by the BPP
members at the time of the raid, the Chairman of the Illinois
Chapter, BPP, FRED HAMPTON, was killed and a BPP leader from
Peoria, Illinois, was also killed. A quantity of weapons
and ammunition were recovered.

It is felt that this information is of considerable
value in consideration of a special payment for informant
requested in re Chicago letter.

~~████████████~~
1 - Chicago

RTP:pas
~~██~~

SEARCHED
SERIALIZED
INDEXED
FILED

FBI request for a bonus for the informant providing the
information leading to the raid.

The author and lawyer Flint Taylor in front of Black Panther headquarters, 1979.

The author; Fred Hampton's mother, Iberia Hampton; and Fred's brother Bill Hampton, 2009.

orally, when Kanter intervened. He held up his open hand toward me from the other side of the table, like a crossing guard signaling a stop. In a well-rehearsed voice, Kanter stated: "I object to the question and instruct the witness not to answer any questions concerning COINTELPRO on the grounds that COINTELPRO is irrelevant."

"Me thinks Kanter doth protest too much," I said to Flint when Piper's deposition was over. "He knows Piper's Racial Matters Squad executed COINTELPRO directives against the Panthers in Chicago. Clearly, they were the ones dealing with black militant organizations."

"Kanter knows it and we know it," Flint agreed. "Now let's figure out how to prove it."

At a PLO meeting in the summer of 1975, we decided that the office could finance only two lawyers in court, Flint and me. Holly and Peter would have to work on other cases when the trial started.

Civil litigation is expensive. Even then, deposition transcripts could run five hundred dollars per day. The December 4th Committee, which included the survivors and supporters, was holding monthly fundraisers to help defray expenses with performers like Chaka Khan, Oscar Brown Jr., and Dick Gregory. Even with that and contributions from the NAACP and the Lawyers' Committee for Civil Rights, plus frequent benefits, we were always short of funds. Our black court reporter, Julian Carter, allowed us to postpone part of the payment for deposition transcripts until after the trial. Only his generosity allowed us to continue discovery.

I called my parents to ask for financial help. They agreed to send me three hundred dollars per month during the trial. My parents, and my dad especially, were proud I was using my law degree for something other than to make money. He had derived much of his satisfaction from the legal work he had done *pro bono*, like working for the Voter Education Project. He was somewhat, though not entirely, put off by the violent Panther rhetoric, but he supported me in my efforts to prove Fred Hampton was murdered. Years later, I discovered Dad kept a file of Hampton newspaper accounts.

Jim Montgomery, the prominent trial attorney who had represented Deborah Johnson after the raid, agreed to represent her at the upcoming trial. He had a deep baritone voice and was a convincing figure in the courtroom. I thought the combination of his trial savvy and our knowledge of the evidence would be a good fit.

We familiarized Montgomery with the federal case we hoped to present, and he agreed to do part of the deposition of Piper's boss, Marlin Johnson.

On September 24, Montgomery began. Johnson had left the FBI and become the CEO of Canteen Corporation, a vending machine company. Mayor Richard J. Daley had subsequently appointed him chairman of the Chicago Police Board, which decided civilian complaints of police brutality. Johnson's deposition took place in the posh conference room of the law firm Sidley and Austin, where he had retained his own counsel in addition to Kanter. Johnson shook our hands as though we were old friends and then sat down with a pleasant smile. He was particularly cordial to Montgomery. Johnson, a little past middle-aged, with a round face and a receding hairline, appeared relaxed, clearly experienced in public relations. He began answering our questions earnestly, as if he wanted to be helpful.

Like Piper, he acknowledged receiving the memo, which bore his initials, stating Mitchell had met with Hanrahan's men and supplied them with weapons information. But Johnson claimed no knowledge of Mitchell obtaining the floor plan of Hampton's apartment and passing it on to the eventual raiders, despite the fact that Mitchell's memo stating this was directed specifically to him.

"I have no recollection of that," was his repeated response to Montgomery's questions about the floor plan. Marlin Johnson had been specifically ordered by FBI Director Hoover to implement the Counterintelligence Program, as had all the FBI office heads (SACs) throughout the country. Montgomery asked Johnson what he did to implement COINTELPRO in Chicago. Johnson looked to his attorney. Kanter didn't miss his cue.

"I object to the question and instruct the witness not to answer any questions concerning COINTELPRO on the grounds that COINTELPRO is irrelevant," Kanter said, repeating his mantra. Montgomery continued patiently but was blocked by Kanter's objections to every question concerning COINTELPRO. Kanter knew Perry would uphold his objections, no matter how specious, if it blocked us from getting evidence of the FBI's involvement in the raid.

By the end of Johnson's deposition I was grinding my teeth and swearing under my breath. Unlike his predecessor, Sheldon Waxman, who had demonstrated some integrity, Kanter unhesitatingly carried out the FBI policy of concealment. By the deposition's end Flint and I ranted at Kanter that we knew he was covering up, and that one day he would be exposed.

We filed another motion asking Judge Perry to order Piper and Johnson to answer questions about COINTELPRO. Again he denied it. He also denied us access to the thirty-four COINTELPRO documents the FBI had given him *in camera* (without our viewing them) months earlier. In July 1975 we appealed. Again, the appellate court refused to overrule Perry.

I felt we had hit a stone wall. But not my partner: "There's more than one way to skin a cat," Flint said a few days later, walking into my office. "Perry can't very well deny us access to files specifically about Fred Hampton. Let's ask for every FBI document naming Hampton, and I bet we'll get some COINTELPRO memos."

I agreed, ready to try Flint's new tactic. We demanded that our subpoena for all the FBI files naming Hampton be enforced. Even Kanter had difficulty objecting.

Perry reluctantly ordered the FBI to produce documents specifically naming Fred Hampton and any of the plaintiffs. A few days later, 193 highly excised internal memos arrived by messenger. Flint and I divided up the new batch of materials in my office. He sat on the other side of my desk while I cleared off some papers. We put our feet up and started reading.

The documents showed the FBI had monitored Fred Hampton on a daily basis and recorded nearly everything he did, from speaking at colleges to serving breakfast to kids.

"The FBI was on Fred like white on rice," Flint commented, partway through his stack. "Their antennae definitely went up when Fred and Deborah rented the apartment on Monroe."

My stack of reports showed the same close FBI scrutiny of Fred's actions. Halfway through my pile I saw a one-page memo from Marlin Johnson to Hoover dated April 8, 1970. It was captioned "Fred A. Hampton (Deceased) et al.—Victims Summary Punishment." Summary punishment was a way of describing the police meting out their form of street justice on the spot without a trial or due process.

"Check this out," I said, handing the paper to Flint. "This is another piece in the conspiracy."

He read it carefully, his eyes focusing intently as they went down the page. When he finished, he looked up excitedly. "I can't believe they wrote this down." Marlin Johnson's memo to Hoover stated:

> AAG JERRIS LEONARD, Civil Rights Division, Department of Justice, at Chicago, advised SAC Marlin Johnson in strictest confidence *that no indictments of police officers are planned in captioned matter.* [emphasis added] The above is based upon an agreement whereby Hanrahan will dismiss the local indictment against Black Panther Party (BPP) members. Hanrahan is to be given 30 days to dismiss this local indictment, which will be based upon the change in testimony of John Sadunas of the Chicago Police Department Crime Lab. Subsequent to this dismissal, BPP victims will then be subpoenaed before the FGJ for their testimony in this case.

"It was fixed!" I exclaimed. "Leonard never intended to indict anyone." As angry as I was, I was also amazed at how smoothly the feds and Hanrahan had closed ranks to protect each other. The Justice Department had impaneled the 1970 federal grand jury in response to the black community's outcry to investigate Hanrahan's raiders for civil rights violations. Attorney General John Mitchell, who we later learned was the White House contact for the Watergate burglars, appointed Jerris Leonard, the head of the Civil Rights Division, to lead the grand jury investigation. At the time, Leonard was reputed to be the liberal in Nixon's Justice Department. In his press statements he assured everyone that he intended to carry out a thorough and impartial investigation.

The document we were reading was dated a month before the Grand Jury concluded and well before the Panther victims were subpoenaed to testify.

"We always wondered why Hanrahan dropped the charges on the survivors so abruptly," Flint said. "Now we know. It wasn't just because they were innocent. It was also part of the deal to prevent his men and him from being indicted."

The concealment of the FBI role in Fred's murder was particularly important in 1970. Disclosure of the FBI involvement would have also led to exposing the Counterintelligence Program.

"I don't think Hoover's orders for every FBI office to develop plans to 'neutralize and destroy' the black movement or his sanctioning of violent means to accomplish this would have washed with the public if they'd known about it back in 1970," I said.

In fact within a year after the Counterintelligence Program was exposed in 1971, it was terminated, at least in name.

The "deal document," as we quickly labeled the April 8 memo, exposed the cozy arrangement between Hanrahan and the FBI. The feds wouldn't indict him or his raiders for civil rights violations, and he would maintain his secrecy concerning the FBI's role in the raid. Their agreement was made *before* the survivors were asked to testify; their testimony would have made no difference.

Few pieces of evidence are more damning or harder to come by, when trying to prove a conspiracy, than an explicit agreement by the coconspirators—in this case Hanrahan and the FBI—to conceal their actions. The FBI produced the deal document under a strict protective order, which prevented us from releasing it or even mentioning it in open court.

"Remember what Leonard wrote in the grand jury report," I reminded Flint. "The Panthers were more interested in police persecution than in obtaining justice. What a fraud. Leonard did a masterful job blaming the victims."

In August 1975 we added as defendants the FBI informant William O'Neal, his FBI control Roy Mitchell, Mitchell's boss Robert Piper, and Special Agent in Charge Marlin Johnson. We hoped to add their superiors in D.C., the FBI heads of COINTELPRO, Attorney General Mitchell, Jerris Leonard, and the estate of J. Edgar Hoover, who died in 1971, after we took more depositions pinpointing their roles.

In the late summer I drove out to Maywood to tell Fred's parents about the new developments. The Hamptons lived in the same two-story brick house where Fred grew up. Every year on December 4, Flint and I, along with Dennis, when he was in town, attended the memorial service for Fred at Reverend McNelty's church, followed by a big spread at the Hampton home. Almost every black political figure in Chicago had participated in the memorials at one time or another. Fred's brother Bill had set up the Hampton Scholarship Fund to select and provide support for one black law student every year. Attendees at the memorial service were encouraged to contribute.

When I arrived at the Hampton home, Iberia, wearing an apron over a flowered dress, greeted me at the door with a big hug. She led me straight to the kitchen, saying, "There's food on the stove." She knew I had grown up in the South and loved her cooking.

At her kitchen table, I devoured fried chicken, a piece of fried catfish, a large helping of macaroni and cheese, and two helpings of collard greens, my favorite, along with a tall glass of sweetened iced tea. She sat and watched, smiling, commenting that she and Francis had eaten before I got there. I begged to hold off on the peach cobbler, and we adjourned to the living room.

The Hampton living room was packed with several large stuffed chairs and two sofas. I could be comfortable in any of them as long as I didn't have to get up soon. Iberia and I sat down on her couch and soon were joined by Francis, who came from the back of the house. He gave me a warm smile when he shook my hand, and said he was glad to see me. He looked a bit wearied by the six years since Fred's death. Still, he had taken good care of himself. He farmed a plot of land in a neighboring suburb a few miles from their home, and went fishing regularly. He and Iberia still drove down to Louisiana at least twice a year. They had not given up their connection to the South and their attraction to its slow, rural lifestyle.

"We've added some new people, new defendants to the lawsuit," I began. "They worked for the FBI and we think they were responsible for setting up the raid."

Iberia's expression always changed when we began talking about Fred or his death. She'd look down at the floor and then raise her eyes up sadly, fearful but wanting to hear more. Her hair was grayer than when I had met her, and many more lines were traced in her forehead. A permanent weariness seemed to have set in.

"Fred was more than a target of the Chicago police and Hanrahan," I told them. "We think his death was instigated by FBI agents carrying out a national program targeting black leaders. FBI Director Hoover ordered those agents to stop—'neutralize' was the word they used—up and coming leaders like your son."

Iberia's expression hardened as I spoke. "I believe it!" she blurted out. "Fred was always out front, always on TV. Sometimes I wished he'd let someone else do the talking." I had heard her say this before. She resented that her son had paid the ultimate price for saying what he believed while others stood behind him and remained unharmed.

"He spoke too much truth for them to let him live," Francis added. "He didn't know how to keep quiet about injustice." His voice trailed off.

"We think the FBI used Hanrahan's ambition to get him to carry out its plan," I said. "He was more than willing." I paused a moment then continued: "Have you read about what they did to Dr. King?"

"Yeah, I read it. Blackmailed him and then suggested he kill his self," Iberia answered.

"The FBI targeted the Panthers even more than Dr. King," I replied. "And Fred was a leader they saw as a particular threat. They watched his every move."

"How was O'Neal connected to this?" Francis asked. O'Neal's role as an informant had received wide publicity.

I explained that O'Neal had been instructed by his FBI handler to go to Fred's apartment and get a floor plan. He did this, marking the location where Fred and Deborah slept, and gave it to the FBI, which passed it on to Hanrahan and the raiders.

"I brought a copy of it if you want to see it." I had hesitated bringing the floor plan with me but felt Fred's parents had a right to know. I pointed out the rectangle on which "bed" was written inside the room O'Neal had designated the "room of Hampton and Johnson when they stay here."

"Lord have mercy!" Iberia declared shaking her head. "They didn't leave nuthin to chance," she said. Tears came to her eyes.

Francis remained only slightly more composed. He was studying the details on O'Neal's sketch. "And that's where all the policemen's shots came together, right at the head of Fred's bed on the diagram," he said, pointing to the same rectangle in the back bedroom.

"Most of the bullets went in that direction," I answered. "But we think Fred was actually killed after Deborah was pulled out of the room. He was shot at close range. The direction of the bullets and the location of the bullet wounds in his head prove this."

Was I being too clinical? This was their son, and I was describing his murder. But they had never shied away from knowing the truth.

"We've added O'Neal and the FBI people in Chicago supervising him to our lawsuit," I continued. "We'd like to include the higher-ups running the Counterintelligence Program in D.C., but so far Perry has blocked us from getting the evidence against them."

"I don't like that judge," Iberia said. "He treats me and Fannie Clark like we're the criminals. He's always calling us the defendants as though we're on trial. He really doesn't like black people."

I told her I wished I could disagree, but the situation was even worse than what she knew. As much as Perry defended Hanrahan and the police, he was even more protective of the FBI. "He goes into a rage whenever we suggest that the raid was part of a federal conspiracy. The very idea is an insult to him. He acts as if his duty is to shield the FBI," I said.

"Are you ever gonna get him to do right?" Iberia asked.

"I doubt it," I responded. "I wish I could be more optimistic."

In spite of our difficulties with Judge Perry, Iberia and Francis were pleased when I described our efforts to sue everyone responsible for Fred's death.

"That's what we want you to do," she urged. "Go after them all." Francis nodded his approval.

I left the Hampton home by way of the kitchen, with a large portion of cobbler in my belly and another on a paper plate to deliver to Flint. When I hugged Iberia good-bye she said, "I love you." Then she added, "Go after everyone who killed my son."

"We will," I answered. "I love you too."

The lawsuit became more real, more human, each time I saw Iberia and Francis. The visits reminded me that the case wasn't about documents or legal motions or conflicts with Perry. It was about killing a young man in his bed, about a family who had lost their son and the movement that lost a leader.

In August, as soon as we added the federal defendants to our lawsuit, Judge Perry confirmed the trial date for January 1976. With only four months lead time and a bar on questioning anyone about COINTEL-PRO, it would be almost impossible to get the evidence we needed to prove that the policy makers in D.C. were responsible for the raid.

That fall Flint and Holly went to Washington to depose Jerris Leonard and the heads of the Counterintelligence Program. By the first week of September, with time for adding new defendants running out, we filed a motion to compel answers to deposition questions, again asking Judge Perry to order the deponents to answer our questions about COINTELPRO.

"He's gonna hold out forever," I told Flint, frustrated by how many times we had to argue the obvious.

"He'll have to," Flint responded, "because so will we."

On September 11, Flint and I went to court to argue our motion before Perry. As soon as we arrived, the shriveled old man with his double hearing aids bounded out from chambers, took the bench, and peered down at us. Our presence pumped life into his shrunken frame.

"*Hampton v. Hanrahan, et al., 70 C 1384,*" Perry's clerk called out. Flint and I walked to the rostrum six feet below the bench. Kanter stood to our left.

For an hour Flint and I argued the obvious relevance of COINTELPRO to the federal conspiracy. Perry sat above us, unfazed. We pointed out that the Counterintelligence Program itself outlined an FBI conspiracy to destroy the Panthers and neutralize charismatic black leaders, and we should be allowed to discover if its mandates led to the raid.

Kanter answered that nothing in the thirty-four documents turned over to the judge or from COINTELPRO itself "even tangentially dealt with what occurred on December 4 or the question of the raid." Judge Perry nodded approvingly.

"Let us see the documents and we'll show you how they are relevant," Flint and I responded.

Judge Perry said he'd heard enough. "I'll rule next week," he announced. Flint and I grabbed our papers and hurried out of the courtroom, shaking our heads in disgust.

A week later, Judge Perry issued his written order: "I have still found that none of these documents that have been submitted to me show any testimony relevant to this case . . . no questions [about COINTELPRO] to the deponents shall be asked."

We were out of patience and just about out of time.

Number One on the "Hit" Parade

It was November 1975, two months before our trial date. We had just moved downtown to the sixth floor of an office building three blocks from the federal court. I traded a noisy cubicle for a spacious office with large windows looking out on busy Dearborn Street. We got a deal on rental space in a building that was due to be razed in a few years.

"Holy shit. Look at these—look what I just got from Arthur Jefferson!" Flint exclaimed, holding up some papers as he came into my office followed by Dennis. Flint dropped the papers on my desk. Arthur Jefferson was a staff member of the Church Committee, the Senate subcommittee headed by senator Frank Church investigating Watergate. Jefferson had told Flint the subcommittee was broadening its investigation to look into other clandestine government activities, including COINTELPRO.

"I met Jefferson in person in Washington in September," Flint said. "He sends me FBI documents they uncover through their subpoena power, and I send him what dribbles we get through discovery here."

I read the four internal FBI memos Flint had dropped on my desk, six pages in all. My excitement rose as I went from one to the next. "These *are* crucial!"

The first document was a memo to FBI Director Hoover written by our defendant Marlin Johnson. It was captioned "Counterintelligence Program . . . (Black Panther Party)." The memo read:

> Chicago now recommends the following letter be sent to Fort, handwritten on plain paper.

> Brother Jeff:
> I've spent some time with Panther friends on the West Side lately and I know what's been going on. The brothers that run the Panthers blame you for blocking their thing and *there's supposed to be a hit out for you*

[emphasis added]. I'm not a Panther, or a Ranger, just black. From what I see these Panthers are out for themselves not black people. I think you ought to know what their [*sic*] up to. I know what I'd do if I was you. You might hear from me again.

A black brother you don't know

It is believed the above may intensify the degree of animosity between the two groups and occasion Fort to take retaliatory action, which could disrupt the BPP or lead to reprisals against its leadership.

The memo documented an FBI effort to exploit the animosity between Jeff Fort, the leader of the Blackstone Rangers, Chicago's largest and most well-armed street gang, and the Panthers. Although we had learned the general contents of the memo earlier, we had not known it was a COINTELPRO document and likely one of the thirty-four Perry had been given and refused to release. A prior effort by Marlin Johnson to have Fred killed was certainly relevant to our case, in which the FBI was claiming it was merely passing on information and had no intent to have Fred murdered.

"For some reason Fort didn't go for it," I said. "Maybe he figured the 'black brother' sounded a little white. Marlin Johnson's not exactly a street person."

"If Fort and the Rangers had retaliated against Fred, the FBI would have walked away clean," Dennis said. "No one would have known they precipitated the violence."

"I wish we'd had this when we deposed Johnson," I said. "I'd like to know how he'd justify this."

Flint pointed to the second document. It carried the same caption, "Counterintelligence Program." Like the Fort hit letter, it bore Marlin Johnson's initials. Dated December 3, 1969, it was a COINTELPRO "periodic progress report." It read:

The BPP continues to be considered the focal point of counterintelligence. Chicago has continued to advise local authorities of instances where BPP members appear vulnerable to arrest on local charges.

In this regard, Chicago letter to the Bureau dated November 21, 1969, captioned "Black Panther Party (BPP), RM" is concerned with the location in Chicago of weapons reportedly purchased legally by BPP members. This information has been furnished to local law enforcement officials. Officials of the Chicago Police Department have advised that the Department is currently planning a positive course of action relative to this information.

The "positive course of action" was the raid planned by Hanrahan's police. The document's COINTELPRO heading demonstrated that the FBI's dissemination of information to the police and Hanrahan was made pursuant to the Counterintelligence Program.

"How can Perry justify concealing *this* memo?" I asked. "This is a COINTELPRO document specifically targeting Fred, and I'm sure it's one of the thirty-four he's been sitting on."

"Perry had to think we'd never see it," Dennis said. "He didn't figure we'd get FBI documents from the Church Committee."

In one of the other two documents, Hoover directed FBI offices to "submit imaginative and hard-hitting counterintelligence programs aimed at crippling the BPP."

"That mandate requires some creativity," Dennis observed drily. "A dirty trick, in fact a crippling trick, every two weeks. I wonder what else Johnson and company tried to do to the Panthers in the year between this memo and when they killed Fred."

The fourth document was a periodic report by the San Diego FBI office dated September 18, 1969. In it, the Special Agent in Charge bragged to Hoover about the "tangible results" already accomplished in the Counterintelligence Program:

Shootings, beatings, and a high degree of unrest continues to prevail in the ghetto area of southeast San Diego. Although no specific counterintelligence action can be credited with contributing to this overall situation, it is felt that a substantial amount of the unrest is directly attributable to this program.

I was appalled both at the candid acknowledgment that "unrest" in the black community was a celebrated part of the program's objectives and that this sentiment would have been memorialized in a letter to Hoover seeking credit for the violent conditions. When I read it today, I am reminded of the CIA's counterinsurgency plan for Central America in the 1980s or the military plan for Iraq. But here the FBI was promoting violence at home against U.S. citizens and groups.

The next day, Dennis cornered Flint and me and read us parts of the motion he had typed out in response to the new documents and Hoover's specific mandate "to prevent the rise of a messiah."

A messianic figure, Fred Hampton, who could and did unite and electrify the masses of black people (and white people!) wherever he went did indeed arise in Chicago. In the atmosphere which existed at the time, with the murders of Malcolm X and Martin Luther King already accomplished, and much of the Panther leadership in jail or exile, Fred Hampton became, to the agents of government responsible for suppression of the movement, Number One on the Hit Parade: and thus he met his end.

Dennis always had a flair for the dramatic. As a lawyer, this found expression in his pleadings and arguments in court. They were often eloquent, always insightful, and sometimes a bit too accusatory for the court's ear. Flint and I frequently toned down his written drafts but always enjoyed the originals.

"I love it," I applauded. "It's Dennis unleashed!"

What Dennis read became paragraph seven of the motion for discovery and disclosure of evidence, which we filed a few days later. We attached the four documents we had received, together with others recently released by the Church Committee, which showed the FBI blackmailing and targeting Dr. King.

At the end, after accusing Perry of being "quite unenlightened by the lessons of Watergate," our motion gave him the opportunity to redeem himself, a way out from of being seen as "embedded" with the defendants.

The court's actions in affording the defendants this protection [from disclosure] are misguided to an extreme degree. We fully sympathize with the chagrin of any person so long accustomed to relying on the honesty and good faith of government officials, when it is so shockingly and undeniably shown to exist no more. But today the frightening ethic which has replaced detachment, trustworthiness, and honor in government is cover-up, deception, and plausible deniability. If the courts of our country or the judges of our country allow themselves to be made tools of this philosophy, then neither the plaintiffs nor anyone else can be expected to maintain respect for the law.

We felt there was nothing to lose by being straightforward, or more precisely, nothing to gain by being diplomatic.

On November 26, I filed the motion—fifteen pages long with fifty pages of FBI documents attached—and hand delivered copies to the pressroom, where each of the Chicago dailies had a desk.

We had developed working relationships with several investigative reporters from Chicago's newspapers: Tom Dolan from the *Chicago Sun-Times*, Rob Warden from the *Chicago Daily News*, and Bob McClory from the *Daily Defender* wrote most often about what we uncovered. They quoted us frequently, usually reporting our courtroom battles sympathetically. Why not? We provided them with revelations of illegal and clandestine government intelligence activities, certainly more newsworthy than the blanket denials from the other side. I returned to the office after filing the motion and called all of our friendly reporters. "Yeah, that's the same Marlin Johnson that Daley appointed to head the Chicago Police Board," I told Rob Warden. "But I don't think he put his anonymous communication with Fort on his resume."

The Fort hit letter made front-page news in all the papers, even the *Tribune*. Everyone in Chicago knew Jeff Fort's name, and no one took the Blackstone Rangers lightly. It was a great story, not without irony. The current head of Chicago's Police Board had assumed the guise of a "black brother," scribbling information in what he thought was black jargon, about a phony death threat in his effort to induce Fort and the Rangers to retaliate violently against Fred Hampton. Johnson's public denial that he ever intended or expected a violent reaction by the Rangers made it even more macabre.

On December 10, 1975, Dennis, Flint, and I walked into Perry's courtroom and sat down at the polished wooden table reserved for plaintiffs' attorneys. The December 4th Committee had put out the word that this was an important court date. The benches for spectators in the rear of the courtroom were full. The press packed the front row. The sketchers for the newspapers began making their drawings of the three of us. Dennis, tall and lean, with a sculpted face, a Max von Sydow profile, but with receding hair going in all directions; Flint with his blond mutton chop sideburns, tinted glasses, and serious but boyish look; and me sporting my dark Afro and bushy beard, a tad overweight, and looking skeptically at the Judge's bench, even before Perry arrived.

The FBI defendants' lawyers, Arnold Kanter and Alexandra Kwoka, were at one counsel table; Coghlan and Volini, the lawyers for the city and county defendants, sat at the other.

Judge Perry scurried out from the back of the courtroom, adjusting his hearing aid as he took his seat on the bench. He was wearing his dark glasses, which he claimed were to prevent the glare, but we thought he actually wore them to allow him to doze through our arguments. The clerk called the case, and the three of us went up to the podium.

The record says we were in court for almost three hours. Dennis, Flint, and I all took target practice at the FBI lawyers and defendants for hiding COINTELPRO and at the judge for letting them do it. This time we had the advantage of having in our possession many of the critical documents the FBI and judge were refusing to release, documents they had previously sworn did not exist or were not relevant.

We tried our best to argue the merits, but Perry only became more irritated and impatient. Then we tried to shame him into correcting his previous efforts to protect the FBI. *How could you allow them to hide these, Judge? And now they have* you *hiding them, too.* We repeated our plea that the trial be continued past the scheduled date of January 5 to allow us time to question the FBI defendants on the new documents, depose their superiors, and add new defendants.

Kanter responded as expected that COINTELPRO had nothing to do with the raid. This led to skeptical looks from the reporters, who had read our motion and seen the attached documents.

Dennis responded that two of the new COINTELPRO memos provided by the Church Committee named and targeted Hampton specifically. Perry nodded. Maybe he was wavering. Perry grabbed his papers. "I'll decide this next week," he said over his shoulder as he walked out. He often got up and walked away if we pressed an argument.

In the corridor outside, I commented to Dennis, "I think we made it into the press, but who knows if we got through to Perry."

Indeed, the press gave a lot of play to the new documents and quoted generously from our motion and our argument. If we had to start the trial without the COINTELPRO evidence, at least the world would know the FBI was responsible for the raid. On December 15, five days after the argument, I walked the three blocks from our new office downtown to the Dirksen Federal Building to pick up Perry's written ruling. I read it outside the clerk's office.

The order urged the defendants to search their files again for "records or exhibits they may have overlooked or misplaced." But Perry refused to release the COINTELPRO documents in his possession or to make the defendants answer deposition questions about the program. He concluded, "The motion is not well taken and that more particularly there is no reason to delay the trial in this cause."

That was it, the court's entire rationale. We filed a last-minute petition again asking the Seventh Circuit to reverse and recuse Judge Perry. We begged them to continue the case to allow us to proceed with discovery around COINTELPRO. Again, our appeal was denied.

Part IV

Injustice on Trial

Opening Day

We sat at the counsel table in the well of the vast Ceremonial Courtroom in the Dirksen Federal Building. After more than five years of preparation, we were starting jury selection.

The thick, dark blue carpet muffled the sounds of the attorneys and clients taking their places at the tables around me. This cavernous space was normally used for the induction of new judges or other special ceremonies. But because there were so many parties, lawyers, and spectators, as well as prospective jurors, Judge Perry had obtained permission to use it for our jury selection. Even the bench was grander than normal, a curved mahogany behemoth that rose five feet above the floor and extended twenty feet to each side, with raised chairs and room enough for several judges in the middle.

The area below was filled with six polished mahogany tables surrounded by cushioned black leather chairs on rollers. The walls were in the same dark brown wood as the tables, and the rich wood and thick carpet created a muted effect, unlike the filthy cacophony of the criminal court building. Business was conducted quietly, in a more sophisticated manner, in the federal courts.

The party with the burden of proof, the plaintiff, always sits nearest the jury. So Flint and I sat at the table only a few feet from the empty jury box. It, too, was surrounded by brown mahogany railings. I had lightly starched my shirts and dry-cleaned all three of my suits. That day I wore my brown wool one. Even Flint's blue suit showed only a few wrinkles. Seated at our table was the large and swarthy Jay Schulman, director of the National Jury Project. His belly protruded from his corduroy sport coat. Jay was a sociologist and statistician from Columbia University. For four months he and his associates had been interviewing registered voters from Chicago and its suburbs, the area from which our jury would be selected.

Jay had used surveys in the Attica, Wounded Knee, and Daniel Ellsberg trials to show that prospective jurors in well-publicized political cases had strong biases and preset opinions about the facts. Schulman's survey of the Chicago area showed that 96 percent of those interviewed had "some recollection of the events of December 4." Two-thirds had already formed an opinion, and a majority of these believed the Panthers were partially or totally at fault.

The survey also indicated that half the people thought the government should use "any means necessary" to destroy groups "which threaten the present system of government." A third said they would not award money for damages to the families of dead Panthers even if the evidence showed the police acted illegally. A vast majority said they would believe the testimony of a police officer over that of a Panther. The survey results did not surprise me and confirmed that we had an uphill battle.

We attached Schulman's affidavit containing his findings to support our motion to allow us extra peremptory challenges. We needed many times the normal number because so many prospective jurors would enter with a bias against our clients. We also gave the judge a list of questions we felt were necessary to get jurors to divulge their opinions and prejudices.

On the other side of Schulman was Jim Montgomery, relaxed and smiling, not a wrinkle in his suit.

"I hope Jim is more effective with Perry than we are," Flint said to me the day before.

"I'm sure he'll be good with the jury," I said. We were pleased to have him on the case.

Herbert Reid, an African American lawyer from the NAACP Legal Defense and Education Fund, sat next to Montgomery. Ever since their May 1972 report, *Search and Destroy*, condemning the raid, the NAACP had supported us, sometimes with funds and now with a full-time attorney for the trial. Reid, a law professor from Howard University, was an able and experienced trial attorney, but he was also in his seventies. We would learn he was prone to naps in the afternoon court sessions.

The seven survivors sat at the table next to us. Their expressions reflected their skepticism about the proceedings. "I hope we get a jury that can see through that old racist judge," Doc Satchel whispered to me shortly after he walked in. Deborah Johnson, still with her Afro, and looking more together and resigned now than when I interviewed her after Fred's murder, sat next to Doc. At our urging the plaintiffs were in their nice clothes, the women in dresses and the men in sweaters. Only Truelock was unshaven, giving a hint of his precarious life on the streets.

The Hampton and Clark families occupied the front row of the spectator section behind us. They wore guarded expressions also. They'd seen Hanrahan acquitted and didn't trust the courts. Six-year-old Fred Jr. sat next to Iberia. He was looking around curiously, swinging his legs back and forth. His large, round face and broad smile already reminded me of his dad. We wanted the jury and the press to see this six-year-old fatherless boy; Fred's brother Bill, a ganglier version of Fred, also was in the front row.

Fannie Clark, Mark's mother, sat next to the Hamptons. She was a stout woman with a matronly air, who wore magnificent hats. Flint and I went over to thank her for coming from Peoria. She gave us each a big hug. "Thank you for what you're doing," she said warmly. Three of Mark's eleven brothers and sisters were sitting with their mother. Behind the Hamptons and Clarks sat the plaintiffs' friends, our friends, and folks working with the December 4th Committee.

The police officer and state's attorney defendants stood around tables in the middle of the courtroom behind their attorneys Coghlan, Volini, and Witkowski, Coghlan's associate. They smiled, patted each other on the shoulder, and joked. Many had been through this before with Hanrahan, when they were facing obstruction of justice charges. They knew the routine: they got paid their regular salaries to wear civilian clothes and watch and doze in the courtroom.

The FBI defendants—Mitchell, Piper, and Johnson—sat calmly in gray suits at their own table across from their attorneys Arnold Kanter, Alexandra Kwoka, and Edward Christenbury, on loan from the Justice Department. Only William O'Neal was missing. The FBI was keeping a tight rein on his whereabouts. The twenty-eight defendants, nine plaintiffs, and ten lawyers filled the buffed mahogany tables. Newspaper and TV people filled in the front rows of the spectator section. Cameras weren't allowed. The sketchers with their large artist pads leaned forward from the front row in the center. Two were drawing Hanrahan, seated by himself. He had dropped out of the public eye after losing his last election. His forehead seemed furrowed in a permanent scowl.

Suddenly, Perry's clerk stood up from his raised stand on the other side of the courtroom and bellowed, "All rise." The door to the left of the bench swung open.

Perry entered and took his seat above us. He looked pleased to see the crowd below. "Be seated," the clerk called again, and there was a rustle of clothing as we all sat in unison. Perry began by hearing the motions we had filed. First, we asked him to order the defendants to tell us if any of the persons we put on our witness list had ever been government informants.

"Motion denied."

I argued our motion for extensive voir dire (questioning of the jury) and asked that we as plaintiffs be allowed extra peremptory challenges because of the prejudices our jury survey had uncovered in the jury pool. Judge Perry listened and then dismissed the National Jury Project's four months of research with one comment: "I think we overemphasize this problem of prejudice because I find when jurors are fully informed, they want to do the right thing." Schulman shook his head in disgust. Perry did agree to question the jurors individually about their recollection of the case but refused to allow us follow-up questions. Perry also ruled we could have only six peremptory challenges, fewer than he allowed the defendants.

Before we could object to his rulings, Perry told the clerk to "call the jury in." The rear doors of the courtroom on our side opened and the first fifty potential jurors entered in single file. They occupied four rows of benches, cordoned off in the center of the spectator section.

I saw only a few black faces, and the average age appeared to be around fifty. It turned out that of the four hundred persons in the special panel, only twenty-three—less than 6 percent—were black. Voter registration lists were 17 percent black. Later we learned blacks called for jury duty were excused much more easily than whites.

Perry told the candidates that the trial "will take many weeks, possibly as much as three months." In describing the incident, Perry referred to December 4 as a "gun battle," the defendants' position. He said, in his most skeptical tone, the plaintiffs "were alleging a national conspiracy to murder Fred Hampton and destroy the Panthers and that the police did all the shooting, and that there was a massive cover-up of the facts by all the defendants." Perry quickly reminded them "these are only allegations." He proceeded to tell the jurors that the defendants "vigorously denied" all our claims and their defense was that they were unexpectedly fired on when they sought to lawfully execute a search warrant.

As the questioning proceeded, Perry dismissed the jurors who claimed it would be a hardship to sit in a lengthy trial. This left housewives, retirees, and those employed by large corporations, which were required to pay their employees' salaries during jury duty. Perry made a mockery of many of the questions we had submitted. He asked all the black prospective jurors, "Are you a member of the Ku Klux Klan?" and he asked the whites, "Are you a member of the Black Panthers?" Ignoring the puzzled looks he got in response, Perry continued. He often referred to African Americans as "colored people," in spite of our objections. Perry did question the jurors individually and asked many of the questions we had submitted. But by disallowing follow-up questions, he had closed the door to exposing the depth of the jurors' biases. Day after day we sat helplessly as he quickly rehabilitated whites who expressed negative feelings about the Panthers or even black people generally. "Can you put your feelings aside and give the parties a fair trial?" was his typical follow-up question. Only the most hard-nosed and clueless racist or someone who didn't want to be on the jury answered in the negative.

The defense attorneys convinced Perry to strike black people who expressed the slightest sympathy for the Panthers or skepticism toward law enforcement. Perry did make it clear at one point in the three weeks of jury selection that he wanted at least one black juror. He told the defendants' lawyers that Florence Smith, a middle-aged, pleasant-looking black woman, was "particularly well qualified."

Ten days after the questioning started, Judge Perry imposed a gag order, prohibiting us from discussing the case with the press. He entered his order in chambers. When Flint and I objected to the gag order in open court, he told the bailiff to remove us from the courtroom.

"He wants a gag order on the existence of the gag order," I griped to Flint as we were escorted out of the courtroom temporarily.

By the fourth week of January, questioning of prospective jurors had ceased, and it was time for us to exercise our six peremptory challenges.

These gave us the right to challenge six prospective jurors without giving a rationale. We excused family members of cops. But we didn't have enough challenges to excuse the heavily bouffanted Judy Norgle, who was dating a cop! Perry refused to excuse her for cause.

"I'm sure she'll be fair," Perry said as Norgle shot us a hostile glance.

After both sides exercised all their challenges, ten people remained in the jury box, nine whites and Florence Smith. Six would be regular jurors, and four would serve as alternates. Our jury's average age was fifty, and most had no more than a high school education. This was not a good start.

"I Am No Solomon"

Jim Montgomery, in a dark tailored suit, squared his broad shoulders and rose to address the judge. His argument was our last chance to get Perry to release the FBI's COINTELPRO documents before we called our first witness. Edward Christenbury from the Justice Department had just reiterated the FBI position; COINTELPRO was "immaterial and irrelevant."

Montgomery enunciated slowly and emphatically, highlighting that our complaint charged that "the raid was accomplished as a result of COINTELPRO." We should have the opportunity to prove our allegations. There was no doubt COINTELPRO targeted the Black Panther Party, and the issue was whether the FBI program lead to the raid. The FBI defendants claimed that they were "innocently in good faith furnishing intelligence to brother law enforcement agencies." We claimed the purpose of supplying the information was to further the illegal goals of the COINTELPRO program including destroying the Black Panther Party and its leadership. Montgomery argued that COINTELPRO was critical to showing the FBI's intent.

Montgomery then gave a succinct history of the Counterintelligence Program and explained that the clear purpose of the COINTELPRO hit letter to Jeff Fort was to get Fred Hampton killed. Montgomery pointed out that the motive and intent of the defendants was a critical part of our proof and COINTELPRO was committed to "preventing the rise of a black messiah."

"We can't rely on the defendants' denial of relevancy, and if the court accepts their claims, you will have precluded us from putting on our case," Montgomery ended, putting the weight squarely on the judge.

When he finished, Perry seemed to soften his position. "I am concerned that the plaintiffs have not seen it," he responded, referring to the hit letter. Montgomery had pressed hard on *our* right to determine what evidence was relevant to our case, not the defendants.

Volini tried to save the day for the defendants, complaining that "no ruling is final," referring to Perry's numerous prior denials of our requests for COINTELPRO information.

Perry responded, "I think these counsel should have an opportunity to look at the material that I have received *in camera*. . . . I am no Solomon; I made a mistake. I have let the defendants determine what is relevant to the plaintiffs' case."

With that Perry pulled a document out from under his papers and read an order he had prepared requiring the federal lawyers to produce the entire Chicago COINTELPRO file as well as all the Chicago FBI files on O'Neal, Fred Hampton, and each of the plaintiffs.

I rolled my eyes in disbelief. Flint had a similar look. The same argument by Flint and me had been rejected so many times. I couldn't believe Perry was actually ordering the FBI to turn over the COINTELPRO files: the ones we had been seeking for two years, through ten subpoenas, seven motions, and six arguments. Looking back, it's clear that Montgomery's argument provided Perry a convenient opportunity to come off his untenable position of denying the relevance of documents he knew would be made public by the Church Committee, if not through other litigation, and that, because of their obvious evidentiary value to us in proving the FBI's motivation to neutralize the Panthers, and Hampton in particular, would only expose Perry's collusion with the federal defendants. Now, he didn't have to admit he was wrong directly to Flint and me, and he could send the message that our lawyering was the problem, not his rulings.

Flint immediately asked Perry to recess the trial until we had received and read the recently ordered documents and questioned the FBI defendants about them. He refused but said we could spend "half days" the next week questioning Johnson outside the presence of the jury.

After court Flint and I went out in the hallway. We congratulated Montgomery. He smiled, knowing he'd done a good job, but he also gave us credit. "You guys did the footwork," he said. "I just finished it off."

The press wanted to know why Perry finally reversed himself. Because we were likely to be quoted, we didn't want to slam him too hard. "Well, let's just say he was slow to understand how important COINTELPRO is to this case," was my response to press inquiries.

Flint and I followed the reporters to the pressroom and briefed them further on why the FBI's Counterintelligence Program was behind the raid and how the release of documents would be critical to proving this. "It started with Hoover," Flint told them. "It ended at 2337, but it was part of a common conspiracy and COINTELPRO provided the directions." We had some of the COINTELPRO documents released to the Watergate Committee, ready to give them. "Yes, I think 'neutralize the BPP' includes killing," I said. "It sends the message while maintaining deniability."

We called Marlin Johnson as our first witness. With COINTELPRO no longer out of bounds, he would have to acknowledge and explain its mandates. He admitted that he received the August 1967 directive to set up a COINTELPRO operation in Chicago whose purpose was to neutralize black leaders and to "prevent the rise of a messiah" who could unite the black movement. Johnson also admitted to receiving Hoover's memo urging FBI offices to use local law enforcement to harass and disrupt black groups, and that he authored the memo to Hoover wholeheartedly approving the goals of COINTELPRO. Nevertheless, contradicting the explicit entreaties in the COINTELPRO memos, Johnson repeatedly asserted that "the purpose of COINTELPRO was to prevent violence." Perry would not let Montgomery impeach Johnson by showing that Dr. King was one of the leaders targeted by COINTELPRO. Because many COINTELPRO memos were titled "COINTELPRO—Black Nationalist Hate Groups," Montgomery asked Johnson for his definition of a black nationalist group. Johnson's answer was "any black organization that had a national headquarters."

Johnson testified that he received and read only the COINTELPRO documents on which his initials appeared, and only a "part" of those. He portrayed COINTELPRO as a minor program run by a small section of his office, barely making the radar screen of someone as busy as himself. Johnson claimed he had no recollection of any specific action he took to implement the program in Chicago. He "did not recall" receiving Hoover's memo calling on all FBI offices to "submit imaginative, hard-hitting counterintelligence measures aimed at crippling the BPP," even though it was addressed and routed to him. The growing chorus to Montgomery's questions was "I don't recall." The COINTELPRO memos addressed to Johnson were admitted into evidence even if Johnson claimed no memory of them.

"How could this guy with such a pathetic memory serve as chair of Chicago's police board?" I leaned over and asked Flint.

On the second day of cross-examination, Montgomery read Johnson the contents of the letter he authorized warning Fort about the supposed hit out on him by the Panthers. He also read Johnson's memo to Hoover explaining that the purpose of his letter was to get Fort to take "retaliatory action" and carry out "retribution against Panther leaders." Johnson insisted a hit was "nonviolent," and no physical harm or violence was intended. "I would never approve any document in this program, *Sir*, where I felt the results of the program would lead to violence." Johnson claimed the "retribution" he intended to follow from his letter meant "disorganization."

"So your intent was not that Jeff Fort blow somebody's head off as a result of this?" Montgomery asked the question on everyone's mind.

"Yes sir, that is correct." Johnson replied, because there was an "FBI understanding" that the program and letter were intended to be nonviolent. I heard muffled laughter from the back of the courtroom.

Montgomery followed up, asking Johnson if anyone explained the FBI understanding to Jeff Fort.

"No."

"Are you aware Fort had only a sixth-grade education?"

"No."

Montgomery asked Johnson what he'd meant by "I know what I'd do if I was you."

"It meant nothing as far as I was concerned. It was just more street language put in there to make it sound more realistic." Johnson crossed and recrossed his legs, directing an occasional inappropriate smile at the judge, trying to defuse the absurdity of his answers.

"What is it that you know about the Rangers that would indicate that no harm would come to the Panther leaders as a result of this letter?" Montgomery pressed on.

"I considered an anonymous letter to be practically nothing. . . . I doubted that it would even be read."

I glanced at the jury. Florence Smith was shaking her head back and forth in disbelief. She knew more about the Rangers than Johnson wanted her to.

That evening Bob Greene, a columnist for the *Chicago Sun-Times*, wrote a satirical editorial entitled, "No Hits, No Guns, No Terror." He interviewed several organized crime experts and asked them for their definition of a hit. Their answers were "a contract for murder" and "to kill, or eradicate."

The next day Johnson continued his vocabulary jumble. One of the COINTELPRO documents he authored praised O'Neal's actions as "an indication of the use of this source (O'Neal) in harassing and impelling the criminal activities of the Panthers locally." Johnson testified that he understood *impelling* to mean *restraining*. There were more snickers in the courtroom. The primary definitions of *impelling*, according to the *Webster's Unabridged Dictionary, 2nd Edition* that was retrieved from the judge's chambers, were "to drive or urge forward to incite to action, to give an impulse to." Johnson claimed he knew nothing of O'Neal's provocative acts.

Johnson denied any knowledge of the floor plan before or after the raid. He also claimed he was never told there were illegal weapons at 2337 and if he had this information, he was required to pass it on to the ATF. Instead, he simply denied receiving it.

Even though it came from SAC Chicago, the acronym for his official title, Johnson claimed no recollection of the contents of the December 3 COINTELPRO memo from himself to Hoover describing the passing of information about 2337 (and the weapons stored there) to the state's attorney. Similarly he didn't know what was meant by the "positive course of action" he expected to be taken in response.

Constant objections by the defense and Johnson's consistent loss of recollection made his cross-examination long and tedious. When Montgomery probed Johnson about the usefulness of a floor plan in a raid, the judge called his questions "speculative." When Montgomery asked Johnson why the ATF was not given the information about a sawed-off shotgun, Perry intervened and said the question was "far afield." Perry told the jury that O'Neal's receiving increased payments because the FBI reported his effectiveness at carrying out the FBI's COINTELPRO objectives was "not an issue."

Toward the end of his questioning, Montgomery came down with the flu. He asked me to finish the cross-examination. February 26 was my first day questioning a witness before this jury. I was nervous approaching the podium in the intimidating atmosphere of the grand federal courtroom. By this time we had moved to a regular courtroom, but the atmosphere was the same.

I asked Johnson what he understood to be the purpose of the federal grand jury, the words coming out hesitatingly at first.

"Leonard told me he was primarily interested in the June 4 raid," he responded. (A blatant lie.) My nervousness and dry mouth vanished as I listened to his absurd answer. Johnson was trying to justify his failure to tell the grand jury about the FBI role in obtaining the floor plan and initiating the raid. He knew the grand jury was about December 4 and he had already admitted meeting with Assistant Attorney General Leonard, who was in charge of the grand jury, several times. Later, I got him to acknowledge that Leonard wanted to know what the FBI told Hanrahan's raiders before the raid. Johnson claimed he never told the grand jury prosecutors about either the floor plan or illegal guns, because he was never told those things before the raid or by the unknown "staff person" who briefed him before his grand jury testimony.

I challenged Johnson's claim of ignorance. "Wasn't it your responsibility to investigate Leonard's request?" I asked. The defense lawyers stood up and objected to give him more time to answer. Johnson asked for the question to be read back three times.

All he could come up with after the delay was "I would have felt they [whoever briefed him] knew, but I do not recall whom I asked." He admitted he never asked Mitchell, the person he knew was involved, or Piper, his supervisor, for information about the raid. Johnson denied knowing about the deal between Hanrahan and Leonard to assure there would be no disclosure of the FBI role, even though the April 8 FBI memo specifically states he was told of the agreement by FBI agent Leonard Treviranus. Perry refused to permit me to confront Johnson either with the document or Treviranus's testimony.

That night a local newspaper described Johnson as someone "whose memory seems to be deteriorating during questioning." His lawyers seemed at a loss on how to rehabilitate him, but Perry did the rehabilitation himself. The next day he told the jury that Johnson "was not evasive at all." This comment was a gross violation of the Judge's supposed impartiality and an invasion of the jury's duty to assess the credibility of the witnesses, but for Judge Perry it was business as usual.

The Deluge

Roy Mitchell, the point man in the FBI conspiracy and O'Neal's handler, walked to the witness box a few feet in front of us on March 11 to begin his testimony. His crew cut was even shorter than at his deposition. His stiff posture and military bearing gave him a straight appearance that contradicted what we knew from his deposition.

In our most recent discovery, we received a COINTELPRO memo that indicated Mitchell instructed O'Neal to create a rift between the Panthers and SDS by circulating racist cartoons and attributing them to SDS. Another showed O'Neal proudly reporting to Mitchell that as chief of security he had devised a "security plan" for Panther headquarters that included nerve gas and an electric chair. Mitchell still denied that he or O'Neal was following COINTELPRO directives. Other Mitchell memos showed O'Neal reporting to him on Fred's daily activities in late 1969, as well as the content and attendance at his speeches. O'Neal told Mitchell about Fred and Deborah renting the apartment in October and that Fred met with national Panther leaders and "would take Hilliard's position on the central staff if he [Hilliard] went to jail."

As Montgomery's inquiries moved forward chronologically to the period before the raid, Mitchell testified about a speech Fred gave in Chicago in November 1969. The cross-examination was going smoothly enough, if not dramatically.

Montgomery: "What information did [O'Neal] give you other than that he was making a speech?"

Mitchell: "Well, he's given me information about Mr. Hampton and a few other Panthers traveling to Rockford, Illinois."

Montgomery: "At some time he told you about his speech—"

Coghlan [*interjecting*]: "I don't believe the witness completed his answer, Your Honor."

Perry: "Well, I thought he had, but if he hadn't, he may do so. Is there something further?"

Mitchell had gotten a cue from Coghlan. He hesitated, but for only a moment. "Yes, Your Honor, when they were contemplating killing a state police officer."

Perry: "I stand corrected, Mr. Coghlan."

Montgomery came over to the table where Flint and I were seated. He leaned over and whispered, "The motherfucker just sandbagged me. Do we have any document reflecting what he's saying?"

"No," Flint and I responded in unison shaking our heads.

Montgomery returned to the lectern. I saw a sinister smile on Coghlan's face.

Montgomery: "Did you make a written memo of that? What you just said?"

Mitchell: "I don't know if it's recorded."

Montgomery: "Have you read anything with that in it?"

Mitchell: "I believe so, yes."

Montgomery: "Where is it?"

Mitchell: "I assume it's in the FBI files."

Montgomery [*curtly*]: "Would you produce it, please? Thank you."

Mitchell was trapped. He had made a striking accusation against Fred Hampton. If there were no report memorializing this, then he would look like a liar. If there was one, we should have received it in discovery. Every day for the next two weeks after cross-examination, we asked Mitchell if he had found the missing Rockford document. At one point he claimed he had "gone through thirty volumes of files trying to locate it," but had not found it.

Flint's ears perked up. "How could he be looking through thirty volumes of files when we supposedly have the complete files, which are less than one volume?"

Kanter jumped in stating emphatically we had received all the files with information from or about O'Neal.

"The entire informant file?" Flint asked.

Kanter: "That's correct."

Taylor: "Could we have an affidavit on that?"

Perry: "That's not necessary."

After two weeks of questioning Mitchell, Perry told Montgomery, "I expect you to conclude with this witness this afternoon." Montgomery focused on the key points in the conspiracy. Roy Mitchell again admitted he had "five to seven" meetings with Jalovec, including a face-to-face meeting at the State's Attorney's Office on the morning of December 1 or 2 with Jalovec and Groth, and there he had told them about illegal weapons at 2337.

Montgomery: "Did you draw them a floor plan?"

Mitchell: "I had notes with me, yes, I do not recall them taking notes, whatsoever."

Montgomery: "Did you show this outline to Groth and Jones?"

Mitchell: "They could have seen it, yes. I took it over there with the purpose of disseminating it to them. They didn't appear that interested in it."

Montgomery: "Did you show it to them?"

Mitchell: "I believe so."

Montgomery: "Did you discuss the possibility of conducting a raid?"

Mitchell: "We never discussed a raid in the five to seven meetings. . . . I did tell Jalovec that Fred Hampton, Deborah Johnson, Louis Truelock, and Doc Satchel frequented the apartment."

By agreement, I interrupted Montgomery's cross-examination and asked Mitchell if he had found the missing memo.

Mitchell: "That document was found last night. It's being prepared. It will be ready sometime this afternoon."

How convenient. Just after he expects to leave the witness stand.

As Mitchell was stepping down, I asked him to tell us where he'd found the document.

Perry: "Now just a minute. Let's put him on the witness stand and get it all."

Perry was hoping to help Mitchell but had inadvertently volunteered him to answer questions on the missing document under oath.

Mitchell [*back on the witness stand*]: "I have found the document, yes."

Haas: "In what file did you locate it?"

Mitchell: "In the file captioned 'Powell.'"

Haas: "Was a copy of that document in the Black Panther file?"

Mitchell knew the FBI had been ordered to produce that file for us in discovery.

Mitchell: "I did not find it there."

A clever nonanswer.

I asked Mitchell why it took him so long to find the Rockford document. He testified that he'd looked for days in the Panther file but admitted his search did not include the time period of the Rockford incident. Mitchell said he then switched to the much smaller Lincoln Powell file and found it in half an hour. We had never asked for the Lincoln Powell file; in fact we had never heard the name, so finding it there would not expose that the FBI had withheld files Perry ordered.

In the afternoon, Kanter sheepishly admitted that copies of the document were also in the files titled "Hampton," "O'Neal," and "Black Panther." "Well, why were they not produced?" Judge Perry asked.

Kanter: "I must apologize, because it has been my understanding. . . . We will take a recess and bring up the whole file."

Christenbury: "I would now, for what it's worth, apologize to the court and to counsel. We did misunderstand the court's order. . . . I apologize for the inconvenience it has caused the court and other counsel."

Court recessed until 9:30 A.M. the next day.

"Sorry we concealed all those documents for so long and told everyone they didn't exist," I mimicked the straight-laced Christenbury in the hallway when Flint and I left court.

"That's OK," Flint replied in the same sarcastic tone. "Just because we are in the third month of the trial and may have to start all over, it's just a slight inconvenience."

"Seriously, what are we going to do if they produce a lot more material?" I asked.

"I don't know," he replied. "We've been fighting so long to get the documents. Now I can't see how we can use them effectively without a long delay."

The next morning, Flint, Montgomery, Dennis (just back from Attica), and I waited in court. Maybe, just maybe, the FBI was going to come clean. I had alerted the media and they were present with sketchpads in hand.

Twenty minutes later both doors at the rear of the court swung open. I heard the rattle of wheels rolling down the corridor outside. A gray cart emerged through the doorway, pushed by Assistant U.S. Attorney Kwoka. Its two shelves were packed with black bound notebooks. There was more rattling from the hallway, and Christenbury entered pushing an identical cart, followed by Kanter wheeling a third one. The procession continued down the aisle of the courtroom past the spectator benches, past the attorneys' tables, and came to rest at the podium before the judge.

Kanter stood next to the carts, looking up at Perry like a disobedient puppy. A quick count showed fifty 500-page volumes from the Hampton and O'Neal files, which should have been produced long ago and certainly in January. The remainder, another 150 volumes, held Black Panther Party files. The parts of those relating to our clients were supposed to have been produced. FBI Agent Deaton testified that Piper and Kanter told him what to turn over. *Let the jury hear that,* I thought. *Concealing evidence is evidence of guilt.*

How could we possibly read, catalog, and use this material effectively two months into the trial? It's impossible. It can't be done. It's outrageous. We need to start all over and they need to pay for their concealment.

With the press staring at him and the withheld evidence before him, Perry repeated that these were documents he had previously ordered produced. Flint said it would take us six months to read and catalogue the material after the FBI copied and excised it, not to mention another several weeks asking the FBI defendants in depositions if they had read or authored the reports. In a quick huddle at a court break, Flint suggested that we ask for sanctions and a mistrial. Montgomery was hesitant to start all over, so we agreed to pursue sanctions only.

Flint walked to the podium. "Your Honor, we want to file a motion for sanctions and contempt against the federal defendants and their lawyers for deliberately concealing this evidence and for violations of the discovery rules. We also want to question Kanter on his role in keeping the documents secret."

Perry looked befuddled for a moment, shifting through the papers on his desk as if the answer were there. Then suddenly he regained his composure and declared, "It was a mistake, negligence on the part of the FBI.

"Call the jury in," he told the clerk, before we could respond.

"Hard to overlook one hundred and fifty volumes," Flint replied.

After the FBI lawyers had removed the carts, the jury was brought in. "There's been a misunderstanding of my rulings," Perry told them. "We are going to recess this case for another week. You should blame me, not any of the parties or their lawyers."

The jurors shook their heads, annoyed and puzzled at another delay. They would have found out the reason that afternoon, but Judge Perry had ordered them not to read the papers. "Government Caught Hiding Thousands of Files," one of the headlines ran. Our jurors were among the few adults in Chicago who were never informed that the FBI had been caught hiding evidence.

O'Neal Gets a Bonus

During the week of recess, the FBI delivered a batch of documents from the newly produced files in court every day. Some showed O'Neal tracking Hampton's every move. Others showed O'Neal involved in criminal activities.

On April 8, during a recess, Flint and I were scanning the newest ones. I stopped short and reread a one-page document. "Flint, this is unbelievable. It's what we've been waiting for!" I said, unable to contain my excitement. I thought we had them at last. I handed the sheet to Flint. It was a one-page airtel, or air telegram, from Piper to Hoover dated December 11, a week following the raid. The document sought a "special payment" to O'Neal because

> he provided a detailed inventory of the weapons and also a detailed floor plan of the apartment at 2337 W. Monroe . . . to local authorities. This information was not available from any other source and proved to be of tremendous value in that it subsequently saved injury and possible death to police officers participating in a raid at the address on the morning of 12/4/69. The raid was based on the information furnished by informant. It is felt that this information is of considerable value in consideration of a special payment to informant.

The document was an admission that O'Neal, not Groth's supposed informant, was the source of information for the warrant and the raid. What was particularly haunting was Piper's cold assessment that a bonus was due the informant because of his role in Fred and Mark's deaths and that local FBI agents were claiming credit for the murderous raid. In the same pile with Piper's bonus request we found a similar memo urging a reward for O'Neal from Roy Mitchell, as well as an FBI memo approving the bonus. In another newly produced document Mitchell described O'Neal as a "counterintelligence agent," which Mitchell had repeatedly denied on the witness stand.

"We should have had these when Mitchell was testifying," Flint said. We have to get sanctions." But Perry refused to grant us even a hearing on the sanctions motion we filed. He accused us of "filing motions in the newspapers" and stalling. He said he would consider the sanctions motion at the end of the trial—when it would no longer be a viable remedy. The FBI was allowed to benefit from its secreting of documents. We were the ones he punished. Perry withdrew his agreement to allow us to recall Mitchell and ordered, "Call your next witness."

"The plaintiffs will call Robert Piper," I said angrily. Because we were still getting documents, I asked Perry to postpone my questioning of Piper.

The Court: "I'm telling you, you've got a witness on the stand and we will not hear anything until you proceed with this witness. Proceed."

Haas: "We would like to have the evidence before we proceed with the witness."

The Court: "Proceed, Mr. Haas. You've had thousands of documents."

When Piper took the witness stand, he still wore that smirk he'd worn at his deposition, but he was no longer shielded by the judge's orders prohibiting questions about COINTELPRO. When I confronted Piper with his paper trail, he admitted to most of the facts that outlined the conspiracy. It just took a long time. Seven weeks in fact, much of which was spent at nights as well as in court reviewing the remainder of the many volumes of files the FBI had finally produced.

During Piper's testimony the FBI produced two new volumes of instructions to FBI agents that bore Piper and Johnson's signatures. These directed FBI agents to "destroy what the BPP stands for," "escalate actions against the BPP," and "destroy the Breakfast for Children Program."

Piper testified that Mitchell had immediately notified him when Fred and Deborah moved into 2337 and that he was passing on information about guns in the apartment to Hanrahan's office and the Gang Intelligence Unit. Piper passed the information to Marlin Johnson because he knew Johnson was "vitally interested in the Panthers and Fred Hampton." A far different image than the aloofness Johnson tried to project. Piper testified that Mitchell told him on December 1 or 2 that the weapons were being returned to Hampton's apartment.

Nevertheless, Piper called GIU head Thomas Lyons and told him that the Panthers were expecting a raid. Lyons assured Piper the GIU would not go ahead.

Piper never informed either the ATF or FBI headquarters that there were illegal weapons in the apartment, which would have required them to take action themselves. Instead, he approved Mitchell's meetings with Groth and Jalovec to set up the raid and provide them the floor plan. On December 3, Piper initialed the COINTELPRO status report to Hoover stating the Chicago FBI office expected a "positive course of action" to result.

Later, when the federal grand jury met, Piper provided the case agent, Treviranus, with negative information about the Panthers and Fred Hampton. He never divulged the existence of the floor plan or that the FBI initiated the raid or was the source for the search warrant.

With Plaintiff's Exhibit 83—the document memorializing his request for O'Neal's bonus—in my hand, I approached Piper. I asked him if he'd authored that document. "Yes," he had. And "yes," O'Neal had provided the information for the raid and "yes" O'Neal deserved a bonus for the results. Piper remained unabashedly proud of the FBI's contribution and enjoyed his opportunity to take credit publicly. In what may or may not have been a slip of the tongue, Piper's exuberance got away from him, and he described the raid as a "success." I stopped questioning him for a moment to contemplate the best response.

"You consider it a success because Hampton and Clark were killed, don't you?" A pause. Piper's lawyers must have been afraid Piper's arrogance might get him to agree, so they intervened and objected to prevent him from answering. I made another effort to confront him.

Haas: "Now, Mr. Piper, was it your belief in 1969 that because the Panthers were a threat, that you and the FBI had a right to violate their constitutional rights?"

The Court: "Objection sustained. [None had been made.] That is not the type of question to ask the witness, and you know it, counsel. It is time you begin to ask correct questions. The difficulty of those questions is that it infers an answer—if the question goes unanswered, it is something the jury may hold against the witness."

Haas: "Your Honor, this is cross-examination of a defendant, I believe."

The Court: "This is cross-examination. Will you shut up?"

Haas: "Well, I object to the court's remarks, Your Honor."

The Court: "Objection noted and overruled. Just one more quip from you, and I will hold you in contempt."

All this took place in front of the jury. At the first recess I responded.

Haas: "Yes, Your Honor, I am forced, I think, because of Your Honor's comments, to move for a mistrial based on what happened this morning. I believe we were . . ."

The Court: "Motion denied."

By June, after six months of trial, only three defendants had testified, although we had uncovered thousands of secreted files. I feared our jury was hopelessly bored and confused by the endless delays and objections as well as prejudiced by Perry's hostile and disdainful remarks. "Panther Trial Slowed by Discovery of Documents" one news story ran, describing the "twenty shelf feet of files" the U.S. attorneys had wheeled into court. Jim Montgomery was beginning to leave courtroom duties to Flint and me as he tended to his own criminal caseload. He saw the trial becoming endless.

The routine was wearing all of us down. My one regular escape from the pressure of the courtroom was yoga. I had learned the ten postures of hatha yoga, beginning with the sun salutations and ending with the headstand. In the morning and sometimes after court at the beach, when it was warm, I would look at the world upside down for five minutes, my head and forearms supporting my body. The world looked different, sometimes clearer. I always finished refreshed. I also was what people considered a polar bear in Chicago. I swam in Lake Michigan most of the year. By June, I swam off the rocks at Lincoln Park and had most of the still-freezing lake to myself.

December 4, Revisited

The seven raid survivors testified during the summer, from June until September, most of it during lengthy cross-examination. Doc Satchel walked to the witness stand hunched over at the waist from his bullet wounds and resulting surgeries and stitches. Slight, with a boyish face, he had left his premed courses at the University of Illinois to join the Panthers and eventually headed up the medical clinics.

On the night of the raid, Doc had been asleep in the front bedroom when the police came to the front door. "I was awakened by what sounded like a knock on the door," he testified. "I began to listen to become alert to what was going on, when I heard gunshots. They sounded as if they came from the front of the apartment."

Doc tried to wake the others in the first bedroom, yelling for them to get down as more shots were fired. He was lying on the floor himself in the dark between two beds when he heard "a rapid succession of shots and noticed that I was hit several times, and I hollered in agony and I heard them [Verlina and Blair] holler in agony also. From the doorway a voice said, 'We got 'em, we got 'em.'"

Doc testified that he yelled, "I'm shot, and I can't move." Then he heard, "If Black Panthers kill police, police will kill Black Panthers." Doc was ordered to stand up and walk out. When he stumbled, the police told him "Get up, Nigger." He dragged himself up and hobbled out. The police pushed everyone into the kitchen. One police officer told Doc, "You won't be able to have kids now," and the other officers laughed.

Doc was shot four times from knee to stomach. His colon was torn up and was partially removed. During his month-long stay in the hospital, he was handcuffed to his bed twenty-four hours a day.

"Would you show the jury the scar from your bullets wounds?" Montgomery asked. Doc raised his shirt to expose an eight-inch gray and scarlet scar running from his lower chest to his abdomen. It was crisscrossed with stitch marks. At Montgomery's request, Doc pointed to the entry points of the two .45-caliber bullets that struck his stomach. The pain, the operations, and his lengthy rehabilitation had destroyed his former buoyancy.

Harold Bell, with his large muscular body, looked stiff and uncomfortable as he took the stand. He testified that he woke up in the living room to the police knock and ran to the back to wake up Fred. "I shook the chairman, I shook him twice, and he just looked up like he was sleeping, just raised his head up and opened his eyes and his head went back down."

Unable to rouse the chairman, Harold crouched in the corner of the bedroom to avoid being shot. A police officer stuck a shotgun into the room, saw Harold, and pulled him out. Harold was pushed to the floor on his stomach, and his hands were cuffed behind him.

Harold testified that the police continued shooting from the kitchen until Truelock called out from the bedroom that there was a pregnant girl in there. During a pause, Truelock and Deborah came out from the bedroom. Harold heard a raider say, "That's Fred Hampton." He saw Gloves Davis in the kitchen, and he and another officer fired into Fred's bedroom. After more shots, he heard a raider ask, "Is he dead?" Then Harold heard, "Bring him out," followed by the thud of something hitting the floor. Harold later saw Fred lying in the dining room, blood dripping from his head.

Harold described the raid as similar to military operations he had witnessed in Vietnam because the raiders moved to a series of vantage points under covering fire, quickly gaining control of the apartment. There was no cross-examination.

In late summer, Louis Truelock, whose testimony was the most problematic of the plaintiffs, was due to testify. Not only did he have a substantial criminal record, he had made the sworn statement to my law partners claiming he'd fired a pump rifle at the police as he ran down the hallway to rouse Fred. This statement had been the focus of Hanrahan's and the raiders' criminal defense.

We had no choice but to call Truelock. If we didn't, the defendants would. Even without his testimony, they could put his statement in as evidence of an admission.

Flint was going to be away during Truelock's testimony. I had no one to watch my back. Montgomery only came to court occasionally now. Herbert Reid's presence in the courtroom was becoming less frequent and he seldom spoke. Herb had signed on for a long trial, but we were in our ninth month with no end in sight. His energy waned.

When Truelock came to my office for his trial preparation, his clothes were disheveled, and it was clear he was living on the streets. His hair and beard had changed from salt-and-pepper to mostly white, and he looked haggard. Still I felt a bond from my first interview, and he trusted me.

"It ain't gonna be fun," I told him. "They're going to grill you about the statement. You remember what that was like in Hanrahan's trial."

"Yeah, and Sears [the special prosecutor] didn't try to protect me. He didn't object to any of their questions."

"Well, I'll do my best to stop them," I said," but the judge doesn't listen to me."

"You know Jeff, I never picked up a gun. I told you that the first day. Later, when people were saying I was the snitch, I wanted it to look like I had done something to save Fred."

I believed Truelock, because of what he told me originally and because there was no pump rifle, bullets, shell casings, or resulting bullet holes that matched a shot from the hallway.

"So keep it simple," I said. "Just tell the jury what you told me when we first talked and what you said today about the statement. We can handle the truth." He relaxed a little.

Truelock told me that it was primarily O'Neal who accused him of setting Fred up. Before that they had been friends, and O'Neal frequently bragged to him about burglaries and robberies he committed. When Fred saw O'Neal carrying a gun, he ordered him to stop and changed his role from bodyguard to errand runner. Truelock said O'Neal once pulled out a satchel full of explosives and told him they could use them to blow up an armory and get some guns. He had putty, blasting caps, and plastic bottles filled with some kind of liquid, which he said was an explosive.

In court Truelock testified that he woke to a knock followed by voices and then gunshots. He ran down the hall to wake Fred.

"Did you have anything in your hands?" I asked.

"No!" He said he couldn't wake Fred up and after a lot of shooting, he called out that there was a "pregnant sister" in the room. After Deborah and he were pulled out and placed in the kitchen, he heard more gunshots and later saw Fred's body lying on the door. He had to walk around it when he was led out the front. He was then taken to the Wood Street station.

"And what happened there?"

"Objection," Coghlan intervened.

"Sustained," Perry responded. The judge wasn't about to let Truelock testify about his overhearing the Wood Street police say, "Rush is next."

I asked Truelock if he ever told anyone from my office that he had fired at the police. He said he had. It was because some Panthers, particularly O'Neal, were labeling him an informant. Truelock then started to describe O'Neal's provocative role in the party. The objections started flying from all the defendants' lawyers that O'Neal's illegal acts were "irrelevant." Perry excused the jury and sustained their objections.

The next day I questioned Truelock outside the presence of the jury. "Panther Misdeeds Urged by FBI Spy" (the UPI headlines) went out all over the country and even made it to the Atlanta papers. The news stories contained Truelock's description of O'Neal's efforts to induce Panthers to commit burglaries and robberies and use explosives. Our jury never heard it.

One morning in September, when Truelock was scheduled to continue testifying, he wasn't in court. Perry came out on the bench and asked where the witness was. I had to admit I didn't know. Three phone calls later, I had no new information. I told the judge I had not been able to reach Truelock, perhaps he was sick. Could we recess for the day? Sensing blood, the defendants' attorneys said if they were not allowed to finish cross-examination, his direct testimony should be stricken, his statement admitted, and the jury should be informed that he had refused to return. I begged for time. Judge Perry gave me until the next morning to produce Truelock or get proof he was dead or in a hospital somewhere.

It was 11:00 A.M. on a very hot day when I went out to find Truelock. PLO had no investigative staff. I drove out to the West Side to the last address I had for Truelock and climbed to the third floor and knocked.

A middle-aged woman in a housedress came to the door. "Does Louis Truelock live here?" I asked.

"Sometimes," she said, "but he didn't come home last night."

"Do you know where I can find him? I'm his lawyer and he needs to come to court."

"Sometimes he stays at his daughter's house, but she ain't got a phone." The woman described the building where his daughter lived, several blocks away.

I was sweating as I entered the unlocked front door of a dilapidated three-story building. There was a strong urine smell in the stairway. *This is the pits*, I thought. *Here I am trying to find my client, who was getting roasted on the witness stand, to coax him back.* At the top of the stairs, I knocked on the apartment door. No answer. Then I heard some rustling noises inside. Another long wait. "Who's there?" a woman's voice finally asked.

"It's Jeff Haas. I'm Louis Truelock's lawyer. He needs to come to court."

A few minutes later Truelock appeared, red-eyed and half awake but a welcome sight.

"Let's go have some breakfast," I suggested.

"Man, I can't take their shit no more," he said over scrambled eggs and toast at a nearby diner.

"You gotta hang in there, not only for you but for the Hamptons and Mrs. Clark."

"You know I'm telling the truth, but the judge don't want to hear it," he said.

I explained that if he didn't finish, they would argue from his statement that he fired at the police. "Only you can testify that the statement's not true."

"OK," he said. "I'll be there."

"Do you want to stay with me tonight, or I can get you a motel room?"

"No, I'm straight."

We agreed I'd pick him up at his daughter's for court at eight the next morning.

I spent the rest of my day worrying whether Truelock would be there. But he was, and even wore a clean shirt. After breakfast I drove him to court. I mumbled something to Perry about Truelock having a bad headache. Perry admonished him to be on time. Truelock resumed testifying. He didn't excel on cross, but he endured. We had just dodged a bullet.

When Jim Montgomery called Deborah to the witness stand, a hush descended on the courtroom. She was a large woman with a big Afro. She identified six-year-old Fred Hampton Jr., sitting with Iberia and Francis, as her and Fred's son. She testified that he often asked about his father, whom Deborah spoke of with reverence, elongating the name "Fre-ed." She fell in love with him the first time she saw him. They had moved into 2337 West Monroe in October, but Fred didn't always sleep there because of security concerns. Sometimes he stayed at his parents' house in Maywood. Fred never used drugs and only "once or twice" had she seen him with a beer. When Deborah found out she was pregnant, Fred wanted them to be together and raise their child. They talked about marriage.

On December 3, they went to bed after midnight. Fred called his parents but fell asleep on the phone. Deborah had to finish the conversation with Fred's sister, Dee Dee. Deborah testified she woke up to gunfire. Harold was shaking Fred, trying to wake him. The bullets were coming so fast that "the mattress was shaking . . . Fred never really woke up. He just raised up slowly and put his head back down." Deborah crawled on top of Fred to protect him. After someone in the room yelled, "We got a pregnant sister in here," the police pulled her out and made her stand in the kitchen. Two police entered the bedroom.

"One of the policeman asked, 'Is he still alive?' I heard two shots, then 'He's good and dead now.'" Deborah broke down in tears several times. She had expected she and Fred would raise their child together, and Fred would support them. Deborah testified that she had no blood on her nightgown as she was pulled out of the bedroom and did not see blood on Fred at that point. Montgomery uncovered the mattress, which had been placed in front of the jury. The top third was covered with dried blood. Deborah broke down crying. She said the blood was not there or on Fred when she left the bedroom.

An Honest FBI Man

The autumn leaves lay wet on the ground in late October when Robert Zimmers, the FBI's most senior and respected firearms examiner, came to Chicago. I met him at his hotel room on Lincoln Park West, across from the zoo. Zimmers had already told the federal grand jury that only one shot could have come from the Panthers. He would be a key witness for us.

Zimmers was a smallish man in his sixties with a short crew cut, and he appeared to be a by-the-books kind of guy. But he was more personable than I expected. He opened his briefcase to pull out his notes and we got to work. Two things stood out as we discussed his findings. One was his objectivity in examining and testing the physical evidence and stating his conclusions. The other was his disdain for the sloppy work and false reports of the Chicago Police Crime Lab. We would later write in our appellate brief, "Of the government officers to become involved in this case, only Zimmers firmly placed his obligation to the truth above his fealty to 'Law Enforcement.'"

He showed me that Sadunas's false matching of the two shotgun shells found in the apartment to Brenda Harris's weapon could not have been an honest mistake. He compared the firing pin marks on those shells with the marks on shells he had test-fired from the shotgun the police claimed Brenda was holding. He put one of the shells found at the apartment under one side of a double-lens microscope and the shell he test-fired from Brenda's weapon under the other. He pulled out photos of the hammer marks. They were totally dissimilar. "Sadunas was experienced enough to see the difference. He must have yielded to pressure."

We spent that evening and the next going over his examinations, test-firings, and each of his conclusions. By the time I put him on the stand, I was confident he knew his stuff and, just as important, I actually understood it. Zimmers was a thirty-year veteran of the FBI, and he'd been selected to work on the Kennedy assassination. His credentials and impartiality would be difficult for government lawyers to challenge. Nevertheless, they had objected to his using the scale model he'd prepared for the federal grand jury until he'd gone back to Washington with the scale model and redrilled several of the holes he had not originally made himself. To stall more, the defendants refused to stipulate that the weapons examined by Zimmers were the ones carried by the cops.

A point of contention throughout the trial had been whether to refer to the events of December 4 as a "raid," as we would have it, or as "the service of a search warrant," the terms the defendants wanted. They often objected when we labeled the incident a "raid," but the defendants' attorneys often slipped and called it a "raid" themselves.

On November 1, 1976, the defendants agreed to a stipulation that the shotgun Zimmers had examined and marked as RZ#51 was the one carried by Officer Jones "on the raid." Two days later when I correctly quoted the same stipulation, Coghlan protested to Judge Perry that I misread the stipulation in a "deliberate, willful, and intentional attempt to prejudice the jury."

Flint said we could clear up the matter quickly if we had access to the transcript. (We had no transcript because we could not afford the three dollars per page being charged for daily copy.)

Taylor: "Judge, we want the transcript brought here." Perry had his own copy.

Perry: "Keep quiet. I will fine you right now if you don't keep quiet."

Taylor: "You are going to make [an] error."

Judge Perry: "Shut up and bring the jury. Be seated ladies and gentlemen. Mr. Haas has deliberately and willfully misread a statement. I direct that you read that statement, that stipulation, correctly."

Because I had in fact read it correctly, I explained to the judge that he was mistaken.

Coghlan falsely stated the stipulation contained the words "the service of the search warrant."

Judge Perry: "Now that is it."

Taylor: "That is not the stipulation, Your Honor, I object to that."

Judge Perry [*with the jury still present*]: "Just a minute. Shut up. Now that is the correct stipulation."

I couldn't read the real stipulation without being held in contempt. I wasn't going to lie and repeat Coghlan's incorrect stipulation. The next question I asked Zimmers ducked the issue and referred to the sawed-off shotgun as "the weapon carried by Officer Jones."

Two days later Flint and I went to the offices of Claude Youker, Perry's court reporter, to purchase the transcript. Youker ushered us into a side office. He said he feared "being bugged."

Youker was well aware of the controversy around the stipulation. Before the trial he had agreed to provide us transcripts on a "pay when you can" basis but had stopped suddenly in February.

Youker found his stenographic notes. "You're right. The words 'weapon carried on the raid' were what they stipulated to."

"There's something else," he said, looking down. "The reason I told you that daily copy was three dollars per page was because Coghlan told me he and the other defendants' lawyers would pay me that rate for each copy if I charged you the same. Normally the three dollar fee would be split among all the lawyers. You should be paying less than one dollar." Youker told us we'd been cut off because Coghlan found out he was giving us the transcript for less and he threatened to stop paying the extra. Youker also said Coghlan warned him "to keep our deal a secret," and that he had been contacting him consistently to make sure we weren't getting transcripts.

Not only had the higher fee kept us from daily copy, the city, county, and feds were paying tens of thousands of taxpayer dollars extra so we couldn't afford it.

I asked Youker if he would include what he told us in an affidavit. To my surprise, he said he would.

When we returned to the office, we agreed Flint would write the transcript motion, and I'd write the one asking Perry to correct his nasty remarks. The first one asked that the defendants' lawyers be held in contempt and that we receive past transcripts at the cost of five cents per page. It further sought to inform the city council and county board that Coghlan's deal had already cost taxpayers more than one hundred thousand dollars and that Coghlan and Volini's legal bill already exceeded $1.2 million. The other motion asked Perry to correct his "grossly prejudicial and erroneous remarks," and declare a mistrial. We charged that Coghlan had read "an imaginary stipulation," and

Judge Perry had "accepted it as the gospel." We tipped off the press to Coghlan's secret transcript deal and gave them copies of our motions. The headlines the following day were "Charge Transcript Fee Gouge in Panther Case," and "New Rip-off Charge at the Panther Trial."

As we argued the motions, Perry sat stone-faced. He ignored my entreaty that every day his prejudicial remarks went uncorrected, their harm was amplified. He gave the defendants ten days to respond to our motions, told Flint and me to "shut up and stop arguing," and ordered me to proceed with Zimmers's testimony.

I was beyond pissed off. As we returned from the lectern, Flint hurled his notebook and papers onto our counsel table. "Something like a handball serve," is the way one reporter described it. His papers slid across the table and hit a water pitcher, which fell to the carpet in front of the empty jury box. The glass lining broke and the water spilled. Judge Perry looked up.

Perry: "All right, let the record show the conduct of both counsel in throwing papers around and one of them—what is it that is broken over there."

Coghlan [*ever the snitch*]: "Sir, there is a broken glass pitcher."

Perry: "All right. Mr. Taylor, you did that, and you are now held in contempt and the court now orders you committed into the custody of the attorney general of the United States for a period of twenty-four hours and orders the marshal to take you into custody forthwith. Court is in recess," said Perry as he left the courtroom.

Flint stood there in shock, looking at the empty bench. The marshals let him gather his papers before they escorted him toward the lock-up.

It wasn't over. Out bounced Perry.

As I went to pick up the pieces of the water pitcher, Perry ordered me to stop and sit down. He then demanded that the jury be brought back into the courtroom to observe the broken pitcher. When they had been marched in and out, with puzzled faces, as no explanation was given, Perry allowed a recess for Volini to photograph the debris. Looking for a way around the ban on the press taking photographs in the courtroom, Perry told Volini the press "may have a copy of the picture that is taken," but to make sure they "pay you for whatever it costs." Coghlan's phony accusation about us misstating the stipulation had paid off big time.

Nevertheless, Zimmers's testimony continued, protracted but unshaken. He explained that when he visited the apartment he had seen an indentation containing gunpowder in the foyer. Zimmers testified that a shotgun blast fired toward the apartment from just outside and to the left of the front door would make the impression he saw and that the powder and wadding found in the impression were consistent with #8 shot, the type loaded *only* into Officer Jones's weapon. Zimmers had labeled Jones's shot number *1* on his diagram.

Zimmers testified that Groth fired through the front door into the living room when the door was opening and the door was also open when Clark's shot was fired. The shot from Mark Clark's shotgun was at a substantial upward angle, consistent with his weapon going off as Clark fell to the floor behind the door. Zimmers also stated unequivocally that the two shotgun shells Sadunas had identified as coming from a Panther weapon actually were fired by Officer Ciszewski, one of the raiders.

Zimmers explained that if Truelock had fired a pump rifle when he was running down the hall, as his statement claimed, there would have to be resulting impact points and expended shells. There were none. And of course there was no pump rifle found. Similarly, if Fred Hampton had fired from the back bedroom, as Officer Carmody claimed, there would have to be expended shells in the bedroom and impact points in the kitchen and there were none.

I had Zimmers come down from the witness stand and walk over to his three-dimensional scale model of the apartment set up in front of the jury. He had constructed the model at FBI Headquarters from his observation of the bullet holes he'd seen, measured, and photographed in the apartment. With a pointer, he demonstrated the absence of any impact points on the west side of the apartment or at the back door. These were the locations where the police had entered. It is where the Panther shots would have struck if they'd fired at the police.

Zimmers resumed the witness stand. He matched the .30-caliber bullet removed from Fred's superficial chest wound to Gloves's carbine. The two fatal entry and exit wounds in Fred's head could have come from a handgun or Gloves's carbine. Zimmers testified that if Fred was lying with his head toward the bedroom door, as everyone had placed him, then the two trajectories were consistent with him being shot at point-blank range from above and at the head of the bed or the doorway. The fatal shots did not come through the wall.

Zimmers refused to give credence to the raiders' implausible theories about bullets and shotgun blasts disappearing out windows, doors, and into thin air, leaving no impact points or shells behind. He was so clear and unyielding in refuting Coghlan's hypothetical scenarios, Judge Perry intervened to tell Zimmers "not to argue the plaintiffs' case," and even told the jury Zimmers "clearly did not want to admit a mistake."

After a particularly difficult Zimmers day, I noticed a tall, thirtyish woman with long brown hair and pale blue eyes sitting on our side of the spectator section. I had seen her a couple times before. I introduced myself. She said her name was Maggie Roche.

"I see they're giving you and Flint a rough time," she said.

"That's a bit of an understatement," I replied. "What brings you here?" I asked.

"I was out of town when I heard Fred Hampton was killed. I've been angry ever since that nothing was done to Hanrahan or the cops. If Hampton were white, they never would have killed him. Their smiles make me sick."

By this time we were walking outside in the hall. Maggie asked me when the informant was due to testify.

"In a couple weeks," I said. "If you give me your number, I'll call and let you know when O'Neal, that's his name, hits the stand."

The next day I called her, and we went out to dinner at a Vietnamese restaurant. Over dinner I learned that Maggie was a public school teacher working with children with special needs.

"That's got to be about as tough as this job," I said.

"It can be, but I chose it over teaching the gifted."

She said that she had devoted her teaching career to working with those most in need and constantly had to fight against the racist policies of the Chicago school board. Fighting racism was something we had in common.

After a couple months of dating, I moved into Maggie's apartment. Although she came from the same Irish Catholic background as Hanrahan and his lawyer Coghlan, she despised their attitudes toward blacks and had rebelled against similar prejudices in her own family. For eleven months my life had been the trial day and night. Other than yoga and swimming, my world had become court and the office. I was lucky to get an afternoon on a weekend to spend outside. It was a comfort and a relief to have someone to be with and talk to about the frustrations of court.

Witness O'Neal

Anticipation grew over William O'Neal's imminent appearance. Those of us close to the Panthers wanted to see how this cocky, streetwise Judas would conduct himself in the courtroom. To my surprise and delight, my mother came up from Atlanta to watch me question him. She too had been following the trial.

Spectators and press filled the courtroom on November 30 as O'Neal, dressed in a dark conservative suit, took the witness stand. Low murmurs of "pig" emanated from our side of the spectator section. The defendants had convinced Perry to provide extra security for O'Neal, and a marshal was stationed next to the door where the jurors entered and exited. At Montgomery's insistence, the marshal was moved out of the jury's path.

O'Neal was calm, polite, and showed little emotion as he answered my preliminary questions with "yes, sir," or "no, sir." The FBI had prepped him well. "I joined the FBI because I believed in law enforcement," O'Neal told the jury, even though I confronted him with his deposition testimony that he had "no other reason than money" for becoming an informant. He also had conveniently forgotten that Mitchell had arranged for criminal charges in his car theft case to be dropped.

When I confronted O'Neal about his building an electric chair and wiring the office to electrocute intruders, he claimed these were done at the urging of Hampton and Rush. He admitted taking the Panthers out for target practice at a friends' farm in Michigan, but glibly added, "Better they shoot at trees than police officers." He denied entirely a plan to construct an airplane armed with explosives to drop on City Hall, and the many burglaries he carried out with Panthers Robert Bruce and Nathaniel Junior. Other provocative and illegal acts he didn't "remember at this time, sir."

O'Neal admitted meeting with Mitchell in November and testified that Mitchell brought with him "gruesome" photos of the two police officers slain that day in a shootout with former Panther Jake Winters. He said Mitchell requested information about the layout of Hampton's apartment, but O'Neal claimed he "didn't know why" Mitchell wanted it. Concerning his next meeting with Mitchell, O'Neal testified, "I don't recall providing him with a floor plan, no sir."

I pulled the large cardboard blow-up of the floor plan out from under the counsel table and put it on an easel in front of O'Neal, where the jury could see it. I pointed to each table, bed, desk, lamp, and dresser and asked O'Neal who provided the location for each item on the blow-up. He admitted it all came from him. "And you provided Mitchell with the information that this was the bed that Fred Hampton and Deborah Johnson slept in when they were there, didn't you?"

"I did," he testified, reluctantly. By the time I had shown him every room, it was clear he could not have recalled so many details without sketching the plan himself while he was at 2337 or shortly thereafter. He would not have done this without Mitchell's request and he must have brought his sketch to their meeting. I asked O'Neal if later he had been concerned that his floor plan led to Fred's death. "I was curious but not concerned," he said. "I think at some point I was curious, and that was about the extent of it."

After expressing such nonchalance over his responsibility for Fred's death, I was surprised when O'Neal admitted approaching Fred's parents asking to serve as a pallbearer. "It was something I did, sir. I don't recall exactly what my motivation was other than an act of condolence. Yes, I felt sorry. I don't like to see anyone killed. I didn't particularly appreciate that he was killed, but it did not make me feel bad."

This ambivalent response made me more determined to probe his motivation. I had always been puzzled why O'Neal had cried more after Fred died than anyone in the Party, and why he had volunteered to be a pallbearer. O'Neal stuck with his claim that being a pallbearer was a genuine act of condolence. His ability to get into the roles and even the feelings of both the informant-provocateur as well as the enthusiastic Panther is what made him so effective and so hard to recognize—a moral eunuch and a schizophrenic.

I probed O'Neal's strange psyche and lack of memory for several court days. December 4 went by with a larger-than-usual gathering at the Hampton home but with no acknowledgment of the day's significance in the courtroom. After the noon recess on Wednesday, December 8, we returned to court, but there was no O'Neal. "A serious problem has arisen concerning the health of a member of the witness's family, who is now hospitalized. It has been necessary to allow the witness to return home for the serious matter," U.S. Attorney Kanter reported.

Perry accepted Kanter's representations without challenge and told the jury a sudden emergency "not connected to our case" had caused the witness to be unavailable.

"I think O'Neal is holding them up for more money," I said to Flint after O'Neal's third day as a no-show.

"He's already been getting eleven hundred dollars per month, plus another eighty-five hundred since July for what they call 'trial attendance,'" Flint said. "How much does he want?"

"Enough to have a new suit to wear every day on the witness stand," I replied. O'Neal had worn seven different suits, all well tailored, dark, conservative, and expensive. "He makes you look pretty shabby."

"Just 'cause your mother's in town and bought you a new suit doesn't exactly make you a clothes horse," Flint shot back. Indeed, when O'Neal had failed to appear on Wednesday, my mother took me across State Street to Marshall Field's and bought me a charcoal suit. "Your outfit shouldn't detract from your cross-examination," she said. My mother had attended two years of law school and was both sharp and critical. I accepted her comment as a compliment to my legal skills.

By Monday my mother had returned to Atlanta. I was wearing the charcoal suit when O'Neal reappeared. We demanded written proof of O'Neal's emergency, and Kanter became more vague in his explanations of O'Neal's absence and refused. Ultimately, Perry denied us the documentation and ordered me not to question O'Neal on the reason for his absence.

O'Neal was on the witness stand for another week. He came back more prepared, probably wealthier as well. He admitted meeting with Kanter and Coghlan and speaking with Mitchell during his absence, furthering our suspicions that he wanted more money.

O'Neal insisted that Mitchell convinced him he had no role in setting up the raid.

"Wasn't what Mitchell told you a lie?" I asked.

After a pause O'Neal responded, "That is possible." He admitted he "may have heard that [Mitchell passed the floor plan on to the raiders] before today." When I asked him what other uses a floor plan would serve besides facilitating a raid, he answered, "The building department used them."

The most emotion O'Neal showed was when he whispered "fuck you" to Flint and me after he descended from the witness stand and walked past our table.

The Shooters

Sergeant Daniel Groth had testified at so many legal proceedings and press conferences that there were major inconsistencies he could not reconcile. This was partly because the theory of the defense had changed. Originally the raiders claimed they did not know that they were raiding a Panther apartment. Later, when indicted, they tried to justify being so heavily armed and firing so many shots by asserting they had detailed foreknowledge of the dangerousness of Hampton and the other Panthers at the apartment. Groth's lawyers' strategy was to have him recall as few details as possible and then harass Flint when he confronted Groth with his prior testimony. Groth was Flint's first major witness.

Groth testified he "could not remember" being told by his informant that it was a Panther crib, or that weapons came and went there. When Flint read his prior testimony to refresh his recollection, his standard answer was "No, that doesn't refresh my recollection." When Flint asked him if his memory had been better when he gave his prior testimony, often within days of the incident, Groth responded cutely, "I don't know that it is or not." When Flint then attempted to read the prior testimony as a statement of a party or to impeach his feigned lack of memory, Witkowski, a Coghlan wannabe, would consistently argue that the prior testimony was not impeaching and move that what was read be struck. Three other defense lawyers would echo his objections. The result was that every ounce of information Groth gave up took ten times longer than necessary. The jury was getting annoyed and bored and Flint was increasingly frustrated.

Taylor [*referring to Groth's former testimony*]: "You sketched out a rough draft of the floor plan of the apartment, did you not?"

Groth: "I don't recall that I did."

Taylor: "Do you recall that you did not?"

Groth: "No, sir."

Taylor: "You numbered those rooms, didn't you."

Groth: "As I sit here now, I can't recall that I did."

Groth had previously testified that he told Hanrahan that Hampton had a .45 and that he showed Hanrahan the search warrant. In court he could not recall this. In his deposition he said Hanrahan had approved the raid plan, but in court when Flint confronted him with his prior statement, Witkowski objected, and Perry sustained the objection.

Flint, who had indexed all of Groth's statements, shook his head in disgust as Groth's lawyers and Perry protected his lack of recall. Adding to his pique, on his first question to Groth about his alleged informant, Groth responded he could not answer because of instructions from his attorneys and "because of a promise to his informant." This was the first time that Groth had mentioned this "promise." It smelled like a Coghlan twist to win the jury's sympathy.

Flint asked more questions to probe whether Groth had an informant. Perry intervened, "The identity of the informant is not relevant anymore because the reliability has been fully established by the facts of the case that the weapons described were found there."

I jumped up and cited a Supreme Court case that said items found in the search could not prove reliability for the search warrant, but Perry ignored me.

Flint kept at it. "You knew Roy Mitchell was Jalovec's reliable informant. Did you have an informant?"

Perry: "I will terminate your questioning if you don't proceed and don't come back to it."

Taylor: "Our position is he is hiding it."

Perry: "I don't care what your position is. An informant has the right to protect his family, even if he is dead."

I had to chuckle at this twisted bit of legal reasoning and newly found right. I still managed to reply, "That's not what the law says. We don't even know if he has a family."

Taylor: "You didn't have an informant, did you, Mr. Groth and still don't?"

Groth: "That is a total untruth."

Taylor: "Well, who is he?"

As the defense lawyers rose to protest, Perry ordered, "Objection sustained. I am terminating your examination of this witness."

Flint was allowed to continue only after an apology and a promise that he would avoid challenging Groth about the existence or identity of his informant.

Groth eventually recalled that he knew it was a Panther apartment where Fred spent many nights, that he told his men that Fred slept with a .45 near him, and that his informant gave him a description of the apartment.

Montgomery asked the last questions. Groth had originally testified that Brenda fired at him from the southeast corner of the living room. What Zimmers had made clear in his testimony and what the model demonstrated was that a shot from the southeast corner would have had to strike a living room wall or door and leave impact points, and none were found. So now Groth claimed Brenda moved.

Montgomery read Groth his testimony at the coroner's inquest.

Question: "Where was Brenda Harris when she fired the shot?"

Answer: "In the very southeast corner of the living room. Yes sir, she was in a semisitting position which is the position she held throughout the time I was in the apartment."

With a straight face, Coghlan rose and objected, arguing this testimony was not impeaching. Perry declared, "Overruled."

Finally, Montgomery asked Groth if he was familiar with the Chicago police regulation that stated, "The following practices are specifically forbidden: firing into buildings or through doors when the person fired at is not clearly visible." Groth, who had fired through the front door and who directed Gorman and Davis to stitch the living room wall, claimed he was not.

Edward Carmody was the only officer to enter from the rear and fire a gun of the caliber that could have caused bullet holes of the size found in Fred's head. We believed he was the officer who shot Fred from inside the doorway to Fred's bedroom. The people in the back of the apartment testified that they heard a thump shortly after hearing shots and then saw Carmody dragging Fred's body out. Carmody admitted he had pulled Fred's body off the bed and into the dining room.

Right after the raid, Carmody had told a TV reporter that as soon as he entered the apartment, Fred Hampton fired at him three times with a .45 from the rear bedroom and that another shot was fired at him from there a few moments later when he was in the kitchen. Carmody's description was the basis of Hanrahan's claim that Fred had shot at the police. It was clear from Zimmers's model that from Carmody's location—either at the back door or in the kitchen—the dining room wall blocked any view of the back bedroom. At the federal grand jury, where Zimmers's model was on view, Carmody admitted his earlier story was a lie. "You didn't see any shots come from the bedroom, sir," I said, "not the one where Hampton was found, no one could shoot from the rear bedroom to the kitchen door?"

He again admitted during my cross-examination that he never saw Hampton fire at him but now claimed he'd never told anyone that.

In his court testimony, Carmody denied shooting anyone. But in his firearms use report, mysteriously never produced for the federal grand jury, Carmody indicated he had "critically wounded" someone. Next to the inquiry "How many feet were you from your assailant or the person you wounded?" he put a question mark.

"And is the reason you put the question mark in there, sir, that you didn't want to put in the two feet away you were from Fred Hampton's head when you fired your shot?"

I've never seen a trial where the prosecutor doesn't confront the defendant with the criminal act he is charged with, but my question upset Perry. Before Carmody could respond to me, Perry defended him: "There is no evidence that would warrant that question and the jury is instructed to disregard it."

I protested, "This was cross-examination."

I asked Carmody if he knew Fred was dead when he dragged him out. "I didn't know," he answered.

"Did he do anything that made him appear alive?" I asked.

"He didn't do anything to appear dead," he snapped back sarcastically.

"Did you do anything to determine if Fred was alive?" I asked.

"No," he replied.

"Did you check his breathing?"

"Sir, I was in a hurry, no."

The evidence was there. In closing argument, we could explain that the reason Carmody never checked to see if Fred was alive was because he had just shot him two times in the head and *knew* he was dead.

40

Facing Hanrahan and Jail

On the walkway outside the Dirksen Federal Building, fifty picketers passed out handbills with the photo of the smiling police officers carrying Fred's body from the apartment alongside a photo of the bloody mattress. The leaflets read, "Hanrahan: Wanted for Murder, Not for Mayor."

Inside the packed courtroom everyone was waiting to see the public figure most identified with the raid. Hanrahan had lost the race for state's attorney and another for Congress. He was now, in February 1977, a candidate for mayor in the Democratic primary running on his tough law-and-order stance.

Perry asked the jury if they had seen the protesters. Judy Norgle raised her hand and stuck up her nose disdainfully, acknowledging she saw them. She recoiled even further when Perry asked if it had affected her, but she insisted she "could be fair." Perry warned the spectators not to display any handbills in court or they would be removed and gave orders to ban the picketing on the federal plaza, something he had no authority to do. "You may be causing very serious damage to the plaintiffs by your posters and picketing," he warned, and threatened a mistrial.

I was pumped to cross-examine Hanrahan. My weariness from thirteen months of trial gave way to a rekindled excitement. Hanrahan was no doubt pumped too. The newspapers reported that his lawyers were seeking to restrain him and dampen his hair-trigger temper with sensitivity training in a mock trial.

The first day, we were like two wrestlers testing each other. Coghlan interrupted at every opportunity, even though I was only asking preliminary questions to elicit Hanrahan's history and close connection to Marlin Johnson and the FBI. Perry excused the jury to hear arguments for most objections. The *Daily News* reporter described the court scene in the afternoon paper: "The jury paraded in and out of the courtroom like ducks in a row during arguments and objections. They have, one lawyer suggested, logged several miles between the jury box and the jury room."

Hanrahan admitted he and local FBI head Marlin Johnson had talked over two hundred times about "wide-ranging" topics but never about COINTELPRO. Hanrahan had stated publicly that a major part of his job as state's attorney was to "sell the police to the public . . . to maintain civilized safe society."

"Our major problem is to overcome antipolice/antigovernment propaganda repeatedly and regularly and professionally issued by the Black Panther Party. It was as a result of that this incident developed," he had told the federal grand jury, implying that the raid was a necessary response to Panther criticism of the police.

"I point to the .45 automatic used by Hampton in attacking the police," Hanrahan had boldly asserted at his first December press conference.

I asked him who'd informed him that Hampton attacked the police with a .45, and his reply was vague—one of the police officers, he said, but he was unable to recall a name. He also could not offer how they had known it was Hampton. I asked him whether, in light of the lack of bullet holes or expended shells from Panther weapons, he still accepted the police accounts.

"I did and I do," he said, with the same fury he had always displayed when his or their account was challenged.

Hanrahan continued to claim no responsibility for the misidentified photos given to the *Tribune* for their exclusive. He could "not recall" who told Bob Wiedrich, the *Tribune* reporter, that the nail heads in the kitchen door were bullet holes from Hampton's firing or who misrepresented the bathroom door to be the bedroom door.

The next day, I asked Hanrahan for his evaluation of the investigation of his officers done by the Internal Investigation Division, the same one that IID chief Harry Ervanian termed a "whitewash" and the "worst I've ever seen."

"Mr. Hanrahan, you do recognize, do you not, that the questioning of your officers was less thorough than the usual case at an IID investigation?" I asked.

Hanrahan sat up straight, squinted his eyes to show his indignation, and replied, "As of this time I certainly do not recognize that, nor do I believe that." I started to impeach Hanrahan with his prior testimony. The defendants objected, and I had to read Hanrahan's prior testimony with the jury excused. "A lot of things went wrong. Admittedly I am not pleased with the IID investigation. I asked, I insisted upon the IID investigation. I am not pleased with the way it was done. I am looking for efficiency, for an excellent product in this building, and I don't want anything less than that."

Perry: "That is what he said in court today."

Volini: "Precisely."

Haas: "Where are we? Are we in *Alice in Wonderland*? What the man has said today was that his only complaint with the IID investigation was the fact that the Panthers [the victims] didn't come forward and make a complaint there. He has yet to—"

Perry: "Oh, counsel, he has not said a word about that today."

Haas: "Judge we are not on the same . . . planet.

Flint had entered during the argument and was watching from the spectator section.

Coghlan: "May the record show that Mr. Taylor was seated in the spectators' row, chortling and chuckling, while Mr. Haas was making his speech, and rose to address the court from the spectator section of the courtroom."

Haas: "Let the record show that Mr. Coghlan . . . is trying to incite the court against us."

Perry: "Shut up."

Haas: "Obviously successful."

Then came the unexpected.

Perry: "I am overruling the objection, I am going to let it be read and let the jury hear exactly what he said. It is the same thing he said today."

Small victory—our sarcasm actually shamed the judge into letting us read Hanrahan's former testimony as impeachment, but not without Perry's belittling remark.

Despite the physical evidence, Hanrahan remained loyal to the police: "I still believe the truthfulness of what the police officers have told me."

"You are going to put on a firearms identification expert to confirm your theories?" I asked.

Objection sustained.

"Are you aware of any report of physical evidence which supports your theory?"

Objection sustained.

"Wasn't it because two persons had been killed in the apartment by police officers that it became difficult for you to continue to arouse the public to support the police?"

"No, it wasn't the fact of those unfortunate killings. It was the tragedy of the orgy of the press and the distortion and the reckless printing of charges and statements by persons who had no knowledge of the facts."

"Didn't it occur to you that your actions stirred up peoples' anger?"

Objection sustained.

I changed subjects. I asked Hanrahan if he had made a deal with Jerris Leonard to dismiss the Panther indictments in exchange for no indictment against himself and his officers. Hanrahan denied the deal, directly contradicting the FBI document that memorialized his agreement with Leonard. When I sought to probe him about the discrepancy, Coghlan and Volini objected and asked for a hearing.

After listening to Coghlan and Volini's argument in chambers but not allowing Flint or me to respond, Perry came out and instructed the jury to disregard my last question to Hanrahan.

Haas: "Mr. Hanrahan, do you know how it was that Jerris Leonard knew on April 8th that the Grand Jury—"

Kanter: "Objection."

The Court: "Now, Mr. Haas, Mr. Haas, wait a minute. You will not go into subject matter any further."

Haas: "I didn't even get to argue it. Well, Judge, the deal—"

The Court: "I said you may not go into it any further."

Haas: "Judge, you can't cover up the cover-up. That is part of our complaint, that they covered up, Judge."

The Court: "Mr. Haas, you are now held in contempt of court for your last remark directed to the court, and I will prepare an order accordingly."

Haas: "All right, Judge. I think all the people who have spoken the truth have always ended up in contempt, and the cover-up goes on and on."

The Court: "I will now turn you over to the custody of the U.S. marshal for contempt, and hold you in custody until tomorrow morning at nine o'clock."

Marshals grabbed me by each arm and escorted me from the courtroom by the side (prisoner) door and into the barred holding cell outside. As I exited, Flint yelled, "I'll try to get you out on an appeal bond."

A few minutes later, the U.S. marshals took me from the holding cell, down the prisoners' elevator to the basement, and then by car to the underground receiving area of the Metropolitan Correctional Center. Moving from the courtroom to the MCC happened so quickly, I didn't realize how angry I was until I arrived. I had decided in advance to question Hanrahan about the deal no matter what the judge tried to do to block it, but still I wasn't expecting to go to jail for it.

The MCC is a modern, triangular-shaped, twenty-story, concrete building with vertical slits for windows, located two blocks from the courthouse. It housed mostly pretrial and presentence detainees in federal criminal cases. I was processed, fingerprinted, and my belongings were inventoried. I was allowed to keep my briefcase after it was searched. I donned a heavily starched orange jumpsuit and was assigned the top bunk bed in a dorm with a low ceiling. It was my first confinement.

What if I had to get out? I couldn't. A tiny bit of the reality of a prison sentence set in, which I had only partially understood while negotiating plea agreements for my clients. *I could do my twenty-four hours, but what about six months or a year? Did one ever overcome the trapped feeling when the cell door slammed shut?*

Later in the afternoon, I was telling the other prisoners, "I'm a lawyer and I'm here because the judge didn't like my questions." Before any of my new roommates could respond, I heard a guard call my name. I was led from the day room to the attorney-client cubicle. Flint was there with a stack of papers. He didn't look happy. Like the stock scene from the movies, I sat down with my lawyer to learn my fate.

"They denied the appeal bond."

"What?" I said, incredulous.

Flint said the appellate judge who denied bond gave no reason; I contemplated a night in jail. I imagined a hellish work release whereby I was in court during the day and in the MCC at night. Flint assured me that we would resume the next day. He handed me my legal pad and a folder with my notes on Hanrahan's cross-examination. Flint looked as glum as I felt when he left the interview room.

That night I lay on my bunk with my chin about six inches from the ceiling. *This is not where cross-examination is supposed to end up*, I thought. *Exposing the deal was important enough to risk being here, but God knows what the jury thinks.* I knew the press would be in court, ready to ask me questions. *What could I say to the press to embarrass the judge?* I spent more time scheming about what I would tell the reporters than preparing for the continued cross-examination of Hanrahan.

At 8:00 A.M. I was released and walked out of the MCC. Flint brought me my suit for a quick change at the office, and we went to court. Before the jury and judge entered, a *Chicago Tribune* reporter approached me. He asked what it was like to be in the MCC. I was ready: "Well, I can't say much for the accommodations, but the company was more congenial than that of some persons in Judge Perry's courtroom." My sound bite made the paper, and I was pleased to get revenge, even if it sounds a bit sophomoric today.

Perry began court with the stern warning, "Now let me make one thing very clear, Mr. Haas. We are not going to have anymore Kunstler-inspired methods of trying this case." I felt proud to be a compared to the famous Conspiracy Seven lawyer but also a little nervous. Kunstler had ended the Conspiracy trial sentenced to four years for contempt.

Despite the fact that I had spent a night in jail for mentioning it, the next day the deal between Hanrahan and Leonard was fair game. Hanrahan was allowed to give his fully prepped denial of there being any *quid pro quo* for his dropping charges. I was not allowed to use the deal document to impeach him, but at least the subject of the agreement was not out of bounds. After ten more days of questioning—or more accurately, two days of questioning and eight lengthy, long-worded, and self-serving days of objections and argument—Hanrahan stepped down. His lawyers were pleased that he hadn't erupted, but they didn't want to press their luck. They had no questions for him.

41

Fred, the "Messiah"

We had three more witnesses. Each presented an important piece of the mosaic. Robert Bruce, a former Panther and friend of O'Neal, was light skinned with freckles. He testified in a quiet voice, almost a whisper. Bruce testified that O'Neal constructed an electric chair, complete with wires and straps, to be used, in O'Neal's words, "to punish and deter informants."

Bruce went on to describe the Rockford trip when O'Neal claimed Fred threatened to shoot a highway patrolman. Bruce said the patrolman was particularly courteous, he had called a tow truck when he saw they were stranded, and neither Fred nor anyone else threatened to harm him in any way. Bruce described how O'Neal was always urging him and others to commit robberies and burglaries. "To go into the streets and get money to live," is what O'Neal called it.

On the morning of December 4, Bruce saw O'Neal crying. "They killed Fred," he sobbed. Later O'Neal and Bruce drove around playing tapes of Fred's speeches.

O'Neal and Coghlan had visited Bruce after the trial started at Bruce's father's house and again at his job. They warned him not to testify, particularly about O'Neal's criminal acts.

Elaine Brown was the leader of the national Black Panther Party in 1977 when she came to Chicago from Oakland to testify. "We wanted Fred to become a national spokesperson," she told Flint and me. "He could say what everyone else did, but say it better. He had the ability to move people, whether college students or welfare women, better than anyone I ever heard." Elaine told us she had visited Chicago before December 4, and Fred had given up his sleeping in his bed so she and Deborah, both of whom were pregnant, would have a place to sleep.

With her full Afro, practiced enunciation, and animated expressions, Elaine was an impressive witness. Her enthusiasm showed when she talked about the Panthers. She explained the Ten Point Program in detail and that "Power to the people" means the people have the right to power over their own lives. "It's what Patrick Henry, Abe Lincoln, and Martin Luther King believed. Then and now," she said.

Elaine testified that in November 1969, when Fred came out to the West Coast, she'd asked him to take her place and speak to an assembly of three hundred UCLA law students. He spoke about forming coalitions with other groups and putting aside racist attitudes. "Have you ever heard anybody just reach you, just reach into your heart, even though you might have heard the words before?" she asked. "I suppose this is what he did that day, and I was so overwhelmed."

Elaine Brown was no slouch as a speaker herself, so her admiration for Fred was that much more impressive.

I had some fears that Bobby Rush, our last witness, might want to disown his Panther days. It was rumored he was aiming for a political career in the Democratic Party. He came into the PLO office in a suit and tie; he still had his goatee and mustache, although better trimmed, and wore the same dark framed glasses. After five minutes of interviewing him, my fears were allayed. "Fred was an amazing speaker and leader, and I held him in awe," Rush said. "They murdered Fred because he reached people when he spoke; lumpen, college students, even law students, they all related to Fred."

Rush began his testimony by mentioning that he was still in school, getting his degree at age thirty.

"I got out of high school at twenty-four-and-a-half and out of law school at thirty-one, so you have plenty of time," Perry responded, more congenial than usual.

"Thank you, Your Honor, that's encouraging," Rush answered. "Fred was the motivating force inside the party. Fred's influence was the greatest. . . . [He had] the dedication of a Malcolm X, the speaking ability of Martin Luther King, and as far as courage, there are few with that type of courage. No one displayed leadership qualities like Fred did at twenty-one."

Rush explained that the Panthers organized poor people, primarily blacks, into a structure to correct problems such as housing and education. They had no military wing. He described the ordinary Panther day—rising at 5:30 A.M. to go to one of the six Breakfast for Children sites to prepare and serve breakfast to the kids and then clean up. Members would spend their days selling Panther papers, soliciting contributions, including food for the breakfast program, or working in the office. They would eat a communal dinner at Panther headquarters and often have political education classes afterward. For most members, it was a full-time job. The party provided money for food and rent from contributions and speaking honoraria. Friendly doctors provided free medical care.

Rush testified that Fred banned the cartoon coloring book that depicted Panthers attacking the police and it was never used in Chicago. When O'Neal told Fred he was building a mortar, Fred called him in front of the entire chapter and told O'Neal he was "crazy and accused him of being a police agent." Fred later told the entire membership that "the electric chair and missile were madness" and ordered O'Neal to dismantle them.

Rush stated that he had visited Fred's apartment on a "daily basis," and would have stayed there the night of the raid except for a family problem at home. My questioning of Rush lasted about two hours. For three days, Kanter and Coghlan's sidekick, Witkowski, tried to dirty-up Fred, the Panthers, and Rush himself.

Rush had said Fred often sounded like a preacher. Kanter asked him, "Ever hear a preacher say, 'You kill a few pigs you get a little satisfaction, but when you kill them all, you get complete satisfaction'?" Rush replied that he had not heard Fred say that, but by "pigs," the Panthers meant "police officers who have no regard for the constitutional rights of individuals," and the Panthers only had the right to kill pigs when attacked first.

Even with Rush's explanation, it was difficult to make Panther rhetoric palatable to our predominantly white, suburban jury. What Fred said in the heat of passion to Panther supporters at a rally was not easy to deal with in a sterile courtroom. Nevertheless, Kanter was mostly ineffective at challenging Rush's explanations.

Witkowski was even more inept as he tried to discredit Rush by replaying the televised statement he'd made at noon on December 4. Responding to Hanrahan's claim that the "vicious Panthers" had opened fire on his unwary police, Rush, angry and outraged, answered, "I don't want to get into a verbal debate with Hanrahan about the words he used. Fred Hampton was lying in his bed and we will prove it. We will prove to the world that Fred Hampton was murdered in his bed." Contrary to the impression Witkowski wanted to convey, that those charges were irresponsible, Rush had gotten his information from me after I interviewed the survivors, and his charges matched the evidence. Witkowski had unwittingly opened the door to my questioning Rush about the source of his information, but Perry refused to allow my follow up.

A Shameful End

When the testimony was over, we argued the admissibility of the final scraps of evidence. Coghlan, Volini, and Kanter were absent from court. Witkowski argued endlessly for several days, giving absurd reasons for why clearly admissible evidence should be left out. On April 13 we found out why: he had been stalling while the defendants' other lawyers had been writing motions to dismiss—two hundred pages worth asserting we had not presented enough evidence against any of the defendants to allow the jury to determine their liability. On that day, they gave us copies and told Perry they were ready to argue.

Perry's response was, "Some of the defendants fired guns. I couldn't with a straight face grant the motions in those cases, so this case has to go to the jury for some of the defendants." He gave us a week to answer their motions.

"They're in a hurry because the mayoral primary is coming up. They want Hanrahan exonerated before then," Flint said over our third beer that night. Judge Romiti's dismissal of Hanrahan's criminal charges right before the state's attorney's election had always seemed rigged, and this looked all too familiar.

"How are we gonna answer their motions?" I asked. We didn't have transcripts to dispute their statement of facts, and Linda Turner, our main typist, was out of town over Easter weekend. Besides, I was exhausted. Perry had said we would take a recess in April, and I was looking forward to the break. I'd hardly had time to take a walk outside for weeks. Maggie and I had planned a short weekend trip to Starved Rock, a park with scenic trails through narrow canyons, an hour and a half from Chicago.

"Let's give Perry a sample of our handwriting," Flint suggested.

"He'll hate mine; that I'm sure of," I responded with a slight smile. Court papers from lawyers were always typed, but we didn't have the time or the typists. The defendants' nine motions to dismiss cited over fifty cases. Attached were hundreds of pages of transcript excerpts to support their factual assertions. The standard on a motion to dismiss is whether the evidence, "taken in the light most favorable to the non-moving party" (our clients, in this instance), was sufficient for the jury to decide in our favor. The defendants argued from an interpretation of the evidence favorable to them, but it would take hundreds of hours for us to sift through the thirty-thousand-page trial transcript to refute their claims.

"We ain't going nowhere," I told Maggie when I got home later that evening. I showed her the three-inch-thick stack of motions the defendants had filed. She wasn't surprised. She had learned to expect the worst.

The next morning Flint dared to ask Perry if we could have access to his copy of the transcript to respond to their motions and extra time to answer them. Christenbury replied haughtily, "Your Honor I grow weary of continually having to pay the price of the plaintiffs' lack of diligence. They have a battery of lawyers to work on it, and there is absolutely no excuse for their now coming in and saying they need additional time. They have had ample time."

I was seething and rose to answer, but Flint spoke first: "The battery of lawyers at the People's Law Office are two lawyers who have been out of law school for two years working to pay our salaries. We are the other two lawyers. We have been in court fifteen months. We are facing the head of the Special Litigation Unit of the Justice Department; the head of the Civil Division of the Chicago office of the FBI, sometimes known as the U.S. Attorney's Office; another attorney from the U.S. Attorney's Office; and a full-time FBI agent, Larry Deaton—all paid by the day.

"We are facing Mr. Volini, paid $350,000 of the city of Chicago's money, and Mr. Coghlan, special state's attorney for Cook County, paid $50 an hour to the tune of $650,000; Mr. Witkowski; John Touhy as special corporation counsel spent three weeks writing this brief at $35 per hour; Mike Conneely, GIU cop assigned full time since May 1974; secretaries, Xeroxes, three copies of the transcript at $9.00 per page. We don't have the transcript. We have to see it only during lunch times and court proceedings."

Perry was not moved and refused to give us his transcript.

For the next five days, Flint and I sat at our conference table surrounded by our notes and the few transcripts we had managed to copy. We handwrote our answers to their motions. My handwriting was notoriously sloppy and my fast printing, which I did hour after hour for several days, was hardly better. I didn't think Perry would read what we wrote, but I wanted to have a filed document refuting the defendants' arguments. Jack Kerouac supposedly wrote *On the Road* in a single sitting, high on LSD. Flint and I wrote our hundred-plus page answer to their motions in five days with only coffee, cigarettes, and outrage to keep us going.

On Wednesday afternoon we filed the accumulation of legal-size, handwritten pages with the clerk and left copies at Perry's chambers and with the defendants.

The next day we were in court opposing the defendants' motions. They again claimed the prosecutors were immune, and they interpreted the evidence favorably to themselves to conclude the FBI was only passing on information and the raiders were merely executing a search warrant when they were attacked with Panther gunfire. They returned the fire in self-defense.

Flint responded by showing how the COINTELPRO-inspired defendants were on a course to destroy the Panthers and neutralize their leadership, and Fred Hampton in particular. They tried to get Fred murdered with the Fort hit letter and then, after two police officers were killed by an ex-Panther, they set up Hanrahan to do their dirty work. Both the bonus for O'Neal and Piper's acknowledgement of the raid as a "success" were further proof of the FBI intention for the raid. He ended by answering Coghlan's argument about us not proving "invidious discrimination," required under the Civil Rights Act.

"Your Honor," Flint said, "when I stood in the blood of Fred Hampton on December 4 as I helped to collect evidence because the police had left after tearing up the apartment, black people were walking through that apartment, and an older black woman, looking around, said, 'It's nothing but a northern lynching.' And that is what it was, and if that is not invidious discrimination, I don't know what is."

I focused on the law. "Judge, I don't understand why we are making such a big to-do over these motions today. They have all been pretty much ruled upon in the past by the Seventh Circuit, and yet we are back as though we hadn't heard fifteen months of evidence." I cited lengthy portions of the Seventh Circuit opinion reversing Perry's earlier dismissal of our case on the same incorrect grounds the defendants were urging upon him again. I pointed out that a conspiracy does not require everyone knowing each other personally or what exact roles they would play. Citing the Supreme Court, I stated, "It is elementary that an unlawful conspiracy may be and often is formed without simultaneous action or agreement on the part of the conspirators." Conspiracy law developed through drug cases was on our side. The importer did not have to know the distributor on the street to be in a conspiracy with him.

Christenbury asserted that the FBI was not in a conspiracy with Hanrahan or the raiders; COINTELPRO had nothing to do with the raid, as Hanrahan and the police didn't even know about it.

Perry recessed at noon and announced he would rule later that day.

Flint and I were sitting in the black leather chairs and I was rocking back and forth when Perry came out from the side door at 4:00 P.M. I made a halfhearted effort to stand and then quickly resumed rocking. The artists from the media were focusing on Perry and sketching noiselessly on their giant pads. The defendants had alerted them to the imminent ruling. We had encouraged the Hamptons and Mrs. Clark and a few supporters to come to court.

"I have a very bad voice," Perry began. "I am not going to attempt to read the orders. There are a number of motions." The volume of typed orders in Perry's hand indicated they must have been written before we submitted our answers.

Perry first denied our countermotions for directed verdicts against the shooters and denied our sanctions motion against the feds.

No surprises there. He'd never even given us the chance to argue the sanctions motion.

Perry cleared his throat. He denied the seven shooters' motions to dismiss their individual counts and ordered us to proceed the following Monday with damages witnesses followed by the defense. He then dismissed the conspiracy count and ended, "The motion as to all other fifteen defendants is granted. The court now stands in recess."

The little man in the black robe scurried off the bench. It took only fourteen minutes for him to gut our lawsuit, exonerating everyone except the seven police shooters. I sat there stunned, looking at

Flint, who looked similarly paralyzed in his chair. *So much work, so much proof, and dismissed so summarily. No justice here,* I thought. On the other side of the court Johnson, Piper, and Mitchell were shaking Kanter's and Christenbury's hands. They were all smiling as they picked up their papers to leave. Hanrahan didn't smile, not even now, but all the other defendants who had been dismissed were patting each other on the back and thanking Coghlan and Volini.

I finally stood up and walked over and explained the dismissals as best I could to the Hamptons and Fannie Clark.

"He just ignored all that evidence," Mrs. Clark said. "He didn't care what Hanrahan and the FBI did to our sons."

Iberia had withdrawn into that shell I'd seen before. Her expression was fixed in a mask of anger and determination.

"He just don't wanna do right," she finally said. That summed it up pretty well.

In spite of Perry's ruling, Hanrahan finished a distant fifth in the mayoral primary the following Tuesday. Hanrahan had convinced few people besides Judge Perry that he was innocent.

Boiling Over

By April, spring had sprung, but we only saw it on our way to and from court. Our world was formal, sterile, and mean. And my attitude wasn't much better. I didn't want to take any more shit from Perry, who'd dismissed so much of our case and years of work with such ease. Our last witnesses, solely on the issues of damages, were Maywood mayor Leonard Chabala, Fannie Clark, Iberia Hampton, and Renault Robinson, head of the Afro-American Patrolmen's League. "One more day," we told the impatient judge.

Mayor Chabala knew Fred in high school when he was part of the Human Relations Council. Chabala testified that Fred had frequently been called upon to calm racial tensions in the high school and had been an especially good communicator. Fred had led the campaign to get a public swimming pool and recreation park for Maywood kids, which was started in his lifetime and was now named the Fred Hampton Pool.

The cross-examination was the expected, "Ever hear Fred say, 'Kill a few pigs, get some satisfaction . . .'?" and "Did Fred know and respect the Constitution?"

On redirect, I asked if Fred knew that under the Constitution "Black people have the right not be killed in their beds or murdered by the police?"

Objection sustained.

Next we called Fannie Clark. She was dressed, as always, in a print dress buttoned to the chin and a large flowery hat. She had sat solid as a rock on the front row of the spectator section most of the sixteen months we had been in court.

Fannie testified that her son Mark was one of eleven children from her marriage to Reverend William Clark, who had died in 1967. Mark completed high school through correspondence and worked at Caterpillar and as a barber and helped support his family from his earnings. Mark had worked for the NAACP, including in their hunger program, and helped start the first Breakfast for Children Program in Peoria. Fannie Clark testified her son was "intelligent, energetic, and dedicated." Mark had found something in his commitment with the Panthers that was missing from the rest of his life. They made him feel pride in himself.

Volini's only question was whether she disagreed with Mark about the acquisition of guns. She said, "Yes, I did."

Renault Robinson had been a Chicago police officer for twenty years. Trim and earnest, he spoke loudly and unapologetically. He and Howard Saffold had founded the Afro-American Patrolmen's League ten years earlier. Its objectives were to improve relations between the black community and the police and to reform the police disciplinary system.

Judge Perry refused to allow Renault to tell the jury how he and Fred had testified at city and state hearings on the issue of police brutality. "The jury is concerned with December 4, not police brutality," Perry said.

Fred was a "self-starter" and spoke about the "betterment of people," Renault testified in a quiet tone. "I saw him as a leader of black youth, offering an alternative to gangs and drugs. I was a pallbearer at his funeral." The defendants did not cross-examine him.

Our last witness was Iberia Hampton. She walked slowly to the witness stand, weary from so many months watching Perry and the defense lawyers trivialize our claims and her son's life. She paused for a moment, and I wondered if she was thinking, was it even worthwhile trying to describe Fred in the atmosphere of this courtroom?

Iberia testified about Fred growing up in Maywood, where he was well liked and had lots of friends. He'd worked in high school and helped support the family. When she and Francis bought a car for their three children, Fred said they couldn't afford it and told them to sell it.

In high school Fred became the leader of the suburban NAACP. He was often called upon to quiet racial trouble and once, "when he intervened at the request of the high school principal, he was arrested by the police."

Iberia testified that Fred wrote her from prison that Deborah was pregnant, and when he got out he said he "wanted me to take care of their child if anything happened." At that point Iberia stopped and put her handkerchief up to her eyes. I was surprised. I had never seen her lose control of her feelings. She put her handkerchief down. "We have supported the child," she said, looking at Fred Jr. sitting next to Francis in the front row. She ended simply telling the jury that Fred had wanted to be a lawyer. There was no cross-examination. We rested our case.

The defense called the chemist, Dr. Morton Mason, who testified that even though two months had passed since Fred's body had been buried in Louisiana, and it had been injected with embalming fluid, which can cause barbiturates to dissolve, he interpreted the February lab tests on Fred's blood to prove that no substantial amount of barbiturates was ever present. He offered no explanation for the earlier, contrary findings by Dr. Berman that Fred had barbiturates in his blood.

Flint had done his homework and confronted Mason with his own lack of knowledge about the temperature of the body since buried, whether the blood and tissue samples were refrigerated, and the pH of the aqueous solution of the samples—all of which are factors that can dissolve or mask barbiturates. When Flint moved to strike Mason's unresponsive comments, Coghlan jumped up in pretend indignation.

Coghlan: "Now since the time he was licensed in 1973, this being 1977, that means he has spent an awful lot of time in the preparation of this case and darn little in a courtroom, and if you ask me, it shows in the type of questions he asks. He just refuses to sit down and look at a law book of trial technique because it is inconsistent with his political views . . . and then he throws the load on Your Honor for his stupidity."

Coghlan went on to accuse Flint, as he had done many times before, of yelling in a high voice and flapping his wrists. It worked. Flint was clearly frustrated.

Taylor [*in response*]: "I am getting a little sick and tired of Mr. Coghlan getting up here and having open license from this court to insult my integrity, to insult—"

Coghlan [*continuing his attack*]: "Would the court reporter show that the remarks preceded by the shrieked "what," and the interruptions of Mr. Taylor were shouted in very high decibels."

Taylor: "You allow Mr. Coghlan to get up here and say these things and insult me . . . my tone of voice, my competency."

Judge Perry: "Bring the jury."

Coghlan: "Let the record reflect Mr. Taylor is yelling in a loud voice. . . . What Mr. Taylor may or may not do in the night is of no concern to me."

Taylor [angrier than ever]: "It is an affront to any decorum in this courtroom to let these attacks go on and to not listen to me. That is all I ask, that you listen to me—not to go to sleep when I make arguments, not to put your dark glasses on."

Flint had crossed another line.

Judge Perry: "Now, just a minute, you know that is a falsehood."

Perry was more outraged at being accused of sleeping during our arguments than at the gay-baiting he had allowed in his courtroom. He never reprimanded Coghlan.

Despite the contradictions in their stories, the defense called each of the remaining shooters to deny wrongdoing. We had called Groth and Carmody. They called Joe Gorman, the raider who wielded the Thompson machine gun.

Stocky, with jet-black hair and a chiseled chin, Gorman talked like someone who liked his job and the opportunities it gave him to use force. After he claimed he saw a bullet "rip through the front door," Gorman admitted firing his machine gun on semiautomatic fire in an arc around Brenda Harris, who was lying wounded on the bed. He also claimed he heard a shot that he was sure came from the north bedroom. He testified that each of the wounded persons—Doc, Verlina, and Blair—rose up like ducks in a shooting gallery, weapons pointing at him, just before he fired at each of them. However, the locations of their wounds were not consistent with them facing him or even being vertical as he had described.

I exposed Gorman's falsehoods, beginning with his claiming to see the hole rip through the front door. Gorman admitted entering behind Groth, Davis, and Jones, so I sought to place figurines on the model to show how he could not have seen what he claimed while standing behind three other police officers. I also wanted to demonstrate that Brenda's alleged shots could not have gone by the four large officers in the doorway without striking one of them. The defendants objected to my using the figurines, on the ridiculous rationale that they had not been used on direct examination, but the judge sustained their objection nonetheless.

My cross-examination was gaining momentum when Volini interrupted. This time he told Perry about a demonstration going on twenty-five floors below, which he said was being led by Fred's brother, Bill Hampton. "Reverse Perry's Racist Outrage," "Stop the Cover-up, Jail the Murderer," and "Coconspirators FBI, Hanrahan, Local Police, and now Perry," were the slogans Volini reported. He said the demonstrations were being "perpetrated by the plaintiffs' attorneys."

I was delighted to see Perry publicly labeled part of the conspiracy, but we could not claim credit for organizing the protest. "Jesse Jackson and Reverend [Charles] Koen are not our clients," Flint said. "There are several hundred demonstrators, not all are our clients." Indeed, a large part of the black community that had followed the trial was outraged by Perry's dismissal of Hanrahan and the FBI.

"I am surprised that you are not out there," Perry responded to Flint, who defended himself by saying that although he was not participating, he had that right.

What made Perry the angriest were the revelations that led to the demonstration. These were contained in our most recent motion seeking Perry's recusal. One year into the trial, Sheldon Waxman, the former U.S. attorney who had defended the FBI, called us. He had encountered Perry at a fundraising dinner as the trial started and asked him if he had seen the recent newspaper revelations of the Church Committee, including the FBI's hit letter to Jeff Fort urging violence against Hampton. Perry indicated that he hadn't seen them and they probably weren't relevant to the Hampton case, anyway. Waxman told Perry, "They seemed relevant to me."

A month later Waxman saw Perry again, and Perry told him, "You were wrong about the material that was in the paper. That stuff wasn't relevant. They'll never be able to prove that the FBI killed those fellas." A self-fulfilling prophecy if there ever was one. We attached Waxman's affidavit about his conversation with Perry to our motion for recusal. The affidavit was widely reported in the press. It led to us receiving another phone call. This one was from Reverend Thomas Strieter, who had read about Perry's conversation with Waxman and had been reminded of a similar conversation he'd had with Perry on May 31, 1976. Strieter had been selected to be the chaplain in a Memorial Day Parade where Perry was the marshal. They rode in the same car. Reverend Strieter told Perry he was from Maywood, and Fred Hampton was one of his constituents. He asked Perry how the trial was going. Perry responded that it was "endless." Later on, Perry volunteered, "If only the lawyers would stick to what happened on December 4, 1969, they might make a case. But this conspiracy involving the FBI and Hanrahan is impossible. This cannot be true. There is no earthly way to establish that."

Together, the affidavits of Waxman and Strieter exposed that Perry had decided both before and during the trial that what we were trying to prove against the FBI was in fact "impossible." One out-of-court admission of prejudgment is worth a hundred in-court biased rulings when it comes to recusing a judge. It's what you need. We had filed the motion to recuse Perry with the accompanying affidavits, knowing they would infuriate Perry but slightly hopeful that he would be forced to refer the motion, and maybe even the case, to another judge.

We asked Perry for a hearing on the recusal motion. The defendants' lawyers moved to strike our motion entirely. Perry denied both and said he took the motion "under advisement."

The next day, Coghlan and Volini fanned the flames of the judge's wrath further by answering our recusal motion, on the judge's behalf, accusing us of suborning perjury. They had an affidavit by the driver of the car, who contested Strieter's version of their conversation. We said we welcomed a hearing on what transpired during the parade.

"Judge, I think the court should really take heed of what is happening here and recognize that the court is no longer a fit and unbiased judge," I said to Perry.

"The conduct of the plaintiffs constitutes an attempt to tear down the judicial structure of the U.S. District Court . . . and to tear down the establishment," Coghlan responded, and Volini pitched in with "Mr. Haas . . . has turned to attacking the lawyers, and now he has turned on the judge. He is saying such terrible and disgraceful things about you, that a weaker man would have folded by now." Coghlan added that I was committing acts of "insolent defiance" and compared me to Hitler and Joe McCarthy. Coghlan's misuse of history was too much to take.

I said he was the one who had borrowed McCarthy's tactics. I then addressed Perry.

Haas: "What we see now is the outright prejudice of the court affecting every single act that goes on here."

Perry: "Well, you don't like anything as far as you are concerned except your way. And you are not going to have your way."

Haas: "I know. My way is a fair trial, and I'm not going to get it."

Perry: "You bet your life you are not going to get it."

Thank you, Judge, for that gracious admission. I had to turn away from the lectern to hide my smile. Coghlan tried to correct the record to show Perry had not intended what he said.

Gloves Davis testified next. He was tall and graceful, almost cat-like in the way he had moved through the front door in the reenactment, and said he shot Mark Clark two times. Davis testified on direct for less than ten minutes, enough to say he saw Brenda Harris fire her shotgun at him, which lit up Mark Clark behind the living room door. He fired and hit Brenda in the leg and turned his carbine toward Mark, who was standing up, and shot him two times. After that, Davis claimed they struggled briefly and Mark fell to the ground dead.

Because the details of Gloves's previous accounts conflicted with the physical evidence, Volini hadn't attempted to bring them out. His strategy was to object to my questions, preventing the clarifying of details, meanwhile harassing me and confusing the jury.

Perry aided Volini's effort by refusing to allow me to have Davis mark his and Brenda's position on the scale diagram of the apartment, although the defense lawyers had used it while cross-examining the plaintiffs. Perry would not let me mention Davis's nickname, Gloves, or explain where he got it, although he had admitted at his deposition that he relished the nickname because it "deterred youth." I argued, but was not allowed, to refer to Davis's sixty-eight prior complaints for excessive force.

Coghlan jumped in. "On the streets, a person with such limp-wristed arguments would be called 'sissy.'"

Recently, when I read the transcript, I was pleasantly surprised to see my response: "I just want to say that I guess on Mr. Coghlan's terms I am a sissy because I don't like to sit around the courtroom and tell dirty, crude jokes about women, which is what he likes to do after court. If that is what being a man is, I would just as soon be a sissy." I had learned something from the women's movement.

As for the cross-examination of Davis, I had a lot to work with. Davis, like Gorman and Groth, had previously placed Brenda in the southeast corner of the living room when she fired. Davis also had testified, "I know very definitely none of the officers fired through that [the living room] door," which I easily disproved by pointing to the entry hole in the panel Groth's bullet had made coming from the outside. Davis also was certain the door was open at ninety degrees during Groth's shooting, again conflicting with the proof that the door was only slightly ajar when Groth shot through it. Zimmers disproved all of Davis's descriptions of Panther firing.

But Davis's biggest contradiction came from his statement that he "never moved out of the living room." One of his .30-caliber bullets made the superficial wound in Fred's chest. Its angle indicated it may have been fired from the south bedroom door. Several of the plaintiffs placed Gloves at the rear of the apartment, and Davis had told Larry Kennon, a black attorney, on the morning of the raid that he'd seen Fred lying in his bed. Larry was a founder and leader of the all-black Cook County Bar Association. He was also a friend and reported Gloves's statement to us.

Moreover, Davis's quick movements in shooting the people in the living room, firing toward the bed where the floor plan showed Fred slept and then proceeding to the rear, supported our position that the defendants' objective from the outset was to murder Fred Hampton. Our stance was also buttressed by Davis's absurd claim that Fred Hampton's being in the apartment "never entered my mind."

George Jones was the other black cop besides Davis who fired. He was soft-spoken and neatly dressed. The defense wanted to end their case with a favorable impression. Although Jones denied firing in the entrance foyer, the physical evidence indicated he had. Whether it was accidental or the signal to attack, Jones likely fired the opening shot as he and the other raiders were poised to strike. During a recess in Jones's testimony, I went into Perry's antechamber to return a transcript. I spotted juror Norgle, looking as unfriendly as ever. In the courtroom, I asked Perry why she was there. Trial judges are not allowed to communicate with jurors without notice to the parties. Perry looked embarrassed. He said he was speaking to Norgle about a friend of hers, a graduating law student who had come into his chambers looking for a job. He had never told us about this. It gave Perry the opportunity to ingratiate himself with this juror by helping her friend.

Coghlan quickly realized his best ally may have compromised himself. He urged Perry to order that none of the lawyers communicate with the young man for "fear of contacting Norgle." Before we could demand a hearing, Perry entered Coghlan's protective order, and we never learned what Perry said to Norgle's friend in chambers.

Jones's direct examination, like the other defendants, was quite short. He attempted to explain the timing of the early morning raid, saying 8:00 P.M. was dangerous in that "highly volatile area," even though he knew the occupants would not be present at that time.

Jones testified he saw Brenda fire a shotgun and fired his weapon, a shotgun, into the north bedroom. That was it. When I asked Jones if he had been told it was a Panther apartment, he answered, "It may have been discussed, but I have no memory of it." He just couldn't recall why these fourteen men armed themselves with a machine gun, shotguns, a carbine, and numerous handguns to serve this warrant. "Could it have been a raid on a seventy-eight-year-old woman's apartment for an unregistered weapon?" I asked. Before he could "not recall," his lawyers objected.

The next day, May 19, Jones's memory was no better. I was already frustrated with his refusal to recall specifics, when Volini had the audacity to argue, "They shouldn't be allowed to pin him down when he does not recall the exact sequence of events."

"He doesn't recall any sequences," I responded angrily. It is the understood objective of the cross-examiner to "pin down" evasive hostile witnesses—exactly what Volini had the temerity to ask Perry to prevent. Perry just smiled and refused to allow us to impeach Jones with the details in his police report.

On May 27 the defense rested, and we began our rebuttal. Flint called our chemist, Dr. Eleanor Berman, to the stand to rebut the defendants' expert's testimony that Fred's blood contained no barbiturates. She systematically analyzed the tests run by the FBI chemist, Mason, and concluded there were several intervening factors that would account for Mason not discovering the barbiturates.

Perry disallowed Dr. Berman's most convincing testimony—that the FBI's tests had isolated a substance that upon further testing may have proved to be barbiturates—because the defendants claimed we had not given them notice.

When Dr. Berman stepped down, and after seventeen months, both sides rested.

44

Rock Bottom

No rest for the weary. Flint and I had two days to put together jury instructions. They contain the law the jury applies in evaluating the facts. Each side submits the instructions they want. Some lawyers say a jury decides with their gut. Others say the instructions are critical, both in determining how the lawyers argue the case in closing and ultimately how the jury will decide. I waver between the two but now believe the instructions are critical in a close case.

Most of our important instructions were rejected, just as our motions had been. The instructions Perry approved were submitted by the defendants and defined the law in such a manner that, if applied, the jury could not possibly find in our favor. For example, Perry gave the defendants' instruction on "assumption of risk," a tort defense, which allowed them to argue that the jury could find that the Panthers' possession of weapons justified their murders. Flint and I realized the jury would have to disobey the instructions to find for the plaintiffs. "Maybe they'll see through him and go with what they know is right," I tried to convince Flint.

"That's giving them a lot of credit," he said. "Maybe Florence Smith will get it, but I don't know about the rest." We divided up closing arguments. Montgomery had called and, despite being gone for most of the past six months, said he wanted to lead off.

At three o'clock in the afternoon of June 15, Montgomery returned to court for the first time in many weeks and began closing argument. The courtroom, which had been largely vacant of late, was packed once again, and the press was back. I wondered if I looked the five years older I felt since the trial started. Montgomery began by telling the jury what the case was *not* about. This included the Panther philosophy, the conduct of lawyers, and revolution. The defendants chose not to conduct the raid at 8:00 P.M. when it was safe. "If they had, Fred and Mark would be alive."

Montgomery described the predawn events. Jones fired first, and then the police burst through the front door. The apartment was secure immediately after the officers entered the "threshold of the living room," but they kept firing. He explained that the defendants were stuck with their original lie that "Brenda had sat on the bed calmly pumping her shotgun," as they entered. There were no shells and no impact points to corroborate their story. He demonstrated how ridiculous the defendants were in trying to move Brenda from where they had clearly placed her originally to a position where it might have been physically possible to fire out the front three doors leaving no impact point. Next he derided "the most ridiculous part of their story," the defendants' claim of how the occupants broke the three cease-fires.

"Throughout the whole of my life," Montgomery said, "in movies or events, I never heard anybody, *anybody*, use 'Shoot it out.' I've heard, 'You're going to have to kill me.' Why say 'shoot it out' and fire one shot? Any idiot wouldn't do that. If you said 'shoot it out,' you would do it. Bring your common experience of life to bear."

Montgomery offered as proof that Fred had never left his bed, an argument I had not considered. The photo of Fred lying in the dining room showed plaster dust on his back. Deborah had described it descending in her bedroom while the police were firing and the bed was shaking. Fred must have been lying on his stomach to end up with the dust on his back.

Finally, he got to Carmody. Both his early statement and written report indicated he saw a hand extending from the rear bedroom firing a .45 at him as he entered. Later he saw the .45 next to Fred's hand as he lay in that room. Carmody was now saying the hand extended from the dining room, which he had called the rear bedroom. But there was no bed in there.

Montgomery continued, saying

When Abraham Lincoln was talking to his cabinet, he asked them, "If I said a donkey's tail was a leg, how many legs would a donkey have?" To a man, the cabinet in unison answered "five." Lincoln responded, "No. You cannot make a donkey's tale a leg by simply calling it a leg. He would have but four legs." You cannot make a dining room a rear bedroom by calling it a rear bedroom.

Montgomery walked over and stood in front of the jury box. "History will look at this case and your verdict. Your verdict is important. You will have the opportunity to sit here and put to rest finally and forever what happened on December 4, 1969."

The next morning, Flint focused on Groth's inconsistent stories about a floor plan. First Groth had claimed, "No, I didn't have a floor plan, didn't have a layout." Later Groth admitted he *did* have a floor plan but destroyed it. Then Flint reeled off the evidence of Fred being drugged, showing how carefully our expert, Dr. Berman, had run her tests, in contrast with the coroner's office representative George Christentopolos, whose experience was "testing mayonnaise for Durkees." The defendants' experts had failed to adjust the pH downward in the tissue samples and had run standards thirty times too high, which masked the barbiturates. Eleanor Berman had gone back and run the same tests as the defense expert, Dr. Mason, with samples containing secobarbital and they did not turn yellow as Dr. Mason said they must if secobarbital, were present.

Flint ended with, "We still haven't heard from Groth's supposed informant."

"You will not go into the question of the informant any further," Perry said.

Two hours later, I asked the jury to come down and gather around the scale model that showed the location of all the bullet holes, while I walked them through the raid. The model was large, and it was easy to demonstrate that the shots the defendants claimed the plaintiffs fired could not have occurred without striking one of the interior walls or the entrance area. There were no bullet holes in these locations.

The model and Zimmers's testimony told the story. Ninety shots to one; no shots from the Panthers except one from Mark Clark's gun at an upward angle as he fell from a police bullet.

"The plain fact is there was no shooting at the rear of the apartment other than by police officers," I said. "The plain fact was that they knew where Fred was, they knew where he slept, and that killing Fred

Hampton was the intent of at least some of the officers who came on this raid."

I argued that Carmody was the only officer who entered at the rear whose weapon could have caused the fatal bullet wounds to Fred's head. Carmody dragged Fred's body into the dining room for all to see, claimed he did not know whether Fred was dead but never checked, and brought his body out to where guns were within easy reach. "Carmody knew Fred was dead because he'd just fired two shots into his head with his .38 snub-nosed revolver."

"When you put it all together, you will find that Edward Carmody went in there to murder Fred Hampton." I sat down.

Volini, the big man with the suit jacket that always bulged over a roll of fat around his middle, walked over to face the jury. "The 1960s was [sic] a violent time, and the Panthers aided the violence. Did police officers have to analyze and understand what 'Off the pig' and 'Power comes from the barrel of a gun' meant? Gilhooly and Rappaport were twenty-five years old when they were ambushed."

I objected. The facts of the November 13 incident were disputed and were not in evidence.

Overruled.

Volini argued that Truelock fired, and the others picked up guns and may have shot. The "shells of the Black Panthers are in the pockets of the lawyers who gathered evidence." This was the first time Volini had made this accusation.

As expected, Volini attempted to convince the jury that the Panthers' possession of weapons was an assumption of risk that exonerated the defendants. He went further: "Fred Hampton assumed the risk of getting shot if he took some drugs."

I objected. This legal theory was a bit much even for Perry, who told Volini he would instruct the jury on the law.

"Watch for the low blows," I whispered to Flint later that afternoon as we watched Coghlan approach the jury. We had come to despise this bully, who flaunted the freedom Perry gave him to make every nasty insinuation he could against the plaintiffs, the Panthers, and Flint and me. Sometimes, when he got excited, Coghlan's mouth would stay narrowly open like a fish. His red cheeks inflated and deflated as he tried to breathe through the opening. Despite his uncharming appearance and unsubtle ways, or perhaps because of them, Coghlan was the most effective of the defense attorneys.

He began by commenting that all the attorneys except Flint and me had conducted themselves "honorably." Quickly he moved to his main theme. "I believe Fred Hampton was a leader and told the truth," he said, "including that he would blow peoples' heads off." A few minutes later we recessed.

The next morning, Perry reversed his ruling of a week before and allowed us to ask for punitive damages. Perry claimed he had ruled against us because we had withheld a key case from him that proved our position was correct. Perry said that he had only discovered the case in reviewing our mandamus petition to the Seventh Circuit. In fact Flint had provided Perry's clerk with the correct citation to the case before Perry ever ruled. But Perry didn't want to admit he'd been so anxious to rule against us he'd made a mistake that might get him reversed on appeal or at a minimum one that would show his bias. The judge interrupted Coghlan's closing argument and gave us five minutes to prepare to argue punitive damages to the jury.

Flint pointed out the defendants' meetings, their planning, the floor plan, and the resulting bullets directed toward Fred's bed—clearly marked on the floor plan—to show intent and malice, requirements for the awarding of punitive damages. I focused on the volume of police shots, the beatings, kicking, and racial slurs inflicted on the plaintiffs after the raid, and the photos that showed how the defendants tore up the apartment when they were done shooting.

"Of all the photos," I said, "the one that demonstrates their intent most clearly is the one of Fred lying on the door, bleeding from his head. Nobody checked his life signs or attempted to help him. Nobody covered him up. They waited for the photographers."

Coghlan countered. "I will tell you how a police officer feels. They don't publicly admit fear but they have it. Police who don't protect their partners end up in the mailroom. No one wants to ride with them. Officer Davis was a tough guy in a tough business. If he had not gone in low, part of him would be splattered where Jim Montgomery said the rifled deer slug was in the entrance foyer.

"What is common to all good policemen is that they would as soon be dead than be known as the guy that backed down when his partner is needed." Coghlan praised Gorman and Groth for their bravery in entering the apartment to back up Davis.

Coghlan's closing argument was based on what Coghlan implied was his own personal knowledge. A lawyer is not allowed to tell the jury about his life or refer to supposed experiences outside the courtroom, but Coghlan got away with it.

I had ten minutes for rebuttal. I told the jury Coghlan had obviously been a cop.

Coghlan jumped up, feigned surprise, and claimed I had brought up a new matter. He wanted time to respond. I objected, but Perry gave him two minutes when I finished.

Going back to the facts after Coghlan's emotional appeal was difficult, but there were some points I wanted to clarify. Coghlan had argued that Jones's shotgun would not fit horizontally in the entranceway, so he could not have fired the first shot. I demonstrated that it could, and if it was held with the butt against the entrance hall door, the barrel would be at exactly the three-to-five-degree angle upward that Zimmers specified was the direction of Jones's shot.

I argued Davis's testimony that Mark Clark was just rising from his chair when Davis shot him was totally improbable. Davis placed Clark and his chair "in the middle of the living room." For Davis's testimony to be true, Clark would have had to fire his shot at an upward angle from below and just inside the living room door, as the ballistics evidence indicated, stand up and move himself and his chair to the middle of the living room, and then sit back down, all in the midst of gunshots from Groth and Davis. The more likely scenario was that Clark had been shot near the living room door and his gun went off as he fell.

My argument ended with a flourish. Perry wrongly accused me of showing the jury a photo that he claimed had not been admitted into evidence, but in fact it had. Perry told the jury, "Listen to me, not Haas."

I responded, "You are the determiners of fact, ladies and gentlemen, thank God."

Coghlan's two-minute rebuttal was well rehearsed.

"I've never been called upon to explain how I worked my way through law school," he said. "I was a police officer from 1955 to 1957. I quit when I got my license. My partner was black and took five bullets in the belly, and I was with him when he died. I did not have what it takes to go through that again."

Of course everything he said was inflammatory, irrelevant, and based on a supposed incident outside our courtroom. After the jury was excused, I moved for a mistrial for Coghlan's "pulsating and probable lie to the jury." Denied. Perry let him get away with it.

Later, Perry spent two hours reading the instructions to the jury, and at 7:15 P.M. on Thursday he sent them to dinner and told them to organize themselves and begin deliberating in the morning. They would remain sequestered at a hotel until they reached a verdict.

I felt some relief but little confidence when the jury finally marched out to deliberate. There was nothing more to be done but collect the admitted exhibits to send to them . . . and wait.

Flint and I had more than our usual two beers that night at John Barleycorn, a Lincoln Park pub, but underneath the momentary warmth and buzz, I feared what our jury would do. It was clear Perry and the defendants expected a quick verdict in their favor. Perry even suggested to the jurors that they might finish their deliberations before the weekend. That would have been on Friday, after only one day of deliberations, a remarkable feat given the lengthy trial.

On Friday, Flint and I went to the office in blue jeans. We sat there nervously, with our suits hanging nearby, ready for the call telling us the jury had reached a verdict. In the afternoon Flint said, "Well, we've kept them out for a day. That ain't bad, given Perry's instructions."

"Whoever heard of 'assumption of risk' in a civil rights suit?" I replied.

"Can you believe Volini argued that if Fred had taken drugs, he assumed the risk of being murdered in his bed?" Flint asked. "By that logic, any black kid on Chicago streets after dark assumes the risk of being beaten by the police."

Our cynical banter continued over the weekend with no calls from court. On Sunday morning, the *Sun-Times* ran a lengthy article with photos of Flint, straight blond hair almost to his shoulders, and me with bushy curls and sideburns. Today I see how young and unlawyerly we looked. Dennis Fisher, *the Sun-Times* reporter who had been covering the case, came to our office the day before with a photographer and interviewed Flint and me. The article called us "Panther lawyers: tight-budget crusaders . . ." and noted that

> even before the trial started, Haas and Taylor were deeply involved in preparing the case. Throughout their effort, they have worked 70 and 80-hour weeks at negligible pay trying to win for the plaintiffs $47.7 million in damages from the police raiders. Their performance hasn't always been polished, but their enthusiasm never has flagged, in spite of what they continue to regard as the hostility of the judge.

"It's like playing in the World Series against the Yankees with their manager as the umpire," Flint was quoted.

I spared the metaphor. "Whether it's his will or his whim, the eighteen months have been excruciating. The law has been turned upside down and stretched every way to defeat us. We can't underestimate the vengeful side of Judge Perry, and no matter which way it goes we think the other side will attempt to put us in jail to cover the cover-up." Perry had taken a number of contempt claims against Flint and me under advisement, and we feared he would give us more jail time when the case concluded. Our efforts to expose the judge's bias were not merely letting off steam, although there was plenty of anger behind them. They were to alert the public that a verdict against the plaintiffs did not follow a fair trial and should have no credibility.

The news story continued. "Coghlan . . . has referred to Haas and Taylor as 'young punks.' Haas and Taylor have called Coghlan a 'Nazi storm trooper.'"

After the recriminations, Flint explained our position more clearly near the end of the article. "We dare to come to the king's throne and say he's wrong. But he's got all the power. We can't forget that. We're just committed to an idea, and every piece of evidence that comes out showing more FBI involvement has told us we must pursue this case. It's a matter of government assassination being exposed."

On Monday, June 20, the clerk called us in. When we arrived in court, Perry passed us four notes sent to him by the jury over the weekend. The first one on Saturday morning came from four of the jurors and asked if they could go to mass on Sunday. Perry told us he responded "only if they all agreed," and they had not gone. The second was sent Saturday afternoon and said the jury was "hopelessly deadlocked and cannot reach a verdict." Perry said he ordered them to continue deliberating, which led to the next two notes on Sunday, which said the same thing, the last one adding, "More deliberations will not result in a unanimous verdict."

Eighteen months and then a hung jury, it seemed a nightmare, but then I thought, *Could we realistically have hoped for more?* It was better than a verdict against us.

Perry should have called the lawyers in after each note. He didn't, I realized, because he didn't want a hung jury. He wanted them to continue to deliberate and decide for the defendants, as his instructions had all but mandated.

The defendants asked that the jury be instructed to continue deliberations and negotiate with each other. Flint and I conferred. Normally, plaintiffs would seek further deliberations that could lead to a favorable verdict. A hung jury is usually considered a victory for the defense. But we knew the atmosphere in the courtroom and the one-sided jury instructions. "Do you really think they understand the judge's bias, so they can discount his remarks, ignore the instructions, and vote damages for Panthers?" I asked Flint.

To ask the question was to answer it. Flint responded, "I doubt it." Neither of us liked our chances with this jury after this one-sided trial. In addition, the jurors' notes had been signed by our presumed nemesis, "Judy Norgle, foreperson." Another bad sign.

Perry asked each side our position. Coghlan and Volini then said they wanted Perry to declare the jury hung, which meant a mistrial, but before he did, they wanted him to reconsider the defendants' motions for directed verdict, which they had filed but had never argued. If their motion was granted, the case would be dismissed based on lack of evidence.

I said that after three days of a deadlocked jury, Flint and I wanted Perry to declare a mistrial, but since Montgomery wasn't there, we needed to recess until we could confer.

Perry called the jury in and asked Judy Norgle, "Are you able to arrive at a verdict?"

"No, we are not, Your Honor," she said emphatically. Perry told the jury they did not need a unanimous verdict on every plaintiff or every defendant to reach a verdict on the others, and they should continue deliberating until he called them back at 2:00 P.M.

Later we met with Montgomery and told him why we doubted more deliberations would work to our benefit. "I don't want to do this again," he said. "I want a verdict now."

I suspected the case was at its end when the jury returned at 2:30 P.M. In addition to Flint, Montgomery, Reid, and me, the rest of PLO was present for our side. The press was there along with as many plaintiffs and supporters as we could reach by phone.

Perry called in the jury. They looked haggard and angry. Florence Smith, the sole black juror, was the only one who looked at us. "I am asking again if you are able to arrive at a verdict," Perry said.

"No, Your Honor, we haven't," Ms. Norgle responded, resolutely.

"Is it likely with further deliberations you will be able to reach a verdict?" Perry inquired.

"We will not." She was unequivocal.

Perry excused the jury and again asked each side its position. Montgomery spoke first. He argued that the length of the trial and animosity between the parties and lawyers might make a verdict "difficult to reach, but they should continue deliberating." Flint and I disagreed. I argued that "Judy Norgle was firm, no hesitation in her response." The jury had been declaring they were deadlocked for three days.

Coghlan also asked that deliberations cease but again urged the court to rule on the defendants' directed verdict motions before the jury was excused.

As soon as he finished, Perry commanded, "Bring the jury."

I sensed something bad was about to happen. I stood up and approached the lectern. "Judge, I don't see any basis for making rulings on those motions at this time. I would oppose that and ask for an opportunity to argue."

Perry: "We have it under advisement. We don't need further argument on them."

Haas: "This is an attempt to preempt the ruling of the jury. I don't think this would be the appropriate time for the ruling."

Perry: "Are we finished now? Bring the jury."
The jury entered and was seated. Perry continued,

In twenty-six years I've never seen a more competent, fair-minded jury. I recognize, I can see it, that there is a tension, there is a division in the jury as I am sure it will pass as you members go from its grip. I have before me under advisement a motion that counsel for defendants have made, and the court feels that as a matter of law that the plaintiffs and each of them has failed to sustain the burden of proof on the issues of evidence on every count remaining in the amended complaint.

Accordingly, the defendants' motion for a directed verdict in favor of each and every defendant against each and every plaintiff is granted, and judgment is entered here together with costs against each and every plaintiff and in favor of every defendant. The jury is hereby discharged from further duty. Each juror is free to talk about the case to the attorneys for the parties and to anyone.

Perry hurried off the bench. I felt a pain in my stomach like someone just kicked me. I glanced at Flint, shaking my head in disgust. He looked angrily at the bench, but the judge was gone. I was stunned. I had anticipated some type of jury verdict or even a hung jury. Instead Perry dismissed the case against the defendants without a jury decision and assessed costs against us. As if the ruling weren't bad enough, we had to watch Coghlan and Volini laughing, getting congratulated, and shaking hands with their clients.

"Let's get out of here," I said, but first I had to say something to Florence Smith, our one black juror. She was walking from the jury box. When I called her name, she turned around.

"I was with you," she said. "I would have held out forever."

"Thank you," I said. "What you did was important." And it was. A white juror heading for the door, who had looked uncomfortable during the trial, also came over and shook my and Flint's hands. It turned out she and Ms. Smith were the jurors willing to vote our way.

In a small conference room off the hallway, we explained what happened to the Hamptons and Clarks. "Perry couldn't do it with the jury, so he did it himself," I told them.

"Is this the end of the road?" Iberia asked. As down as I was, I replied, "No way."

Flint added the one bit of good news. "Since Perry decided it, the evidence will be considered favorably to us on appeal. We won't have the burden of overcoming a jury verdict."

"We owe Florence Smith a tribute," I said. "If the jury had found for the defendants, we would have an almost impossible burden." As soon as I said it, I realized the legal distinctions made little difference to our clients or hardly to us at that moment. They seemed insignificant next to the overwhelming fact that after seven years, our case had just been dismissed.

Iberia told me years later that she did not "see any hope for any of us." She and Francis had missed one or more days of work every week for eighteen months to attend the trial. Now the judge had thrown out their son's case. Iberia and Fannie both wore that expression of tired outrage, a familiarity with suffering that black people have had in America; a look that says, "I see what your justice system did again." Herb Reid understood that look and said he and the NAACP were not giving up.

On the first floor, I told the press how Perry had made himself the jury, and Flint explained how absurd it was for Perry to dismiss a case on the grounds that there was insufficient evidence to go to the jury, while the jury itself was deadlocked. Montgomery said nothing. I could tell he blamed us for the verdict as much as the judge. He headed back to his office. Herb Reid came back with us to PLO. There we slumped down in the hard chairs of our conference room. For once, there was silence. In spite of the hope we conveyed to our clients, I felt we had hit rock bottom.

For two days I stayed home feeling terrible. The free time and walks outside I had longed for were not comforting. On Thursday, PLO lawyers gathered in our conference room. We were not a happy crowd. "Things could be worse," Dennis said. "The jury could have acquitted the defendants."

"That's true if we ever get to appeal," I said. "Perry is going to make us pay the defendants' costs. This could be tens of thousands of dollars."

"We've gotta appeal," Flint interrupted. "The bastard can't get away with this."

"I'll work on it," Chick added. "I've already done a lot of the research."

"And who's gonna pay for the transcript we need to read and cite in our brief?" I asked.

"I'm sure it's over thirty-five thousand pages." Nobody answered.

"It's gotta be done," Dennis said. "We have too much evidence to let Perry win."

"If we get the right appellate panel, we have a chance," Flint perked up.

"Do you think Fred would quit?" someone threw out. We all knew the answer. That comment pulled me up. Fred wouldn't have given up, so how could we, who were representing him and his legacy?

"Don't mourn. Appeal." Someone threw out, a takeoff on the union rallying cry, "Don't mourn. Organize." I had to laugh and declare the mourning period over.

"I'm in," I said. "Let's get that transcript and nail Perry's ass."

"One good thing," Flint added. We get to consolidate our entire case in one appeal. There's nothing left before Perry, thank goodness." I could see he relished another shot at proving the FBI conspiracy.

It's a truism that what appears to be our worst nightmare often turns out to be a blessing. So it was with Perry's ruling. Had he not dismissed the shooters, we would have been left with another trial against them, still in front of him—a trial we would probably never win.

Before things got better they got much worse. First, Judge Perry ruled our clients must pay the defendants' costs, consisting mostly of the time and expense of the FBI's reproducing the documents it had hidden and even some transcript costs. Perry assessed their costs at one hundred thousand dollars. On top of that, he set an appeal bond of another hundred thousand, creating what appeared to be an insurmountable financial obstacle to prevent us from appealing his dismissal. Perry continued the sentencing on the pending contempt citations against Flint and me until after any appeal, reserving the right to incarcerate us later.

The final blow, the least expected, came by messenger from Jim Montgomery. It was a letter announcing that he would now be the *sole* attorney for Iberia Hampton, Deborah Johnson, Verlina Brewer, and Brenda Harris.

When we talked to the other plaintiffs, we found out what happened. Montgomery had told each of them he no longer wanted to work with us and that our tactics only led to infuriating the judge and prolonging litigation and would not result in winning the case either by way of settlement or trial. He implied he could negotiate a settlement if they would accept his exclusive representation, but he would also require that they sign a new fee agreement, raising the percentage of his contingency fee from one-third to 45 percent.

The letter from Montgomery was demoralizing. I understood why our strategy of confrontation did not look like it would bring success. Montgomery offered accommodation, which works in most civil cases, but I believed that our defendants would not settle until we gained the upper hand. For now they were riding high.

"Do you think Montgomery has been offered a deal if he separates from us?" I asked Flint and Dennis.

"I think he hopes he can cop a deal," Dennis said. "But I don't think there is one—not now, anyway."

"Why would Coghlan and Volini want to settle now after they have a verdict? Their gravy train is guaranteed through the appeal and ten more hung juries," Flint said.

"They're certainly not going to settle until we get an appeal going, and right now that's problematic," Dennis added. "We have to get over the hurdle of the appeal bond."

45

Out of the Abyss

We still represented **Fannie Clark,** as well as Doc Satchel, Harold Bell, Blair Anderson, and Louis Truelock. We didn't have a lot of time to bemoan the division of plaintiffs. We had to file the notice of appeal and draft the motion to convince the Seventh Circuit to overturn Perry's requirement of an appeal bond, and time was running out.

Dennis and Chick helped Flint and me research and draft the motion. We argued our clients' indigence; the importance of being permitted an appeal; the political, legal, and public significance of the case; and the strength of the evidence—enough to cause the jury to be divided even after a one-sided trial. Perry's appeal bond was a vengeful effort to prevent us from exposing and reversing his unjust rulings.

Although Montgomery's time for challenging the appeal bond had expired, he filed nothing for the other plaintiffs. We had warned him of the deadline. I feared that his plaintiffs, including Iberia, would have to post the appeal bond or, more likely, forfeit their right of appeal when they could not raise the bond. Obtaining and even winning a new trial without Iberia, not to mention Deborah, Verlina, and Brenda, would be sad indeed.

A few days later, the appellate court struck down the appeal bond. Fortunately, they didn't restrict their order to our plaintiffs. We were free to challenge on appeal all of Perry's dismissal orders, his contempt citations, and his vindictive awarding of costs. We were back in business, or at least in court.

Writing an appeal from a thirty-five-thousand-page transcript, which we did not yet have, seemed an overwhelming task. The brief required a statement of facts with each factual assertion backed up by a citation to the trial transcript. This was followed by legal arguments, supported by facts and the law. Sorting and prioritizing the issues was a huge task. Most important was demonstrating that we had enough evidence to warrant at least a jury's verdict on all our claims, including conspiracy.

Our first objective was getting a copy of the trial transcript that the other side had received every day during the trial. We filed a petition to proceed *in forma pauperis* (as poor persons) before Judge Perry. He quickly denied the motion, gratuitously stating that the appeal was "frivolous" and "without merit." We then went to Claude Youker, Perry's court reporter. He agreed to provide us copies of the trial transcript to be paid for when and if we got the money. Then Perry did us a favor, unwittingly of course. He wrote a twenty-five-page "Summary of the Facts," which he sent the parties with an accompanying letter. "Because of the complexity of this case and the extensive documentation involved," he wrote, "I am of the opinion that copies of the summary may help the attorneys for all parties in organizing the appeal."

Perry's summary was nothing more that the defendants version of the evidence. He wrote that the purpose of COINTELPRO was to prevent violence and accepted as fact that Groth obtained his information from his own reliable informant. *Thank you, Judge Perry*, I thought. His summary proved he had considered the evidence in the light most favorable to the defendants, the opposite of what the correct legal standard required.

As soon as the trial transcript arrived, Flint, Dennis, and I began working with Chick and other PLO members to write the brief. Flint spent whole days at Lake Michigan reading and outlining the transcript and writing up the facts, while I reviewed and corrected the emerging statements of fact. We received some legal and financial support from the NAACP and their counsel, Jim Myerson, in New York. The National Council of Churches raised money for transcript costs. Given the publicity of the trial, Flint and I had plenty of calls for representation, but we only had time to take a few cases. When I wasn't writing the facts for our brief, I was defending paying clients in criminal court to support the office. Flint was becoming an expert on civil rights law, interpreting new decisions for civil rights' attorneys.

In the fall of 1977, PLO moved. Our old building was torn down, and our new offices on the sixteenth floor of the Fisher Building were even closer to the federal courts, where we were beginning to take on more civil rights cases. Maggie and I still lived in her apartment on Roscoe Street, and our relationship coalesced around our new son, Roger, and the excitement of raising him.

That fall was a blur of reading transcripts, gleaning salient facts, writing them down coherently, and carefully citing each fact to the relevant page of the transcript. For three months I wrote in longhand, as did Flint. Linda Turner typed up our drafts. Her willingness to stay up all night as we made corrections and she retyped each draft made it possible to meet our deadlines. Dennis and Chick did much of the editing and rewriting, and others helped with the legal argument.

The brief ended up 274 pages long with 100 pages of appendices. Dennis supplied the adjectives, and Fred's inspiration had a hand in writing it. We began the section entitled "The Massive Prejudice of the Court Below" with Perry's declaration from page 33,365 of the transcript about a fair trial: "You bet your life you are not going to get it."

Our brief was an indictment of government wrongdoing and cover-up. It is at least as applicable today as when it was written. We gathered the injustices we'd seen, the realizations that came from trying to expose them, and our eight years of frustrations into its final passages.

[Perry] conducted a trial, which was an agonizing reenactment of the raid, and cover-up—a counterintelligence action in which the Defendants again cooperated to neutralize and disrupt the Plaintiffs and their lawyers in the Courtroom by discrediting them to the jury, whom they constantly sought to misdirect. The Federal Defendants again stayed in the background, hiding their involvement while encouraging the State Defendants and their counsel to do the dirty work. In their corner was the trial Judge who unfailingly supported their cause because he was committed to its triumph.

This Court must see to it that the conspiracy proceeds no further, as well as holding those shown to be responsible accountable. Plaintiffs have sought to prosecute this case for eight years in the public interest as well as their own. FBI racial counterintelligence was a star-spangled blueprint for genocide, and still is if allowed to exist, and if those who operate it are still allowed to do so. They still have the mission of neutralization against their perceived political opponents, and they still demand immunity for their operations. They still purport to be protecting the country; and they still do not accept the Bill of Rights.

For all this, the undersigned demand detailed and determined redress, to be ordered and guaranteed by this Honorable Court through the full and timely exercise of its judicial responsibility, upon the authority of the truth and the People of the United States, until full justice is finally done.

All Power to the People.

Montgomery filed a short brief adopting some of our research and arguments. He focused on getting a new trial against the shooters. He didn't join in our accusations of Perry's prejudice.

In their answer filed sixty days later, The FBI defendants claimed that they were immune from liability because they were acting within the scope of their official duties as FBI employees carrying out the Counterintelligence Program. This was an ironic twist given their years of denial that COINTELPRO was relevant. Taken to its logical extension, this defense would allow FBI agents to destroy and neutralize the Panthers, or any other political organization, by violent means. They asked for *carte blanche* to commit murder and violate the Constitution with impunity. It is the "good German" defense of "just doing my duty" that was rejected at the Nuremberg trials. It is similar to the immunity being claimed today for those who ordered and implemented torture at Abu Ghraib and Guantánamo Bay detention centers based on their carrying out the government-mandated torture policy.

Our reply brief warned that the urge to grant immunity to all government wrongdoing was a fascist impulse: "The court must reject these 'I was only following orders' assertions out of hand. To do otherwise would sanction a program of official lawlessness of a magnitude never before contemplated and a viciousness never before seen."

The state defendants' answer contained an egregious attempt to protect Groth from having to name his purported informant. They argued that disclosure would be "a disastrous blow to law enforcement . . . and dry up police sources." In our reply brief, we countered, "The defendants' contention that the anonymity of the informant must be protected at all costs is really nothing more than an attempt to shield themselves from liability."

Finally, all the defendants strongly objected to the sanctions we asked the court to impose and the interim fees we sought. Our reply brief answered their objections:

Unless this Court exercises its statutory and equitable powers and provides Plaintiffs with the resources with which to continue the battle, the

Defendants' economic war of attrition against the Plaintiffs will continue and the dollar bill will prove more powerful than the Bill of Rights.

Janis Joplin sang, "Freedom's just another word for nothing left to lose." When we wrote the reply brief, we had lost everything but the freedom to speak the truth. We argued that the defendants were broadly inviting the court to join in the conspiracy to cover up their crimes. And on our eighty-fourth page, we concluded:

> This Court must fully accept the reality that a mere acknowledgment of the wrongdoing which has taken place is not enough; decisive, comprehensive action is required to prevent the ultimate success of the conspiracy. It cannot be left to these indigent Plaintiffs and exhausted lawyers to return to the beginning, and face the richly financed resistance of three governments, still bent on suppressing the truth.
>
> The Plaintiffs must be armed on remand with all of the evidence, and with enough money to carry through; and it must be made clear to the District Court that the law, the rules, and the truth will be upheld.

On August 18, 1978, Flint, Dennis, and I rode the elevator to the top floor of the Dirksen Federal Building to argue the appeal. We had been practicing our argument for days in front of Chick and Jon Moore, who had recently joined the office and had worked on the reply brief. We signed in as three of the appellants' attorneys. Montgomery's signature was already there as the fourth. Thomas Fairchild, Luther Swygert, and Wilbur Pell were the names of the judges listed to hear each of the three cases.

"We're two out of three," Flint said excitedly when we found a small briefing room and sat down at the table. We had researched the judges. We had a good draw.

We couldn't have done better than Judge Swygert. He was regarded as the most liberal judge on the circuit. Thomas Fairchild, the chief judge, was more in the center but was solid on the Civil Rights Act and the Constitution. He was part of the panel that reversed Perry in 1973 after Perry had dismissed our case the first time. The third judge, Wilbur Pell, was an archconservative who belittled civil rights claims. We had little chance with him, but we hoped he would not have much influence on the other two.

"We have a shot with this bunch," Dennis said. I was relieved. I couldn't imagine arguing before a panel of three judges like Perry, if indeed three of his kind even existed. It was my first appellate argument and I was nervous as hell.

At 9:00 A.M. we entered the large, heavily carpeted courtroom. There was a table for counsel on each side, and in front was the podium with a microphone, well below the bench where the three judges sat. We put our papers on the appellant's table on the right, next to Jim Montgomery. The rows of benches for the spectators behind us were full, with the front rows reserved for the plaintiffs, defendants, and the press. My mother had again come up from Atlanta, and she was sitting behind Iberia.

Some of the familiar tension returned as we faced Coghlan and Volini for the first time in more than a year. Next to them were Touhy, Witkowski, and Harland Leathers, a Justice Department attorney who argued for the FBI. Jon Moore and Chick Hoffman had brought Zimmers's scale model into the courtroom at 8:45 A.M. and placed it below the bench.

We all stood as the three judges walked in from the left and assumed their places in their high-backed leather chairs. Chief Judge Fairchild was in the middle and stated the rules: Ninety minutes for each side; the clerk would turn on the white light on the podium when there was a minute left, and the red light would come on when time was up. Time would be strictly enforced. The lawyers did not have to repeat the evidence because the judges had read our briefs, but both sides were free to emphasize specific facts they felt were important.

Montgomery spoke slowly and dramatically, with pauses after each salient fact. He walked over and pointed to the rooms in the scale model to show the judges where each event had occurred. He described Fred "being shot in his bed as he lay drugged and asleep," and the two fatal shots "coming from the doorway of his bedroom," while pointing to these locations. The large appellate courtroom reverberated with his deep, rich voice as he highlighted Brenda's testimony. She had seen "Mark Clark fall toward the floor after a shot from Davis, and she saw the flash of Mark's gun as he was falling." Montgomery emphasized that after the police had shot Brenda and Mark and secured the living room, they had total control of the apartment and should have stopped firing.

I spoke next, afraid that I'd be asked about a case whose facts I couldn't remember. I always had a tough time connecting the facts of a case with its title. I described the specific actions of each FBI defendant and explained how they fit together to set up the deadly raid. The acts themselves were sufficient for a jury to find them part of the conspiracy. When we added that they were operating pursuant to COINTELPRO mandates to destroy, disrupt, and cripple the Panthers and neutralize their leadership, the evidence was overwhelming.

As Flint walked up to face the judges, he picked up the silver pitcher resting on the podium and poured water into a glass. He looked up but kept pouring as the glass overflowed, spilling water on Flint and the carpet. Recalling the earlier contempt order surrounding the water pitcher in the trial court, Judge Fairchild interjected, "I knew we shouldn't have an open pitcher here." Everyone laughed, including Flint. For a brief moment the charged atmosphere was broken.

Flint continued and focused on the cover-up as evidence of the defendants' guilt. He emphasized the contrast between the federal grand jury, where Johnson, Piper, and Mitchell never mentioned the FBI role, and the bonus documents where they claimed credit for the raid and its "success." When we finished our arguments, the judges had asked us very few questions.

John Touhy had a much harder time. After a long, boring recitation having to do with the peripheral defendants, the judges became impatient and questioned him about the discrepancies between the physical evidence and the raiders' testimony. He wasted a lot of time explaining that Volini would answer their questions. His cocounsel finally passed him a note telling him to sit down.

When Volini started, little time was left. He repeated the raiders' version of the opening event; Brenda fired her shotgun at the incoming police. Judge Fairchild confronted him with Brenda Harris's testimony denying this. Volini tried to discredit her, but Fairchild kept asking, "Isn't the credibility of the witnesses for the jury to decide?" Every time Volini repeated the raiders' testimony, Fairchild and Swygert confronted him with the conflicting accounts and physical evidence.

Volini became more and more frustrated and finally blurted out, "Who are we fooling here?" We're "nitpicking," he said, referring to the judges' questions. He regressed to his trial litany of how dangerous the Panthers were and how many unregistered guns they possessed.

Judge Swygert stopped him. "Are you saying the Panthers have no constitutional rights?"

Volini paused and tried to backtrack. "No, Your Honor, I wouldn't suggest that."

Swygert confronted Volini with Hanrahan's statement that Hampton had fired at the police from the back bedroom. Volini was forced to admit that no one had told Hanrahan this.

After Volini, Witkowski defended Groth's refusal to name his informant. He argued that we had failed to provide enough evidence showing his nonexistence to make Groth release the name. This seemed absurd; everyone knew proving a negative is almost impossible, particularly when the person with knowledge is shielded from questioning. Fairchild forced Witkowski to agree that if the informant did not exist, this would undermine the entire basis for the raid. Fairchild asked him, what was the reason Groth had withheld the name? Witkowski hesitated then replied, "Danger to the informant." He didn't dare argue the nonexistent "danger to other persons" privilege that Coghlan had concocted for Perry.

Justice Department attorney Harland Leathers started by saying the FBI defendants were immune because they were carrying out national policy and acting pursuant to their duties. The "acting under orders" defense. Swygert asked, "Are you saying that they could act illegally and still be immune? Would they have immunity if they gave Hanrahan a gun and told him to shoot Fred Hampton?"

Leathers tried a new strategy, arguing that the FBI defendants did not participate in the raid and were only passing along information. Fairchild responded, "If the FBI gave a floor plan to someone planning a bank robbery, wouldn't they be accountable?"

Leathers answered that the FBI had no knowledge of any illegal activity and no intent to cause any. Fairchild asked, couldn't the FBI assume after November 13 that the police might want revenge? Didn't COINTELPRO indicate an intent to destroy the Panthers and their leadership? Weren't these questions for the jury to decide? Leathers responded by repeating that the FBI defendants had acted lawfully.

As he finished, Leathers said he was appalled that in our reply brief, we accused him of a "fascist" mentality when he's claiming that the FBI was immune from liability for its actions pursuant to COINTELPRO because they were doing their duty and carrying out national policy.

When Dennis rose for rebuttal, Pell asked him if the court would also be part of the fascist conspiracy if it upheld Perry's rulings. This question looked like trouble.

We could not ignore the fascist aspect of COINTELPRO, Dennis replied, with its claim of absolute immunity for government misconduct. COINTELPRO was "so outrageous" that it "can't be properly characterized" any other way.

Pell again challenged Dennis on his terminology, but Dennis continued. He shared our dilemma with the judges. "We were constantly forced to choose between exaggeration and restraint in describing the most notorious event of our lives and the most incredible train of events following it."

I feared Swygert and Fairchild would feel the need to protect Pell against Dennis's characterizations of the FBI.

After a few more back-and-forths, Fairchild intervened and told Dennis to focus on the facts of our case, not the abstract labels. Dennis balked at first, saying we could not ignore the threat that COINTELPRO imposed nationally. He then described specifically how COINTELPRO had led to the December 4 raid. He ended with a plea to the court not merely to reverse Perry but to arm us with the necessary tools—interim attorney's fees and sanctions—to have a fair chance at the next trial.

"This case will be taken under advisement," Fairchild announced. The judges stood and walked out. Flint, Dennis, and I gave each other positive nods. We shook hands with Montgomery; he had been at his best. As we exited, I saw my mother talking to Iberia.

"I hope you get some justice," my mother said. "Jeff's told me how much you've had to take."

"Well, he and Flint have had to take it also," Iberia responded. "They deserve to win."

Part V

Vindication

46

A Victory

Atlanta in April is as beautiful as any city in the world. The white dogwoods, the multicolored azaleas, the pink flowering quince all come to life everywhere, particularly in the Chastain Park area where my parents live. It was still chilly and gray in Chicago when Maggie and I came to my parents' house for a visit in 1979 with one-and-a-half-year-old Roger and Maggie six months pregnant. My dad watched incredulously as Roger donned a hat and cane and did an amazingly graceful version of a tap shoe routine he'd learned to mimic before he learned to talk.

On the Monday afternoon of a particularly gorgeous day, Maggie and I were visiting friends of hers who lived outside Atlanta. We were in the kitchen of their home when the phone rang. "It's for you," Maggie's friend said. I had left the number where we would be with my mom. I took the phone and walked out onto the steps outside.

"Jeff, we won," I heard Flint say. "The decision came down today."

"What, are you kidding?" I asked, knowing he wasn't.

"No, it's real and it's amazing. We won on everything. A new trial against all the defendants, sanctions against the feds, Groth has to name his informant, and even our contempts were reversed."

"And—," I started to ask.

"Yes, they got rid of Perry and even awarded us interim fees. It's incredible, from the little I've read so far. Swygert wrote the opinion and adopted our uncompromising view of the case and analysis of the evidence."

I was elated.

Flint added that Pell had written a vicious dissenting opinion attacking us, and he expected that the defendants would seek a rehearing from the entire Seventh Circuit. A chilling thought, too demoralizing to contemplate at that moment.

"I only wish I was at PLO to celebrate," I ended. "Congratulate Dennis, Chick, Jon, and Peter for me," I said. "They made it possible. And of course you, Flint, you've been the best." I was crying.

"You weren't bad yourself," Flint said. We laughed.

Maggie had heard my excitement and came outside. "We did it," I said. "We won everything."

She was so happy tears came, and we hugged. She'd been through a lot. I had hardly relaxed since the trial. "Call your parents," Maggie said. "No, let's surprise them when Dad gets home."

That night I told them to sit down. When they did I said, "Guess what? Mom, that call you forwarded was from Flint. We won!"

I have never seen my dad happier. His smile and hug made me feel it was OK I didn't get into Harvard. I'd still done well practicing law. Mom wanted to know the details, so I told her all I knew.

The next day the opinion arrived. Flint had included some press clippings. I took the whole packet into my dad's study, sat down in his comfortable black reclining chair with the matching ottoman, and read. "New Panther Trial Granted, Survivors Get Another Chance at Hanrahan," the *Chicago Defender* headlines declared over the photo of Fred's bloodstained bed. The *Tribune* and *Sun-Times* had similar headlines.

I began reading Judge Swygert's opinion. After a few pages of his opinion, it was clear he understood the implications of our evidence and grasped how the conspiracy worked. He understood the significance of Mitchell's placing the floor plan in the one file where it could be destroyed; Jalovec's acknowledging to Mitchell that his information was *the* source for the raid; and the manner in which the federal grand jury was used to cover up the FBI's role.

Judge Swygert rejected the defendants' arguments that the FBI defendants and the raiders couldn't be in a conspiracy because they didn't know each other. He wrote:

> The participants in the conspiracy must share the general conspiratorial objective, but they need not know all the details of the plan designed to achieve the objective or possess the same motives for desiring the intended conspiratorial result. . . . Plaintiffs did offer sufficient evidence to warrant a jury determination of whether a conspiracy existed.

We had always alleged a single conspiracy including both the execution of the raid and the cover-up. Swygert said we could show two conspiracies—

the first conspiracy was designed to subvert and eliminate the Black Panther Party and its members . . . the second conspiracy harassed the survivors of the raid. Moreover, the postraid conspiracy was intended to frustrate any redress the plaintiffs might seek and more important to conceal the true character of the preraid and raid activities of the defendants involved in the first conspiracy.

Swygert directed, "the trial court upon remand should provide jury instructions that will insure the jury is aware of the alternatives of finding single or multiple conspiracies in the evidence presented by plaintiffs." Swygert intended for a jury, not the next trial judge, to decide the case.

Judge Swygert rejected Hanrahan's claims of absolute immunity, stating it did not apply when he was supervising police officers or holding press conferences prejudicing defendants' rights to a fair trial. Neither did the FBI defendants have immunity from the Civil Rights Act when they acted in conspiracy with each other and with local officials to violate established constitutional rights.

The court ruled that we had made a case under Section 1985 of the Civil Rights Act, "Conspiracies involving racial or discriminatory intent." Swygert commented, "The statute was intended, perhaps more than anything else, to provide redress for victims of conspiracies impelled by a commingling of racial and political motives. And this is precisely the sort of conspiracy alleged by plaintiffs in this case."

Judge Swygert's pronouncements on the nature and scope of conspiracies to violate civil rights remain a primer of civil rights and conspiracy law today. So do his findings that state actors who fail to intervene to protect the civil rights of citizens are also liable. Thus, the nonshooters who witnessed the Panther beatings after the raid but did nothing to intervene could be held liable.

In addition to reinstating our case and ordering a new trial, Swygert made three other rulings that greatly improved our posture in the lawsuit.

First, he rejected Groth's claim of an absolute informant privilege. "A considerable amount of evidence was introduced leading to the conclusion that either Groth did not have an informant and merely repeated the information he had received from Jalovec in the affidavit for the warrant, or that O'Neal was Groth's informant." Swygert acknowledged that if Groth's informant did not exist, the warrant would be invalid, supported only by "misrepresented triple hearsay, and this would further bolster plaintiffs' conspiracy claims" and "highlight the importance of the federal defendants in the alleged conspiracy."

Amen, he's got it right there.

Next Swygert took on the issue of the FBI defendants' violations of pretrial discovery: "Moreover, sanctions should be imposed against the federal defendants and counsel representing them at the first trial for repeatedly disobeying court orders to produce documentary material."

This was too good to be true. I'd love to see Kanter's and Christenbury's faces when they read this. I had to call Flint.

"I just read the part about sanctions. What do you think this means?" I asked.

"Dennis and I have been talking about that," he said. "It's interesting that Swygert cared more about enforcing Perry's discovery orders than Perry ever did. We think we should get the next trial judge to consider entering judgment against the FBI defendants and fining their lawyers. If not, the next jury should be told the FBI hid evidence, and they may consider that as evidence of guilt."

"They all sound good to me," I replied. "And well deserved."

"Have you gotten to our contempts yet?" Flint asked.

"Coming up," I replied. "I can't wait." I hung up and kept reading.

Swygert described the circumstances that led to Flint's contempt, including Perry's erroneous accusation that I had "deliberately and willfully misread the stipulation," his refusal to provide us with a transcript, and his refusal "to correct the record immediately." He continued with, "These combined circumstances apparently caused Taylor to reach the breaking point of his patience and forbearance." Swygert noted that the incident occurred while the jury was in recess. "While we do not intend to condone Taylor's gesture of anger, we are convinced . . . there was no interference with the conduct of the trial. There was no obstruction in the administration of justice."

One down. Let's see what he says about me.

Haas was held in contempt for saying "we can't cover up the cover-up." After saying this, he tried to explain: "that is part of our complaint that they covered up, Judge." The judge, however, took the remark as personally directed at him. In the context of what happened before, the judge, in our opinion, had no reason to interpret the remark in that manner; and should have given Haas the benefit of every doubt.

Thank you, Judge Swygert.

He went on to cite with approval the principle stated in the Seventh Circuit's reversal of Kunstler and Weinglass's contempts in the Conspiracy Seven trial:

Attorneys have a right to be persistent, vociferous, contentious, and imposing, even to the point of appearing obnoxious, when acting on their client's behalf. An attorney may, with impunity, take full advantage of the range of conduct that our adversary system allows. Accordingly, we find the contempt citations are unwarranted when considered in their factual setting.

Vindicated again. A long time comin', but it sure felt good.

Swygert also awarded us interim attorneys' fees for winning the appeal and declared that the case should be reassigned to a new trial judge, who should give the "retrial high priority."

"Perry's history!" I exclaimed.

"It won't be nearly as good theater next time," Maggie said, with a whimsical smile, "but your chances of surviving are much better."

Swygert's opinion in *Hampton v. Hanrahan* (cited at 600 F. 2d 600) remains among the most famous civil rights decisions ever rendered. Pell's vituperative dissent conceding he had not read the entire record was a sharp criticism on Swygert and an outright attack on PLO and the Panthers. It reminded me of how easily the opinion could have gone the other way. Nevertheless, it was time to celebrate, and the day I got back to Chicago we partied well into the night wearing freshly lettered T-shirts proclaiming, RIGHT ON, LUTHER! compliments of Chick Hoffman.

47

Onward

By the time the Seventh Circuit decision came down, the aftermath of another event was demanding more of my time than the Hampton case. On July 22, 1978, a few weeks before our Hampton oral argument, there was a riot at Pontiac Correctional Center in central Illinois. Three guards had been stabbed to death and the prison was on indefinite lockdown. After Attica, I had represented prisoners in a number of suits challenging conditions in Illinois prisons. The century-old maximum-security prison in Pontiac was among the worst in the state.

Two days after the riot, or rebellion as we called it, I visited prisoners I knew at Pontiac. They urged me to get involved in defending whoever would be charged with the guards' deaths. Prison officials were publicly stating they would seek the death penalty. For the next six months, I drove the one hundred miles to Pontiac Correctional Center at least once a week.

First, I gathered information on the conditions there, which included weeks and then months of twenty-four-hour-a-day lockdowns in tiny cells five tiers high in a steel cell house that was brutally hot during the day and freezing at night. Food, often containing rat feces and human hair, was passed to the prisoners through chuckholes in their cell doors.

PLO brought a suit challenging the continued lockdown. After we provided the court with prisoners' firsthand accounts, we convinced Judge John Powers Crowley to accompany me to the prison for a surprise visit. The prison had been on twenty-four-hour lockdown for two months. He and I walked the intensely hot galleries strewn with stinking, uncollected garbage, watching comatose men sleeping in their underwear at noon. Judge Crowley did not want to tell me his impressions informally, but he kept shaking his head, and I could tell he was mortified. The next day he ordered that the lockdown be lifted.

The success of our lawsuit and the sympathetic and dramatic TV footage of the conditions at Pontiac Correctional Center turned the public's sympathy from the guards and toward the prisoners as people came to understand the riot as a spontaneous response to inhumane treatment. Nevertheless, by the middle of 1979, the Department of Corrections charged seventeen prisoners with conspiracy to riot and murder. As the lawyer who had been visiting regularly since the riot, I had earned the confidence of most of the defendants. I was in the best position to organize the Pontiac Brothers legal team. With seventeen men facing the death penalty, I couldn't abandon them. There were other PLOers to help with the Hampton case, and the new trial seemed far away.

The Pontiac defense occupied the majority of my time from late 1978 through the criminal trial, which began two years later. I played Flint's role, marshaling and indexing the documents, and with Michael's help, drafting many of the legal motions. I met with the defendants regularly in Pontiac and helped them recruit lawyers who would work for a joint defense. The Cook County Bar Association, Chicago's black lawyers organization, encouraged their members to help the Pontiac Brothers. We wanted quality lawyers for all the men charged as quickly as possible to avoid the defendants getting nervous and suspicious and testifying against each other in exchange for leniency.

The follow-up legal work on the Hampton case fell heavily on Flint and Dennis, with backup from Chick and Jon Moore. Both were excellent writers and researchers. Jon had joined the office to work on the Hampton appeal and had proved his merits working on our reply brief. I was still available to read their motions, strategize, and argue in court, but the defense of the Pontiac prisoners was becoming as intense as the Hampton trial had been. Also needing my attention was our second son, Andrew Hampton Haas-Roche, who was born on September 5, 1979.

Flint's stature in the legal community and his self-assurance grew with the Hampton trial and especially the appeal. He and other Lawyers Guild members started the *Police Misconduct Litigation Manual*, which remains the most highly regarded primer for civil rights attorneys. The first issue was devoted to an analysis of Judge Swygert's opinion.

Flint tackled the new legal challenges in the Hampton case, more determined than ever. The defendants were petitioning the entire

Seventh Circuit to reverse Swygert. They needed a majority of the eight circuit judges to get a rehearing. Flint took the lead in answering the multiple arguments contained in the defendants' briefs, which were basically rewrites of the issues they lost in the original appeal. On September 12, by a 3–3 vote, the rehearing was denied. If the two judges who'd recused themselves had remained on the panel, Swygert's decision would have likely been revisited and very likely reversed.

A month after the court of appeals ruling, the *Chicago Sun-Times* reported that Judge Pell, who wrote the scathing dissent and who voted for a rehearing, had been an FBI agent and remained active in the Society of Former Special Agents of the FBI. This group lobbied for and funded the legal defense of former FBI director L. Patrick Gray, accused of illegal surveillances of radicals, as well as Thomas Kearney, an FBI agent charged with illegal mail opening and wiretapping. Pell had excluded his FBI stint and membership in the former FBI support organization from his official resume.

When the Justice Department informed Judge Perry it had decided not to appeal Swygert's reversal of Flint and my contempts, Perry was so disappointed he wrote his own brief to justify his actions and uphold his contempt findings. This unprecedented partisan action by the trial judge did more to show "he was an activist seeking combat," as we had described him in our appellate brief, than anything we could have done. I was delighted when the Seventh Circuit denied his plea.

Following Swygert's instructions, Flint submitted a bill for our appellate work. He calculated he had put in 1,532 hours at $80 per hour and I had put in 542 hours at $90. Together with hours from the rest of our office and a multiplier because of the difficulty of the work and the uncertainty of getting paid, we sought $500,000 in appellate fees. John Coghlan, who had received more than twice that amount personally, was quoted in the paper, saying, "I'm pleased to see that for once they are not posing to be in this thing for the public good. I'm glad to see they like the buck the same as the rest of us do. It reinforces my opinion of human nature."

Despite this endorsement of our humanity, Coghlan filed strenuous objections to our receiving any fees, and the Seventh Circuit set our fee award at one hundred thousand dollars.

As expected, Coghlan and Volini, who had already received over two million dollars of public money, filed for *certiorari*, or leave to appeal Swygert's ruling to the U.S. Supreme Court. Putting more resources into defending Hanrahan and the raiders was met with strong resistance from black members of the Cook County Board of Commissioners and the City Council. A *Chicago Daily Defender* editorial captured the majority black sentiment:

> The major decision makers at the Cook County and federal government levels deserve contempt for their decision to fight the Black Panther ruling. . . . Essentially, this means all of us taxpayers will continue to pour millions of dollars into an endless and futile effort. . . . As a small, vocal segment of the public, we state our resentment of this action. We believe the folks out in the street resent it too. There is no real doubt about what happened on Dec. 4, 1969. The only doubt is when our exalted public officials will stop playing games at our expense.

We answered the government's petition to the Supreme Court on behalf of our five plaintiffs and hoped that our pleading would stand for all the survivors because Montgomery filed nothing on behalf of the four he was representing. We still had received no money, and the lengthy briefs in the Seventh Circuit and again in the Supreme Court were time consuming and exhausting. Michael and I were getting paid thirty-five dollars per hour by the state of Illinois for the Pontiac defense. That kept PLO afloat.

We feared that the defendants would get the four judges they needed to have the Supreme Court grant *certiorari* and take the case. Justice John Paul Stevens, a liberal justice formerly from the Seventh Circuit, had removed himself because he wrote the first Hampton opinion reversing Perry. We filed a brief to disqualify the very conservative justice William Rehnquist because he had worked in the Justice Department during the time of the federal grand jury and had been the chief attorney for Attorney General John Mitchell, a potential defendant in our case. Rehnquist refused to step down.

On June 2, 1980, more than a year after Swygert had ruled, the Supreme Court, by a 7–1 vote on the shooters and a 5–3 vote on the federal defendants, refused to take the case. Justice Lewis Powell issued a scathing dissent with respect to the federal defendants, reminiscent of Pell. He wrote that our objective was not monetary damages but "a larger target—the FBI." Not surprisingly, Rehnquist joined Chief Justice Warren Burger and Powell in the dissent. Despite the decision upholding our opinion, the court reversed Swygert 7–1 on awarding interim fees, with only Justice Thurgood Marshall dissenting. Again, we had no funds to pursue the case and unpaid bills from the first trial.

When the Supreme Court denied *certiorari*, I was preparing the defense of Joseph Smith, one of ten Pontiac Brothers set to go on trial in September 1980. Each man faced the death penalty, and each had his own lawyer. Michael had convinced the trial judge to remove the case to Chicago, and the ten defense lawyers were meeting on a daily basis to prepare. I had never done a death penalty case, and here I was one of the chief counsel in what some called the largest death penalty case in U.S. history.

After seventeen months of Perry, I felt I could handle just about anything in court. I was by no means alone. The Pontiac Brothers had interviewed and recruited many of the top black criminal lawyers in Chicago and nationally for the defense team.

The family and friends of the men on trial, together with those concerned with Illinois prison conditions, formed the Pontiac Brother Defense Committee. They sent out a steady stream of information about the overcrowding and abhorrent conditions in Illinois prisons. "Put the state on trial" was our motto, and hundreds of spectators, mostly from the black community and many from families of prisoners, came to support the men on trial.

In August 1980, I hauled my boxes of Pontiac files to Twenty-Sixth Street, where the Pontiac defense team had been given an office and where the defense lawyers met regularly. The trial was set to start the next month. "I'm sure you can handle Hampton," I said to Flint, as I was about to embark on another long and contentious trial.

"No problem. Got it covered," my less-than-effusive but dogged partner replied.

Flint had been studying and cataloging the transcript and the record to implement Judge Swygert's orders that Groth must disclose his informant and the new judge must consider sanctions against the feds. Jon Moore and Chick Hoffman also worked with Flint.

In September, as the Pontiac trial was starting, Flint and his team filed a new interrogatory and document request on Groth to name his informant, to produce documentary proof that he had an informant, and to schedule his deposition. Ten days later they filed a motion to amend our complaint to add Hoover's estate, former attorney general John Mitchell, Jerris Leonard, and the FBI heads of COINTELPRO as defendants.

The Hampton case was reassigned to Judge Milton Shadur, a liberal judge and scholar of constitutional law. We were optimistic. On September 25, 1980, he set the first status date. Flint opened the session appropriately: "Ten years later, here we are back in court—the city, state, and federal governments are still spending millions of taxpayers' dollars to defend this murder." That was as far as he got.

The defendants had filed a motion to recuse Shadur. They argued that he was prejudiced because one of his former law partners had been a member of the Lawyers' Committee for Civil Rights, which had written an *amicus curiae*, or friend of the court, brief in support of the special prosecutor seeking to indict Hanrahan in 1971. Before Shadur could take any action, he had to resolve the recusal issue. He announced he would rule in October. Frustrated, Flint told the press as he walked out, "They're trying to get rid of the only judge who might be fair."

In October, Shadur wrote in an opinion that he believed he was impartial, but his "impartiality might be said to be questioned" because of the position of his former law partner. He declined to keep the case. Shadur was a stickler on the law and very protective of constitutional rights. We appealed, claiming there was insufficient basis for him to remove himself, but the Seventh Circuit judge refused to reverse his decision.

Judge John F. Grady, a former federal prosecutor with a reputation for issuing tough sentences to criminal defendants, was assigned the case. Grady was a large man with a particularly big head and thick bushy hair with a lock that frequently dropped over his forehead. He had an imposing manner reinforced by a deep voice. Grady was known as a no-nonsense judge. At the first court date, he addressed the lawyers: "It will be a long, arduous trial. It will cause the reliving of events extremely painful to people in this community. Settling out of court would be an act of legal statesmanship."

Grady recessed the case for two weeks to give the parties an opportunity to explore settlement options. I liked Grady's instinct to settle, but I knew the defendants weren't worried enough yet to offer real money. We'd have to change their prospects for the new trial.

48

Seize the Time

Flint and Dennis, now returned from Attica, began our offensive by writing and filing a fifteen-page motion for sanctions against the FBI. Flint had chronicled each deceptive statement the defendants and their attorneys had made, providing dates on which the documents were produced that proved their withholding of evidence. He also listed every hour we had wasted in depositions and at trial questioning FBI witnesses while the documents we needed were deliberately concealed. Flint calculated these at 2,861 hours pretrial and 1,871 hours at trial. Only Flint had the patience and persistence to prepare such a detailed compilation. It was necessary because Judge Fairchild had amended Swygert's order to say sanctions *might be* issued rather than *must be*, and we had to convince Grady to punish the FBI for its obstruction in the first trial.

Flint's motion asked for production of all FBI documents still withheld, default judgment against the FBI defendants, and an attorneys fee award to compensate for the unnecessary time it took to obtain materials that should have been produced early in discovery. We hoped to prevail on this motion and put the FBI in such a bad trial posture that they would have to settle.

The next Sunday, I took the afternoon off from working on the Pontiac trial, now in its third month of jury selection, to meet with Flint and Dennis. We sat in the conference room, flipping the Bears game on and off at breaks. The city wasn't offering more than fifty thousand dollars, and the FBI was saying it had no authority to indemnify the FBI defendants, who could pay only small amounts out of their pockets.

"Sounds like settlement isn't going anywhere," I said.

"It won't until we hold their feet to the fire," Dennis responded. "They think they can stall and play us off forever and still hang another jury.

They haven't been taught their lesson yet. I think they should pay big time for their arrogance. Three million sounds about right."

That seemed like a lot. Not too long ago we were tossed out of court.

"Let's go for it," Flint said. "If Grady gives us half a chance, we can really tighten the screws." His determined expression reinforced his words. "Let's see what they say after Groth has to give up a name for his supposed informant and after Grady rules on sanctions."

I marveled at Flint's will. We all knew there was no easy way home. He was fully aware of the continued imbalance of resources and our empty bank account. But the lure of winning, of proving the conspiracy, trumped everything else.

"Let's tell Montgomery to tell the defendants we're not interested in chump change," Dennis said. "Scheme on."

On the next court date, Flint reported to Grady in chambers that the defendants had offered nothing and were not serious about settlement. The plaintiffs wanted answers to the three motions we filed. Grady, who was used to having his suggestions followed, wasn't happy but he couldn't force the defendants to settle; not yet anyway. He set schedules for their responses.

The defendants' attorneys answered our motion to add the FBI and John Mitchell, the estates of Hoover and Clyde Tolson (an associate director of the FBI who was also Hoover's lover and heir), and the heads of COINTELPRO by arguing that the statute of limitations had run out and also that they were immune from prosecution. After lengthy briefs by both sides, Grady ruled in our favor. On August 4, 1981, he allowed us to join and charge as defendants in the conspiracy John Mitchell, Hoover's estate, Jerris Leonard, and the D.C. heads of COINTELPRO— everyone we wanted with the exception of the FBI itself, which he ruled had sovereign immunity as a federal agency. Adding the new defendants opened the door to more discovery about COINTELPRO in D.C., at FBI headquarters. *Strike one against the defendants*, I thought.

After lengthy briefing, and reading Flint's detailed compendium, Grady determined that sanctions against the FBI defendants were warranted. These included allowing us to put on evidence at the second trial that they had intentionally concealed evidence at the first trial, which the jury could construe to be evidence of their guilt. This ruling was devastating to the defendants on two fronts. It acknowledged a pattern of concealment by the defendants and their attorneys, which was greatly embarrassing to the FBI and U.S. Attorneys' Office, and it undermined their credibility in their denial of responsibility for the raid. The FBI's mantle, its arrogant assumption of propriety and good faith, would not be available at a second trial. *Strike two.*

The third avenue opened by the Seventh Circuit was Groth being forced to disclose a name for his supposed informant. Coghlan sought a sweeping protective order preventing us from following up with discovery after Groth disclosed the name of his informant. Coghlan asserted that further investigation would present great danger to the informant and his or her family. Grady entered the protective order temporarily.

Meanwhile, our Pontiac jury, nine out of twelve of whom were black, returned their verdict. I sat with nine other lawyers and ten men facing the death penalty as the clerk read the verdicts. "Not guilty for Albert Jackson on murder count one. . . . Not guilty for Lawrence Talbert on murder count one. . . . And finally, forty "not guilty" verdicts later, "Not guilty for Joseph Smith on murder count one." The jury found all the defendants "not guilty" on every count.

I looked at the relieved faces of the men on trial. Then there was jubilation—crying and hugs and thanks to the jury. The Pontiac Brothers' families were ecstatic as well. From possible death to freedom, many of them were released that afternoon. We had a dinner celebration with most of the jurors present. I was still high from the Pontiac verdicts when Flint came to tell me Groth's answer to our simple interrogatory, "What is the name of your informant?"

"They named Babatunde, just like we figured," Flint said.

"Big surprise," I said, "naming the dead man we thought they would. He can't deny it."

"But I think we can," Flint said. "They're gonna have to come up with some corroboration. Grady is going to be suspicious that after all these years of claiming how dangerous it would be to disclose the informant, they're now claiming a dead person."

Several days later we were in Judge Grady's plush, carpeted chambers. Flint and I had expected Groth to name Babatunde, but Grady was visibly shaken when Flint announced in the judge's chambers that the person Groth named had been dead for ten years. Grady shook his head, and his big hands opened palms up in a gesture of, what is this?

He was sitting at the end of his conference table with Flint and me on one side and Coghlan and Volini on the other.

"The impression I have had all along is that we have some live person there whose physical safety was allegedly in danger. Now, we have somebody who's been dead for ten years, a very different picture than I have been given up until now," Grady said, shaking his head in disbelief. Coghlan was fidgeting in his chair, trying his best to look earnest. He begged the judge to extend the protective order until Babatunde's mother decided if she needed protection. Grady reluctantly agreed. It gave Coghlan time for one last effort.

While the protective order remained in effect, Coghlan, together with uniformed Chicago police officer Michael Conneely, paid two visits to the home of Babatunde's mother, Theresa Morgan. From statements we obtained later from her, this is what happened: Coghlan told Mrs. Morgan that they were looking into the death of her son, which they claimed was part of a recently reopened investigation. He told her that Babatunde had given information to the police that provided the basis for the raid on Hampton's apartment in 1969 and this was about to be publicly announced. Mrs. Morgan later told us she was very upset and very suspicious.

On his next visit, Coghlan told her that he had information that Panther Milton Boyd murdered her son because he was the informant who caused Fred Hampton's death. Coghlan concocted the story that Boyd had struck her son in the head, detonated explosives near him, and drove his car away. To convince her, Coghlan drove her past the spot where he said Babatunde had been murdered.

Coghlan persuaded Mrs. Morgan to come to his office, where he introduced her to Sergeant Groth, whom he identified as "the one who knows [your son] was an informer." After Groth left, Coghlan dictated a statement he showed to Babatunde's mother. In Coghlan's typed statement, Mrs. Morgan stated that her son was a police informant and that the Morgans felt their lives would be in danger if this was disclosed—and they wanted police protection. Coghlan tried to persuade Mrs. Morgan and her remaining son to sign it by telling them that their lives were in danger from Hampton's friends.

Theresa Morgan refused to sign Coghlan's document despite his threats and entreaties. "Coghlan became angry and gave us cab fare to return home," she said. On his next appearance before Grady, again in chambers, Coghlan sought an extension of the protective order, claiming there had been an unexplained fire at Ms. Morgan's home sometime in the past. He sought to imply that the Morgans had already been victims of retaliation and thus needed protection.

Grady was growing impatient. He told Coghlan, "Given the plaintiffs were proceeding on the theory that there was not an informant for Groth, [Grady] could not imagine how his family could be in danger." Grady continued addressing Coghlan: "If there was any real danger to the relatives of a person who had been dead for several years, they would have felt the effects of it before now, and in a more palpable sense than an unexplained fire." He dissolved the previous protective order.

But Grady was not done. He wanted to know how long Coghlan had known Groth would name a dead person, since Coghlan had represented to Judge Perry, to the Seventh Circuit, and to Judge Grady that disclosure would endanger the life of the informant as well as other persons. If Coghlan knew the informant was dead, his representations would have been false and made in bad faith. The noose around Coghlan's neck was tightening. He turned redder than usual.

He cleared his throat before looking at the judge and answered, "I had *not* been told by Groth who the informant was. I had been doing my own figuring it out." Coghlan should have stopped, but now he was nervous and talked too much. "The reason I suspected him came from a statement Groth made on a deposition question that one of the meeting places, as I recollect, was a West Side elevated train." Coghlan claimed he connected Groth's "meeting" with his informant when he found out Morgan had worked as a conductor on the West Side El.

As we left Grady's chambers, Flint said to me, "I don't think Groth ever said anything about meeting his informant on a West Side El."

"I think Coghlan made that up," I answered. We went back to the office, where Flint and I reviewed the transcripts from Groth's deposition. After an hour we finished scanning them. There was nothing there about meeting his informant at or near a West Side El.

Two weeks later, at his deposition, Groth claimed an implausible lack of memory about anything that could be verified with respect to Babatunde being his informant. The worse his memory got, the clearer it became that not only was Babatunde not his informant but that he never had one. Groth testified—"testilied" would be more accurate—that he uncovered key information that the Panthers murdered Babatunde, but he could not substantiate or recall any of it. Significantly, he never reported his supposed information to the police or state's attorney.

The final piece in the puzzle came to us a week after Groth's deposition. On August 20, 1982, Flint and Sherman Randall, an investigator who worked on the Pontiac case, went to visit Theresa Morgan. When Flint introduced himself as a lawyer for the survivors in the Hampton raid, she looked relieved. "You know my son had nothing to do with that, don't you?" she said. "Those men tried to get me to say he was an informant and the Panthers killed him. There was no reason he would have been helping the police kill those boys."

"Do you mind if we tape what you say?" Flint asked.

"Not a bit," she said, and continued talking about Coghlan's visit.

"He never identified himself as a lawyer for Groth and Hanrahan. He acted like he was doing an investigation with the police. He took me to his office to sign a statement he wrote up. I refused to sign because it wasn't true and because my son wasn't here to talk for himself. That lawyer was trying to fool us."

Throughout her taped statement, Theresa Morgan made it clear she did not believe her son had ever been an informant and resented Coghlan's assertion that he was.

When Flint returned to PLO, he came into my office and played the tape of Theresa Morgan's interview. "That's a new low, even for Coghlan," I said, "telling Mrs. Morgan that her son was an informant and had been murdered. He has no shame."

"Well, we got him this time," a smiling Flint said, holding up the tape.

Flint amended our complaint to include the facts of Groth and Coghlan's ten-year deception of the courts with a false claim of privilege and how, when that was about to be exposed, Coghlan had attempted to mislead and frighten a witness into signing an untrue statement to cover their fraud and perjury. A few days after we filed the amended complaint with these allegations, Coghlan resigned. The newspapers reported that the county fired him. *Strike three.*

We were on a winning streak, having greatly bettered our position for the next trial. On the other hand, we still had no money and a case that would likely polarize a jury, making it difficult for a unanimous verdict.

Our posttrial interviews showed that only one juror besides Florence Smith wanted to assess damages against the police. There was the additional reality of our clients, who had been waiting thirteen years and had received no compensation for their injuries and losses. Many of them would not turn down real money if it were offered.

Montgomery had noted our success and had become quite solicitous of our work, complimenting Flint regularly with "nice job" each time Judge Grady ruled in our favor. But Montgomery also said that despite the improved position we were in legally, his clients wanted to settle, and he was duty bound to try to get the defendants to offer money.

Flint, Dennis, and I, together with the rest of PLO, called a meeting to weigh our position, much improved due to the recent successes. There is a point in civil litigation, after you have obtained an advantage strategically, when you must decide whether to cash in or roll the dice and try for the most at trial.

"I'm more than willing to keep going," Flint said as we sat around our conference table. "I really want to take John Mitchell's deposition and find out what he and the White House knew about COINTELPRO."

"I want to take it all the way to the top, too," I responded. "But when John Mitchell and the other defendants get new lawyers, they could delay the case for months, probably years. They'll claim the right to read the trial transcript and the thousands of pages of deposition testimony to get up to speed."

"Montgomery has been talking to the other side," Dennis said. "He says we'll be lucky to get two million. He's gonna make a deal no matter what we say. I think they should pay us three million dollars if they don't want to go to trial."

"If we do settle, a third should come from the FBI no matter what claim about agents not being indemnified," I said. "They can find a way, even if they have to pass legislation."

"Dan Webb, the U.S. attorney, would also like to settle this case and remove the taint of cover-up from his office," Flint added.

For so long it seemed our clients would never collect anything. But when I thought about the depth of the FBI conspiracy, Fred and Mark's deaths, the bullet wounds, and the thousands of hours we had put in, Dennis's number was no longer unrealistic. And of course it didn't really pay for the killing of Fred and Mark. Nothing would.

I had been running the prospect of settlement by our clients. "Doc is as loyal as ever and Fannie Clark is also," I reported. "They will go with whatever we propose." I thought Harold and Blair would also, and Truelock was always broke, so he'd probably support a settlement.

"I think our clients would be pleased with a substantial settlement," I continued. "We can't begrudge them that. And it wouldn't hurt for us to get paid for the last thirteen years, either. We can't finance the case forever. Can you live with a settlement, Flint?"

There was silence in the room. Flint didn't want to stop fighting, maybe didn't know how. He could go on forever. He shrugged, "If that's what people want, but I'm gonna keep pushing until a deal is signed."

Before our next court date in chambers, we went into a small conference room and discussed with Montgomery what we wanted. He said the defendants were now thinking in terms of "serious money."

"We want to get three million for all of us," I said.

"I would like to get that too, but my clients want to settle," he told us emphatically. "Coghlan and I have already discussed two million, and it's likely to work. I'm going to tell Grady we're in serious negotiations."

I had a mixed reaction. He wasn't demanding the three million we wanted, but two million still seemed like a hefty settlement. It was three times what the plaintiffs in the Kent Sate shootings settled for and would be one of the highest settlements in civil rights history. There was a difference between what we wanted and seeing real money on the table. The two million looked better than anything we had imagined months before. It would be enough to make people understand we'd won, but we agreed that it wasn't what the plaintiffs deserved or what we wanted. We would have to run it by our clients. We had always told them it would be their decision.

In chambers, Montgomery indicated that the two sides were making progress toward a settlement. We didn't contradict him. Robert Gruenberg was representing the FBI defendants, and with the certainty of sanctions being leveled against his clients at the next trial, he no longer dismissed our demand that the FBI put up one-third of the settlement. Grady hinted again that the sanctions he would invoke for their malfeasance at the first trial would be severe. Volini and Witkowski said the city and county would only pay if the feds paid their one-third.

"Any settlement will have to include money from the FBI," Flint said.

Gruenberg said he would do his best to get authorization for the FBI to pay its share.

"How much are we talking about?" Grady asked.

"Two million for all the plaintiffs is what we have been discussing," Montgomery said. Grady nodded as if he thought that might be an appropriate figure. Flint and I didn't object.

"I don't know what Montgomery's been told, but my clients haven't agreed to pay a third of that figure," Volini said, playing hardball to the end. But now he was bluffing. There was political pressure on the city from the black community to settle.

"Our clients haven't approved any settlement either," I pitched in. "We need time to discuss it."

"Well, I'm going to have all of you consult with your clients and then come back to see where we are. My position is clear," Grady said, looking at the defense lawyers. "This case should be settled. If I have to bring your superiors, the decision makers, in here to do it, I will."

"It sounds pretty good to me," Doc said when I called and told him we were negotiating in the range of two million dollars. "How much will each one of us get?"

"We haven't done all the numbers yet, but you will get more because of your injuries, around $150,000 after our fees and costs. And we're trying to get Fannie Clark at least $200,000."

"Whose gonna pay?" he asked.

"All of them," I said, "the city, county, and feds."

"Is some of it coming out of Hanrahan's pocket?"

"Unfortunately, no. The county will pay his bill. None of the defendants have to pay themselves. It's a drag, but at least we'll get paid."

"It don't seem right that the people who shot us pay nothing."

It always pisses off victims of the police to learn that taxpayers foot the bill. "It isn't right," I said. "But the police contract requires they be indemnified. I wish we were getting money from them too. It might deter them next time."

"Sound's OK, I guess." Not a totally enthusiastic endorsement of our twelve years of work. Then Doc added, "I know you guys did your best, and what you did was incredible. If the others say OK, it's OK with me."

As I hung up, I realized it might actually be over soon. I felt strangely ambivalent. We were about to win, or at least settle. We had presented enough proof of the conspiracy and the murders to force them to pay damages. But none of the perpetrators had to pay themselves. None of them had been convicted. Not even Carmody, who we believed shot Fred and who admitted dragging his body out for all to see. Not Hanrahan for endorsing Fred's murder, not the FBI for plotting the whole thing.

The negotiations went on for several weeks. On July 25, 1982, the *Sun-Times* headlined a story, "After 12 years, Panther Suit Nearing Settlement." Inside, the story stated unidentified sources claimed the negotiations were "positive" and that all lawyers were to submit their claims for fees at the next August court date.

Both sides had in fact been weighing the same number, $1.85 million. But when we submitted our claims for fees, we hit a snag. Montgomery wanted 45 percent of his clients' one-half of the settlement. We would presumably get the one-third share of our clients' settlement money, based on the agreement we had signed with all the plaintiffs at the beginning of the case. Flint calculated that we had done more than 90 percent of the work, and put in over 90 percent of the time. We didn't think Montgomery should get two-thirds of the legal fees.

Grady brought all of us together in chambers on October 6.

"I understand the plaintiffs and defendants have agreed to settle for $1.85 million with one-third coming from the city, one-third from the county, and one-third from the federal government," Grady announced. It seemed simple, anticlimactic. The money would mean a lot to our clients, but did it make up for what had been done and the decade spent uncovering it? However, once settlement negotiations begin, they have their own momentum. We weren't going to stop now.

"We have a fee dispute with Mr. Montgomery, but we don't believe that should hold up the settlement," I told Judge Grady.

"Have you prepared a document reflecting the settlement?" Grady asked.

Montgomery had brought three copies of the settlement agreement setting forth the terms. "I have it here," he said.

Grady looked at it hurriedly and then passed it around the table for each of the lawyers to sign. Flint, Dennis, and I looked at each other. *Last chance to bail out,* I thought. But we signed the paper as it passed our side of the table, and Montgomery signed it as well.

"We'll need your clients' signatures on releases," Grady said, standing up. "As soon as you get them, bring them to my clerk. I'll enter an order dismissing the case."

News of our impending settlement, and the amount, reached the press a few weeks later from an undisclosed Justice Department source. "$1.85 Million Accord Reached in 1969 Black Panther Case," the *Los Angeles Times* reported on October 24, 1982. At the same time, the county board was about to vote to approve the settlement. "Pay and move on," was the official position.

On Sunday, November 14, the *New York Times* did a follow-up article on the settlement. Bill, Fred's brother, was quoted: "At times when we had to go to court almost daily it seemed that we should just give up. But we in the family knew we were right, that the police were wrong, so we kept praying and kept fighting."

Flint commented in the article, "The case may be almost over in the legal sense but it will live on as a reminder to people of how far the government can and will go to suppress those whose philosophies it does not like."

Assistant U.S. Attorney Gruenberg denied that the settlement was an admission of responsibility and said it "was intended to avoid another costly trial." This is what the government says when it settles, regardless of the size of the payout. Hanrahan refused to comment.

Still it was not over. Nothing came easy. Montgomery's clients refused to sign the releases. He claimed they objected to us getting paid for the time we put in for them, but we couldn't check this out because his new retainer gave him the exclusive power to negotiate with us. On November 24 we appeared in Grady's chambers. Bob Gruenberg, who had worked to get the FBI to come up with its part of the settlement, warned Grady that he was "worried" the federal government might renege and withdraw its offer.

Grady was riled. He did not want the deal to collapse. He looked at Montgomery, and in the sternest tone he could muster said, "There is no one who can predict what might happen here, and it seems very plain to me that these plaintiffs [Montgomery's clients] are making a mistake by not signing these releases."

On December 2, Dennis, Flint, and I sent a memo to Montgomery's clients, the Hamptons, Deborah Johnson, Verlina Brewer, and Brenda Harris: "We firmly believe that PLO is legally, morally, and in every other way entitled to be fairly paid for the work we did for our former clients both before and after we represented you directly; and that it would be morally and legally wrong for Jim Montgomery to receive 45 percent of half of this settlement fund while we are left with one-third of the other half."

We attached a breakdown of the hours of pretrial, trial, and appeal. PLO attorneys expended thirty-seven thousand hours and Montgomery slightly fewer than four thousand. The breakdown stated: "The record shows that we did at least nine-tenths of the work on the case as a whole. . . . We feel that we should receive at least three-fourths of the combined lawyers share." Our memo also said the settlement should include reimbursement to the organizations that had paid expenses— the Center for Constitutional Rights, the Lawyers' Committee for Civil Rights, the National Jury Project, and the NAACP—as well as James Carter, whose firm of black court reporters we owed nine thousand dollars, and, finally, Robert Zimmers, for the remainder of his expert fee.

"December 4 is almost here again, and we shouldn't let it pass with the entire settlement, and everything it means to all of us for the past and future, still hanging fire," our memo concluded. Two months later, on February 28, Grady called. He had the signed releases. We could pick up the settlement order.

Later that day, almost thirteen years after we filed our suit, Dennis, Flint, and I stood in front of the news cameras at our office and read our press release. We gave credit for the settlement to the court of appeals, the work done before Judge Grady, and "the continuing community concern particularly among black people." We ended:

> It is entirely appropriate that the legal portion of this case has been con-
> cluded during Black History month, for the murders of Hampton and
> Clark by the agents of three governments is a most significant event not
> only in black history but also in the history of this city and in history as
> recorded by all people of conscience. We intend to continue to keep the
> memory and meaning of December 4 alive, so that it will be more difficult
> for government officials to conspire to murder two black leaders and to
> destroy the movement, which they led.
>
> FLINT TAYLOR
JEFFREY HAAS
DENNIS CUNNINGHAM

Epilogue

It's Mother's Day weekend 2005 in Haynesville, Louisiana. Iberia and Francis have asked me to come for their annual family reunion. They want me to see where they grew up, where Fred spent his summers when he was young. Where he is now buried. I arrive at the family home on Saturday morning. It is a simple wooden, one-story house with wood panels and linoleum floors. Outside is a huge oak tree, which gives us shade on this hot, humid day. We sit on folding chairs, sipping lemonade.

On the dirt road in front of us, Tennessee walking horses are parading up and down in twos and threes. Suddenly they break into the elaborate prance that they are known for. Bits of dirt flash about their hooves. Iberia's nephew, who still lives on the family compound, hosts a horse show with Tennessee walkers every year. Family members and friends who left Louisiana come back with their horses in trailers and compete in a horse ring around the bend in the road from Iberia's house. Before the show, the riders are putting the horses through their paces.

"Things are a lot different now from when Iberia and I grew up," Iberia's sister Marie tells me. She shakes from an advanced case of MS. "Black kids ride the school bus now, and there's one school for everyone. It isn't like when Iberia and I grew up. We had to walk the five miles into school on Sunday night and stay with an aunt until after school on Friday," she said. "And coming home, the white kids on the school bus would throw mud at us and call us names." She still carries the hurt. Her story reminds me of watching my classmates in Atlanta yell "nigger" at the black kids going to the symphony. "Even though most everybody left the country, our family kept this place here. I still come on weekends from Baton Rouge," Marie said.

Fred's cousin, Charles White, comes up to us. Apparently he's heard that one of Fred's lawyers is here. I'm not hard to find, being the only white person among the scores of black families celebrating.

"So you were one of our family's lawyers?" he asks.

"For a long time," I say. "It took us thirteen years to prove they murdered Fred."

"Fred and me did 'most everything together when he came down here. We stood on our heads in the shallow end of the lake and we rode horses. I sure hated it when he got killed. I was gonna move to Chicago to be with him." He paused. "But I've done all right staying here. Got jobs mostly working on oil rigs, and I love the horses. I wasn't cut out for city life."

Francis is fanning himself with a paper plate and tells me a story of his grandfather.

"Uncle Wylie, that's what they called my grandfather, heard the Klan was coming after him one night," Francis said. "Nobody messed with Uncle Wylie. He told my father and his brother to get behind the house and shoot at anything white that moves. Uncle Wylie sat in a chair inside the front door with his double-barreled shotgun in his lap. When them Klan boys came up on the front porch, Uncle Wylie opened the front door and faced them with his shotgun. They took off running so fast and made such a commotion that Uncle Wylie's son, my uncle, shot one of them white-faced cows running away." We both laughed.

I could see Francis recounting that story to Fred as a boy with the same chuckle. "Fred had a lot of Uncle Wylie in him," Francis says.

I look at the etched lines on the faces of Iberia and Francis. I can see fifty years of Chicago winters, working in the industrial plant at Corn Products, raising a family, teaching their children to stand up for what they believed—and then having a son shot down by Chicago police. Despite everything, they are still at home in Louisiana.

Every year on the Saturday before Mother's Day, Iberia's family visits Fred's grave. This is my first time joining them. It's hot and I'm already sweating at 11:00 A.M. when I step into the Hampton car. We join the caravan heading for the cemetery in the country. The graveyard is near the church, long since destroyed by fire. The Church was where Iberia and Francis first met at Sunday services. Fred's grave, like the others around it, is set in a clearing with a grove of pine trees behind, much like the landscape around the Georgia farm where I grew up.

I squint from the sun as Iberia and I approach the tombstone. It has several pockmarks.

"Some people came and fired shots to deface the tombstone the year after we buried him," Iberia said. "People down here heard about Fred. A group of Panthers came down for the burial and stood around guarding his body in the church. The sheriff almost went crazy, arming his deputies and surrounding the church, but there was no trouble."

Fred's granite tombstone had a pair of outstretched hands, palms upward. On it are carved the words, "Fred said, 'If I were free, what would I spend my life doing?'" I don't know where the quote came from. I walk a short distance away, leaving Iberia to stand there silently facing the tombstone, and watch her put down the fresh flowers she brought. Someone brings her a chair, and she sits down looking straight ahead at the tombstone, chin resting on her hands.

It is twenty-two years since Flint, Dennis, and I announced the settlement. The case did not end with our press release. It took three more years to resolve our fee dispute with Montgomery. Eventually, Judge Grady ruled our way. The plaintiffs shared two-thirds of the $1.85 million dollars. Our office got paid some $450,000, less than $15.00 per hour for the over 300,000 hours we put in. Still, it was a lot of money for us back in 1986, and it kept the People's Law Office going.

By the end, all the plaintiffs—including Montgomery's clients—understood who earned them the settlement. Mrs. Clark told us when she came to get her check, "My family and I will never forget the work you did. You won, and you showed the world that Mark was trying to do something to make things better." Doc kept in regular contact, even after he moved from Chicago. In 2004, I interviewed Brenda Harris in a West Side apartment. Her Afro was showing a bit of gray, and her youthful face was drawn, but her voice was as soft as ever, and her slight, fragile appearance reminded me of her nickname, China Doll. She's now a Muslim and a nationalist. Life has not been easy for Brenda, who left college at the University of Illinois to join the Panthers.

"There were so many people who joined so quickly. We had no way to check them out," she said over the sound of a space heater churning along to keep us warm. "We talked so much about guns, and most people didn't know how to use them. We didn't have enough classes in black history or a clear idea about the role of women."

"How were women treated?"

"Some of the brothers hit on us. But not Fred, he wouldn't allow women being put down, and he gave women a lot of responsibility. He understood we did a lot of the work."

"What happened after he was killed?" I asked.

"After he was killed, the party floundered. We lacked leadership. A lot of people were scared after the raid. I left in October."

"Did your injuries heal?"

"My fingers are still stiff from the bullets. I never played the violin again."

Deborah Johnson, who now goes by Akua Njeri, worked as a paralegal at PLO in the late 1980s and worked with us to organize the twentieth anniversary commemoration of Fred's death. After the ceremony late at night on December 4, 1989, many of us went from the event to 2337 West Monroe, by then a boarded-up and dilapidated building. It was not planned, but Dennis, Flint, and I pried open the back door and twenty or so of us went inside. It was pitch black. We took everyone on an eerie tour with flashlights. "This is where Fred died," Dennis said, standing in the bare dining room, repeating what Skip had said on that spot twenty years earlier in front of Mike Gray's camera.

Iberia, Francis, and Bill Hampton were honored guests at PLO's twentieth and thirtieth anniversary celebrations and received standing ovations both times. PLO and the entire progressive community in Chicago have paid tribute to Fred Hampton's brief but indelible impact as well as his family's loss.

Jim Montgomery's professional reputation continued to grow after the case. Mayor Harold Washington picked him as Chicago's corporation counsel. Several years ago, Jim and I participated in a trial practice seminar at the University of Chicago Law School. His hair was gray and there were more wrinkles, but he still had that broad smile.

"How are you, and how is good old Flint?" he asked, his deep, baritone voice bringing back the days in Perry's courtroom. "You guys are still fightin' the good fight, I hear," he said amicably.

"Flint's fine," I said. "It's been a long time, but it's good to see you." I meant it. His cordiality made me forget the fee dispute and the arguments. We talked about cases, Chicago's political situation, Harold Washington's death, and the trial seminar as though there had never been a rift. Montgomery later affiliated with Johnnie Cochran and returned to representing civil rights plaintiffs.

Shortly after his reversal by the Seventh Circuit, Judge Perry and his cohort Judge Julius Hoffman were prohibited from taking complex cases and those requiring more than five trial days. Perry retired in 1983 at the age of eighty-seven and died the following February.

Edward Hanrahan never publicly accepted the settlement. On the day we gave our press statement, he responded by saying the Panthers were rewarded for their "lawbreaking and irresponsible charges," and he said the settlement shielded the "FBI's deception of the federal grand jury, the State's Attorney's Office, and the public."

Hanrahan remained bitter at the FBI—as well as the Panthers and us—and disappeared from the public scene in Chicago. In ensuing years, Flint and I occasionally saw him standing hunched over with a briefcase in the Dirksen Federal Building elevator on his way to the federal law library, a dreary relic of the person he had been in 1969. We always recognized each other, but Flint and I never could bring ourselves to say hello. Nor could he. His 1972 prediction, "Monroe Street will be my obituary," turned out to be accurate, at least politically. In early 2009, I attempted to interview Hanrahan, but he did not respond to my call. Five months later, on June 9, he died at age eighty-eight. His obituaries focused on his role in the Hampton raid and cover-up and the fatal toll these took on his political career.

In the late 1980s, William O'Neal agreed to be interviewed on camera for the PBS *Eyes on the Prize* television series documenting the civil rights movement. In the documentary he describes arriving at the Panther office with Bobby Rush on the morning of December 4, after the raid:

> We both were speechless. We just walked through the house and saw where—what had taken place and where he'd died—and it was shocking. And then I was, you know, I just began to realize that the information that I had supplied leading up to that moment had facilitated that raid. I knew that, indirectly, I had contributed, and I felt it, and I felt bad about it. And then I got mad. You know, I had—. And then I had to conceal those feelings, which made it worse. I couldn't say anything; I just had to continue to play the role.

Years after the trial and not under oath, O'Neal finally acknowledged his responsibility for the raid. Shortly thereafter, on January 17, 1990, he ran in front of an oncoming car at 2:00 A.M. on the Eisenhower

Expressway on Chicago's West Side. When I read the short column in the newspaper describing his death, I felt no joy and no sadness, only the recognition that even O'Neal must have had a conscience.

Iberia is still sitting at Fred's grave and someone announces, "It's time for lunch."

I get back in Francis's car and we head to Iberia's house. My plate isn't big enough to get all the chicken, corn bread, greens, and catfish I want, but Francis follows me to the table with a smaller plate containing the macaroni and cheese and candied sweet potatoes I'd passed up.

"Fred would like it here, too," Iberia says after she sits down with us. "But he wouldn't have been content. He had to be doing something for someone else. He could never sit still."

"He was never happy if someone else was being mistreated," Francis adds. "That's why he wanted to be a lawyer. But he couldn't wait."

"The sixties were a hard time to wait," I say. "It seemed like the world was exploding. There was no sitting on the sidelines."

"Not everyone paid the price Fred did," Iberia says. She was right. Bobby Rush is now a fourth-term U.S. congressman. Rush never disavowed his membership in the Panthers or his admiration for Fred. He was the first to proclaim that the FBI and federal government murdered Fred. Others who had protested Fred's murder had also risen to prominence. Danny Davis, an alderman when he decried Fred's murder, is now in the U.S. Congress. Harold Washington, who was a state senator when he loudly and persistently demanded an independent investigation of Fred's death, became mayor of Chicago in 1983. In fact it was the coalition of blacks and progressive whites and Latinos that came together to protest Fred's murder and to unseat Hanrahan that later coalesced into the force that elected Washington as Chicago's first black mayor.

But another legacy of Fred's death was that Chicago's West Side deteriorated further into a haven for drugs and gangs. Fred was an inspirational leader with the ability to reach street kids and get them involved in supporting and building their communities, not preying on them.

I didn't want to explore the diverse legacies of Fred's assassination with Iberia. She was still bitter. "We should own city hall for what they did to my son," she blurted out at one point. On Sunday morning at a communal breakfast, I am welcomed. I say goodbye to Francis, Iberia, and her family, and they invite me back for next year.

Maggie and I separated in 1983. By the time we realized our relationship had become a routine focused on the kids, it was too late to reclaim. Moving out and away from living with Roger and Andrew was the most wrenching experience of my life. But we continued to share the parenting, and I discovered there is life after divorce.

In 1988, Mariel Nanasi, a law student from Denver, came to work at PLO. I first noticed her when she propped her red, calf-length boots on my desk and asked me why I thought law would change things. We made a date to discuss this and ended up starting a relationship. We're still discussing her question. My work and my love life have always been intertwined. We now have two children and have been married almost twenty years. And yes we are still very much in love.

In 1989, Flint and I, together with John Stainthorp, who had worked on Attica and joined the office in 1980, were on trial once again in the Dirksen Federal Building. The three of us had just won a large civil rights verdict, and with the proceeds of our attorneys' fees we bought the building where PLO is presently located on Milwaukee Avenue at Division and Ashland. Janine Hoft, Stan Willis, Michael Deutsch, and Jan Susler were now partners, and Erica Thompson would be shortly. We were suing Jon Burge, a Chicago police commander who tortured black suspects using electroshock and "dry submarino," a technique similar to water boarding, in which a plastic bag is placed over the victim's head to prevent breathing until the victim loses consciousness. Many of Burge's victims spent the best parts of their lives on death row because of the false confessions he and his cohorts extracted.

After twelve years and two lengthy trials with another hostile, racist judge, who held both Flint and I in contempt and who maneuvered a verdict for Burge, we obtained a reversal in the Seventh Circuit and eventually got a summary judgment from a judge similar to Grady and a settlement of 19.8 million. Again it was a very lengthy, hard-earned legal victory against publicly funded attorneys. The exposures and our organizing to publicize them eventually led to Burge getting fired. Many people on death row had their convictions reversed, and our lawsuit played a large role in Governor Ryan's pardoning or commuting to life

everyone on Illinois death row in January 2003. Flint and PLO continued seeking compensation for Burge's victims and in 2008 announced a
19.8 million-dollar settlement for some of them. In October 2008 Burge
was indicted for the federal crimes of perjury and obstructing justice. A
jury found him guilty on June 28, 2010.

I now live in New Mexico, having left Chicago in 2001. Leaving was
not easy. I spent the major part of my adult life there. It's still my city. But
life in the shadow of Taos Mountain was different, spectacularly beautiful, muse to lofty thought. Yet the beauty here also makes me remember
the cold gray of Chicago, the El train rumbling close to the apartments
where I lived, and driving down Lakeshore Drive looking up at the sky-
scrapers and catching glimpses of the gray-green lake with whitecaps
on my way to the Loop. Half my years in New Mexico have been spent
writing about Fred Hampton. My memory of him and our pursuit of his
killers remain the defining points of my life.

Some of us are born with courage. Others, like me, need models to
help us stand up. I would like to think I picked up some of Fred's daring,
determination, and commitment, as many others did. After Mariel and
I moved to Taos, we learned that former secretary of defense Donald
Rumsfeld had several estates here and frequently visited. She and I, with
help from local activists, formed the Action Coalition of Taos (ACT).
We organized a march and demonstration of three thousand people,
the largest in northern New Mexico history, to protest the Iraq War. We
chanted and marched to Rumsfeld's house. There, at sixty years old, I
stood precariously perched on his fencepost, my ankles held by friends.
Self-conscious after all these years, I wondered what I was doing there.
Then I flashed back to Fred speaking out at the church and remembered
his words, "If you don't struggle, you don't deserve to win." Reenergized,
I declared Rumsfeld "a war criminal for waging aggressive war, the same
crime we prosecuted and executed Nazis for at Nuremberg. The crowd
repeated, "Rumsfeld's a war criminal." A charge that has been repeated
often since. It is the moment I am most proud of in Taos.

Like others who heard Malcolm X, Dr. King, and Fred Hampton
speak in the 1960s, I learned that fighting injustice and inequality is the
struggle of our lives, and perseverance in this struggle is what makes
our lives valuable.

In 2006 the black aldermen and alderwomen on Chicago's City Council introduced a resolution to name the block of Monroe Street where the raid occurred Fred Hampton Way. The proposal was about to be approved when the Fraternal Order of Police objected. A bitter fight ensued between black and white aldermen, and the resolution was defeated. Mayor Richard M. Daley refused to take a position.

The conflict in city council demonstrated how strongly Chicagoans are still divided over the killing of Fred Hampton. By contrast, the suburb of Maywood has continued to operate the Fred Hampton Memorial Pool for more than thirty-five years. In 2007 a bronze statue of Fred was unveiled outside its gates in a ceremony presided over by local officials. Many of the people who knew Fred and protested his murder back in 1969 were present and spoke. Flint was one of them.

"I'm glad the pool and his statue are in Maywood. This is where Fred lived," Iberia told me when I visited her in 2008. Francis had just passed away. "I didn't want the place where Fred was killed named after him, anyway. It made me sad."

It was also sad visiting the Hampton home without Francis there, even though the collard greens, sweet potatoes, and cornbread were as good as ever.

"Fred's son came by the other day," Iberia told me, thankful, but regretting that she and Francis had had little contact with their grandson in the past ten years. Recently, Fred Hampton Jr. has been working closely with Aaron Patterson, one of Burge's torture victims, and speaking out against the still unpunished torture by Chicago police. He is chairman of the Prisoners of Conscience Committee, in which his mother, Akua, is also active.

"Are you going down to Haynesville for Mother's Day this year?" I asked Iberia.

"I'm gonna try," she said. I knew she'd make it.

A few minutes later, I stood up to leave. We hugged, and I started toward the door, but there was a question I had to ask her.

"After all these years, what do you think our lawsuit proved?"

Without hesitation Iberia replied, "They got away with murder."

Acknowledgments

To Those Who Worked to Uncover the Assassination

Although this book describes events from my perspective, I want to make it clear that the People's Law Office and I never acted alone. We always had help. The list of individuals who actively worked to help expose and condemn the murders of Fred Hampton and Mark Clark includes other lawyers, students, community activists, reporters, film-makers, elected officials, and many ordinary citizens.

Within a few hours of the raid, PLO lawyers, law students, and several volunteers began gathering, tabulating, and securing evidence. Renault Robinson, leader of the Afro-American Patrolman's League, went to the scene, examined the bullet holes resulting from shots coming into the apartment, and quickly condemned the raid as a "police murder." After seeing the bullet holes in the apartment walls and hearing the survivors' descriptions of the raid as a military-style surprise attack, Bobby Rush, Fred Hampton's coleader of the Panthers, declared to the public and press that the FBI and its director, J. Edgar Hoover, were responsible.

It took the next thirteen years and the sustained efforts of hundreds of dedicated people to fight against the deliberate cover-up by the Chicago police, Hanrahan's office, and the FBI and finally prove the conspiracy accusations correct. The Chicago Panthers and the seven survivors of the raid, Doc Satchel, Harold Bell, Brenda Harris, Verlina Brewer, Bill Hampton, Akua Njeri, Louis Truelock, and Blair Anderson, kept the issue in the public spotlight. I also want to clearly recognize that the unnamed thousands from the black community—as well as many white people of conscience—who stood in line to view the murder scene, who walked solemnly past Fred Hampton's casket, who attended his memorial service, or who voted to defeat and oust Hanrahan in the next election, played critical roles.

Attorneys Eugene Pincham, Sam Adams, Kermit Coleman, and Warren and Jo-Anne Wolfson were our early mentors and helped us represent the Panthers after the raid. Jim Montgomery taught us about trial technique and devoted huge chunks of his time and practice to vindicating the rights of the victims of the December 4 raid. Herbert Reid of the NAACP and Howard Law School came to Chicago and assisted us through the long trial. Arthur Kinoy, Bill Bender, and Morty Stavis of the Center for Constitutional Rights and Rutgers Law School helped us to shape our complaint, answer numerous motions to dismiss, and ultimately keep our litigation alive. Many other lawyers and legal groups gave us substantial help and support along the way, including James Meyerson and Nathaniel Jones of the NAACP; Tom Geraghty and Jonathon Hyman of the Northwestern Legal Clinic; Jay Shulman from the National Jury Project and Diane Rappaport, Sarah Vanderwicken, and Liza Lawrence, who assisted Shulman with our jury selection in Chicago; Larry Kennon and the Cook County Bar Association; Susan Rutberg; Sybille Fritsche and Nancy Preston of the Lawyers' Committee for Civil Rights; the Chicago Council of Lawyers; the National Lawyers Guild; and attorneys Stephen Seliger, David Thomas, Barry Spevak, and Kenneth Tilsen, who helped on the appellate briefs.

Fred Hampton's life and the raid that ended it were captured for all time in the film footage by Mike Gray and the Film Group. It is dramatically incorporated in their subsequent documentary film, *The Murder of Fred Hampton*, directed and edited by Howard Alk. Norris McNamara took photos of the raided apartment for the defense.

A group of local and national reporters refused to accept the police's version of the event. They delved deeper and played a critical role in informing the public about what actually happened. The Chicago reporters were Chris Chandler, Brian Boyer, Lu Palmer, Rob Warden, Tom Dolan, Betty Washington, Hank Di Sutter, Lillian Calhoun, Bob McClory, Dennis Fisher, and Ron Dorfman. They were joined by John Kifner and Nathaniel Sheppard of the *New York Times*, Francis Ward of the *Los Angeles Times*, and Salim Muwakkil of *In These Times*.

The December 4th Committee—which was often headed by Akua Njeri (previously named Deborah Johnson), Fred Hampton's fiancée—was made up of raid survivors Doc Satchel, Harold Bell, Brenda Harris, and Verlina Brewer, and community activists Prexy Nesbitt and David Saxner. They kept the public and media informed about the trial, brought people to court, and held fundraisers for legal costs.

Public figures who spoke out loudly to condemn the raid included then state representative Harold Washington and then alderman Danny Davis, former congressman Abner Mikva, former alderman Leon Despres, former Supreme Court justice Arthur Goldberg, former attorney general Ramsey Clark, former NAACP executive director Roy Wilkins, and Reverend Jesse Jackson. The list is longer than I can include here but also includes Reverend Tom Strieter and the Maywood Town Council, Howard Saffold, attorney Tom Todd, and Mary Powers. Dick Gregory and former Black Panther Party leader Elaine Brown also protested Hampton's assassination to a national audience.

Two people who did their jobs with integrity rather than joining the government cover-up were assistant U.S. attorney Sheldon Waxman, who turned over the FBI's floor plan in spite of his implicit instructions to keep the organization's role in the raid hidden; and Robert Zimmers, the FBI firearms expert, who proved the falsity of the police's version of the raid by accurately connecting the bullet holes, bullet fragments, and shell casings to police weapons. He also exposed that the Chicago Crime Lab deliberately falsified their findings to fit the police's story. Herbert MacDonnell and Eleanor Berman were also experts who acted with honor.

I want to acknowledge the courage and legal acumen of Judge Luther Swygert, who took the time to carefully and thoroughly read the massive record, analyze the compelling evidence of government conspiracy and cover-up, and write a careful, incisive opinion on the facts and the law. The decision was implemented by Judge John F. Grady, who likewise recognized the strength of our evidence and was willing to impose sanctions against the defendants for their efforts to obstruct its production. Their tenacity in upholding the basic principles of civil rights and constitutional law must be contrasted with that of Appellate Judge Wilbur Pell. He dismissed our claims and our proof as "unbridled, denigrating attacks on public officials," while he acknowledged he never read the record. He also never divulged that he had been an FBI agent, which would have allowed us to get him dismissed from ruling on the appeal.

Of course I must recognize my partners, comrades, and fellow workers at the People's Law Office, who had the vision and perseverance to pursue the case legally and in the public forum for so many years and against tremendous odds. To Skip Andrew, who had the presence of mind to go to the scene within minutes of the police's departure and film the gathering of physical evidence the police left behind. To Dennis Cunningham, who provided the vision and political will to pursue the case to its end. To the many PLOers who worked on the case over the years—they are too numerous to name, but especially to then law students Seva Dubuar, Jack Welch, and Ray McClain, who helped gather evidence, and to my law partner Donald Stang and attorney Marc Kadish, who assisted the criminal defense of the survivors. To Nancy Dempsey, Mary Frank, Victory Kadish, and Reverend Jim Reed, who also went to the scene early and helped collect evidence. An especially big thanks to Peter Schmiedel and Holly Hill, who devoted two years to our trial preparation; to Charles Hoffman, Jon Moore, and Michael Deutsch, who, with help from Mara Siegel and Ralph Hurvitz, worked assiduously to prepare the many trial briefs and appellate pleadings; and to Linda Turner, who typed them all.

And of my brilliant and irrepressible partner Flint Taylor I am proud to express the highest praise and respect. His steadfast pursuit of the truth was the engine that kept the litigation going until we prevailed.

Finally to Pat Handlin and Maggie Roche, Flint's and my respective partners, who not only put up with us during this long episode but also supported and encouraged us.

There is something else I must say. In many ways the whole is greater than the parts. PLO has stood up to confront and expose government illegality and atrocities for forty years. The inspiration for us, like for many others, came from the Vietnamese liberation and other anti-colonial struggles, from the black struggles for equality and power of the sixties, and from women's challenge to patriarchy. Much has been written about the supposed excesses of that period, and most of it has been exaggerated and even manufactured in an attempt to return to the "good old days" of unbridled colonialism, explicit segregation, and accepted patriarchy. There were some mistakes, and I have included my criticisms of our actions and myopia. But for many of my comrades—at PLO and elsewhere around the nation—and me, it is the light, energy, and fervor of those times, so well articulated and symbolized by the short but inspiring life of Fred Hampton, that has driven our lives and commanded us to pursue justice.

To Those Who Helped Me Write the Story

While writing is a lonely pursuit, I have benefited from the input, ideas, criticism, encouragement, and support of many writers and friends, all of whom made this book possible.

Kira Jones, Summer Woods, Allegra Huston, and Henry Bauer read my first efforts at telling this story and encouraged me to continue writing. Bill Ayers and Bernardine Dohrn convinced me that this book had to be written and that I should take the time to do it. My Bennington College MFA-program mentors were critical in helping me interweave my own story with the historical events I witnessed. My writing circle in Taos kept me going with directed criticism and strong support. This group included Connie Josefs, Veronica Golos, Helen Rynaski, and Monique Parker. I owe a special thanks to my friend, writer David Perez. He has been my main editor, collaborator, and critic. When the manuscript was done, Bill Ayers, Sandy Snyder, and my Bennington classmate Wendy Call gave generously of their time and thoughts, putting in many hours editing and commenting on this book.

I also want to express my appreciation to one of my fellow cofounders of the People's Law Office, Dennis Cunningham, who remains a visionary and a comrade. He did a final reading and shared with me his knowledge, analysis, and memories of the events of so long ago.

Bradley Greene, aka Abdul Shanna, has been a constant source of information on life inside the Chicago Panthers. And I thank former Panthers Bobby Rush, Yvonne King, Lynne French, Billy Brooks, and Brenda Harris for sharing their experiences as Panthers and their recollections of Fred with me. I also want to thank Mumia Abu-Jamal for writing up and sharing with me his impressions upon visiting 2337 West Monroe Street shortly after the raid.

Flint Taylor was particularly helpful in finding transcripts and documents from the PLO historical files, and his daughter Kate scanned the entire thirty-seven-thousand-page trial transcript onto CDs, which made them accessible to me from fifteen hundred miles away.

I also want to thank my wonderful agent, Frances Goldin, who responded to my initial query with "How could I say no?" as if there were any doubt the book needed to be published. Frances has become a friend and someone I greatly respect. I want to thank Susan Betz of Lawrence Hill Books for publishing my account and guiding me through the steps necessary to complete it.

In addition to thanking those who helped me during the writing and production processes, I must thank Fred Hampton's parents, Iberia and Francis, who, together with Fred's brother Bill and sister Dee Dee, took me in as a son and welcomed me in their Maywood home. So did their family and friends in Maywood and Haynesville, Louisiana. They were all so willing to share with me their experiences with Fred and what he meant to them.

I was continually encouraged to write the best book I could by my mother, Betty Haas, who, well into her nineties, remains a dedicated and scrupulous reader of my work and provides valuable criticism and support.

Finally, to my wonderful wife, Mariel Nanasi, I thank you for the endless hours during which you tolerated my preoccupation with the book, including my 4:00 A.M. risings to meet deadlines, your continued willingness to read and comment on drafts, and your love and support during the four years it took to complete. And of course to my loving kids, Justin and Rosa, who were willing to share their dad so I could complete this project, and to my older sons, Roger and Andrew, who constantly asked about the progress of the book and supported my writing.

Glossary

appeal bond (civil case): The money required to be posted to allow the losing party to pursue the appeal.

appeal bond (criminal case): The money required to be posted to allow a convicted person to remain out of jail during his or her appeal.

"Black Nationalist Hate Groups": The FBI's all-inclusive term for U.S.-based black civil rights and human rights organizations (included the Southern Christian Leadership Conference and the Black Muslims).

Black P. Stone Nation: A black Chicago street gang previously known as the Black Stone Rangers. Jeff Fort led the gang from 1968 to 1969.

Black Panther Party, Black Panther Party for Self-Defense (BPP): A national black liberation organization formed in Oakland, California, in 1966 by Huey Newton and Bobby Seale.

COINTELPRO: The FBI acronym for a series of covert action programs directed against dissident groups. With regard to large sectors of the black movement COINTELPRO's stated objectives were to "expose disrupt, misdirect, discredit, or otherwise neutralize the activities of black nationalist, hate-type organizations and groupings, their leadership, spokesmen, membership, and supporters."

Conspiracy Seven Trial (originally the **Conspiracy Eight Trial**): The federal criminal trial of people the government claimed led the demonstrations at the August 1968 Democratic Convention in Chicago. The contentious trial lasted from September 1969 to February 20,

1970. Bobby Seale was severed as a defendant to be tried separately on November 5, 1969, after Judge Hoffman sentenced him to four years in prison for contempt.

FBI field offices: Local offices of the FBI in major U.S. cities.

Gang Intelligence Unit (GIU): A special unit of the Chicago Police Department charged with monitoring and arresting Chicago street gang members engaged in criminal activities.

mandamus: A legal procedure in which one party asks the higher court to order the lower court to take or refrain from some action.

Pentagon Papers: The Department of Defense's secret history of the Vietnam War. The document was leaked by Daniel Ellsberg, a former defense department analyst, to the *New York Times* and the *Washington Post* and first published in the *New York Times* on June 13, 1971. The papers contradicted the optimistic picture of the war put forth by officials; their publication outraged President Nixon and national security advisor Henry Kissinger.

Racial Matters Squad (RMS): FBI squads mandated to target black organizations and achieve COINTELPRO objectives. Robert Piper was head of Chicago's Racial Matters Squad in 1969.

recusal: The act of removing a judge from hearing a case.

Southern Christian Leadership Conference (SCLC): The civil rights organization founded and headed by Dr. Martin Luther King Jr.

Special Agent in Charge (SAC): The designation for an FBI agent heading a local field office. Marlin Johnson was the SAC of Chicago in 1969.

Special Prosecutions Unit (SPU) of the Cook County State's Attorneys Office: A police unit created by State's Attorney Edward Hanrahan to enforce his "War on Gangs." The unit executed the December 4 raid.

Student Nonviolent Coordinating Committee (SNCC): A civil rights organization founded in the South that confronted segregation and advocated black power. Stokely Carmichael was one of its leaders.

Students for a Democratic Society (SDS): A leftist student organization founded in Ann Arbor, Michigan, in the early 1960s.

Watergate: The White House scandal that began with the arrest of five men for breaking into and entering the Democratic National Committee headquarters at the Watergate office complex in Washington, D.C., on June 17, 1972. FBI and Senate Watergate Committee investigations revealed that this burglary was one of many illegal activities authorized and carried out by Nixon's staff. The discovery of Nixon's attempts to destroy the White House tapes, which proved his early knowledge of the break-in, led to his resignation on August 8, 1974.

Weathermen: The radical faction of Students for a Democratic Society (SDS). The Weathermen took control of SDS and its national office in Chicago in the summer of 1969 and called for violent confrontations with the police. In 1970 they became the Weather Underground Organization and took credit for several bombings of U.S. buildings in retaliation for the Vietnam War and police violence toward blacks.

Young Lords Organization (YLO): A former Puerto Rican Chicago street gang that opposed the expulsion of Puerto Ricans from and gentrification of Lincoln Park, a Chicago neighborhood. They formed an alliance with the Chicago Black Panthers and Young Patriots.

Young Patriots: A group of primarily Southern, white youth relocated to the North Side of Chicago that opposed urban renewal and set up a health clinic. The Young Patriots (now disbanded) formed an alliance with Chicago's Black Panthers.

Sources

My primary sources for this book have been my own observations, experiences, and memory, which are admittedly subjective. However, when documented accounts of events are available, such as trial and deposition transcripts, I relied on these. This process required reading, or in many cases rereading after thirty years, the entire thirty-seven-thousand-page trial transcript, many of the deposition transcripts, hundreds of FBI documents, thousands of pages of motions and attachments, all the appellate briefs and Hampton court decisions, and transcripts of the tapes of the oral argument in the Seventh Circuit.

I base my accounts of events at which I was not present on personal interviews and written descriptions of those events by persons who were present. My descriptions of Hanrahan's criminal trial, from which I was excluded because I was a potential witness, are based on Michael Arlen's book *An American Verdict*. Courtroom testimony comes directly from the official transcript from that trial. My interviews include lengthy conversations with Fred's parents, Iberia and Francis Hampton, in Maywood, Illinois, and in Haynesville, Louisiana, at a family reunion; with Fred's brother Bill and sister Dee Dee; with numerous childhood and adult friends in Maywood and Chicago; with relatives and friends of Fred Hampton in Haynesville; with former Panthers from Chicago, Oakland, New York, New Haven, and Philadelphia; with Mark Clark's mother, Fannie Clark, and his sister Eleanor Clark; and with the survivors of the raid.

Real names are used throughout this book, with the exception of jurors "Florence Smith" and "Judy Norgle," which are pseudonyms used to protect the jurors' identities.

I relied on numerous newspaper articles from the *Chicago Sun-Times, Chicago Tribune, Chicago Daily News,* and the *Defender* to show what was being reported and the public reaction. Some of the more significant articles are listed below.

Additional Sources

Abu-Jamal, Mumia. "Memories of Chicago, 1969." Letter to author, 2007.

Arlen, Michael J. *An American Verdict.* Garden City, NY: Anchor Press/ Doubleday, 1974.

Ayers, William. *Fugitive Days: A Memoir.* New York: Beacon Press, 2001.

Berlet, Chip. "Perry Ex Parte Messages in Panther Case Revealed." *Chicago Lawyer,* December 1979.

Branegan, Jay. "Taxpayer Panther Case Bill Put at $2.1 Million." *Chicago Tribune,* August, 20, 1979.

Brown, Elaine. *A Taste of Power: A Black Woman's Story.* New York: Anchor Books, 1992.

Canton, Susan. "Fred Hampton: A Political Assassination." *First Principles National Security and Civil Liberties* 2, no. 3 (1976).

Carmichael, Stokely. *Ready for Revolution: The Life and Struggles of Stokely Carmichael (Kwame Ture).* New York: Scribner, 2003.

Churchill, Ward and Jim Vander Wall. *Agents of Repression.* Cambridge, MA: South End Press, 2002.

Cunningham, Dennis, Flint Taylor, and Jeffrey Haas. Press release announcing settlement, February 28, 1983.

Davey, Monica. "Chicago Divided Over Proposal to Honor Slain Panther." *New York Times,* March 5, 2006.

December 4th Committee. *Fred Hampton: 20th Commemoration.* Chicago: Salsedo Press, 1989.

December 4th Committee. "Wanted For Murder Not for Mayor." (flyer, February 1977).

DeZutter, Hank. "The Death of Fred Hampton: A Special Report." *Chicago Journalism Review* 2, no. 12 (December 1969).

Foner, Philip S. *The Black Panthers Speak.* New York: De Capo Press, 1995.

Frank, Leo and Lucille Frank. Letters to and from Herbert Haas, 1915. Leo Frank Exhibit and Archives, Bremen Jewish Heritage and Holocaust Museum, Atlanta.

Giovanni, Nikki. "The True Import of Present Dialogue, Black vs. Negro." *Black Feeling, Black Talk, Black Judgment.* New York: William Morrow & Company, 1979.

Gray, Mike and Howard Alk, dirs. *The Murder of Fred Hampton*. VHS. The Film Group and Facets Multimedia, 1971.

Greenberg, Cheryl L, ed. *A Circle of Trust: Remembering SNCC*. New Brunswick, NJ: Rutgers University Press, 1998.

Greene, Bob. "Laundered Box Score? No Hits, No Guns, No Terror." *Chicago Sun-Times*, February 12, 1976.

Harr, Jonathan. *A Civil Action*. New York: Vintage Books, 1995.

Hampton, Henry, prod. *Eyes on the Prize II: America at the Racial Crossroads*. Blackside, 1990.

Hampton, William, Delores and Paul Smith, Dorothy Smith, Tom and Doris Strieter, Joan and Ted Alpert, "The Essence of Fred Hampton." Maywood, Illinois, 1994.

Hanrahan Press Conference. WBBM-TV Chicago, a CBS affiliate. December 4, 1969, 11:00 A.M.

Jones, Thai. *A Radical Line: From the Labor Movement to the Weather Underground, One Family's Century of Conscience*. New York: Free Press, 2004.

Kifner, John. "White Paper on the 'Police Murder' of Fred Hampton and Mark Clark." May 9, 1970. Chicago.

Kunstler, William M. *Deep in My Heart*. New York: Morrow, 1966.

McClory, Robert. "Agent Provocateur." *Chicago Magazine*, February 1979.

———. "Judge Walks out in Panther Trial." *Chicago Defender*, August 11, 1976.

———. "Why Don't Jeff Haas and Flint Taylor Just Give Up?" *Chicago Reader* 7, no. 42 (August 4, 1978).

Lindell, Rebecca. "After Raid, Blacks Leave Democrats' Machine." *The Monitor*, Fall 1989.

Oney, Steve. *And the Dead Shall Rise: The Murder of Mary Phagan and the Lynching of Leo Frank*. New York: Pantheon Books, 2003.

Orwell, George. "Why I Write." *Gangrel* (London), Summer 1946.

"Panther Case Revisited." *Chicago Sun-Times*, August 25, 1975.

"Panther Chief, Aide Killed in Gun Battle." *Chicago Daily News*, December 4, 1969.

Paton, Alan. *Cry, the Beloved Country*. New York: Scribner, 1948.

People's Law Office, Lawyers and Staff. "People's Law Office—20 Years Working with People and Their Movements for Justice and

Liberation." Chicago: Chicago Chapter National Lawyers Guild, November 18, 1989.

———. "People's Law Office—30th Anniversary Working with People and Their Movements for Justice and Liberation." Chicago Chapter, National Lawyers Guild, November 13, 1999.

"Reenactment." WBBM-TV Chicago, a CBS affiliate. December 11, 1969.

Sayles, James. "Fred Hampton: August 30, 1948—December 4, 1969." *Vita Wa Watu, A New Afrikan Theoretical Journal*, Bk. Eleven (August 1987).

Sheppard, Nathaniel. "Slain Black Panther's Family Pressed Legal Fight Because 'We Were Right.'" *New York Times*, November 14, 1982.

Taylor, Flint, Margaret Van Houten, and Chip Berlet, "Counterintelligence." Chicago, National Lawyer's Guild. Task Force on Counterintelligence and the Secret Police. Vol. 1, 1978.

Till-Mobley, Mamie and Christopher Benson. *Death of Innocence: The Hate Crime That Changed America.* New York: Random House, 2003.

United States District Court, Northern District of Illinois. "Report of the January 1970 Grand Jury." Chicago, May 1970.

U.S. Congress. "The FBI's Efforts to Disrupt and Neutralize the Black Panther Party." *Supplementary Detailed Staff Reports of Intelligence Activities and the Rights of Americans: Book III: Final Report of the Select Committee to Study Governmental Operations with Respect to Intelligence Activities United States Senate*, Washington, DC: U.S. Government Printing Office, April 23, 1976. Report no. 94-755, vol. 3, pp. 185–222.

Warden, Rob. "The Panther Lawyers." *Chicago Lawyer* 5, no. 12 (December 1982): 4–7.

———. "A 'Nonperson' at Panther Trial." *Chicago Daily News*, December 2, 1976.

Wiedrich, Robert. "Exclusive." *Chicago Tribune*, December 11, 1969.

Wilkens, Roy and Ramsey Clark. *Search and Destroy: A Report by the Commission on Inquiry into the Black Panthers and the Police.* New York: Metropolitan Applied Research Center, 1973.

Hampton Case Citations

City of Chicago et al. v. Hampton, 415 U.S. 917 (1974).

Hampton v. Hanrahan, 339 F. Supp. 695 (N.D. Ill. 1972).

Hampton v. Hanrahan, 484 F. 2d 602 (7th Cir. 1973).

Hampton v. Hanrahan, 600 F. 2d 600 (7th Cir. 1979).

Hanrahan v. Hampton, 446 U.S. 754 (1980).

Hampton v. Hanrahan, 499 F. Supp. 640 (1980).

Hampton v. Hanrahan, 522 F. Supp. 140 (1981).

Index

Index

Index

Index

About the Author

Attorney **Jeff Haas** has spent his career working for justice. In 1969 he and three other lawyers set up the People's Law Office, whose clients included the Black Panthers, SDS, and other political activists. Haas went on to handle cases involving prisoners' rights, police torture, the wrongfully accused, Puerto Rican nationalists, and protestors opposed to human rights violations in Central America. He lives in Santa Fe, New Mexico, with his wife, Mariel, and children, Justin and Rosa, and continues to represent victims of police brutality. He is one of the founders of Another Jewish Voice of Santa Fe, which promotes a perspective on Israel and Palestine different from that of traditional Jewish organizations, and is chair of Eco-Viva, supporting community-led sustainability programs in El Salvador.

Also Available from Lawrence Hill Books

Eye of the Hurricane
My Path from Darkness to Freedom

Dr. Rubin "Hurricane" Carter, LL.D.
with Ken Klonsky
Foreword by Nelson Mandela

978-1-56976-568-5
$26.95 (CAN $29.95)

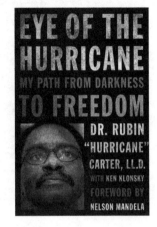

"Outspoken, uncompromising, and ultimately accurate. Dr. Carter's autobiography presents the unique and passionate vision of a unique and passionate man."
—Sister Helen Prejean, author of *Dead Man Walking*

"When a judge is responsible for freeing a person whom he believes has been wrongly convicted of murder, he worries whether he will live to regret or be proud of that decision. When it comes to Rubin Carter, I have no regrets. . . . He is a testament to the human spirit."
—Judge H. Lee Sarokin

The Sixteenth Round
From Number 1 Contender to Number 45472

Rubin "Hurricane" Carter

978-1-56976-567-8
$16.95 (CAN $18.95)

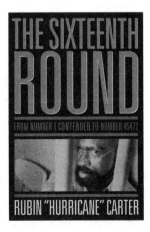

Now back in print

"A document of life lived in the center of hell."
—*Sports Illustrated*

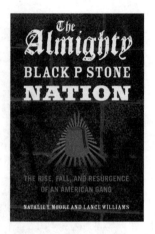

The Almighty Black P Stone Nation
The Rise, Fall, and Resurgence of an American Gang

Natalie Y. Moore and Lance Williams

978-1-55652-845-3
$26.95 (CAN $29.95)

"Fascinating. . . . A compelling account of the evolution of one of America's largest gangs as an illustration of the dangers of government efforts to frame gang activity as terrorism." —*Publishers Weekly*

"A powerful exposé of disturbing realities underlying enduringly misunderstood urban legends." —*Kirkus Reviews*

"The best and most accurate book on a contemporary Chicago gang ever written." —John Hagedorn, author of *People and Folks: Gangs, Crime, and the Underclass in a Rustbelt City*

Available at your favorite bookstore, (800) 888-4741, or www.lawrencehillbooks.com